Living and Learning

Living and Learning

Essays in Honour of J.F.C. Harrison

Edited by

MALCOLM CHASE and IAN DYCK

SCOLAR PRESS

Published by
SCOLAR PRESS
Gower House
Croft Road
Aldershot
Hants GU11 3HR
England

Ashgate Publishing Company
Old Post Road
Brookfield
Vermont 05036
USA

British Library Cataloguing in Publication Data

Living and Learning: Essays in Honour of
J.F.C. Harrison
    I. Chase, Malcolm II. Dyck, Ian
    941.082

    ISBN 1–85928–110–9

Library of Congress Cataloging-in-Publication Data

Living and learning: essays in honour of J.F.C. Harrison/edited by
    Malcolm Chase and Ian Dyck.
        p.   cm.
    John Harrison, a bibliography
    Includes bibliographical references and index.
    ISBN 1–85928–110–9
    1. Great Britain—History—19th century. I. Harrison, J.F.C.
    (John Fletcher Clews) II. Chase, Malcolm. III. Dyck, Ian.
DA530.L58   1996
941.081—dc20   95–20583
                                                         CIP

ISBN 1 85928 110 9

Typeset in Sabon by Raven Typesetters, Chester and
printed in Great Britain by University Press, Cambridge

Contents

Notes on Contributors

John Belchem is Reader in History at the University of Liverpool. His postgraduate research, supervised by John Harrison and Asa Briggs, formed the basis of his book '*Orator Hunt*': *Henry Hunt and English Working-Class Radicalism* (Oxford, Clarendon Press, 1985). His most recent publication is *Popular Radicalism in Nineteenth Century Britain* (London, Macmillan, 1995).

Malcolm Chase is Senior Lecturer in History in the Department of Adult Continuing Education at the University of Leeds. His study of radical agrarianism before the Chartist Land Plan, *The People's Farm* (Oxford, Clarendon Press), was published in 1988. His other publications as an editor are (with Christopher Shaw) *The Imagined Past: History and Nostalgia* (1989), and more recently *The Life and Literary Pursuits of Allen Davenport* (Aldershot, Scolar Press, 1994).

Gregory Claeys is Professor of the History of Ideas at Royal Holloway and Bedford New College, University of London. Among his many publications are *Citizens and Saints: Politics and Anti-Politics in Early British Socialism* (Cambridge University Press, 1989) and an edition of the works of Robert Owen (London, Pickering and Chatto, 1983).

Ian Dyck is Associate Professor of History at Simon Fraser University, British Columbia. He is author of *William Cobbett and Rural Popular Culture* (Cambridge University Press, 1992), and of articles in *Rural History* and *History Workshop Journal*. He also edited *Citizen of the World: Essays on Thomas Paine* (New York, St Martin's Press, 1988).

Phil Gardner is Lecturer in Education, and Fellow of St Edmund's College, Cambridge. Formerly a postgraduate student with John Harrison at the University of Sussex, his book *The Lost Elementary Schools of Victorian England* (London, Croom Helm) was published in 1984.

Alun Howkins has published widely on rural history, including two books: *Poor Labouring Men* (London, Routledge, 1985) and *Reshaping Rural England* (London, Harper Collins, 1990). He is Reader in the

School of Cultural and Community Studies at the University of Sussex, and an editorial collective member of *History Workshop Journal*.

William Lamont is Professor of History at the University of Sussex, where his interest in millenarianism and popular religious history of the early modern period intersected with his colleague John Harrison's interest in the modern period. He has published widely on Puritanism, Richard Baxter and the Muggletonians; his *Puritanism and Historical Controversy* will appear shortly.

Peter Lineham teaches History at Massey University in New Zealand. He is a graduate of the University of Sussex, where his research was supervised by John Harrison. He has published widely on the history of popular religion in eighteenth-century England.

Iain McCalman's *Radical Underworld: Prophets, Revolutionaries and Pornographers in London, 1795–1840* (Cambridge University Press, 1988), began with John Harrison's encouragement when he was a Visiting Professor at Australia National University, Canberra. Professor McCalman is now Director of the Centre for Advanced Study in the Humanities there.

Rohan McWilliam is a lecturer at Anglia Polytechnic University, and previously held appointments at the Universities of Kent and Essex. He is the author of a forthcoming book on the Tichborne cause and mid-Victorian popular radicalism, his research into which was begun under the supervision of John Harrison.

Edward Royle is Reader in History at the University of York, and author of several books on nineteenth-century secularism and radical politics, including *Victorian Infidels* (Manchester University Press, 1974) and *Radicals, Secularists and Republicans* (Manchester University Press, 1980). He has also published on the history of religion in Britain since the eighteenth century, with special reference to local studies of Yorkshire.

Dorothy Thompson is a Fellow of the Institute for Advanced Research in the Humanities at the University of Birmingham, and the author of many works on politics and gender in the Victorian period, most recently *Outsiders: Essays in Class, Gender and Nation* (London, Verso, 1993). She co-edited, with John Harrison, a *Bibliography of the Chartist Movement*, published in 1978 (Brighton, Harvester).

E.P. Thompson completed the essay that is printed here shortly before his death in 1993. His best known work, *The Making of the English Working Class* (London, Gollancz, 1963) was written while teaching for the University of Leeds Department of Adult Education and Extra-Mural Studies. His last book, *Witness Against the Beast: William Blake and the Antinomian Tradition* was published by Cambridge University Press in 1993.

Malcolm R. Thorp is a member of the History Faculty at Brigham Young University, Utah. His research into popular religion continues an interest first encouraged while a student of John Harrison's at Wisconsin. He edited (with R.L. Jensen) *The Mormons in Early Victorian Britain* (Salt Lake City, University of Utah Press, 1985).

Eileen Janes Yeo was John Harrison's research assistant at Wisconsin. She now lectures at the University of Sussex, and is Chair of the Society for the Study of Labour History. Her book *The Contest for Social Science: Relations and Representations of Gender and Class* was published in 1995 (London, Rivers Oram Press).

Acknowledgements

We would like to thank the other authors of the contributions in this volume, whose commitment to the project has been crucial. Other friends, former pupils and colleagues of John Harrison also supported the venture: we would like to thank particularly Asa Briggs, Ken Inglis, Roy Shaw, Barry Smith, Martha Vicinus and the late Jack Ravensdale. At Scolar Press Alec McAulay's enthusiasm has been sustaining, while Caroline Cornish has been as pleasant and skilled a desk editor as we could have hoped for. The Department of Adult Continuing Education at the University of Leeds as well as the Department of History at Simon Fraser University have been particularly supportive. Special thanks are due to Shirley Chase and Anne Hales.

CHAPTER ONE

John Harrison: an appreciation

The Editors

John Harrison has made a significant and highly regarded contribution to our understanding of modern British, and American, social history. At the heart of his achievement as a historian lie three books which stand out as works not only of enterprising and detailed research, imaginatively executed, but also as seminal influences on subsequent scholarship in their fields. The first of these, *Learning and Living* (1961) is, even in its fourth decade, still the most influential and widely read work in the field of adult education history. (In the 1980s it was reliably rumoured to be the most stolen book from the library of the extra-mural delegacy of one distinguished university, a situation hopefully eliminated by the availability of a new edition since 1994). *Robert Owen and the Owenites in Britain and America: The Quest for the New Moral World* (1969) was central to the transformation of labour history on both sides of the Atlantic. It set new standards of scholarship and critical analysis, and was a pioneering work of comparative history. The comparative method was refined further in *The Second Coming: Popular Millenarianism: 1780–1850* (1979). This illuminating study of millenarian religion helped to refocus the critical attention of historians of popular movements. Yet with typical modesty John Harrison observes in its conclusion: 'We see only as through a glass, darkly. At the end of this book it is apparent how little we know about what ordinary people "think and feel".'[1]

Many readers would wish to contest this last statement, precisely because John – as much as any historian of the nineteenth century – has opened up the history of 'ordinary people', their thought and feelings. His work is anything but doctrinaire, and it has eschewed preoccupation with narrow, male-dominated, labour movement institutions. Furthermore, as the late Edward Thompson (a colleague at the University of Leeds and happily author of one of the essays in the present collection) wrote: 'John Harrison writes always for an informed general public and not for examiners or fellow specialists; and he writes always with clarity, in an unhurried, authoritative, economical style.'[2]

As the author of several widely-acclaimed textbooks, John Harrison can also claim credit for helping to create that informed general public to which Thompson referred. *The Early Victorians, 1832–1851* first appeared in 1971 as part of a series, *History of British Society*, edited by Eric Hobsbawm. It has never been out of print and, as *Early Victorian*

Britain 1832–1851 (the title of the paperback edition issued in 1979), has become a staple feature of both A Level and undergraduate reading lists. The mid-Victorian volume in this series was furnished by John's colleague, Geoffrey Best. Together, their books were widely acclaimed, the trilogy being completed by John in 1990 with his *Late Victorian Britain, 1875–1901*. In the intervening period he published *The Common People: A History from the Norman Conquest to the Present* (1984). Having taught British history across a broad span, in both adult education and the American university system, John was well placed to embark on such a venture. It can be seen as fulfilling one of the defining objectives of his work, namely to produce a 'new type of history of the common people', based solidly on the experiences and perceptions of the people themselves. Most recently, John Harrison has produced *Scholarship Boy: A Personal History of the Mid-Twentieth Century* (1994), drawing on his own experiences and perceptions to rescue – as he playfully puts it in the introduction – the lower-middle classes from the enormous condescension of intellectuals and literati: but beneath the humour lies a serious point, that the lower–middle classes have received little attention from historians, compared to rulers and decision-makers; and 'unlike the working class, whose history has been enthusiastically recovered by several generations of labour and socialist historians, the lower-middle classes still await a devoted chronicler'.[3] John Harrison does not claim to be that chronicler, but future social historians of twentieth-century Britain will henceforward be in his debt, just as those of eighteenth and nineteenth centuries long have been.

In retrospect it seems natural, even inevitable, that John Harrison should have been destined to be a historian from an early age. Many essays of this nature include some kind of defining childhood anecdote precisely to establish such a trajectory. If such is wanted here then it might be John's discovery, at a bookstall in the Leicester Corn Exchange, of a copy of Richard Baxter's *Saints Everlasting Rest* of 1657, purchased for the not-insignificant sum (to a 1930s teenager) of 2s. 6d. (12.5p). Shortly afterwards John won a Bronze Medal from the Local Education Authority for a history of the Fletchers, the Derbyshire yeoman family from which his mother was descended. She was a qualified uncertificated teacher, and his father was a railway parcels office clerk. It was a supportive family, but that John would receive a higher education was far from being a foregone conclusion. Nor was it clear that such an education, if reached, would be in history, for John was (as he remains) deeply interested and widely read in literature, especially poetry. At Selwyn College, where he went as an Exhibitioner in 1939, he studied mainly Tudor and Stuart constitutional history, developing an interest in modern history largely as an adjunct to political interests pursued through the Left Book Club and Cambridge University Socialist Club. If his thoughts turned at all to an academic career it was more likely to have been in international relations. A deep shadow, of course, was thrown over all of this by the Second World War, and John's undergraduate years came to an abrupt halt when he was called up in October 1941.

The world into which ex-Captain Harrison (formerly of the King's African Rifles) plunged in 1947 was a very different one from Kenya, Uganda and Mauritius where he saw service. He had returned from military service to Cambridge in 1946 to take Part II of the Law Tripos. The decision to study law in preference to history (in which he had been awarded the BA under wartime regulations in 1942) was prompted by an intention to pursue a career in educational administration. He had been successively Batallion Intelligence Officer, Regimental Adjutant and a General Staff Officer (Grade III). Moreover he had recently married. The decision to pursue a career in administration was then a sensible one, and John was only deflected from it when after just two terms he secured a First in Part Two of the Tripos. A career of scholarship seemed to beckon. None the less his first civilian job – albeit brief – was as a schoolmaster in Leicester, work he combined with teaching in an adult school on Sundays. The latter seems to have confirmed him in the career he should take, and like many of his generation he consciously chose university adult education in preference to undergraduate teaching. The influence of H.L. Beales who, along with other staff members of the London School of Economics, had been removed to Cambridge during the war, may also have been at work here. Certainly, Beales was a formative influence on the historical research John Harrison would later undertake.

So it was that in September 1947 John Harrison joined the Department of Adult Education and Extra-Mural Studies of the University of Leeds. Here he spent the next 14 years. 'Here' is something of a misnomer. Initially his appointment carried specific responsibilities for York, Selby and Goole, while throughout his time at Leeds the classes he taught were scattered across an area that stretched from the Tees estuary to Skipton. In the main his teaching was to evening classes organized by the WEA in the towns and villages of the North Riding, but he also taught breakfast-time classes in a Teesside Working Men's Institute, scheduled to accommodate the back-shift from the local steelworks. Though he always taught some history, many of his classes were in international relations; and a significant portion of his time was devoted to work with trade unions, notably the National Union of Agricultural Workers, of which he was a member. This, combined with the fact that his petrol coupons were stamped 'J. T. C. Comm' led to suspicions in the village where the Harrisons lived that he was a communist agitator. The abbreviation, however, stood for Joint Tutorial Classes

Committee, a co-ordinating body on behalf of the University and the Workers' Educational Association. Prior to this, whilst living in a suburb of York, a school of opinion had emerged to the effect that John was a cat burglar – logical enough in its way, for he had a wiry physique, no proper job in his neighbours' eyes, and he went out most nights.

As I have learned from my own work for the Leeds Extra-Mural department in the 1980s and 1990s, the memory of John's teaching is still green in Cleveland and North Yorkshire. It is abundantly clear that he had a real rapport with his students: steelworkers, trade unionists, housewives, teachers, clerical and mill workers. Furthermore he had joined what at the time was widely regarded as one of the finest departments of its kind in the country. He was quickly struck by the sheer enthusiasm and devotion which permeated the department, and no less struck by the forceful personality of its architect, Sidney Raybould. Obsessive, argumentative, and apparently without any interests beyond his work save for Yorkshire cricket, Raybould was the antithesis of John in temperament; but John's first book warmly acknowledges his 'very great personal inspiration'. Raybould for his part nurtured his young colleague's career, securing for him the commission to write *A History of the Working Men's College, 1854–1954* and making him his deputy in 1958. The year before this Raybould had supported John Harrison in taking up a Fulbright Award to research and teach at the University of Wisconsin's School for Workers.

In retrospect that interlude can be seen as a watershed in John's career, but at the time he still seemed destined to remain in English adult education. Several things seem to have inclined him to reconsider this. Raybould was a consummate university politician and a breezy and efficient administrator. He was also highly proactive in the cause of adult education. He fought for his staff to be accorded equal status with 'internal' faculty, and to be allowed freedom of time for research and scholarship; but he largely saw that research as centring on adult education. It is evident that John Harrison vindicated Raybould's vision of what a university adult education teacher should be; but it was unlikely he would want to remain confined to it, while his appetite for a proactive, creative role in adult education policy seems to have been limited. John's creative energies were rather directed at the research which would culminate in *Learning and Living*, research that was grounded in extensive reading in the records, publications and ephemera of a wide range of self-made social institutions of the working class, as well as in what had yet to be coined 'oral history'. He was already assuming a profile beyond the extra-mural world, as is evident in his becoming the secretary at the inception of the Society for the Study of Labour History. Once *Learning and Living* was in the press, John seems to have been momentarily at a loss for a direction to follow. For a time he was engaged to write the official history of the Post Office Engineering Union, a worthy project for a labour historian but not one, perhaps, where John Harrison's creative capacities as a historian would have been deployed to their fullest effect. One senses that both this commission and the task of managing an adult education department (John was Acting-Director at Leeds in 1960–61), were relinquished with few regrets when he crossed the Atlantic for a second time in the summer of 1961.

For the next nine years John Harrison held a professorship in the Department of History at the University of Wisconsin, Madison, returning for a year in 1963–64 to London to pursue research into Robert Owen and the Owenites. His interest in the subject dated back to one of his earliest publications, based on research begun with the encouragement of Lance Beales and G.D.H. Cole. This was a study of the Leeds Owenite and educationalist James Hole, published by the city's Thoresby Society in 1954. An appreciation of the importance of the Owenite dimension is of course readily apparent in *Learning and Living*. However, it was access to the American dimensions of Owen's career, as well as the extensive collections of the Wisconsin university library that made possible the ambitious programme of research that culminated in the 1969 study, the now standard work on the subject. In what he has described as a research cottage industry, John Harrison was ably assisted by successive research assistants, Eileen Janes Yeo among them. The bibliography accompanying this collection of essays makes clearer the extent of that cottage industry. It can be seen as informing and underwriting something of a sea-change in the discipline of labour history, and as opening up popular politics to techniques and perspectives of the history of ideas in a way which – familiar though it may seem now – broke new ground in the late 1960s and 1970s.

M. C.

* * *

John Harrison remarks in his fine autobiography that 'every book is in some degree an intellectual or spiritual biography'.[4] The same is true of this volume in the sense that the editors and contributors are friends, students or colleagues of John Harrison who have in some way benefited from his scholarship and tutelage as well as his warm and generous personality. Indeed, so agreeable is John that only once can either of us recall seeing him as much as mildly annoyed, and this was but a sideways glance at a farmer who was taking it upon himself to remove a stile in a remote part of a South Downs right of way. 'Oh well,' remarked John a hundred yards later, 'with my tall legs I probably don't need stiles'. Tall legs are indeed a John Harrison trait; so too are humour and good will.

As students of John Harrison we thought that we were familiar with most aspects of his rich and varied life, but not until seeing his autobiography did we fully appreciate the extent and diversity of his achievements as a soldier, husband, teacher and writer – indeed the period to which the editors belong is not reached until the latter half of John's career as Professor of History at the University of Sussex (1970–1985). Yet whenever we encounter other students who have worked with John Harrison – whether in North Yorkshire, Wisconsin or Sussex – we inevitably learn that they were treated with the same degree of respect and regard that we received. All members of the Harrison alumni, though now scattered around the globe like so many seeds in the wind, are full of praise for the high intellectual and human quality of John's counsel and supervision.

Since John can always be counted on to offer sensible and even-handed advice, students have requested his good sense on any number of topics. During John's Wisconsin days, for example, many American students looked to him for advice about the Vietnam War – an uneasy situation for anyone, least of all a relative newcomer to America. For my part, I recall looking to him for hints and clues about the ideological menu that was scrolled before Sussex students during the Margaret Thatcher years. The political vitality of Sussex during these heady days was instructive and energizing, but there were times when it seemed rather doctrinaire and unrelenting. Mrs Thatcher's agenda pressed us from one side and the Militant Tendency from another, while the 'two Davids', standing resolutely in the middle, scolded both extremes. Although I was not particularly inclined to play at political theatre or fight the battles of the billboards, I found that John, often by example more than words, served me with cues that invited a 'get on with the job' approach. Not always did I follow this advice but I would not want to imagine my fate without John's encouragement and example.

When Malcolm Chase and I first conceived of this collection of essays I confess that I stole another look at the justly acclaimed volume in honour of G.D.H. Cole,[5] partly because Cole encouraged some of John's early research and partly because I wished to arrive at some sense of how social and labour history had evolved between the Cole and the Harrison generations. But I got even more than I expected out of the volume because this time I discovered the section of reminiscences, particularly those of Hugh Gaitskell – a student of Cole's at Oxford during the 1920s. Although not in search of omens regarding my chances of becoming leader of the Labour Party, I was struck by some remarkable similarities between Gaitskell's relationship with Cole and mine with John Harrison. I learned, for example, that Cole was a keen country walker but Gaitskell not, and that the latter only agreed to undertake a walk with Cole on account of the fame of his tutor. I can say as much about John's first invitation. A country walk to nowhere in particular, I wondered – what was the point? Meantime I prayed that John might heed his wife Margaret's suggestion that his students might be 'too occupied with other things'. Not a chance of it – off we marched with boots, lunch and ordnance survey map – and with John taking two strides (long legs remember) for every three of mine. Yet the grief was short-lived, for precisely as happened with Gaitskell, I became a passionate convert to the English country walk. I can honestly say that John has taught me as much about the habitat of rural England as about historical research, and that I am at one with Hugh Gaitskell's remark about G.D.H. Cole, namely that it was not so much what John said about the countryside as 'his obvious feeling for it' that was so inspirational and rewarding.[6]

Gaitskell goes on to tell us what all biographers and introducers of *festschriften* might care to know – that the process of rural walking somehow induces candour from the parties involved. Among the things that Gaitskell learned from Cole's impromptu remarks was that his tutor was a steadfast 'little Englander', and perhaps even a closeted old-style Tory on account that Cole, when passing by a large landed estate in Hampshire, astonished his student by launching into 'a panegyric of the English aristocracy'. Similar episodes come to mind from my own walks with John Harrison, such as when, in an unguarded moment, I announced in a puffed-up manner that Britain might have had no alternative but to send the task force to the Argentine after all, or on another occasion, that the Tory 'wets' were fundamentally different from 'dry' Tories. John smiled but his subsequent silence spoke disapproval. While some of us might have untold streaks of paternalism or some symptoms of cultural nationalism, John does not, for here is someone who has devoted much of his life to the education of adult learners, and who is wholly committed to the principle that education is characterized by personal freedom, integrity and self-reliance within a context of sharing and pure community.

Tolerance, co-operation and understanding describe John Harrison's accomplishments as a person and scholar. Not surprisingly they also describe his own historical heroes and heroines. Upon entering his study one's eyes are drawn to four large portraits: Paine, Owen, Cobbett and the millenarian Richard Brothers. This cast of radical thinkers is well represented in John's writing, though it is a mark of his understanding of the many different paths to the 'new moral world' that he should always preserve the individuality and integrity of the historical personages with whom he is dealing. John Harrison will not dissolve Cobbett's 'little Englander' sensibilities into Paine's internationalism; nor will he beat and cajole Brothers' millenarianism with Owenite secularism. On John's walls, as in his books, historical portraits are gathered and compared and analysed but never suffocated.

Our aim in this volume is to encompass the three principal fields of John Harrison's research and writing. The first theme is popular belief – a phrase which brings a smile as we reflect on Willie Lamont's anecdote at the start of his fine essay on Victorian Muggletonianism, and a sense of loss when we reflect that Edward Thompson's essay, treating of the Muggletonian Roger Gibson, was also his last piece of historical writing. Peter Lineham illuminates Antinomian Methodism with special reference to the tradesman William Cudworth, while Malcolm Thorp takes a close look at the very popular but now largely forgotten preacher and millenarian Robert Aitken. John Harrison has always said that historians could do worse than to take contemporary popularity as a nudge to research. Like others in this volume, Iain McCalman takes this advice to heart in his intriguing examination of the extraordinary prophesier Lord George Gordon. Was he 'mad' after all? Perhaps no more than Edmund Burke.

Our second theme is education or more accurately learning – the latter term being preferable on account of the focus here being on non-institu-tionalized instruction. Edward Royle conducts us from the world of belief to the secular chapel, and within this context to the instructional philosophies of the Huddersfield 'infidels'. Moving along the axis of learning and secular belief we arrive at so-called fringe movements – always upheld for study by John Harrison – and here ably represented by John Belchem's examination of the association between political reform and vegetarianism in the Manx press. Finally, to conclude the learning theme, we are reminded by Phil Gardner that pupils need instructors. Focusing on elementary schooling in the late nineteenth and early twen-tieth centuries, he explores the processes which prompted children them-selves to become teachers.

The last and broadest theme can loosely be described as studies in the platforms and ideologies of particular social movements, chiefly Chartism. The authors of these chapters pose a variety of questions about the way that historians represent and articulate ideas, such as who are 'the people' after all? Dorothy Thompson asks precisely this question about the high noon period of Chartism. Alun Howkins takes us into the countryside and poses a similar question: who was 'Hodge', and how and why did he evolve into a rather less ignoble figure during the last third of the nineteenth century. My own piece focuses on rural England too, with my ultimate question being whether historians have paid sufficient atten-tion to the representation of town and country in contemporary thought. Gregory Claeys follows John Harrison's lead by bringing America into the picture in his study of the evolution of British radicals' understanding of the United States during the first half of the nineteenth century. Eileen Janes Yeo carries us back towards Chartism, strongly advancing our knowledge of that movement by asking gender-based questions regarding what is arguably the best known working-class autobiography, that of William Lovett. Malcolm Chase is similarly concerned with the way that historians represent and dissect popular movements such as Chartism – why, he expressly asks, has the Chartist Land Plan been ignored when so many lent it ardent support? Finally, Rohan McWilliam shows us that historiographical detours have also been made around G.W.M. Reynolds's participation in the Chartist movement. Rohan studies all facets of Reynolds's interesting career, and in the process seeks not to dodge but to understand the links between escapist mass culture and radical ideologies.

John Harrison has always encouraged the daring and bold question, the examination of the periphery to get at the centre. We confess, then, that the people in our story might appear at first glance to resemble a cast of misfits – millenarians, 'infidels' of various sorts, vegetarians, 'mad' radical leaders, 'plodding' farm workers as well as women in movements that many men thought should not have women. We hope that the people, subjects and questions taken up here are worthy of a passing grade in what John Harrison calls the ultimate test of popular history: 'The test always must be: what at the time did common people feel was important to them, and what, with the privilege of hindsight, seems to have been significant for the common people beyond their generation and environment?'[7] These are large questions, but throughout his career as a teacher and scholar, John Harrison has put nothing less to himself, to his students and to his sources.

I.D.

Notes

1. John Harrison, *The Second Coming: Popular Millenarianism, 1780–1850* (London and New Jersey, 1979), p. 230.
2. Edward Thompson, *The Guardian*, 13 September 1979.
3. John Harrison, *Scholarship Boy: A Personal History of the Mid-Twentieth Century* (London, 1995), p. 2.
4. Harrison, *Scholarship Boy*, p. 177.
5. Asa Briggs and John Saville (eds), *Essays in Labour History: In Memory of G.D.H. Cole* (London, 1967).
6. Hugh Gaitskell, 'At Oxford in the Twenties,' in A. Briggs and J. Saville (eds), pp. 6–20.
7. John Harrison, *The Common People: A History from the Norman Conquest to the Present* (London, 1984), p. 15.

CHAPTER TWO

A New Jerusalem: the elusive dream[1]

William Lamont

John Harrison and I used to teach a joint seminar at the University of Sussex on popular millenarianism. On our way to a class one day we were confronted by an agitated University Chaplain. With clerical collar bobbing, he asked us: 'What time does The Second Coming start?'. The World Turned Upside Down indeed! When John Harrison wrote his book under that seminar title an obscure sect called the Muggletonians was given a characteristically sympathetic hearing. But he wrote about them before the recovery of their archive, which would throw new light not only on their seventeenth-century origins but on their later history. We know now much more about 'Ancient' Muggletonians as a result; 'Modern' Muggletonians have been, however, largely neglected. This essay is written to redress that imbalance and may seem an appropriate tribute to pay to a historian who has all his life written memorably about the common people, whose focus of studies has been largely Victorian England, and whose sympathies have always been powerfully engaged with the autodidactic artisan.[2]

Muggletonianism in mid-Victorian England was indeed at some sort of crossroads. There was a numbers crisis. We have no authoritative evidence of the total size of the sect, although there is much impressionist testimony to shrinking numbers. The London-based list of members attending the annual dinner, however, carries with it dangers of distortion. Thus a newspaper report for 1919 contrasted the 'mere handful' of attenders at the London dinner with up to 40 attending the comparable occasion in Derbyshire. Although Derbyshire was probably second only to London as a Muggletonian base, there were other known areas (like Southampton, Bristol, Pembrokeshire and Salisbury) with a Muggletonian crop of believers. But awareness of its shrinking base – which at least is irrefutable – led members in Victorian England to take drastic remedial action. How to do so without becoming evangelists (like the Quakers they despised) is part of the Victorian crisis which I wish to describe in this essay.

There was also a philosophical crisis which struck at the heart of the movement itself. The Frost family, who were Derbyshire brassfounders, moved to London around the year 1800, and were to be among the wealthiest and most influential families in the movement. We shall see nevertheless that James and Isaac Frost, for all their financial clout, were not able to impose their will upon Thomas Robinson, a shoemaker down on his luck, who was saved from the workhouse (as he acknowledged in a graceful letter of 1885) only by the charity of his fellow worshippers, and whose wife acted as caretaker for 21 years in the Muggletonian Reading Room and Library, set up in New Street, Bishopsgate, in May 1869.[3]

How the Victorian Muggletonians coped with these two crises has, I hope, an interest in its own right. But it also raises wider historical issues of continuity, between seventeenth-century visions and their later articulation, which I want to touch upon at the end of this essay.

Let us begin with Lytton Strachey's famous essay on Muggleton in 1924, to see how far modern discoveries have changed historical perspectives.[4] Errors jostle with epigrams in eight sparkling pages. The sect, he tells us, began when God spoke to a London tailor, John Reeve, (on three successive mornings in February 1652) and told him that he and his cousin, Lodowicke Muggleton, were the Two Last Witnesses from Revelation. However, 'in a few months' Reeve was dead, and Muggleton was 'left alone to carry on the work'. The 'few months' were actually six years and the work that Muggleton was left to carry on, according to Strachey, was this: 'He never ceased, in sermons, in letters, in books, in pamphlets, to declare to the world the divine and absolute truth. His revelations might be incomprehensible, his objurgations frenzied, his argumentations incoherent – no matter; disciples gathered around him in ever-thickening crowds.' Muggleton's own estimate was that he made one convert in his lifetime (cousin Roger). The 'ever-thickening crowds' of disciples numbered 248 attenders at his funeral in 1697, and it was downhill all the way subsequently from that high point. He once speculated if there ever had been a prophet who travelled *less* than he had. Strachey tells us that 'inquiring magistrates were browbeaten with multitudinous texts': not after the Restoration, when passivity reached the point where followers (erroneously) thought he had recanted his whole set of beliefs under pressure. How then did he survive? Strachey puts it down to the half-hearted nature of Stuart persecution: 'heretics shall be tortured – not to death oh no! but . . . to some extent'.[5] That is one view of the Merry Monarch, though not of his latest biographer, who, comparing the body count of imprisoned Quakers and Marian martyrs, wonders whether it is 'a matter of personal taste whether a moment of agony at a stake is a worse end than a slow decline, penned upon stinking and verminous straw'.[6]

Strachey called Muggletonianism 'an exclusive faith, certainly'. We would say, certainly not: it was actually freed from the usual sectarian conceit that only believers are saved. The Muggletonian propensity to curse the enemy fell into 'duesetude' over time, according to Strachey, thus obscuring two important points: how early it was challenged from within (Arden Bonell's revisionism begins in the early eighteenth century), and equally how long it continued to be used as a weapon *in extremis* (infidel Richard Carlile, Sir Walter Scott and a Swedenborgian were to be among their last scalps). Strachey's essay then has not worn well (except in its readability). But his tone is not one of unremitting mockery. When he says that he 'would be sorry if the time ever came when there were no more Muggletonians'[7] (perhaps that stage has been now reached for us after the death of The Last Muggletonian, Philip Noakes, in 1979), we feel that he means it. He has, moreover, a historical sense. The Muggletonians, he insists correctly, should be seen in their context. They belonged to a unique moment in English history in the 1650s when 'prophets and prophetesses ranged in crowds through the streets of London, proclaiming, with complete certainty, the explanation of everything'. The options were illimitable: 'one could become a Behmonist, a Biddelian, a Coppinist, a Salmonist, a Digger, a Traskite, a Tyronist, a Philadelphian, a Christadelphian, or a Seventh Day Baptist, just as one pleased'.[8] Did Strachey have in mind persons like Lawrence Clarkson, a Muggletonian who could be said to have tried *everything* first?[9] Now Strachey is here practising 'horizontal' history – a term used by Professor Collinson to distinguish this sort of contextual approach from that of the 'vertical' denominational historians. It is what Christopher Hill was to do so well in *The World Turned Upside Down*,[10] though Strachey's lists of names and groups become flesh and blood humans in the imaginative recreations of a master historian. The technique, however, of both men is actually similar, and how superior that technique does seem to that of those 'vertical' historians who fit the Muggletonians into some sort of rogues' gallery of crooks and eccentrics! Dr Aikin's *Memoirs of Religious Impostors, from the Seventh to the Nineteenth Century*, published in 1823, for instance, smuggles Lodowicke Muggleton in between Mahomet and Joanna Southcott.[11]

However Collinson is not saying something as crass as: 'horizontal' history good; 'vertical' history bad. He certainly wants to show how history is reinvigorated when the blinkers of denominational history are removed, but he is no less sure that 'those who write from within the tradition with theological awareness and spiritual sensitivity, have much the better chance of getting it right'.[12] The history of the Quakers has been distorted by its attracting too many 'vertical' historians;[13] the history of the Muggletonians, we might say, by too few. One might even argue there have been none, but that is to reckon without the major contribution of Alexander Gordon.

Gordon was a Unitarian historian actually, but he was also a sort of honorary Muggletonian. That, in Victorian England, a Unitarian could conceivably *be* a Muggletonian says much about the evolution of the sect. Gordon wrote about them in two successive years in Liverpool: *The Origins of the Muggletonians* (1869) and *Ancient and Modern Muggletonians* (1870). The lectures are very different in quality. The first is highly derivative. Gordon, a modest man, recognized that much of it was no more than a straight 'transference' from the text of Muggleton's posthumous memoirs, *The Acts of the Witnesses of the Spirit*.[14] In Muggletonian historiography, however, this was in fact a breakthrough: to take Muggleton seriously enough to plagiarize him was an advance on Aikin's 'Imposter' or, for that matter, Macaulay's 'Mad Tailor'.[15] As Strachey would do later, he gave a 'horizontal' perspective when he compared Muggleton to Fox and Boehme. But he did more: he offered also a glimmer of a 'vertical' perspective. He compared seventeenth-century Muggletonians with Unitarians of his own day. It was a daring opening salvo to give his 1869 audience. 'Unitarianism', he pointed out, 'raises questions of salvation'; 'Muggletonianism' on the other hand 'raises no theological ideas whatever'[16] – how could it, with such a silly name? Gordon invited his audience to shed such condescension.

We don't know what impact the lecture had on its audience. We do know the impact it had on his subject. Muggletonians – so used to derisory dismissal – warmed to a man who, from the outside, could recognize Reeve's 'purity and tenderness of mind' and acknowledged a 'sneaking kindness'[17] to Muggleton (this a bit too patronizing for one believer, though).[18] Two momentous decisions followed. Unbeliever Gordon was admitted to the annual dinner; he was allowed a week's access to what he would call in his second lecture 'the curious store of manuscripts in the possession of this singular community'.[19] This was the phrase which alerted E.P. Thompson to a potential treasure trove, and in turn would lead him to Philip Noakes's collection in apple boxes on a Kent farm, at Matfield – and to their ultimate resting home (in 88 volumes) in the British Library Manuscripts room.

Gordon was not the only non-believer to attend a believers' dinner, although he thought that he was. A letter earlier in the 1860s records a gift of £5 for poor believers from a Mr and Mrs Wilson, who were attenders from outside the faith. But it was rare (Gordon, for instance, would himself be asked only once more, as late as 1914). And it was controversial. Gordon's host was J.D. Aspland and he wrote a letter of apology to a coreligionist afterwards:

> I must now tell you that I was really quite unhappy about the affair,
> I felt that I had put myself forward in asserting and inviting Mr
> Gordon and I felt the opposition to Mr Gordon's presence at the

holiday was partly a censure upon me for making my self too busy. I
still believe nothing could have happened more opportunely for the
good of the Church than Mr Gordon's introduction to us.[20]

To see good in Gordon's introduction to the sect, to contemplate let-
ting him loose in their precious archive (if only for a week), is all part of
the process of opening up, which was occurring at this period of mid-
Victorian England (the move from assorted pubs to a central Reading
Room in 1869 belongs to the same tradition). Gordon in 1870, when he
gave his second lecture, could speak now, not just about 'Ancient'
Muggletonians, and 'origins' of the movement, but about 'Modern'
Muggletonians. He could draw upon the archive, and, as far as we know,
no embargo was placed by Muggletonians on what he said. There was,
however, curiously, a self-imposed embargo. He could have fully
redressed, in his second lecture, the imbalance he had stressed in his first,
when 'Unitarianism' could be a concept to raise questions of salvation
which 'Muggletonianism' could not. But the Liverpool Literary and
Philosophical Society had its own embargo on a dangerous area marked
out as 'theology'; as their guest, Gordon honoured their scruples, he even
approved of them.[21] Thus he is aware in 1870 of the importance of
Muggleton's break with Reeve on theology in 1661, and aware too of the
many schisms in the movement which arose subsequently from it. These
are issues we shall explore later, but it is important now to recognize that
Gordon himself could have explored them, and made the necessary
connections, and he chose not to do so.

How did Gordon stumble on the Muggletonians? That is probably the
way that he would have expressed it. Serendipity is his chosen explanation. A chance meeting with 'William Ridsdale of Mansfield, a very cour-
teous old gentleman' in 1860 led to introductions to London leaders of
the sect. He picked up one of Muggleton's printed works in 1865 on a
Liverpool bookstall (George Borrow in *Lavengro* describes a similar
chance encounter with a Norwich Muggletonian antiquarian bookshop
owner).[22] He even, to his astonishment, when inspecting one of
Muggleton's books (seized upon his arrest in 1676) found that the
official in charge of the library at St Paul's Cathedral was himself a
Muggletonian.[23]

There was, however, a less serendipitous explanation which throws
interesting light upon the religious milieu of the time. When Gordon
came to London, Robert Brook Aspland, 'editor for many years of
Unitarian journals', was a formative influence.[24] His cousin, J.D.
Aspland, would be Gordon's troubled host at the annual dinner (his
commonplace book, through the generosity of a twentieth-century lady
called Muggleton, now joins the rest of the British Library Archive in
the Manuscripts Room).[25] When he died in 1877 Gordon wrote this

obituary notice of his friend: 'Differ as we may from the "believers in the Commission of the Spirit" we cannot fail to recognise whenever we see it, fidelity and conscientious principles, and a faith illustrated with good works and adorned with charity.'[26] This common ground is invoked by another Muggletonian, William Cates, in a letter to Gordon in 1869: 'I likewise as a Muggletonian thank you for the candid manner you have shown our principals [sic] to the world against the Bias, and unjust remarks of great writers, such as Macaulay.'[27]

Strachey had written of the sect's 'exclusivity' (which we have said is false). But they were non-proselytizing (unlike the Quakers) – which is sometimes taken to be the same thing as exclusivity but which is not. Were then the overtures made to Gordon, from Aspland and Cates, some breach with ancient principles? We need to be sure what these principles were. One thing we can be sure of: they were not those of the Skoptsky, a nineteenth-century Russian millenarian sect. They believed that, once 144 000 of the elect have been gathered – now that *is* exclusivity – the kingdom of heaven will arrive, and unbelievers would be decapitated. In his *Sociology of Religion* Stark claims to have found in the Muggletonians 'ideas very close – surprisingly close – to those which dominated the Skoptsky'; a closeness which has eluded the writer of this present essay.[28]

The Muggletonians did not think small is beautiful. After all, something like half the world (and of those, all who died as children) would be saved. Within that band, it is true, were the fortunate few (the Muggletonians) who had assurance of salvation which came from following the prophets, but, crucially, assurance was not coterminous with salvation. Nevertheless, Muggletonians clearly did have an obligation to widen the number of those who had that assurance. That obligation was, however, in its turn tempered by another consideration. As Muggleton put it, in a letter of 1682, 'God only opens the gate of Heaven to those who knock themselves.'[29] Philip Noakes would open the gate of his retirement home at Matfield to Jehovah's Witnesses callers, but he was reticent in conversations with his wife and two daughters. For they could be saved – like children generally – by being unconquerably ignorant; to know, and then to reject, the message of the prophets was, however, to incur certain damnation.

Some skilful tight-rope walking was needed accordingly. Muggletonians could neither evangelize, in the accepted manner, but equally they could not keep aloof. Thus Robinson sternly reminded a fellow-believer: 'The candle of Truth is not lighted to be hid under a bushel of worldly excuses.' The Frost brothers' printing of the works of Muggleton and Reeve in three volumes (and presentation of them to the British Museum) was one way to light the candle of Truth. The Muggletonians

would indeed prove to be quick on the trigger with responses to defamatory press comment. Thus Robinson put Augustus Jessopp right about
Boehme's influence on the group.[30] He also informed *Chambers
Encyclopaedia* they were wrong in 1881 to think that the sect was now
extinct.[31] He explained to the Reverend E.S. Anthony, who had
answered an advertisement placed by the Muggletonians in *The Inquirer*,
that they had been misrepresented so often that they thought it right to
vindicate their principles, and to advertise for sale the prophets' Works.
In 1843 the reprinting of a large number of the seventeenth-century texts
was halted, not by scruples about the propriety of such actions, but by
more mundane considerations. The books were not selling. Accordingly
a thousand copies of lists of extant unsold material were distributed,
with descriptions of their content. 'How can the truth be spread', wrote
the brothers Frost, 'if the Saints are not moved to spread it?'[32] But the
truth did spread, however haltingly, and sometimes even reached the
most exalted quarters. On 13 December 1881, Gladstone (then Prime
Minister) wrote in his diary that he was reading 'Muggletonian Hymns!!'
And on 14 January 1882 he wrote to a Mr J. Salkeld. There is no copy of
the letter, but his secretary noted in the Letter Book: 'Mr J. Salkeld.
Books. Muggletonian Hymn Book, uncut, how much?'[33]

But believers had to spread the truth with tact. They had to be sure of
the motives of their interlocutors. Fred Noakes, the Last Muggletonian's
father, would not disclose much in answer to the enquiry of a Mr
Montague, since he felt that the motive was prurient curiosity. He would
have responded differently if he had felt that the question had been
prompted by spiritual hunger. Noakes and his wife were both of the
faith. All four of their children knew that their parents were Muggletonians but only the youngest son, Philip, became one himself. The oldest
son wrote to his parents from behind the lines on the Western Front in
the First World War: 'It is not that I am any more inclined to accept
[Reeve and Muggleton] as inspired men, for my reason will not let me do
otherwise than consider you mistaken in some of your beliefs, but they
were undoubtedly good men.' Even so, he would enthusiastically discuss
predestination and the parable of the tares with his father. Philip's
daughters only remember him discussing his beliefs in a very general
way. His seemingly contradictory willingness to confide in E.P.
Thompson, after an initial hesitation, sprang, one suspects, from a recognition of the integrity of the historian's motivation. It was not spiritual
hunger, as the prophets had defined it, but Thompson's passionate desire
to recover the links between the Muggletonians and William Blake was
more than mere curiosity (and perhaps a similar intuition had led
Aspland, in the previous century, to put his trust in Gordon?).

To tell or not to tell? Philip Noakes (like Aspland) was a member of an ever-shrinking religious group – by his time the crisis had become even more acute, of course. Something of the isolation which he felt was experienced earlier in the century by one Alfred Hall, who had emigrated to the United States of America when still a young man. He was born in Derbyshire in 1845 and would live on until his eighty-fifth year, in December 1930. His daughter, in a letter to Philip Noakes's father in 1936, would recall his 'little Chest wherein he kept his clear Spiritual Books and Letters' which 'he did treasure very highly'. She also added that she had all 'the precious books and letters he gave to me': a source which we still have to track down. Hall's wife had died young, giving birth to her eighth child, and when the oldest girls had reached adolescence, Hall recognized that they needed a female influence. He felt, however, unable to marry outside the faith, and here was his problem. He knew of no other Muggletonians in the USA. He wrote to Thomas Robinson for advice. Robinson's reply was eminently practical as usual, and had the commonsense sensitivity which is the mark of Muggleton's own advice to his seventeenth-century correspondents. A wife would be of great benefit, but since he cannot marry a fellow-believer, he must not attempt the risky business of conversion. He should find a woman who would be a companion but (with eight children already in the family) she should be past child-bearing age, and have no children of her own.

In the event Hall never did remarry. There is a rather sad self-portrait in a letter of 1914, which sees him attending lectures ('even entered Bible classes'), in the hope that he might 'drop a word in season'. The tentative note is striking. As he said in an earlier letter to Robinson, he 'had been more careful of late in casting pearls before swine'. Robinson tried to put his own sense of isolation in perspective in a letter in 1883: 'We have had but two converts here for many years. I was a convert and married a Believer, and of our family two Daughters and one Son hath with his wife been converted since coming of age.' The sense of isolation comes through other Muggletonian letters. In 1887 Sarah Ann Huntley's niece moved away to Coventry with a husband who, although not of the faith, was tolerant. 'I am sure it is a comfort to you', wrote Sarah Ann, 'being so many miles from your family and friends. You must help him on quietly, reading to him the six principles.' This might be called conversion by stealth. The Six Principles were indeed all that Muggletonians at any time were required to believe; they had been published first by Reeve and Muggleton in 1654. The First Principle was that God became the Man Jesus: the Unitarian ark of their covenant. The Second Principle was that angels were created as 'pure reason': the antithesis of the Seed of Faith. The Third Principle was that devils were produced by the imagination of men. The Fourth Principle was that the Fall of Eve brought forth the two Seeds of Faith and Reason. The Fifth Principle was that Heaven was a local place above the stars (as Alfred Hall wrote to Isaac Frost in 1880: 'I never did believe in the imagination of the Newtonian principle'). The Sixth Principle was that hell was internal, and the soul mortal.

In their isolation the later Muggletonians teased out the implications of the Six Principles in the surviving tracts of Muggleton and Reeve, and in the letters of Muggleton particularly, but also those of later followers, which were deposited in the archive which one believer, Alexander Delamaine, had begun to assemble as early as 1682.[34] Mrs Wratten, incarcerated in a nineteenth-century workhouse, had only the letters of Thomas Robinson and Mrs Huntley for spiritual nourishment. Mrs Huntley took her some of the prophets' writings from the seventeenth century: 'I shall be glad to hear whether the Matron or others have inter-fered with you in reading *The Mortality of the Soul*. If not I shall be pleased to bring the *Eleventh of Revelations* on Friday 6th.'

There were other ways open to believers to break out of their isolation, which stopped short of crude evangelizing (Alfred Hall's letters drip with contempt for the contemporary American evangelist, Billy Sunday: 'believe me, if I could hate, it would be even that very word'). Occasionally a newspaper article would inspire one or other of the believers to write to the author. John Cates wrote in 1893 to the Reverend Alexander Smith, whose article 'Why Go to Church?' had appeared in *The Pall Mall Gazette*. Cates saw similarities between his own beliefs and those of the minister. Sarah Tricker, another believer, commented: 'I feel so pleased to see we have one who can defend our faith.' John Cates's three letters to the *Daily Telegraph* in 1904 were intended for inclusion in a correspondence then raging under the title, 'Do We Believe?' But, as Cates lamented in a letter to Fred Noakes, 'we cannot in the ordinary sense of the term make converts, the faith must be born in them'. In the 1930s Fred Noakes himself would send copies of his mother's pamphlets to the Religious Editor of the *Daily Express* (who had expressed dissatisfaction with his own religious beliefs) in the hope that he would find ease therein. His letter concluded with the wish that he might have touched, in the recipient, a responsive chord; if not, the 'pre-cious pearls' were to be handled with care. The *Daily Express* did not print the letter; Noakes did not even receive a reply. What we now know of the later Muggletonian history supports the claim for the group made by a member in 1870: 'the exclusiveness was not sought, it was compul-sory'. The writer instanced the refusal of *The Times* to insert advertise-ments of the prophets' Works, 'because as they said they were contrary to the received opinion of the Age'.[35]

What we have seen, thanks to the recovery of the Muggletonian Archive, is how critical the mid-nineteenth-century period was in the total history of the movement. It saw a strenuous effort by a religious group, declining dangerously in numbers into small pockets of family worshippers, to demonstrate by looking outwards that their beliefs were not 'contrary to the received opinions of the Age'. The Frost brothers' three-volume publication of the works of Muggleton and Reeve, their presentation of them to the Trustees of the British Museum, the invitation to Gordon to their dinner and his 1870 lecture on Modern, as well as Ancient, Muggletonians – all these testify to a genteel evangelizing (within the limits of their suspicion of the very concept of the evangelist) which would have its fruits in Gordon's picking up of a Muggletonian pamphlet in 1865 on a Liverpool bookstall, or in the Prime Minister of the day's scouring of bookshops for Muggletonian hymns.

The 1870 anonymous writer, who criticized *The Times* for its snobbery, had a good case to make for Muggletonianism, in its revised form, as being in harmony, not in conflict, with the secular tendencies of the present age. This was the case which in fact he did make.[36] Theirs, he said, was a movement which entirely ignored all forms of public worship. They denied the omnipresence of God: 'they do not (as many do) think that God is a vast spirit without a body, in everything and everywhere at the same time'. They thought that praying was a waste of breath. They had no use for sumptuous buildings for rites or ceremonies. They denounced 'Priestcraft of every denomination'. They only attended two great commemorative festivals: February (when God had spoken to Reeve) and July (when Muggleton had been released from prison). They had monthly meetings, on the first Wednesday of every month, when they conversed together, sang spiritual songs of their own invention, and gave thanks for the special privileges they enjoyed. They attacked the new Victorian fad of spiritualism: 'from the first the Muggletonians made their fearless attacks upon that Hydra-headed-Monster Superstition'. And this, as the writer pointed out, was in line with their seventeenth-century predecessors' scepticism about witches, hobgoblins and ghosts: all written off by them as products of men's imaginations. The Muggletonians of 1870, like their predecessors of 1652, knew that the soul perished with the body, and that matter pre-existed the Creator.

What the writer concealed was that this harmony between 'Ancient' and 'Modern' Muggletonians had been won at the price of bruising internal struggles.[37] Muggleton himself broke with his co-founder Reeve on an essential theological point, Reeve's belief that God took 'immediate notice' of His followers. Muggleton's claim was that Reeve had been won over to his contrary view by the time of his death in 1658. It was this view which Muggleton developed in his outstanding letters to his followers (*pace* Lytton Strachey, Muggleton's greatness rests on his power with the pen, not with the voice). It is this claim which would be contested in a series of schismatic challenges (Buchanan and Medgate, James Birch, Martha Collier) right up to 1870 and beyond that date too. The 1870 writer had to acknowledge there had been these divisions, and equally had to acknowledge there had been the difference over the issue of 'immediate notice' between Muggleton and Reeve. What he did not do was relate these two divisions or acknowledge their centrality in Muggletonian dogma.[38] Gordon, for his part, recognized in his 1870 lecture that the rejection of 'immediate notice' was important to Muggleton, but his own self-denying ordinance on theology (which we discussed earlier) meant that its wider significance was not brought out in his lecture.

Of course, it could be argued that by then the days of rival prophets were over: James Birch and Martha Collier belonged to the end of the eighteenth century, to the period of Jacobin agitation. But this misses a wider point. Muggleton and Reeve co-wrote *A Divine Looking Glass* in 1656. Muggleton drastically revised it in 1661 to bring its doctrines in line with his new philosophy, that God took no 'immediate notice' of His subjects. This was the issue that rival prophets in the next two centuries took up, and they took it up in the name of John Reeve. The Frost brothers can be acquitted of Jacobin-baiting, or of suspecting rival prophets in the wing, when they took the issue up again on the other side in the middle of the nineteenth century. Their desire to house the prophets' Works in the British Museum is part of that process of semi-evangelizing which has been described in this essay, but the lengths to which they went to secure the 1661 edition of *A Divine Looking Glass*, not the 1656, in their package to the Trustees, tells us something else:[39] about a crusade to align Muggletonianism with the Unitarian world of the Asplands and the Gordons of Victorian England. Hence the almost hysterical terms in which champions of the earlier edition were seen as a party: they portrayed the conflict as one between 'Reevonians' and 'Old Believers'. And hence their readiness to send their daughters as lobbyists to get the signatures of influential men like Robinson to a petition asserting the inviolability of the 1661 text. Robinson tried to defuse the issue – 1661 changes, he argued, had to be made to evade the Restoration censor (which was true);[40] his commonsense caution won him accolades from later critics;[41] but the issue did not go away: it still worried believers as late as 1933.[42]

It worried believers, because Robinson was only half right. Muggleton's was a political compromise in 1661 but one with immense theological consequences. When Muggleton tells the first rebel on this issue, Buchanan, that, if there was no God to reward the virtuous or to punish the vicious, 'yet could I not doe any otherwise than I doe',[43] he is, perhaps, foreshadowing Kant's doctrine of the autonomy of ethics; he is, certainly, redirecting the movement on a Laodicean course of survival.

And this was not happening in an ideological vacuum. In the same year that Muggleton rewrote *A Divine Looking Glass*, George Rust was warning that Calvinist stress on God's powers of intervention was producing a backlash in men, leading them to wish 'either his *not being*, or his *non-concerning* himself in the affairs of men'.[44] Or, we might say, leaving them with the choice of atheism or Muggletonianism Mark Two.

In the process what is obscured is Muggletonianism Mark One. Theirs would not be the only body of beliefs which went underground at the Restoration. The success of Restoration historiography in snuffing out an alternative tradition is admirably documented in a little-known but excellent monograph, Royce MacGillivray's *Restoration Historians and the English Civil War*.[45] We are not here talking about the familiar process of excavating the radicals (though that too), but of stripping away the protective post-Restoration layers to recapture that moment in history when action could be expected at the centre, and holy commonwealths could be the goal, Cromwellian magistracy their instrument. For that is what the 1656 text was about: a deeply providentialist work, hailing Cromwell as the chosen vessel of God, and all who opposed him as spiritual rebels.[46] This was not just political dynamite at the Restoration; it was by then seen as theologically flawed. But the sentiments were those shared with others: Winstanley, Harrington and Baxter – whatever their profound differences with each other – had also looked to Cromwell to produce holy commonwealths.[47] Even as careful a historian as Professor Speck in his contribution to the recent volume, *Images of Oliver Cromwell*, takes at face value Baxter's post-Restoration distancing from the Protector.[48] Baxter's private papers, though, tell a different story: of a commitment to Cromwell, and to a 'Holy Commonwealth' under him, which was in turn rooted in the pastoral successes of his Kidderminster ministry.[49] Dorchester for a period, we now know, became England's Geneva under its minister, John White.[50] This was the company to which Muggletonianism belonged in 1656, and no subsequent revisions could excise that memory – at least from some of those who came after them.

That memory would be perpetuated in 'Reevonian' efforts throughout the history of the movement to keep the 1656 text alive. The ferocity of the backlash of the opposing 'old Believers' is only intelligible by recognizing the importance (particularly in Victorian England) they attached to aligning themselves with the Unitarian currents of the day. The resolution was there to fashion a sect which could invite a man like A.P. Gordon to their annual dinner.

All of this seems a long way from Blake's 'New Jerusalem', and yet it was the Muggletonianism that Blake may have inherited from his mother which the late Edward Thompson saw as a possible element in his radical 'anti-hegemonic' philosophy. For this he has been scolded by Perry

Anderson, who sees rather Blake's anti-heroic reaction to Jacobinism as more in line with the quietism of the sect.[51] Anderson is half right; but only, as this essay shows, half right. For he is ignoring – as Thompson did not – the powerful opposing current within Muggletonianism which taught that it was not quixotic to dream of building a 'New Jerusalem'. That lesson was never totally forgotten, even if it was to find seemingly trivial expression in a never-ending spat over which edition of a seventeenth-century tract was preferable to the other.

Notes

1.   The main documentary source for this essay is the Muggleton Archive: (British Library) Additional MSS 60168–60256. Through John Harrison's kindness I was introduced to the widow of The Last Muggletonian, Philip Noakes (now Mrs Jean Barsley), and the essay draws upon, in addition, family papers which she placed at my disposal with great generosity. These are in the form of loose papers and exercise books which do not lend themselves to attribution. Where unreferenced quotations are made in what follows they are all drawn from Mrs Barsley's private collection. Her daughter, Carole Malone, and another Muggletonian descendant, Hilary Clark, also gave valuable assistance, which I am most happy to acknowledge.

2.   The finest assertion of autodidacticism comes from this letter of Mrs S.A. Huntley to Mrs F.E. Noakes in August 1901: 'I well remember when I *thought*, I knew, 55 years ago at the age of 17. I was staying at Putney, it was a lovely night, the Moon and Stars shining lovely. Opposite the Parkfield Cottages was a high land and many of the Villagers were standing there, amongst them was a University gentleman, who began to tell us the Stars were worlds etc. until I could stand it no longer and told him differently by the Scriptures. At last he got into such a rage, he said – who are you to contend with a man brought up at the University? I said this is the difference – you were brought up in the University on earth and I in the University of heaven.'

3.   The plaque commemorating the opening of the Reading Room (along with a portrait of Muggleton) can now be found in the Quiet Room of the Meeting House of the University of Sussex (donated by Mrs Barsley). It is referred to by A.P. Gordon, *Ancient and Modern Muggletonians* (Liverpool, 1870), p. 57.

4.   Reprinted in Lytton Strachey, *Portraits in Miniature* (New York, 1931), pp. 11–20.

5.   Ibid., pp. 15, 16, 17.

6.   Ronald Hutton, *Charles II* (Oxford, 1989), p. 457.

7.   Strachey, *Portraits*, p. 18.

8.   Ibid., pp. 11–12.

9.   Lawrence Clarkson, *The Lost Sheep Found* (London, 1660), *passim*; on whose career, see Barry Reay, 'Lawrence Clarkson: An Artisan and the English Revolution', in C. Hill, B. Reay and W. Lamont, *The World of the Muggletonians* (London, 1983), pp. 162–86.

10. Christopher Hill, *The World Turned Upside Down* (London, 1972).
11. M. Aikin, *Memoirs of Religious Imposters, from the Seventh to the Nineteenth Century* (London, 1823).
12. Patrick Collinson, 'Towards a Broader Understanding of the Early Dissenting Tradition', in R.C. Cole and M.E. Moody (eds), *The Dissenting Tradition: Essays for Leland H. Carlson* (Ohio, 1975), p. 26.
13. A signal exception is Barry Reay, *The Quakers and the English Revolution* (London, 1985).
14. Lodowicke Muggleton, *The Acts of the Witnesses of the Spirit* (London, 1699).
15. T.B. Macaulay, *History of England* (London, 1849–65), vol. 1, p. 164.
16. A.P. Gordon, *The Origins of the Muggletonians* (Liverpool, 1869), p. 1.
17. Ibid., p. 7.
18. (British Library) Additional MS 60170 (W. Cates to A.P. Gordon, 16 October 1869), no foliation.
19. Gordon, *Ancient and Modern*, p. 1.
20. (British Library) Additional MS 60170 (J.D. Aspland to W. Cates, 9 February 1871), no foliation.
21. Gordon, *Ancient and Modern*, p. 1, calls the restriction 'a very salutary law of this Society'.
22. George Borrow, *Lavengro* (London: Everyman Library, 1961), p. 138.
23. H. McLauchlan, *Alexander Gordon* (Manchester, 1932), p. 56.
24. H. McLauchlan, 'Alexander Gordon (1841–1931), Biographer and Historian', *Essays and Addresses* (Manchester, 1950), p. 293.
25. (British Library) Additional MS 61950 – donated by Miss E. Muggleton, to whom I am also indebted for help in writing this essay.
26. (British Library) Additional MS 60170, no foliation (obituary notice by Gordon on J.D. Aspland, 10 August 1877).
27. Ibid., (W. Cates to A.P. Gordon, 16 October 1869).
28. W. Stark, *The Sociology of Religion* (London, 1967), vol. 2, p. 112.
29. (British Library) Additional MS 60171, fo. 907 (Muggleton: Elizabeth Faggerter, 16 June 1682).
30. (British Library) Additional MS 60170, no foliation (Robinson to Gordon, undated, on Jessopp's maligning of the group). Cf. Augustus Jessopp, 'The Prophet of Walnut-Tree Yard', *The Nineteenth Century*, vol. 16, July–December 1884.
31. Ibid.; *Chambers Encyclopaedia*: 'The census of 1851 showed no trace of them and they are supposed to be now completely extinct;' Robinson received an apology from *Chambers Encyclopaedia* on 11 August 1881.
32. Cf. Mrs S.A. Huntley to Mrs F.E. Noakes, 7 September 1891: 'Father spent £800 in printing the Books and distributing them, I never heard that one was sold, or that one came to the truth through those three beautiful Pamphlets, although so well circulated in all parts of England.'
33. (British Library) Additional MS 44545, fo. 89. I owe both these references to the kindness of the Editor of *The Gladstone Diaries*, Dr H.C.G. Matthew.
34. Known to believers as the 'Great Book', but now more simply as (British Library) Additional MS 60171.
35. (British Library) Additional MS 60170, no foliation.
36. Ibid., this long anonymous piece, written on 1 January 1870, and entitled, *Faith and Practice of the Muggletonians*, is of first-class importance.

37. Ibid., see this disingenuous gloss: 'Many of the believers have their own
     particular views . . . but they do not affect the six principles.'
38. Ibid., on the Birchite schism in the previous century over 'immediate notice'
     the writer says 'as soon as those who had the ability to expand their partic-
     ular ideas fell off and died – their creed died with them'.
39. (British Library) Additional MS 60168, no foliation, has Joseph Frost's
     letter to the British Museum Trustees of 24 February 1853 defending the
     1661 edition ('feeling that every authors work should be kept entire as he
     leaves it') which was appended to the first volume of the Collected Works.
40. Ibid.; Thomas Robinson to Joseph Frost, 22 July 1857, contains the very
     full explanation of why Robinson wouldn't sign the Frost daughters' peti-
     tion, outlawing the 1656 edition of *The Divine Looking Glass*.
41. Mrs Isaac Frost, Senior to Thomas Robinson, November 1880 – 'in the
     same clear manner that you explained the cause of the Prophet Muggleton
     leaving out that part of the Divine Looking Glass, which in after years was
     again printed in that book'.
42. Mrs F. Lee to Mrs F. Noakes, 9 February 1933: 'You are most likely quite
     right in regard to Muggleton's revision of 'A Divine Looking Glass' and
     again we know printing was difficult to get done and very expensive to the
     believers in those days.'
43. (British Library) Additional MS 60171, fol. 1043.
44. George Rust, *A Letter of Resolution Concerning Origen and the Chief of
     his Opinions*, Marjorie Hope Nicolson (ed.), (New York, 1933), p. 136:
     quoted in John Stachniewski, *The Persecutory Imagination* (Oxford,
     1991), p. 334.
45. Royce MacGillvray, *Restoration Historians and the English Civil War* (The
     Hague, 1974).
46. John Reeve and Lodowicke Muggleton, *A Divine Looking Glass* (London,
     1656), p. 81, for example: 'Thus those which art spiritually rational mayest
     know, that it is neither Chance, nor Fortune, nor natural Endowments, nor
     deep Subtlety, nor Silver, nor Carnal Weapons, nor any Power in Men, nor
     Angels, is the cause of exalting Oliver Cromwell, in a Place of so great Con-
     cernment. But the mighty God of Israel hath brought it to pass, to manifest
     his prerogative Will on Earth, as it is in Heaven; that his Natural Wonders
     may be as visible unto Men in this World, as his spiritual Wonders are
     visible, I say unto Angels, Moses and Elias in That World To Come.'
47. William Lamont 'The Left and its Past: Revisiting the 1650s', *History
     Workshop*, 23, Spring 1987, pp. 141–53. My quarry in that article – and
     this essay – is not merely the recovery of a repressed radicalism in post-
     Restoration England, but a repressed *Cromwellianism*.
48. William Speck, 'Cromwell and the Glorious Revolution', *Images of Oliver
     Cromwell*, R.C. Richardson (ed.), (Manchester, 1993), p. 53.
49. Richard Baxter, *A Holy Commonwealth*, William Lamont (ed.),
     (Cambridge University Press, 1994).
50. David Underdown, *Fire from Heaven* (London, 1992).
51. E.P. Thompson, *Witness against the Beast* (Cambridge, 1993); Perry
     Anderson, 'Diary', *London Review of Books*, 21 October 1993, p. 25.

CHAPTER THREE

Roger Gibson and American Muggletonianism

E.P. Thompson

Without doubt there were some Muggletonian believers in North America in the eighteenth century, although we know little about them.[1] There were few enough of them in England, and it is probable that the only 'church', with regular meetings and records, was that in London. In any case there were no church premises, the faithful hiring rooms in public houses for their meetings and for singing their 'divine songs' set to the popular tunes of the day. There was no Muggletonian national structure, and the London church acted as a corresponding centre for isolated groups of followers, whether in Britain or overseas.[2] Some of these letters were preserved and copied for circulation among the faithful, and that is how the letters of Roger Gibson have survived.[3]

Gibson, a New London (Connecticut) merchant, was an occasional correspondent with the London church between 1773 and 1795. The port of New London was the site of the colony's custom-house and hence a busy merchant centre, and Gibson seems to have been well-to-do. He was in origin a native of Scotland and it is not known when he settled in Connecticut.[4] The border country of Connecticut and Rhode Island was then a hotbed of Protestant sectarianism, and New London had been an epicentre of the Great Awakening.[5] One might speculate that if Muggletonians crossed the Atlantic in the seventeenth century they might have been tempted to settle in Rhode Island, during the tolerant regime of Roger Williams. However, no continuities can be shown, and Gibson wrote in 1773, 'there are none here who understand this Commission or Doctrine . . . except one Man . . . who has professt this faith for thirty Years'. This was Captain Samuel Champlin from Rhode Island, who (we learn from a subsequent letter) was responsible for Gibson's own conversion, and who himself had been converted as a result of purchasing some of the prophets' books which he met with by accident at a public sale. But Champlin disappointed the puritanical Gibson, who was

> sorry that he has made so little progress all this time, by some parts of his conduct to give offence; indeed I can have little or no Unity with him, but leave him to which of the two Seeds which shall gain the predominance in him, to determine his State of Election or Reprobation; I lent him some of the Books which he had never seen

and told him when he had perused these, he might have others. He
indulges himself too much in Vain Sports and Pleasures of this life, to
the neglect of his necessary business, whereby he is reduced to a low
Ebb of Fortune, and made him in some Instances fraudulent. He has
two Young Men of his Sons who are in a prosperous Way and assist
him.[6]

It is evident that this was by no means the beginning of Gibson's
correspondence with the London church, which had been sending him
books, and which was enquiring about other contacts. Did Gibson know
of one Fleeming in Boston? Or of the 'Woman Bacon' in New York? She
was a servant maid, who had received books from the church. Gibson
replied:

> I remember about eleven years ago, I was at a House in New York,
> the Masters Name was Joseph Griswold a Distiler, who goes to no
> place of Worship, but from what principle he refrains, I know not;
> there I saw a Woman reading a Book, which I endeavouring to look
> to, she held it from me, it is possible, this was the Woman . . .

Gibson promised to enquire for Griswold next time he was in New York.
So slender were the links between the faithful! For some unexplained
reasons the letter concluded with gossip not about New London but
about Old:

> There is one Samuel Pike a noted Preacher in London of the Sect of
> the Independents Called Sandemanians, these Pharisees cast him out
> of their Synagogue (as I have heard) because he would not give his
> Daughter's Portion to their Church, and that she herself voted for his
> Excommunication, that Sect Uses the antient policy & fraud of the
> Papists, which is surprising impudence in these days.

Gibson hoped that the knowledge of the Commission of the Spirit could
be conveyed to Pike, for he might well be in a state of mind to turn to the
true faith.[7]

Gibson wrote to the church again on 23 May 1774. His letter does not
survive, but there is a copy of the church's reply.[8] Gibson had fulfilled his
promise when he went to New York:

> I am very glad to hear you have found out Mrs Bacon your
> Conversation may be a means to help her, for I perceive you have
> Raised a prayer in her and if She faint not She will be answ'red, but
> never can Expect it while She is under the power of a False Ministry,
> for as God gave all for our Redemption So he will have all the Whole
> man or none; I am of great hopes She is of the Royal Seed, for the
> Elect are fearfull their Name is not in the book of life, while the Seed
> of Reason, takeing hold of a Commission, are for Crouding into
> Heaven . . . Mine and the Church's Respects to her . . .

Of others mentioned in Gibson's previous letter, Samuel Pike, the
expelled Sandemanian, was dead, and so also was Mr Gray, who had

provided Mrs Griswold with books. John Middleton, the correspondent, added a comment: 'I perceive that Sect of the Rogereen's are acting over what the Ranters & Quaker's did att the Bigining.'[9]

Gibson's next letter was dated 30 June 1777 and it commences: 'the present War hinders all correspondence . . . but we medle not with Politics'. Samuel Champlin had 'got the better of his Foibles' and the two had been joined by a third believer, Nathaniel Rogers: 'We three meet every Sunday, for our mutual edification in love.' Gibson had heard that Mrs Bacon was well, but she lived 150 miles from him, and he had not seen her for several years. There followed some critical comments on her limited understanding of the true faith. She understood the cardinal Muggletonian doctrine that God is Christ. But

> she has no understanding of the differences of the three commissions, the power of a Commission, and how that there is no true Faith, but in the Commission then in being. I cannot help being surprised at her Ignorance, when I consider her good capacity, and the opportunity she has had for upwards of 14 Years, of all the Writings of the 2 last Prophets

that God had sent into 'this bloody unbeleiving [sic] world'.[10] However, there was hope that she might become more enlightened in time, if she did not 'confuse her mind with human Writing'. The letter then discussed the difficulties of corresponding or of conveying books. There was no post 'except when a Flag of Truce comes to this place'.[11]

Gibson's next letter may not have been until July 1785.[12] It commences: 'On account of the unhappy war lately ended, by the wofull Separation of two Countries, whose mutual Interest it was to be united, our correspondence has been interupted & I have been in great trouble & a bad state of health since the peace.' He had hoped to send a contribution towards reprinting the works of the prophets, but:

> When New London was burnt on Sept 6th, 1781, by the British Troops, my dwelling House, furniture, Clothing & Marchandize, books of accot.s, & Library of books, valuable Papers, as obligations, &c., were all destroyed in the Conflagration, so that I had nothing left me, but a Small farm about six miles From Town, & my outstanding debts, many of which I must lose by Saving only two of my Ledgers, &c in Consequence of the war, the Insolvency of many, & migration of others to I know not where: however I am trying again in my old Age to begin the World (as saith the proverb) for rebuilding my House in order to carry on som small trade for my farm will not do, having no help of my own and uncapable of Labour, it takes almost the whole for that & the Taxes which are most oppressive, before the war we know not what Taxes was here, they were then so trifling, but now we know the Difference.[13]

He had managed to save a recent consignment of books, except for *The*

Testament of the Twelve Patriarchs and Thomas Tomkinson's *A System of Religion*.

There was some news of other believers. 'My Son is a true believer . . . which is a great comfort to me, but there is no other of my family cares to know aney thing of the matter.' Samuel Champlin had died in 1779 'in great faith and Confidence of the truth of this Commission . . . some foibles he had, but who are without their failings?'

> Although there are many who tacitly aprove of the doctrine of this Commission, yet I know of none who proffesses openly the true faith (tho' there may be many & I not know it) but Mrs Bacon of New York, Colonel Stanton of Charlestown, State of Rhod Island about 30 miles from this & Nathaniel Rogers here; I have heard that there are several Believers Scattered about in America but Who they are I know not.

However there was news of one local convert:

> One Isaac Walden a true believer of this Commission, to whom I Lent the books by degrees, was very much concerned on Account of the Ignorance of the Proffessors of Religion, and imposture therein, Among all denominations, and Som in imitation of John Robins.[14] This friend desired my Assistance to have the Transcendant Treatise here reprinted which was done April 1783, a thousand copies were reprinted & they are all Sold, and not twenty left.[15]

Gibson concluded by criticizing the London church for not making the printer of the reprinted works of the prophets place his name on the title pages,

> for I am sure the liberty of the press has never been Allowed in great britain, since the Reign of William the 3d. Both Spiritual & temporal Tyrony had got a deadly blow, & may it never rise, the late revolution here has had this good effect, for before one could not have got the transcendent treatise reprinted, in this state.

The reply of the London church came not from his previous correspondent, John Middleton, but from Benedict Shield. The reason for this becomes immediately apparent. There had been a serious schism in the London church, and a body of about 30 had seceded to follow James Birch, a watch-maker, who claimed to have 'immediate notice' that he was to lead a 'second call' of the Third Commission. Gibson's former correspondent was among the secessionists, and Shield hastened to notify Gibson of the awful heresies of 'this Great Rebel and his Adherents', upon whom had been pronounced the 'sentence' of eternal damnation. Shield added his condemnation of a smaller group of secessionists, under Martha Collier, also around the issue of 'immediate notice', although stopping short of claiming a 'second call'. The air over the Atlantic was blue with the denunciation of the heretics.[16] Gibson was evidently highly regarded by the London church and the secessionists, as a major contact in the USA and perhaps as the major importer of Muggletonian books.[17] John Middleton and James Birch both wrote to him, putting the case of the seceders. Their letters are lost, but from Gibson's replies to Shield and to Middleton, it is clear that he upheld the position of the orthodox within the church.

The arguments are lengthy and repetitious, but the letters touch on other matters of interest. Gibson appears to have still been in touch with Mrs Bacon who 'Lives House-Keeper at a Distiler's Country Seat' 20 miles from New York. He had received (after some difficulty)[18] a box of books, which he hoped to distribute among people who live 'from thirty to upwards two hundred Miles from this, at different points of the Compass, and in sundry States' so that (he exulted) 'the sound of the Commission of the Spirit is gone through the most half of the United States of America, and to some of those under the British Government'. This had been assisted by the copies of the *Transcendent Spiritual Treatise* which they had reprinted:

> It was not so well printed, nor on so good paper as the London Edition, Isaac Walden had the chief hand in it; for his Occupation is a pedlar and a repairer of pewter, Tin, Brass & Copper Utensils; Travels through many places and meets with other Travelers going to & fro; I likewise in endeavouring to Collect my Debts, had occasion to go into different States, and always taking a Number of the above Books we reprinted, disposing of them to all who were disposed to buy them.

As for the recent box of books, Isaac Walden would take them around on his next circuit. The letter includes also an eloquent statement of Muggletonian expressions of faith in such a thinly scattered situation:

> As we have no Outward Ordinancies of Worship, nor bound to Meetings, it is not in the power of all the Devils who govern the world to hinder our Meetings, which are, when we Meet in the Streets, or in the Fields, or Change, in a House Public, or Private, or in a Vessel, by Water, or on the Land, we can Mutually Edify one another and consult what is for the good and Benefit of one another both in Spirituals and Temporals. Yet in a Place where there are two, or three, or more they may appoint time and place for Meeting, but this is at their Election.[19]

The letter to John Middleton was firm in the orthodox faith, and hoped for his repentance, but was friendly in tone. It provides a little more evidence of Gibson's attitude to the revolution, which turned largely upon his merchanting interest:

> Please to acquaint Thomas Joseph that there never was much encouragement for the arts he and his son profess in this part of America where I am: the Southern parts are more opilent and do

have such things but now even they are upon a plan of Oeconomy. It
has been of the most Mischievous consequence both to great Brittain
and America, the Universal Credit given by the British Merchants to
the American Merchants. They ought not to have Credited us more
than we sent Effects to pay for, had it not been for that we would
have been one people perhaps for ever, for they made us fat and we
kicked. I was offered any Credit I pleased, but I refused, as I choosed
to keep within the bounds of my small Capital.[20]

This run of papers also includes a list of 48 books, some in sheets and
some bound, sent to Gibson in July 1786 and paid for (£2. 18s. 10d.) in
April 1789. There are 14 titles in all, taking in the main Muggletonian
texts.

Gibson's letters to the seceders, Birch and Middleton, were copied and
laid before the believers at their meeting at the Blue Boar in Aldersgate
Street, and other copies were sent into the country. Benedict Shield
reported that 'all Rejoice in your Strength of Faith'.[21] Gibson replied in
April 1788 – his son had to write the letter as his shoulder was dislocated
– transcribing a further letter to him from James Birch. It is a ranting
tirade against 'the foam, spit and spue of all the new-born of Death and
Hell', claiming himself to be a Messenger of Jesus with special powers.
Birch was kind enough to tell Gibson that he had a serpent's head and
scorpion's heart and was riding on the ass of Reason, and assured him
that he would be cast into a lake to burn in wrath. This correspondence
with the home country was providing Gibson with scant comfort.[22]

This schism clouded the correspondence for a year or two.[23] The last
letter of Gibson's to be preserved is that of an ageing man, but it is of particular interest. He had lost all his contacts in New York:

> They are all either dead, or gone elsewhere, the late Revolution has
> caused great changes here, and in other parts of the World, and may
> turn out for a General good, tho' in such Cases the consequence is
> Evill to many, of whom I am One, but Liberty of Conscience is
> Established in these States here to the greatest Extent, which is one of
> the greatest Naturall Rights of mankind.

The Muggletonians generally kept quiet about their faith and did not
proselytize, placing all their confidence upon keeping the published
works of the prophet in circulation. Gibson again complained that the
reprinted works carried no printer's name nor place of sale:

> In my youth I was very inquisitive about Religious Matters, being
> concerned that I might obtain Salvation, and being very Sceptical
> with regard to Revelation, Occasioned by the difft. opinions of the
> Several Sects Called Christians, & I thought the Bible was one of the
> most Inconsistent Books that ever I read in the Doctrines thereof ...
> tho' the Morals inculcate therein, Excelled all others, whether
> Pagan, Mohomedan, Jew, or Christian; for I had read those called
> the best Authors among them all.

He had remained in this state of impartiality, unconnected with any denomination nor frequenting any form of worship ('but only for Amusement'), and 'neither believing nor disbelieving any thing about Religion . . . but only Morall Virtue', until Samuel Champlin had lent him some books of Reeve and Muggleton. This effected his conversion, and he was determined to have all the books himself if they were possible 'to be had at any Rate'. He wrote to a correspondent in London 'who tho' of the Quaker denomination was as great a Sceptick as formerly was myself', who found out the Muggletonian meeting and passed on to it Gibson's request for books. He added that he had 'a great affection' for John Middleton, as he was his first correspondent with the church: 'my heart bleeds for him'.

But Gibson's efforts to win converts through books were not going well. He had disposed of few of the last box of books. He had loaned out several, but although the readers 'aprove of them above whatever they heard or saw before, yet the Love of this World and things thereof, takes up their Minds from Attention, and except two, a Man and his Wife, there is none that I know of who is come openly to own his Faith . . .'

> but Scepticks & Deists approves of it as the best System of Revealed Religion that ever they saw or heard of, and som (like Agripa) say, they are almost persuaded to become Muggletonians, yet they do not purchase any of the Books, which is a sure Sign, that the Spirit of corrupt Reason the Devil predominates in them . . . The Proffessors of Religion are in General, so prejudiced by their Leaders, that they will neither see nor hear . . . In providence there seems to be a general disposition stired up in the Minds of Mankind in many places of the World, to Assert their Naturall Rights and Properties, in oposition to Spirituall & Temporall Tyrany & Imposition; if they persevere and Succeed, it may bring about a general knowledge of this Commission of the Spirit. The Believers who formerly lived in this Township are either dead, or removed to other Places, so there are now none here who openly proffess this Faith but myself & Son.[24]

Thus Gibson's correspondence concludes, much as it had continued, on a note of vague euphoria coupled with modest realism. More letters probably passed, since the archive contains a copy of a letter from Thomas Pickersgill to Gibson in 1795, which, after much pious recital of Muggletonian doctrine, acknowledges his request for books, informs him that 26 miscellaneous books are being sent, and concludes:

> You Inform us of James Durham living at New York. He as sent a letter to is friends lately, that he going to Return to England. And as for the Trobles of the Nation & Diferint powers at war, we have nothing To do with, but I believe the prophets words, is Coming to pass Quickly.[25]

One cannot with any confidence draw large conclusions from this

material. It may perhaps afford the most comprehensive account of
Muggletonian influences in North America in the late eighteenth century.[26] If there were other centres of the faith these would probably have
come to the notice of Gibson or of the London church. The exchanges
have their own inherent interest, and show the great difficulties of trans-
planting a strange heresy across the Atlantic. I do not know that
Muggletonian ideas had any influence in America; they did not collide
with any intellectual genius, as they might have collided in England with
William Blake.[27] But there is one line in Gibson's last letter which pro-
vokes sober reflections: 'I am informed there are many believers of this
Commission in Several of the Southern States.' This is a question which
requires more expert investigation than I am able to give to it. That antinomian oppositions between works and faith, law and grace, were often
present in the black churches of the south is a commonplace. Genovese
tells us that a white clergyman complained (1832) that 'many of the
blacks look upon white people as merely taught by the Book; they consider themselves instructed by the inspiration of the Spirit'.[28] This opposition between the 'Letter' and faith is central to Muggletonian doctrine.
But we can go closer still. Genovese, referring to the Mississippi Valley
Baptists, writes: 'So far did one wing go that its famous two-seed doctrine, according to which Eve produced two seeds only one of which
originated with God, has quite sensibly been classified by some scholars
as thinly-disguised Manichaeanism.'[29] But this is also undisguised
Muggletonian doctrine, according to which Satan copulated with Eve,
giving conception to Cain, through whom the seed of the devil (or
Reason) entered into the human race, whereas the seed of 'the woman'
was the seed of God or of faith, conveyed through Abel and Seth. Hence
these two seeds wrestled in the human species (and in individuals) for
predominance, and it was predetermined that one or other must gain
ascendancy. A version of this doctrine was preached by Daniel Parker of
'Two-Seed-in-the-Spirit' fame and his followers in Tennessee and
Kentucky: 'The bad seed, or spirit of the serpent or devil, entered Eve
when she fell, and by her was transmitted down the stream of life.'[30]

I do not know that this doctrine can be recovered from any other
source than Muggletonianism, short of questing back to Cabbalistic, or
to gnostic and Manichaean origins. From what source did Elder Dan
Parker gain his inspiration? His 'anti-mission' Baptists were familiar with
the language of seventeenth-century antinomians, some of which would
have warmed Blake's heart: 'Money and Power are the principal members of the old beast.' These doctrines were chiefly espoused by poor
whites, and one may guess at the convenience of the doctrine of Two
Seeds as legitimation of racism. But, then, the doctrine could, without
any modification, be reversed and taken over by blacks. In Muggle-

tonianism, the doctrine of the two seeds, the uncompromising defences of spiritual autonomy against the 'kingdom of the Beast', combined with a political quietism which might seem to be splendidly constructed for slave religion: and the naturalistic symbolism of Eve and the Serpent might also connect with survivals of Afro-American animism. Did copies of Isaac Walden's reprinted *Transcendent Spiritual Treatise* find their way to Kentucky and Tennessee? But I have long trespassed beyond the evidence, and must leave the enquiry to others.

Notes

1. I am much indebted to Professor Jon Butler for a sight of his forthcoming entry on 'Protestant Pluralism' for the *Encyclopedia of the North American Colonies*, and also to Professors John Demos, Philip Greven, J. Jefferson Looney, David Montgomery and Richard Simmons, for much helpful advice.
2. There is an account of the eighteenth-century London church in my *Witness against the Beast: William Blake and the Moral Law* (Cambridge, 1993), ch. 6.
3. In the British Library, in Additional MSS 60168–70.
4. He is referred to as 'from Glasgow' in Francis Manwaring Caulkins, *History of New London, Connecticut* (New London, 1895), p. 457 n. From his correspondence it appears that his sister lived in Edinburgh. In the *Diary of Joshua Hempstead* (New London County Historical Society, 1901), p. 633, there is a reference in 1754 to the marriage of 'Mr Roger Gibson an old Countryman', which might possibly be him.
5. See Harry S. Stout and Peter Onouf, 'James Davenport and the Great Awakening in New London', *Journal of American History*, 71, (3), December 1983.
6. Roger Gibson to Benedict Shield and friends, New London, 2 November 1791.
7. Roger Gibson to John Middleton, New London, 4 March 1773.
8. John Middleton to Roger Gibson, 5 July 1774.
9. The Rogerenes were a dissident group led by John Rogers, which split off from the Baptists in 1677 in Rhode Island and which also won support in New London; John Rogers Bolles and Anna B. Williams, *The Rogerenes: Some Hitherto Unpublished Annals Belonging to the Colonial History of Connecticut* (Boston, 1904).
10. According to Muggletonian doctrine, Reeve and Muggleton were called as prophets of a Third (and last) Commission, which was embodied in the faith of believers.
11. Roger Gibson to John Middleton, New London, 30 June 1777.
12. Roger Gibson to John Middleton, New London, 4 July 1785.
13. *The Public Records of the State of Connecticut, 1783–4* (Hartford, 1943) record a memorial from Roger Gibson (p. 415) pleading for an abatement of taxes in view of the burning of his house, buildings and property on 6 September 1781: the memorial was successful. That Gibson's losses were considerable is confirmed by his being listed among the largest of the New

London sufferers (at £884 18s. 6½d.) entitled to claim shares in the compensation secured by Connecticut's 'Western Reserve' (subsequently Ohio): see ibid., *1789–92* (Hartford, 1948), May 1792, pp. 449, 467. Another sufferer (p. 466) was Lodwick Champlin: he and Joseph Champlin may have been Samuel Champlin's sons.

14. John Robins, a Ranter and pretender to divinity, was sentenced to eternal damnation by Reeve and Muggleton in 1651, and hence entered into Muggletonian mythology: see Christopher Hill, Barry Reay and William Lamont, *The World of the Muggletonians* (London, Temple Smith, 1983), pp. 67–70.

15. This was John Reeve, *A Transcendent Spiritual Treatise*, sometimes attributed to Reeve and Muggleton, first published in 1652, reprinted 1711 and 1756 (London). It may have been the only Muggletonian work printed and published in North America: it is the only item so published noted in the National Union Catalogue, and *The Eighteenth-Century Short Title Catalogue* (London, British Library, 1992) cites the second edition, New London (Conn.), printed by James Springer for Isaac Walden, Carter's Island, 1797.

16. For this heresy see William Lamont, 'Lodowick Muggleton and "Immediate Notice" ', in Hill, Reay and Lamont, ch. 5.

17. Benedict Shield to Roger Gibson, London, 4 July 1786.

18. The letters carry many details of the hazards of the transatlantic passage and carriage of books, of customs and postage, of the difficulties of transmitting remittances during the state of war, etc. All this will be well known to historians of America.

19. Roger Gibson to Benedict Shield, no date (in response to Shield's of 4 July 1786).

20. Roger Gibson to John Middleton, New London, 19 January 1787.

21. Benedict Shield to Roger Gibson, London, 4 September 1787.

22. Roger Gibson to Benedict Shield, New London, 18 April 1788.

23. There are two further letters on the controversy. Gibson to Shield, New London, 6 April 1789, and Shield to Gibson, London, 29 June 1789. Both concerned payment for books and James Birch's secession.

24. Roger Gibson to Benedict Shield, New London, 2 November 1791.

25. Thomas Pickersgill to Roger Gibson, London, 4 September 1795.

26. London church members had a little correspondence with fellow believers in North America in the nineteenth and twentieth centuries: see, for example Thomas Robinson (of Camberwell) to Mrs White (New York), 1845, copied in British Library Additional MSS; also Hill, Reay and Lamont, *The World*, pp. 4–5.

27. See also William Lamont's essay, Chapter 2 above, on the later incidence of Muggletonianism in America.

28. Eugene Genovese, *Roll, Jordan, Roll* (New York, 1972), p. 214.

29. Ibid., p. 243.

30. Elmer T. Clark, *The Small Sects in America* (New York, 1965), pp. 199–204. Also Walter Brownlow Posey, *The Baptist Church in the Lower Mississippi Valley, 1776–1845* (Lexington, Ky), pp. 70–1.

CHAPTER FOUR

The Antinomian Methodists

Peter Lineham

John Harrison in his writings has consistently argued for the importance of religious values on social life, particularly from minor religious traditions. He has shown how religion's ideas, forms and attitudes shaped social values and structures. This approach deserves to be employed more extensively by historians. In this essay I want to trace a curious group, the Antinomian Methodists, who came from the mainstream of popular religion, even though they were Methodism and Calvinism 'off the rails'. Semmel in his pioneering study of the social significance of Methodism suggested that much of Wesley's theology was shaped by a desire to rebut antinomianism.[1] Yet antinomianism is regularly viewed only through the eyes of its opponents. Antinomian Methodism, although it attracted few wealthy followers, was a familiar option in the community of the poor. Unlocking its logic and forms can explain something of the intellectual world of early industrial England.

The earliest Methodist antinomian

George Whitefield knew the environment of the transatlantic great awakening well, and he never anticipated many problems from extremes of Calvinism in England. America was a different story. Writing to an American friend about opposition to the revival he commented that '*sinless perfection* hath been propagated in England, and *Antinomian principles* suffered to spread among you'.[2] Certainly there was a fair measure of 'false fire' in the Great Awakening, and its extremism and the moral lapses led to damaging accusations of antinomianism.[3] But Whitefield soon discovered he was wrong about England. He met William Cudworth.

Cudworth was born in London in 1717 or 1718. He was a tradesman, who at the age of 20 read *The Sincere Convert* by Thomas Shepherd (1604–49), a Puritan critic of Hutchinsonianism in Massachussets Bay. Thus he encountered the doctrine of the imputed righteousness of Christ.[4] A sermon by an old-fashioned Scottish Calvinist minister in London, the Reverend William Crookshanks, induced Cudworth to join the Swallow Street church, where Crookshanks ministered. Cudworth became a zealous conservative dissenter and student of the Puritans. A typical religious zealot, he was contemptuous of the evangelical focus on the forgiveness of sins.[5] Underneath he was a classic candidate for evangelical conversion. Early one Friday morning in May 1743, pangs of spiritual distress drove him to Whitefield's Tabernacle. There he heard the young preacher, John Cennick, speak on 'Jesus Christ the same yesterday, today and forever'. A moment of awakening resulted, as he discovered that by faith he could receive Christ.[6] He had found a Methodist route to the Puritan vision of faith in the divine promise.

Cudworth immediately began a religious society for his friends at Swallow Street.[7] This burst of evangelical enthusiasm led him to be accused of antinomianism. He is supposed to have said: 'If I embraced my hands in my father and mother's blood, it would not startle my assurance.'[8] His minister in Sunday sermons sought to stem the tide towards Methodism. He warned his congregation not to accept the doctrine that assurance of faith was possible.[9] Cudworth responded in no uncertain terms to this sermon, declaring that, 'justifying faith is the very coming, the very reliance, (a sort of assurance you seem to have no idea of at present) . . . that those who do so shall be saved'.

A few years later, in 1748, Crookshanks was dismissed from the ministry but in 1743 Cudworth was forced out and subsequently the session excommunicated him.[10] Cudworth's religious society and friends left too and by October 1744 they had hired a former Huguenot church in Peter's Yard, Castle Street, near Leicester Fields, close to Cudworth's house in St Martin's Lane.[11] Meanwhile John Cennick at the Tabernacle befriended the eager convert, and appointed him a teacher at the Tabernacle school. He met Whitefield and was received by the Tabernacle Conference as a lay preacher in January 1744, and his chapel was adopted as a Whitefieldite preaching place.[12] In the September 1744 meeting of the English Calvinist Methodist Association, Cudworth was appointed to assist Herbert Jenkins care for the London societies.[13]

The Tabernacle had a rough time in the mid-1740s, despite the support it had from a huge number of London artisans. Calvinist Methodism's blend of Puritan theology and Moravian experience proved a volatile combination, particular because it was dispensed by somewhat immature preachers. Cudworth introduced them to high Calvinism. They were soon startled by his insistence that assurance was not a distinct experience, but was an aspect of faith. The appeal of Methodism, whether Calvinist or Arminian, was usually its offer of an experience of assurance that faith was real. Cudworth argued that faith contained in itself all the assurance one needed.[14]

Whitefield heard about Cudworth's views before he went to America in August 1744, but he took no action.[15] A few months later some members of the Tabernacle expressed anxiety about Cudworth's orthodoxy

and asked what was going on in his chapel in Peter's Yard.[16] Howel
Harris, Whitefield's deputy, agreed that the next quarterly meeting of the
English Calvinist Association should be held in London so that it could
consider the issue. That meeting on 12 December 1744 erupted into a
debate between Harris and Cudworth. Cudworth in preaching to the
association, criticized the Tabernacle's doctrines as 'legal' not evangelical.[17] John Cennick supported him. He had written a preface recom-
mending Cudworth's edition of the writings of the antinomian Puritan,
John Simpson,[18] and he now declared to the association that he 'had
more outward light in conversing with Bro. Cudworth'. Harris sought to
impose Whitefield's sermon on the marks of faith as a doctrinal standard,
but Cudworth rejected this solution. Harris was horrified but others were
not yet willing to discipline him.[19]

   The crisis grew when the chief woman labourer at the Tabernacle,
Elizabeth Wood, complained to others that Cudworth had no 'knowledge or faith and not much grace'.[20] Did the Tabernacle have to tolerate
his errors? Two orthodox Calvinist preachers, Thomas Adams and
Herbert Jenkins, demanded that members be admitted only if they could
prove their conversion by their behaviour.[21] Cudworth responded with a
pamphlet which rejected all outward guarantees of conversion. Another
preacher wrote the introduction to the work.[22] Respectable Calvinists
were outraged. James Erskine, the Scottish MP, complained that
Cudworth denied the believer's responsibility to grow in godliness, and
thus confirmed Wesley's charge that Calvinists did not take sin
seriously.[23]

   Cudworth's position nevertheless appealed to many because it contrasted sharply with the religious moralism of the age. When the
Tabernacle society split over the issue in April 1745, his party was the
larger one.[24] The preachers were less sympathetic, and Cudworth needed
Cennick's protection.[25] Howel Harris soon returned to London and
asked Cudworth to preach on 'how he received his knowledge of Jesus
Christ, and what trials he has met within that account'.[26] Harris was convinced after hearing him that 'either he was never awakened or else is
now asleep and has not the care of the churches on him', and refused to
preach again at the Tabernacle if Cudworth was admitted there.[27] Harris
later told Whitefield:

> it was press'd deep in my heart that he was not to labour with us &
> so aft[r] much time spent together in endeavouring to come together &
> understand each other I was oblidg'd [sic] to declare that I must go
> off if he would come in, & so it was agreed that he sh[d] depart
> quietly.[28]

On 31 May a trial was held and Cudworth was accused of 'antinomianism that drunk into his spirit'. Cennick then reluctantly agreed to exclude

him from the Tabernacle pulpit, although for his own part he continued
to preach at Cudworth's own chapel.[29] The Tabernacle published a letter
by the interfering, but orthodox Calvinist, Mrs Dutton, to persuade
members of Cudworth's errors.[30]

The next quarterly meeting of the English Calvinist Association on 12
June 1745 at Frogford, Wiltshire, implicitly condemned Cudworth, but
permitted him the dignity of resignation.[31] Cennick disapproved, and
preached for his chapel the next Sunday. Cennick had, however, decided
to join the Moravians, and they insisted that he broke off his contact with
Cudworth, who had allowed a renegade Moravian to preach in his
chapel.[32] Cennick later admitted that his support of Cudworth had made
the split in the Tabernacle worse.[33]

In Whitefield's absence the Tabernacle society had lurched from crisis
to crisis. Howel Harris believed that Cudworth was to blame, describing
him as 'an enemy to the work of the Spirit in us'.[34] Whitefield on his
return to England in 1748 wrote coldly to Cudworth: 'by what you have
published and I have perused, you have unhappily fallen into some principles, which are contrary to the revealed will of God'.[35] Years later
Whitefield conceded that his antinomianism 'seems only to be speculative',[36] but would not allow him back in the fold.[37] For his part
Cudworth was frustrated at the Calvinists' deference to the evangelist,
insisting, 'Mr Whitefield is but a man, and his preaching or not preaching
a thing does not make it to be true or false.'[38]

Cudworth's connexion

When Cudworth and his society seceded, they decided to form a dissenting church. So in June 1745 Sunday worship commenced at the former
Huguenot chapel at the corner of Black Eagle and Grey Eagle Streets in
Spitalfields. In December 1745 Cudworth was ordained and the church
formally established.[39] The former French chapel in Peter's Yard,
Leicester Fields, which he had used in 1743 and had a license as an episcopal chapel, joined his connexion in 1746.[40] In 1747 Cudworth
acquired another former French chapel in Henjoye Street, Wapping and
later opened other preaching places in Petticoat Lane and Angel Alley.[41]
Then in 1754 Cudworth leased a site in Margaret Street, near Oxford
Circus, and erected a house and a pentagonal meeting house, the New
Chapel, Cavendish Square. Ben Franklin later described this building as
'a perfectly phenomenal ugliness, wherein it was doubtless aided by the
architectural monstrosity of its design'.[42]

The new connexion was unstable. Initially Cudworth attracted many
hearers at the expense of the Tabernacle but few of them stayed.[43] The

connexion split twice in the late 1740s.[44] It became a church on the radical fringe, and rejected the name Methodist.[45] Wesley attacked Cudworth in print in 1745, further isolating him.[46] In retaliation on 2 July 1747 Cudworth's supporters cheated Wesley of his normal outdoor pulpit in the Moorfields.[47] Yet Cudworth acted as a mediator between Cennick and the Tabernacle when Cennick seceded.[48] He attracted dissident preachers from other Methodist connexions, for example Heatly from Chatham.[49] In 1751 he re-established links with the now disgraced Howel Harris.[50] His fellow-teacher in the Tabernacle school, William Allt, became one of his preachers in 1745.[51] So did William Collins, a former Moravian and former Calvinist Methodist, but in June 1747 he seceded with the Wapping congregation.[52]

The final split of Cudworth from the Methodists was provoked not by his theology but his ecclesiology, when he published a pamphlet in mid-1745, which Howel Harris summarized as 'about order &c ag^t our way'.[53] It declared that the biblical pattern was congregational independence. In June 1747 the members of Cudworth's chapel signed a covenant outlining their convictions about baptism, the Lord's supper and hymn singing (a Methodist rather than a dissenting practice).[54] The church followed Moravian and Presbyterian precedents in appointing lay elders, deacons, elder-women, deaconesses and choirs.[55] Cudworth's 1746 *Collection of Hymns* used on its title page a delightful Moravian engraving of a neat but crowded sheepfold enclosed by railings. In place of the front gate lay a lamb holding a cross and a banner reading 'salvation'.[56] Underneath are the words:

> This keeps the fold secure,
> The Lamb stays at the door;
> We count him all our own, –
> Flesh, blood & what he has done.

Subsequent hymns continue the theme. At the very time that evangelical independent dissenters were becoming more connexional, Cudworth chose another direction.

Cudworth's refusal to identify the elect by their good works led him into ecclesiastical experiments. He believed that believers were directly taught by the apostles the true ways of Christ, and his church called itself the Hearers of the Apostles and Prophets.[57] Since he believed that very few people truly understood the gospel, Cudworth felt that the true church was necessarily small. National churches were a particular abomination in his eyes, and he criticized the Methodists for not declaring themselves separate from the state church.[58] The Cudworthian approach influenced other Antinomians particularly the Walkerites of Dublin who in turn influenced the early Plymouth Brethren.[59]

Cudworth's followers were not the only Antinomians. The Moravians were often accused of antinomianism by other Methodists because of the Lutheran aspects of their theology, whereas Cudworth admired them, described his doctrine as 'mostly Lutheran', and viewed Christ as the lamb of God. The Hearers of the Apostles had the temerity to complain that the Moravians did not preach the blood and wounds of Christ sufficiently![60] The two groups differed primarily over their patterns of leadership.[61] Some early Moravians explored the Cudworthian option as they grew frustrated with their German masters, but the Moravian authorities kept careful note of those who attended Cudworth's church and in June 1746 rebuked them.[62] Cudworth hoped for some understanding between the two groups and wrote to argue the case:

> The Lord has called a few of us together in his name & fellowship, & are all of one heart & one mind, our doctrine is Christ alone, whom each of us knows for himself, & being delivered from the schemes of men, we find thro' the holy scriptures a blessed increase of true wisdom & spiritual understanding . . . & to be united in heart with all them who loved the Lord Christ in sincerity. We are therefore desirous of as intimate an acquaintance, friendship & union as you are pleased to admit of, believing that your advice & counsel may be of great pleasing to us.[63]

The Moravian leadership was utterly unsympathetic. James Hutton wrote sharply to Cudworth rejecting the proposal.[64] Cudworth later wrote a pamphlet against the Moravians in order to define his differences with them.[65]

Cudworth was primarily a Londoner, but he itinerated regularly as far north as Manchester. He was travelling in Staffordshire at the time of his death in 1763.[66] Curiously the Leicestershire revival from which the Arminian Baptists emerged, owed much to him. William Kendrick, one of its first leaders, although originally a Wesleyan and then a Moravian, in 1745 seceded to Cudworth, while another pioneer, Stephen Dixon, also knew Cudworth,[67] and he was noted throughout the county as a preacher and debater.[68] Eventually Leicestershire Methodists rejected his theology, but significant pockets of antinomianism remained and there was a Cudworthian chapel in the Nottingham area as late as 1777.[69]

James Wheatley

Cudworth's most significant impact in the provinces was in Norwich, through the renegade Wesleyan preacher James Wheatley. Wheatley had itinerated for Wesley from 1742,[70] and became a very prominent Wesleyan preacher. John Wesley admitted the fact:

this man became a most popular preacher. He was admired more and more wherever he went, till he went over the second time into Ireland, and conversed more intimately than before with some of the Moravian preachers. The consequence was that he leaned more and more to their doctrine and manner of preaching. At first several of our preachers complained of this: he by slow and imperceptible degrees brought all the preachers then in the kingdom to think and speak like himself.[71]

Wesley's information was partly right. In November 1750 Wheatley met the Moravians while visiting his brother in Yorkshire,[72] but he also had longer-term contact with the Calvinist Methodists. He attended a meeting of the English Calvinist Methodist connexion in September 1746 in Gloucestershire without authorization from Wesley,[73] and Howel Harris had 'sweet conversation' with Wheatley when visiting Plymouth in February 1747.[74]

Other Wesleyan preachers rejected Arminianism, but Wheatley was one of the few to be disciplined, and only because in June 1751 he was accused of sexual improprieties. He eventually admitted sexual misdemeanours with five women, but accused other preachers of similar failings.[75] This provoked a crisis for Wesleyan Methodism, and four other itinerants were suspended. Although it was a case of practical antinomianism, Wesley suspected there were theological causes, perhaps Cudworth was involved. The suspended preachers 'preached Christ' and 'preached the gospel', and criticized other preachers as 'legal wretches' or 'doctors of divinity'.[76]

Wheatley established himself as a preacher in Norwich late in August 1751. By late 1751 revival had broken out in Norwich. Thousands flocked to hear him preach and about 2 200 people joined his society.[77] He opened a meeting house on St John's Timber-hill, and called it the Tabernacle. Yet in the face of intense mob hostility, he looked not to the London Tabernacle but to Cudworth for help.[78] Cudworth visited in December 1751 in the company of a Mr Silverthorn. He was nearly murdered in an outdoor field shortly after his arrival, and he and Silverthorn were burned in effigy to the shrill cries of 'blasphemy, imposter, schismatick, antichrist'.[79] He returned to Norwich so frequently in the fifties that he became known to posterity as 'Cudworth of Norwich'.[80] Wheatley's followers were soon called 'dear hearers', no doubt in imitation of the Hearers of the Apostles in London.[81]

This assistance did not solve Wheatley's problems. The anti-Methodist violence persisted because Cudworth did not have the public prestige of Wesley or Whitefield to defend the converts. Perhaps rumours about Wheatley and Cudworth worsened the criticisms.[82] Wheatley later accepted help from other sources, and when a new tabernacle was erected, he accepted a gift from the Countess of Huntingdon. Whitefield preached at the opening in April 1753, and returned early in 1754.[83] Wheatley also invited the Moravians but they rebuffed him.[84]

Then came a new crisis for the Norwich society. In December 1753 Wheatley was accused of adultery with one of his converts. The accusations became public in July 1754.[85] Wheatley was attacked in print and was expelled from his own society, although Cudworth defended him in print.[86] The case was a *cause célèbre* in the summer of 1754, and in November 1754 it went to the Consistory Court in Norwich. In February 1756 Wheatley was ordered to do public penance in a linen cloth with a paper pinned to his breast, saying he was a 'lewd, debauched, incontinent and adulterous person' – the very essence of an Antinomian.[87] He appealed to the Court of Arches in 1757 but was found guilty and excommunicated. He appealed again to the High Court of Delegates in Canterbury in 1759 and seems to have been found guilty in November 1759.[88] After that Wheatley went abroad.

In the midst of the scandal in July 1754 the Wesley brothers arrived in Norwich.[89] They decided to recommence Methodism in the town, and a chapel ironically named the Foundry was opened, and attracted some of Wheatley's congregation.[90] Charles Perronet, who had already published an account of the Norwich riots, supported Wesley with an open letter to Wheatley.[91] Wesley privately urged that Whitefield should take charge of the Tabernacle society.[92] Cudworth would not abandon his friends.[93] Like Wesley he wrote to Whitefield about developments, and Whitefield agreed to provide supply preachers for the Tabernacle pulpit from 1755,[94] but Cudworth wanted to preach next time he visited, and orthodox Calvinists thereafter were sometimes excluded.[95] Wheatley soon resumed control of the much reduced society using as his assistant Robert Robinson, but Robinson separated from the Tabernacle in 1758, repulsed by Wheatley's morals, and became a distinguished Baptist minister in Cambridge.[96] When Whitefield visited Norwich in 1762 and 1767, he preferred to avoid the Tabernacle.[97]

The break with Whitefield led Wheatley to offer the Tabernacle not to Cudworth but to Wesley in November 1758.[98] It was a strange turn of events. Wesley decided to unite the Tabernacle and Foundry societies. It was a bizarre experiment, given that antinomianism was Wesley's *bête noir,* and Arminianism was beyond the pale for Cudworth. Yet Cudworth urged Tabernacle members to join in the union, and Wesley permitted non-Anglican celebrations of communion in the Tabernacle, allowed meetings to clash with church services and baptized some converts by immersion.[99] Once again there was a crisis because Cudworth would not abandon Norwich. In 1759 Wesley found him preaching in the branch Tabernacle at Forncet and they had a frosty meeting.[100]

Hatred of the Wesleyan doctrine of perfection was rife in the Tabernacle.[101] Wesley tried to put the best construction on events, conscious that the membership of the society was very large. Yet the members could not be reconciled to Arminian theology and Wesley became irritated: 'For many years I have had more trouble with this society than with half the societies of England put together,' he complained. 'With God's help, I will try you one year longer; and I hope you will bring forth better fruit.'[102] He withdrew permission for Communion to be celebrated in the chapel, and the membership promptly declined. By October 1764 the numbers were so low that he surrendered the lease on the Tabernacle, concluding that Arminian Methodism was incompatible with other viewpoints. Yet those in Norwich who went with him remained afflicted with antinomianism.[103] The Tabernacle transferred to the Countess of Huntingdon's connexion. Wheatley was preaching in the Birmingham region in 1763 and still had close women associates. He died in 1776.[104]

Wheatley outlived Cudworth. In his last years a friendship developed between him and James Hervey.[105] Hervey was famous on account of his evangelical writings, and was a high Calvinist. He sought to use his influence with Whitefield and Wesley to bring Cudworth back within the pale, but they were unconvinced. When Hervey died in 1759, Cudworth lost a friend whose judgement he respected. Cudworth died in June 1763 after a sudden illness while itinerating in Staffordshire. His deathbed letter to his wife and family became a popular antinomian document.[106]

After Cudworth's death his small connexion fell apart, although the chapel in Margaret Street remained to the end of the eighteenth century. The leading London Anglo-Catholic church of All Saints Margaret Street was later erected on the site. The Peter Street congregation negotiated a merger with the Swallow Street Presbyterian church in 1778,[107] and thus the Hearers of the Apostles united with the body from which they had originally split. Others including the Sandemanians and Rellyeans inherited the reputation of Antinomian Methodists.

The significance of Cudworth's theology

Cudworth was inherently a controversialist, and indulged in pamphlet warfare with many popular religious writers, among them Ann Dutton, James Relly, William Law, Dr Free, Robert Sandeman, Wesley and Whitefield. His writing was blunt and unvarnished, but 'very sophistical and adapted to deceive unwary souls'.[108] Howel Harris commented: 'I believe Bro' Cudworth's spirit ye most still and selfish and incorrigible yet

I believe his Light was originally from the Holy Spirit, and his own wisdom stop'd in secretly.'[109] How did Cudworth define antinomianism? His hymns explain the appeal of the doctrine for the Hearers of the Apostles. One can imagine his congregation singing the following hymn enthusiastically:

> Before I knew the Lamb of God,
> Had made me perfect in his blood,
> My soul continually did lie,
> In unbelief and misery.
>
> I saw my heart, day after day,
> After the vainest objects stray,
> My nature vile, I full of sin,
> A wretch polluted and unclean.
>
> And tho' the preachers often said,
> Consider not thy body dead,
> But hear what Jesu's word doth say,
> Thy sins, poor soul, are wash'd away.
>
> Yet still I staggered at the word,
> And disbeliev'd my loving Lord,
> But when a frame I did possess
> I then thought Christ my righteousness.
>
> Sometimes believing, as I thought,
> And sometimes faith, and sometimes not,
> I daily strove, but all in vain,
> I fell, and fell, and fell again.
>
> But when I look'd not to my sin,
> But to the blood that made me clean,
> I then the promise could receive,
> I then the saviour did believe.[110]

Here is the offer of a freedom in life that religion often promises but fails to deliver. This was coupled with a rejection of natural reasoning as unchristian. Cudworth's writings were criticized for their 'ignorance and ranterism of enthusiasm'.[111] He must not be dismissed as a libertine, however, unlike another Calvinist Methodist seceder, James Relly, with whom he is often confused. Cudworth wrote to the Norwich newspaper denying an allegation that he was turned out of Whitefield's societies for immorality.[112]

His antinomianism was an incidental product of Calvinist federal theology. As Christopher Hill has commented, antinomianism 'attended on Calvinism like a shadow'.[113] His heroes were the antinomian Puritans of the seventeenth century, including John Eaton, Walter Marshall,

Tobias Crisp, Samuel Richardson, John Simpson and John Salt-marsh.[114] Cudworth was well read in this tradition. Concerned that Wesley's 'Christian Library' was redefining the past, he planned an evangelical library, an abridgement of many reformed and puritan writers.[115] He took much trouble to circulate the writings of Walter Marshall.[116] Cudworth was very critical of most contemporary writers. His curious work, *The Polyglott*, tabulated the views on assurance, grace, works and the death of Christ expressed by Wesley, Whitefield, Relly, Glas and Sandeman, and (on the other side), Hervey, Cudworth and Marshall.[117] Evangelicalism was in a sense a recrudescence of the Puritan tradition, and at the heart of Calvinist Methodism lay a renewed emphasis on the doctrine of justification on the basis of imputed righteousness.

Cudworth took this emphasis and pushed it to extremes. He insisted that imputation, not repentance, enabled sinners to go free.[118] He saw faith as a persuasion of heart created by the gospel.[119] Faith had no guaranteed external evidence. The source of assurance lay not in feelings or good works but the voice of God from outside assuring the person that they were of the elect. The Methodist position on assurance had nudged nearer to that of the Antinomians than that of traditional Calvinists, but Cudworth insisted that 'feelings' were only valid when God spoke externally to the person. He took the position that true Christians should 'appropriate' their faith and sense their personal interest in Christ's work.[120] Ann Dutton, a high Calvinist, sensed in his views a suspicion of experience. His notion was, she thought, based only on rational deduction.[121] But it was a rationality which rejected the Enlightenment.

Antinomianism is normally interpreted as a rejection of the obligation to keep the moral law. This is not quite fair. Antinomians believed that Christian ethics were for Christians alone. Wesley in 1745 wrote against Cudworth a *Dialogue between an Antinomian and his Friend*. In this he cleverly caricatured the antinomian position: 'Obey! Law! Works! Commandments! O what legalness is in your spirit ... [I am free] from sin and hell, and the devil and the law.'[122] In reply Cudworth penned *A Dialogue between a Preacher of Inherent Righteousness and a Preacher of God's Righteousness*, insisting that he had nothing against good works, but these were nothing to do with salvation.[123] Welsey, who was deeply concerned about the implications of the doctrine of imputed righteousness, complained that: 'your type of speaking ... is a dangerous way of speaking, exalting people in pride, keeping many in the sleep of death, and throws others into fatal slumber, and stops them in the midst of their Christian course'.[124] Rumours that living in sin was tolerated at Peter Street chapel were however unjustified.[125] Cudworth denied any hint of practical antinomianism in his thought: 'We affirm constantly, that they which have believed should be careful to maintain good works.'[126] His concern was that when good works were given spiritual significance they killed spiritual vitality. Godly life arose from the joy of being justified.[127]

Cudworth's writings forced evangelical Calvinists to wrestle with issues of ethics which they tended otherwise to neglect. He trod a narrow line, even in his terms. He saw sin as inevitable, refused to regard moral endeavour as spiritually significant, but expected that the gospel would induce believers to observe good behaviour. It did not always happen.

So what was the significance of Antinomian Methodism for social history? Arguably this sectarian position encouraged a freedom of spirit and an alienation from the establishment which aligned it with radicalism. William Huntington S.S. must be seen in this context. The overlap of Methodism and Calvinist independency gave resilience to some of the intellectual debates among English artisans. Many artisans earned their spurs in debating these doctrines, and were liberated by such rarefied theological disputes. In Norwich and Leicestershire these ideas had widespread currency.

Cudworth cannot be dismissed as a gadfly, and the antinomian option was not just a debating point. It gave new life to an old theological option. Although Cudworth's direct impact was short-lived, the debate over antinomianism remained common right through the century.[128] It was a classic issue for those emphasizing justification by faith.[129] This explains much about the experimentation on the fringes of popular religion. When social historians want to understand how sectarian religion worked, they too often ignore its theology. The shape of antinomian theology defined the kinds of action it inspired.

Notes

1. B. Semmel, *The Methodist Revolution* (London, 1974), pp. 45–6; there is a useful critique in D. Hempton, *Methodism and Politics in British Society, 1750–1850* (London, 1984), pp. 22–3.
2. Whitfield to B——, 5 February 1742 in G. Whitefield, *Works* (London, 1772), vol. 1, p. 367.
3. C. Cherry, *The Theology of Johnathan Edwards: A Reappraisal* (Bloomington, new edn, 1990), p. 205.
4. W. Cudworth, *A Short Account of the Dealings of God in the Experience of William Cudworth* (London, 1754), pp. 3–5.
5. Ibid, pp. 6–7.
6. Ibid, pp. 8–9.
7. W. Cudworth, *A Second Part of the Experience of William Cudworth* (London, 1754), pp. 4–6.
8. Ibid, p. 4.
9. W. Crookshanks, *Steadfastness in the Faith Recommended* (London, 1743), pp. 5, 8, 12–14.

10. E. Welch (ed.), *Two Calvinistic Methodist Chapels, 1743–1811: The London Tabernacle and Spa Fields Chapel* (London Record Society, 1975), nos 9–10; J.C. Whitebrook, six articles on William Cudworth, Dr Williams Library, London, article no. 2; Cudworth, *Second Part*, p. 22.

11. J.C. Whitebrook, 'French Chapels in London', *Notes and Queries*, 24 April 1926; Welch, *Chapels*, no. 12.

12. Welch, *Chapels*, no. 3.

13. Moravian Church House, London [hereafter Mor CH] A3 file 5: Cennick 'Account', 5 September 1744, no. 23.

14. National Library of Wales, Aberystwyth, Trevecka Letters, no. 1291: J. Pugh to H. Harris, 14 February 1745. See also T. Beynon, *Howell Harris's Visits to London* (Aberystwyth, 1960), pp. 63–4.

15. Cudworth, *Second Part*, pp. 12–16.

16. Welch, *Chapels*, nos 11–13.

17. Trevecka Letters, no. 1246: Cennick to Harris, 25 October 1744, Beynon, *Howell Harris*, pp. 62–3.

18. J. Simpson, *Man's Righteousness No Cause or Part of his Justification* (London, 1745), p. iii.

19. Beynon, *Howell Harris*, pp. 65, 70, Trevecka Letters, no. 1279: Harris to Whitefield, 11 January 1745, reprinted in G.M. Roberts (ed.), *Selected Trevecka Letters, vol. 1 1742–47* (Caernarvon, 1956), pp. 160–1.

20. Beynon, *Howell Harris*, p. 64; Welch, *Chapels*, no. 21.

21. For Adams see Welch, *Chapels*, no. 29; for Jenkins see Trevecka Letters no. 1441; Jenkins to Harris, 11 April 1745.

22. W. Cudworth, *Some Reasons Against Making Use of Marks and Guidances in Order to Attain the Knowledge of Any Interest in Christ* (London, 1745).

23. Trevecka Letters no. 1306: Erskine to Harris, 20 March 1745.

24. Welch, *Chapels*, no. 28.

25. Cudworth, *Second Part*, pp. 20–2.

26. Welch, *Chapels*, no. 32.

27. Beynon, *Howell Harris*, pp. 69–71.

28. Trevecka Letters no. 1372: Harris to Whitefield, 8 November 1745, reprinted Roberts, p. 178.

29. Beynon, *Howell Harris*, pp. 69–70; Welch, *Chapels*, no. 35.

30. A. Dutton to H. Jenkins, n.d., in *Christian History* (London, 1748), pp. 158–9.

31. Beynon, *Howell Harris*, pp. 72–3; Cudworth, *Second Part*, p. 21, insists he was not condemned.

32. Ibid, p. 23; John Rylands Library (J.R.L.), Manchester, Eng MS. 1054 – Moravian Church, Minutes of Provincial Conferences, p. 2; Mor CH, British Pilgrim House Diary (hereinafter Br. Diary), p. 793 (29 July 1745); Mor CH: Cennick to Hutton, 30 August 1745.

33. Mor CH, Br. Diary, p. 900, Cennick to London Moravian Brethren, 30 November 1745.

34. Beynon, *Howell Harris*, pp. 128, 132.

35. Whitefield, *Works*, vol. 2, p. 149 – plainly referring to Cudworth.

36. Whitefield to Harris, 2 May 1746 in *Christian History* (1747), pp. 10–11; Whitebrook articles, no. 6.

37. Whitefield to Harvey, 9 December 1756, in *Works*, vol. 3, p. 194.

38. W. Cudworth, *Truth Defended and Cleared from Mistakes and*

Misrepresentations (London, 1746), p. 18.

39. Cudworth, *Short Account*, p. 23.
40. See the cover of [R. Fowler], *The Copy of a Letter Sent to Matthew Henderson* (London, 1746); J.R.L. Eng MS 1054, p. 5.
41. J. Eaton, *Abraham's Steps of Faith* (London, 1745), title page; J.C. Whitebrook, *William Cudworth and his Connexion, (1717–63)* (London, 1918), p. 1.
42. Whitebrook articles, no. 5.
43. Trevecka Letters, no. 1551: E. Wood to J. Kelly, 23 October 1746; no. 1516: Harris to Whitefield, 30 August 1746 (printed in Roberts, p. 193), no. 1535: Elizabeth Whitehead to Harris, 6 October 1746, (printed in Roberts, p. 206); Beynon, *Howell Harris*, p. 99.
44. W. Cudworth, *The Sentiments of a Church of Christ* (London, 1748), pp. 9–13.
45. W. Cudworth, *The Doctrine of Our Lord Cleared From False Glosses* (London, 1761), p. iii.
46. J. Wesley, *Dialogue Between an Antinomian and his Friend* (London, 1745).
47. Mor CH: Br Diary, p. 1142 (1 June 1748); Whitefield, *Works*, vol. 2, p. 149.
48. Mor CH: Cennick to the Brethren, 16 November 1745.
49. Mor CH: Br Diary, pp. 985–6 (22, 26 June 1746).
50. Trevecka Letters, nos 2019–21: Cudworth to Mrs Griffiths, 30 November, 3 and 11 December 1751.
51. Trevecka Letters, no. 1605: William Allt to James Kelly, 17 January 1747. See also 'The General Baptists of Lancashire', *General Baptist Magazine*, 1 (1798), p. 228.
52. Cudworth, *Sentiments*, pp. 9, 12–13; Welch, *Chapels*, no. 14; J.R.L. Eng MS 1054, p. 11; Mor CH: Br Diary, p. 618 (12 September 1744); Trevecka Letters, no. 1530: Dixon to Harris, 20 September 1746.
53. W. Cudworth, *Some Observations Concerning the Church of Christ* (London, 1745); Trevecka Letters, no. 1372: Harris to Whitefield, 9 November 1745, printed in Roberts, p. 178.
54. Cudworth, *Sentiments*, p. 9; Cudworth, *Truth Defended*, pp. 47–54.
55. Cudworth, *Second Part*, pp. i–viii.
56. *Budingische Sammlung* (Budingen, 1742), title page.
57. Cudworth, *Doctrine*, p. iv.
58. W. Cudworth, *Observations on Dr Free's Speech* (1759), pp. 1–8.
59. I.S. Rennie, 'Aspects of Christian Brethren Spirituality', in *Alive to God: Studies in Spirituality*, J.I. Packer and L. Wilkinson (eds), (Downers Grove, 1992), pp. 190–209.
60. Mor CH: Br Diary, p. 1099 (13 March 1747); W. Cudworth, *Some Observations on the Antiquity of the Present United Brethren* (London, 1751), p. iii.
61. Cudworth, *Church of Christ*, pp. 21–2.
62. Mor CH: Br Diary, pp. 766 (12 July 1745), 822 (30 August 1745); Mor CH: 'Minutes', conference 2; Cennick to Hutton, 17 June 1746.
63. Mor CH: Br Diary, pp. 907–8, (6 December 1745); Cennick to the Brethren, 20 November 1745.
64. Mor CH: Br Diary, p. 908 (11 November 1745).
65. Probably Cudworth, *Antiquity of the Present United Brethren*.

66. Whitebrook articles, no. 6; W. Cudworth, *A Collection of Hymns* (1746), p. 24.

67. D. Benham, *Memoirs of James Hutton* (London, 1856), p. 91; Mor CH: Br Diary, 27 September 1743; Mor CH: Dixon to Ockerhausen, 17 July 1752; Mor CH: London Congregation Diary, vol. 1, pp. 71, 77 (February 1743).

68. 'General Baptists of Lancashire', p. 229; (W. Cudworth), *A Copy of a Letter Sent to the Revd. Mr K*** Concerning Repentence* (London, 1752).

69. See W. Cudworth, *A Collection of Hymns for the Use of the Hearers of the Apostles* (Nottingham, 1777).

70. J. Wesley, *Works, vol 20 Journal and Diaries III (1743–54)*, W.R. Ward and R.P. Heitzenater (eds), (Nashville, 1991), p. 23 – note for 12 April 1744; Fulneck, West Yorkshire, Moravian Archives, Congregation Diary, p. 387 (16, 27 November 1750); Fulneck, Elders Conferences, p. 68 (29 August 1752); E.J. Bellamy, 'Norwich Methodism in the 1750s with special reference to James Wheatley', University of Bristol MPhil. thesis, 1986, p. 26.

71. J. Wesley, *Works, vol 26 Letters II, 1740–55*, F. Baker (ed.), (Oxford, 1982), pp. 286–7, writing a letter to a friend, 20 December 1751.

72. Fulneck Diary, pp. 387 (16/27 November 1750), 428 (9/20 December 1750).

73. Welch, *Chapels*, no. 69; Beynon, *Howell Harris*, p. 115 (19 September 1746).

74. Ibid, pp. 125–6 (13, 15 February 1747); Trevecka Letters, no. 1614: Harris to Wesley, 14 February 1747, printed in Roberts, p. 220.

75. Wesley, *Works, vol. 20*, pp. 393–6; C. Wesley, *Journal*, T. Jackson (ed.), (1849), vol. 2, pp. 82–4 (11–28 June 1751).

76. Wesley to an Evangelical Layman, 20 December 1751, in *Works*, vol. 26, p. 487.

77. Trevecka Letters, no. 2021: Cudworth to Madam Griffith, 11 December 1751; Cudworth, *Second Part*, p. 24.

78. C. Perronet, *A Summary View of the Doctrines of Methodism, Occasioned by the Late Persecution of the Methodists in Norwich* (Bristol, 1752), p. 18; *True and Particular Narrative of the Disturbances and Outrages in the City of Norwich* (1751), pp. 27–8; (A.H. Seymour), *Life and Times of Selina, Countess of Huntingdon*) (1844), vol. 2, pp. 329–31.

79. *True and Particular Narrative*, pp. 10, 12, 15.

80. W. Cudworth, *A Defence of Thereon and Aspasio* (1760), pp. 14–15; Cudworth, *Second Part*, p. 24.

81. C. Wesley, *Journal*, vol. 2, p. 111 (7 August 1754).

82. *True and Particular Narrative*, pp. 1–10.

83. Seymour, *Life*, vol. 2, pp. 332–4; Whitefield letters of 17 and 18 April 1753, and to W[heatley], 19 January 1754 in *Works*, vol. 3, pp. 10–12, 61.

84. Fulneck, Elders' Conferences, p. 68 (29 August 1752).

85. Bellamy, 'Norwich Methodism', pp. 154–9; G.W. Picher, *The Rev. Samuel Davies Abroad*, (Urbana, 1967), p. 124.

86. T. Keymer, *The Wolf in Sheep's Clothing* (Norwich, 1754); (J. Wheatley and W. Cudworth), *Reply to the Scandalous Papers of Mrs M____ n and*

Mr T ___ K ___ (Norwich, 1754); T. Keymer, *The Former Sycophant Displayed: Being an Answer to Mr Wheatley's Reply* (Norwich, 1754).
87. L. Tyerman, *The Life of the Rev. George Whitefield* (1876), vol. 2, pp. 125–6.
88. See D.S. O'Sullivan, 'The Case of James Wheatley, Methodist', *Norfolk Archaeology*, 36 (1977), pp. 167–75.
89. Wesley, *Works*, vol. 20, pp. 488–92 (8–18 July 1754); C. Wesley, *Journal*, vol. 2, pp. 100–13 (8 July–13 August 1754).
90. J. Wesley, *Journal*, N. Curnock (ed.), (Epworth, 1909), vol. 4, pp. 197–8 (27 February–1 March 1756); Seymour, *Life*, vol. 2, pp. 334–5.
91. Perronet, *Summary View*.
92. Whitefield to Wesley, 9 August 1755 in Whitefield, *Works*, vol. 3, p. 132.
93. [W. Cudworth]. *A Letter From a Brother at London to the Society Belonging to the Tabernacle at Norwich* (Norwich, 1754).
94. Whitefield to Worsley, 9 August 1755, and to n.k., 26 August 1755, in Whitefield, *Works*, vol. 3, pp. 133–5.
95. Seymour, *Life*, vol. 2, p. 340.
96. Tyerman, *Life*, vol. 2, pp. 407–9; Seymour, *Life*, vol. 2, pp. 338–9; G.W. Hughes, *With Freedom Fired: the Story of Robert Robinson, Cambridge Nonconformist* (1955), pp. 14–15.
97. Whitefield to Keen, 31 July 1762 and 11 April 1767, in *Works*, vol. 3, pp. 279, 344; Seymour, *Life*, vol. 2, p. 338.
98. Wesley, *Journal*, Curnock (ed.), vol. 4, p. 290 (3 November 1758), p. 295 (20–21, 24–25 December 1758); T. Mallard, 'Notes on the Countess of Huntingdon's Churches', Chesthunt College, Cambridge, Archives, G 3/14.
99. Wesley, *Journal*, Curnock, (ed.), vol. 4, p. 302, (21 March 1759), pp. 350–2 (3–9 September 1759), p. 363 (27 December 1759–3 January 1760).
100. Ibid, vol. 4, p. 302–3 (25, 27 March 1759), W. Cudworth, *The New Testament Church*, (1764), p. 2.
101. Wesley, *Journal*, Curnock, (ed.), vol. 4, pp. 431–3 (18 January–2 February 1761); T. Jackson (ed.), *Lives of the Early Methodist Preachers* (1871), vol. 1, pp. 253–4.
102. Wesley, *Journal*, Curnock, (ed.), vol. 5, p. 36 (16 October 1763), pp. 99–100 (12 October 1764).
103. Ibid, vol. 5, pp. 243–5 (30 November–5 December 1767); Jackson, *Lives*, vol. 6, pp. 261–2.
104. Beynon, *Howell Harris*, p. 200 (12 October 1763).
105. Whitebrook articles, nos 5, 6.
106. W. Cudworth, *Christ the Only Foundation* (2nd edn, 1763), p. 21.
107. Whitebrook, *William Cudworth*, p. 2.
108. Trevecka Letters, no. 1681: Button to Harris, 23 July 1747.
109. Trevecka Letters, no. 1367: Harris to Adams, 5 November 1747.
110. Cudworth, *Hymns* (1746), pp. 66–7.
111. R. Finch, *A Free Examination of Mr Cudworth's First Thoughts on the Doctrine of Election* (1747), pp. 13, 43–4; (W. Cudworth) *Nature and Grace or Some Essential Differences* (1763), pp. 1–10.
112. Bellamy, 'Norwich Methodism', pp. 152–3.
113. C. Hill, 'Antinomianism in 17th Century England', in *Collected Essays of Christopher Hill*, vol. 2, (1986), p. 177.

114. P. Toon, *The Emergence of Hyper-Calvinism in English Nonconformity, 1689–1965* (1967), p. 30.
115. Cudworth, *Thereon and Aspasio*, p. 3; Eaton, *Abraham's Steps*, pp. 2, 12–14; Simpson, *Righteousness*.
116. Cudworth, *Sentiments*, pp. 22–4; W. Marshall, *Christ Our True Principle of Holiness* (1753); Marshall, *The Gospel-mystery of Sanctification* (7th edn, 1761), pp. iii–x.
117. W. Cudworth, *The Polyglott: or, Hope of Eternal Life, according to the Various Sentiments of the Present Day* (1761).
118. W. Cudworth, *Free Thoughts Upon the Doctrines of Election, Fall of Man, and Restoration by Christ* (1747), pp. 17–31.
119. [W. Cudworth], *A Friendly Attempt to Remove Some Fundamental Mistakes* (1756), p. 25.
120. Cudworth, *Thereon and Aspasio*, pp. viii, 130–1.
121. A. Dutton, *A Letter to Mr William Cudworth* (1747), pp. 5–10, 23.
122. J. Wesley, *Dialogue*, p. 6.
123. Cudworth, *Use of Marks and Evidences*, pp. 3–12.
124. J. Wesley, *Second Dialogue Between an Antinomian and His Friend* (1745), p. 11.
125. Beynon, *Howell Harris*, p. 130 (18 March 1747).
126. W. Cudworth, *A Preservative in Perilous Times* (1758), p. 47.
127. Cudworth, *Sentiments*, pp. 6–7.
128. For example, 'Brief Memoir of Rev. Richard Denny', *Evangelical Magazine*, October 1813, pp. 365–7.
129. Jackson, *Lives*, vol. 5, pp. 15–17.

CHAPTER FIVE

Prophesying Revolution: 'mad Lord George', Edmund Burke and Madame La Motte

Iain McCalman

Throughout the first year of the French Revolution *The Times* could not decide who was the greater lunatic, Lord George Gordon or Edmund Burke. The former had fortunately been locked in Newgate prison the previous year, but Burke was still loose. The newspaper thought he belonged in Bedlam because of his obsession to impeach Warren Hastings; it reported that he was having his head read and had checked into a lunatic asylum strapped in a strait-jacket.[1] Burke's *Reflections on the Revolution in France*, published in November the following year, seemed to many of its readers to confirm this brutal diagnosis.

Some who found things to like in the book remained puzzled that Burke should have produced it. How did one explain what Jefferson called 'the revolution of Mr Burke', an abrupt political tack from advocating parliamentary reform, religious toleration and American liberty to denouncing France's fledgling efforts at liberty.[2] Why had he turned so violently against the Dissenters and reformers with whom he had worked in the past? And even when events in France began to align with his predictions, there remained the extremism of the book's tone. Its language seemed so emotionally incontinent, equating preachers and atheists, lawgivers and madmen, Dissenters and Jew brokers – saturated with references to lunatics, criminals and cannibals. How could one seriously compare the elderly and respectable Unitarian preacher Dr Price to the Civil War regicide Hugh Peters? And why the sudden bathetic rhapsody to the beauty and virtue of Queen Marie Antoinette. Friends like Philip Francis were also worried by the structural looseness of his text. It seemed such a disordered narrative, leaping from polemic against Price, to the melodramatic storming of the Versailles palace and the epiphany to the Queen. What connected these diverse plots; what story was Burke trying to tell?

Burke's friends attributed his extremism to excess of genius, or temporary derangement from overwork. His enemies declared him mad, a crypto-Catholic, or a pensioned ministerial scribbler.[3] Most modern analysts have treated the work as a piece of pure political theory consistent with Burke's earlier thought, or as an equally abstract literary construct manipulating language with rhetorical brilliance. More historical and contextual explanations rightly stress Burke's social incongruence and political isolation. Conor Cruise O'Brien's new biography plausibly re-emphasizes Burke's repressed Irish and Catholic sympathies,[4] yet even here many puzzles and contradictions remain. Some of these, I believe, can be illuminated by a passage overlooked in the book's many analyses. Towards the end of his attack on Price, Burke suddenly shifts his target. In England, he says:

> We spurn from us with disgust and indignation the slanders of those who bring us their anecdotes with the attestation of the flower-deluce on their shoulder. We have Lord George Gordon fast in Newgate; and neither his being a public proselyte to Judaism, nor his having in his zeal against Catholic priests and all sorts of ecclesiastics raised a mob . . . which pulled down all our prisons, have preserved to him a liberty, of which he did not render himself worthy . . . We have rebuilt Newgate and tenanted the mansion. We have prisons almost as strong as the Bastile, for those who dare to libel the queens of France. In this spiritual retreat, let the noble libeller remain. Let him there meditate on his Thalmud, until he learns a conduct more becoming his birth and parts, and not so disgraceful to the antient religion to which he has become a proselyte; or until some persons from your side of the water, to please your new Hebrew brethren, shall ransom him.[5]

Reading this on the first day of publication, Dissenting minister Theophilus Lindsey declared that Burke had obviously been terrified into madness by the Gordon Riots.[6] This partisan and somewhat cruel accusation seems to me to offer a key insight into the genesis of the *Reflections*. I want to argue that Burke's interpretation of the riots and their leader, Lord George Gordon, informed his thinking about the nature of revolution and its potential threat in Britain and abroad. He and some contemporaries, Gordon included, saw the riots not as an isolated eruption of disorder but as a failed revolution. Lord George Gordon is the archetypal revolutionary figure who stalks through the pages of the *Reflections*. He is the ideological and narratological device Burke used in order to construct and connect his fictions of the regicide enthusiast and the regal martyr. This curious coupling between Dissenting rationalist, noble incendiary and ravaged Queen – the ingredients of an unprecedented and uniquely conceived total revolution in the social order – came together in Burke's mind not only through the immediate impact of the Riots, but also through Gordon's notorious actions and publications in the decade following them.

Why did Burke see the Gordon Riots as revolutionary? For a start he knew their leader well; they had been close friends working together in the Rockingham interest.[7] Probably the two poorest men in Parliament, they loathed slavery, suspected Crown influence and sympathized with the oppressed Americans. Yet Burke had been increasingly disturbed by Gordon's adoption of the apocalyptic anti-papal rhetoric of Protestant libertarianism which erupted after the granting of rights to North American Catholics. This became a domestic issue in 1778 when the North government engineered a petition for minor Catholic Relief from loyal Scots Catholics so as to recruit fighting Highlanders to the armed forces.[8] Burke's genuine wish for toleration, particularly if extended to Ireland, exceeded his dislike of North's cynical motives, and he championed the measure. Not so Lord George; he thrilled to the discovery of this 'dark secret' and told the King that the public would not tolerate 'the diabolical purpose of the bill . . . to arm Roman Catholics for the American war'.[9]

It was actually the Scottish public, led by a popular faction within the Kirk, which instigated a successful resistance to Catholic Relief. According to a contemporary Scottish account Gordon 'transformed himself into the habit and appearance of a strict Presbyterian' on becoming president of the burgeoning Protestant Association. His parliamentary speeches and publications resounded with the apocalyptic rhetoric of a latter-day Covenanter.[10] Waning Presbyterian support when the Scottish bill was dropped only encouraged him to develop a quasi-republican programme based on a 'Political Presbytery', land redistribution and repeal of Scottish taxes and duties.[11]

Gordon tapped a wide vein of Scottish discontents; support ranged from Highland crofters to discontented Glasgow merchants.[12] His future secretary and biographer Robert Watson, an Elgin hirer's son, construed him as a vehement Scottish nationalist, and Scottishness was certainly never better invented than in Gordon's earlier campaign for the seat of Inverness. He learned Gaelic, wore tartan, played the pipes, danced the fling and extolled Ossianic primitivism.[13] Open contempt for 'people of fashion'[14] like his place-seeking brother also extended his appeal from Scotland to England. His unpowdered hair and plain dress, refusal of courtly manners, denunciations of luxury and corruption and rejection of political bribery and faction touched deep dissatisfactions and cultural yearnings among the excluded middling sort of London and the larger provincial towns.[15] A master of populist theatricality, he embodied and articulated nativist and patriot sentiments which many modern analysts now idealize as romanticism.[16]

Gordon's campaign to repeal Catholic Relief in England centred on Protestant anti-popery, an ancient popular emblem of English liberty and superiority, which in the climate of 1780 also carried a powerful revival-

ist charge. Recent studies of the Gordon Riots stress the religious and
political motives of the rioters as against the socio-economic interpretation
of Rudé.[17] Gordon's biblical handbills, pamphlets and print caricatures
evoked a demonology of Babylonian scarlet whores, horned papal beasts,
conspiratorial Jesuits and servile peasants.[18] Methodist preachers, led by
Wesley, encouraged him with a Protestant martyrology of persecutions,
burnings and massacres.[19] Rational Dissent also gave its qualified blessing
in Priestley's *Free Address* published immediately after the riots. He agreed
that Catholicism was 'a bloody persecuting religion' and praised Gordon's
religious zeal 'unawed by civil power and regardless of all political parties',
disputing only 'the means used to secure you your great object' since toleration would extinguish Catholicism more effectively.[20]

Dissenting preacher and Middlesex reformer Dr Bromley similarly
blended anti-papal religion with radical politics. Gordon worked hard to
harness such County Reformers.[21] Prominent Dissenters and City
Radicals like Alderman Frederick Bull, Brass Crosbie and John Oliver
signed his petition and mobilized the City Council behind his cause.[22]
Priestley and Price, though not themselves signatories, associated with
this group and with Burke's *bête noire* Lord Shelburne, a covert anti-
popery sympathizer rumoured to have encouraged the rioters.[23] No
wonder Burke exploded in the aftermath of the riots:

> We ought to recollect the poison which, under the name of antidotes
> against popery . . . has been circulated from our pulpits and our
> presses . . . These publications have tended to drive all religion from
> our minds, and to fill them with nothing but a violent hatred of the
> religion of other people, and, of course, with a hatred of their per-
> sons; and so, by a very natural progression they have led men to a
> destruction of their goods and houses, and attempts on their lives.[24]

Burke spoke from bitter personal experience because Gordon had repeat-
edly identified him as an enemy of the Protestant cause. He was saved
from the June mob only by a combination of personal courage and military force. Susan Burney heard him pleading agonizingly outside his
house, 'I beseech you gentlemen, I beg . . .', before having to draw his
sword to rid himself 'of these terrible attendants'.[25] He could dramatize
revolutionary violence so vividly in 1790 because he had been present at
its dress rehearsal. Other literati who also experienced the riots at close
hand often responded in ways which similarly foreshadow elements of
the *Reflections*.

They too strained for language and imagery to evoke what Dr Johnson
called 'this time of terror'. Burke called it 'a desperate attempt, which
would have consumed all the glory and power of this country . . . and
buried all law, order and religion under the flames of the metropolis of
the Protestant world'.[26] The metaphors of crime, madness, cannibalism

and bestiality which initially shocked some readers of the *Reflections*, are prefigured in scores of observers' letters. Commentators ransacked their vocabularies for suitable similes to describe the 'mad dog' and 'lunatic apostle' Gordon. Walpole tried Kett, Masaniello, Jack of Leyden and Lord George Macbeth before settling, like most, on the Puritans. Gordon's long lank hair reminded him of Lilburne, while Holcroft found the 'meagre figure, plain clothes and biblical style of address' more reminiscent of William Prynne.[27] Gibbon simply stated that 'forty thousand Puritans such as there might be in the time of Cromwell have started out of their graves . . . '.[28] It was as if these men and women of the enlightenment had suddenly glimpsed beneath the placid waters of modern Nonconformity, a primitive and ferocious enthusiasm,[29] underlined for Burke by his loss of the seat of Bristol at the instigation of a Dissenter faction.[30] Gibbon wrote that 'the month of June 1780 will ever be marked by a dark and diabolical fanaticism which I had supposed to be extinct, but which actually subsists in Great Britain perhaps beyond any other country in Europe . . . '.[31]

Burke attributed the underlying motive of the rioters to envy – religious, social and economic – dwelling in his first post-riot speech on the spectacle of women rampaging through the streets like 'monsters',[32] precursors perhaps of the 'harpies' storming the Versailles palace. The most typical rioter, he claimed soon after, was a Protestant cobbler 'debased by . . . poverty' and eager to exalt himself by bullying others.[33] Still more culpable were the quasi-educated preachers and literary hacks – the 'political men of letters' of 1790 – whose envy of the civilized and propertied led them to disseminate Gordon's propaganda. These 'miserable agents' of a 'dirty faction' in Edinburgh comprised scribbler-preachers like James Fisher whose attempt to blame the riots on Catholics prompted Burke to demand that the government sniff out the habitats, connections and practices of all Protestant petitioners.[34]

This reactionary reflex is instructive. Burke was beginning the political reorientation which was to earn him the nickname of *le Newgatien Burke* among French pamphleteers in 1790.[35] Some commentators noted the symbolic significance of the ease of Newgate's destruction. At that moment, one volunteer soldier observed, the riots ceased to be simply a religious issue and became a matter of state survival.[36] Yet if Newgate offered itself as a symbol of the haplessness of the state, the Crown's deployment of professional soldiers seemed to many Whigs the riots' worst consequence. Like Burke in 1790, they predicted that tyranny would succeed anarchy.[37] Surprisingly, Burke's Bristol speech exulted in this strengthening of Crown power,[38] an indication that Mr Burke's 'revolution' had begun, for nothing could be more repugnant to a genuine Whig. Wraxall hinted as much in a retrospect of 1815, pointing out that

Burke's falling out with Fox of 1792 had been foreshadowed in 1780.[39]

Burke thought that military force had prevented a terrible insurrection. Neo-Puritanism might have sparked the riots, but modern democratic ideas had fanned the flames. Gordon's rhetoric and political connections suggested the involvement of American revolutionaries, an idea encouraged by government spies.[40] Radical Thomas Holcroft echoed the Attorney General in speaking of Gordon's conspiracy to overthrow monarchy, constitution and 'the very existence of empire'.[41] Wraxall attributed the failure of insurrection to the King's decisiveness and the loyalty of British professional soldiers.[42] Burke later speculated that:

> had the portentous comet of the Rights of Man . . . crossed upon us in that internal state of England [in 1780–82] nothing human could have prevented our being irresistibly hurried out of the highway of heaven into all the vices, crimes, horrors and miseries of the French Revolution . . . Such was the distemper in the public mind, that there was no madman, in his maddest ideas and maddest projects, who might not count upon numbers to support his principles and execute his designs.[43]

Between the Gordon Riots and the French Revolution that same madman worked to effect the junction that Burke so feared – of Dissenting enthusiasm and the abstract rationalist principles of the enlightenment. Nothing seemed madder than Gordon's conversion to Judaism in the late 1780s; it attracted scorn from newspapers, prints, chapbooks and ballads, and even featured in burlesque speeches at the annual Garrat Mock Election.[44] To some Dissenters, however, Gordon's philo-semitism simply echoed an old Puritan prophetic tradition. Biblical claims that the millennium would be preceded by conversion and restoration of the Jews to their homeland and glory had long offered Puritans a compelling analogy or identification with the people of Israel, inspiring both scholars and Fifth Monarchists. Restorationist or philo-semitic prophecy resurfaced strongly during the 1780s among rational Dissenters like Price and Priestley, as well as urban artisan seekers like William and Catherine Blake. Elsewhere I have argued that Priestley's Letters to the Jews of 1786 inaugurated a feverish popular debate over the advent of a spiritual or literal new Jerusalem.[45]

Scottish Presbyterianism introduced Gordon to this powerful apocalyptic idiom which – like its Huguenot counterpart – pivoted the suffering and restoration of Israel against the conspiracies and oppressions of the Papal antichrist. Critics noted his mounting chiliasm in the aftermath of the riots. Romilly was appalled in 1782 by a new rash of handbills in 'the style of the Puritans of the last century' fomenting anti-Catholic disturbances in Ireland.[46] He even publicly defended the sanity of the King's failed assassin Margaret Nicholson in 1786,[47] then promptly had himself excommunicated by the Archbishop of Canterbury under the banner of Dissent.[48] Government prosecution finally halted his prophetic mission in 1787 after he incited Newgate convicts with handbills denouncing capital punishment and transportation as contrary to the laws of Jehovah.[49]

Both Price and Priestley published notorious millenarian sermons in 1787 and it seemed natural for the press to link Gordon with Priestley's quest to summon a restorationist conference between Dissenters and Jewry.[50] When ministerial engraver James Sayers produced the first English caricature to attack the French Revolution in February 1790, he also depicted Price, Priestley and Lindsey as seventeenth-century preachers praying for the French National Assembly to a congregation comprising Fox and Paine, a bearded Jew despoiling the sacred symbols of the Established Church, a Cromwellian soldier and mad Margaret Nicholson.[51] Six months later the *Reflections* similarly parodied philosemitic prophecy by likening Price to a Fifth Monarchist preacher spouting Moses's vision of 'a promised land' from 'the Pisgah of his pulpit'.

Lord George's much publicized political actions seemed also to shadow Price's. After a visit to France in 1782, he campaigned remorselessly against such tyrannical, warlike and Popish European monarchies. He bombarded press, politicians and foreign consulates with propaganda, including tracts on finance in the vein of Price, attacking inflationary paper currency and burdensome loans.[52] His reforming friends ranged from SCI dignitaries to more plebeian activists like Thomas Hardy and Robert Watson, both future leaders of the LCS.[53] Even an effective life sentence in Newgate for libelling the French Court did nothing to lessen his political visibility. He received a throng of revolutionary visitors, corresponded with Grégoire, Marat, Brissot and Robespierre, and boasted of involvement with revolution in Poland, Bohemia, Ireland and Holland. He published addresses to the National Assembly in 1789 and 1790 which condemned their King and praised Jewish emancipation, leading to rumours that Palais Royale extremists sought his liberation 'as a fellow sufferer in their cause'.[54] *The Times* treated him as a perfect doppel-ganger for Radical Dissent, commenting in November 1789:

What a pity Lord George Flame could not be present at the Revolution meeting to join . . . with . . . the rest of the worthies who composed that glorious congratulation to the National Assembly. He no doubt would have thrown so many flammable materials into the political cauldron, as would have set both nations in a BLAZE.[55]

But the blaze which Burke worked to extinguish was as much sexual as political, and it had also been fanned by Lord George Flame. Britain had long been a centre for French exiles specializing in political-pornographic blackmail against the royal Courts. Marie Antoinette had become a target by 1784 at least,[56] but – as in France – this trickle of political smut became a torrent and a serious matter of state with the repercussions of the Diamond Necklace affair in 1785.

When two adventurers of suspect noble lineage used a disguised prostitute to persuade ambitious Cardinal Rohan that he had bought the Queen's favours with a costly diamond necklace, France's *ancien régime* seemed to have reached its nadir of corruption. Countess Jeanne de La Motte's subsequent prosecution generated the most publicized trial report of the century, rivalled only by stories of her subsequent sufferings when branded with a V for *voleuse*, the customary punishment for prostitutes. An engineered escape from prison brought her to Britain in 1788 where she produced a flurry of memoirs and addresses which circulated widely on both sides of the channel.[57] These remorselessly attacked the Queen's political and sexual morals, equating her debauchery with wider political tyranny, conspiracy and corruption.

Gordon meanwhile had taken up the cause of another refugee from the affair, the flamboyant mason, mesmerist and con man Count Cagliostro, whose own version of the scandal was also being skilfully marketed in Britain and France.[58] The Count could hardly have chosen a worse advocate: Gordon forced a confrontation with French officials, then published a letter accusing the 'Queen's Bastile Party' of 'perfidious cruelties' against innocent Cagliostro.[59] When prosecuted in 1787 for libelling the French Queen, Gordon's 'indelicate' claims and lewd asides did nothing to help his case. Neither did his published defence which paired Marie Antoinette with Catherine of Russia, also supposedly 'gloating with desire'.[60] La Motte's lurid accusations were simultaneously filling newspapers on both sides of the Channel. By early 1789 Mirabeau doubted whether constitutional monarchy could survive this tide of scurrility, claiming later that 'Mme de La Motte's voice alone brought on the horrors of July 4 and October 5.'[61] Some French newspapers even pretended that she led the women into the Versailles palace and so into the pages of Burke's *Reflections*.

It is in this context that we should read Burke's emotional defence of Marie Antoinette. He sought to intervene in what French historian Lynn Hunt sees as a central site of political conflict between the old and new order – a struggle over the symbolic attributes of the Queen's body.[62] Gordon depicted Marie Antoinette as leader of 'a contemptible designing junto' of courtiers who attacked liberty throughout Europe and instigated his imprisonment. She stood for the feminine traits of duplicity, greed and ruthlessness that had supposedly infected the Courts of the *ancien régime* since the time of Louis XV. More fundamentally, she

represented the old familial-based Court policy where women had something of a public role, and which had now to be replaced with a purely
masculine republican fraternity. To Robert Watson the fall of the Bastile
constituted 'the preliminary step to the overthrow of that imperious
woman' and her overthrow in turn symbolized 'a step to universal emancipation'.[63] Burke explicitly attributed such smears to coffee-house
libellers, Dissenting pulpits and Lord George Gordon.

Strictly speaking Burke exaggerated in linking Gordon with La Motte;
the noble libeller belonged with Cagliostro's rival politico-pornographic
syndicate. Yet they used the same publisher and their smut content was
similar. A street chapbook made the essential point: 'the poor Queen of
France, to us who ne'er did ill / was attacked by Lord Gordon with his
venemous quill'.[64] And Burke was not above using sexual innuendo himself. His reference to La Motte's *fleur de luce* carried a double erotic
charge since it branded her a whore and reminded readers that her
violent struggles had stripped her naked, forcing the executioner to burn
her breast.[65] Linking Gordon with a supposed prostitute also reactivated
public scandals from his libertinist past, the source of Mrs Montague's
famous quip that 'the Whore of Babylon was the only whore Lord
Gordon ever disliked'.[66] This reminds us also that Gordon's propagandists had made extensive use of anti-popery obscenity in 1779–80.
Burke's voracious political mind excelled in such detail. By reassembling
these materials with rhetorical brilliance, he connected Dr Price the
rational Dissenter to the bigoted enthusiast, enlightenment revolutionary, lunatic Jew and libertine pornographer Lord George Gordon. Such,
it seems, was the progression from reason to revolution.

Though Burke's juxtaposition of Price, Gordon and Marie Antoinette
might have been intellectually and ethically dubious, he was right at least
to take the supposed lunatic seriously. Historians have failed to do so.
Burke identified Gordon as a distinctive and dangerous revolutionary
figure. Gordon's blend of neo-Puritan enthusiasm and enlightenment
rationalism constituted one of the most fertile sources of ideology and
energy which the British state had to combat between 1780 and 1840,
producing a succession of revolutionary prophets and discourses.
Another shrewd counter-revolutionary Robert Southey made exactly this
point in his *Letters from England* of 1807, sensing like Burke that the
radical enthusiast not only embodied a peculiarly British response to cultural and political crisis, but also articulated a new and appealing con-
stellation of ideas, feelings and discourses which we might today call
romantic. Southey's youthful friend Coleridge had once fitted the mould;
his prophetic 'Religious musings' expressed anti-papal restorationist
longings as ardent as those of young engraver-poet William Blake who

exulted in 'The Glad Day' of 1780 when England's Bastile went up in smoke. Some of Gordon's supporters were to attach themselves to the radical-revolutionary prophet Richard Brothers in 1795 and after him to Thomas Spence and his insurrectionary successors. Spence struck several commemorative copper tokens of Gordon: one depicted him as the Puritan hero of 1780, another as the Newgate martyr of 1793 supported by the words, 'The beginning of opression (sic)'.[67] That too was prophetic in its way.

Burke's sensitivity to this threatening new romantic-revolutionary figure stemmed in part from his own social and psychological susceptibility. It was also no accident that he and Gordon should have begun as friends and collaborators. They were so alike – ethnic and social outsiders with intensely emotional and volatile personalities; extremist visionaries often accused of being madmen and Quixotes; millenarians touched by, yet recoiling from, the enlightenment. What divided them ultimately was the ancient allegiance and discourse of Protestant anti-popery; it helped make one a prophet of revolution, the other of counter-revolution.

Notes

1. *The Times*, 24 January, 11 February, 24 February, 2 March, 3 April, 1 June, 16 September, 6 October 1789.
2. L.G. Mitchell, 'Introduction', *The Writings and Speeches of Edmund Burke. Vol. 8, The French Revolution, 1790–4* (Oxford, 1989), p. 21.
3. For comments on his madness from William Windham, Dr Milner and others, see Gary Kelly, 'Revolution, Crime and Madness: Edmund Burke and the Defense of the Gentry', *Eighteenth-Century Life*, vol. 9 (1984), pp. 25–6; Mitchell, *Writings and Speeches*, p. 25; F.P. Lock, *Burke's Reflections on the Revolution in France* (London, 1985), p. 134.
4. Conor Cruise O'Brien, *The Great Melody: A Thematic Biography and Commented Anthology of Edmund Burke* (London: Sinclair Stevenson, 1993), pp. 3–86.
5. Edmund Burke, *Reflections on the Revolution in France* (Harmondsworth: Penguin, 1969), pp. 179–80.
6. Quoted in Iain Hampsher Monk, 'Review', *History of Political Thought*, 12 (Spring, 1991), pp. 179–83.
7. *History of Lord George Gordon . . .* (Edinburgh, 1780), p. 5. For this early part of Gordon's political career, see also Robert Watson, *The Life of Lord George Gordon: with a Philosophical Review of his Political Conduct* (London: H.D. Symonds, 1795), pp. 18, 86, 119; William Vincent [William Holcroft], 'Anecdotes of the Life of Lord Gordon', *A Plain and Succinct Narrative of the Late Riots and Disturbances in the Cities of London and Southwark* (London, 1780), p. 59; J. Irving, *The Book of Scotsmen* (1881), in *British Biographical Archive*.
8. Robert Kent Donovan, 'The Military Origins of the Catholic Relief Programme of 1778', *Historical Journal*, 28, (1985), p. 82.

9. J. Paul de Castro, *The Gordon Riots*, (London, 1926), pp. 19–20.
10. Donovan, 'Military origins', pp. 31–2; *History of Lord George Gordon*, pp. 9–10, 25–8; 'Speech to the House of Commons, 1778', 'Appendix', in Vincent, *Narrative*.
11. P[ublic] R[ecord] O[ffice], P[rivy] C[ouncil] R[eports], 1/3127, esp. examinations and correspondence of Ralph Bowie and Reverend David Grant; PRO, T[reasury] S[olicitor's] papers, 11/388/1212, Lord George Gordon's Correspondence – Summary; see also, Watson, *Gordon*, pp. 13–17; Eugene Charlton Black, *The Association. British Extraparliamentary Political Organization, 1769–1793* (Cambridge, Mass.: Harvard, 1963), pp. 149–53.
12. Robert Kent Donovan, *No Popery and Radicalism. Opposition to Roman Catholic Relief in Scotland, 1778–1782* (New York and London: Garland, 1987), *passim*.
13. *History of Lord George Gordon*, pp. 4–5; Watson, *Gordon*, pp. 6, 11.
14. British Library, Additional MS 42129, 'Lord George Gordon's Narrative', fo. 34; Watson, *Gordon*, pp. 2–4.
15. Colin Haydon, 'The Gordon Riots in the English Provinces (1780)', *Historical Research*, **63**, (October 1990), pp. 354–9.
16. For the best analysis of this nascent cultural revolution, see Marilyn Butler, *Romantics, Rebels and Reactionaries. English Literature and Its Background 1760–1830* (Oxford: OUP, 1981), esp. pp. 1–68; Gerald Newman has perceptively called Gordon's Protestant Association 'a popular counterforce against what was felt to be the un-English conduct of the upper classes in Parliament', Gerald Newman, *The Rise of English Nationalism. A Cultural History, 1740–1830* (New York: St Martins, 1987), p. 209.
17. Nicholas Rogers, 'The Gordon Riots Revisited', *Historical Papers* (Canada, 1988), pp. 32–3.
18. See for example, the handbills collected in PRO PC/3127, and caricatures in Dorothy George, vol. V, nos 5534, 5643, 5671–2, 5703, pp. 319, 381, 401–2, 420.
19. James Barnard, quoted in Rogers, 'Gordon Riots Revisited', p. 21; for other examples of Dissenting and Methodist involvement, see Dorothy George, *British Museum Catalogue of Political and Personal Satires* (London, 1938), vol. V, pp. 406–7, 410–11, 506–7.
20. Joseph Priestley, *A Free Address to Those Who Have Petitioned for the Repeal of the Late Act of Parliament in Favour of Roman Catholics* (Birmingham, 1780), pp. 3, 6, 11, 21.
21. See for example, George, *Catalogue*, vol. V, nos 5633, 5644; PRO TS 11/388/1212, Examination of Fisher, 10 June 1780, fos 4–5.
22. PRO TS 11/389/1214, Petition of Protestant Subjects of the Cities of London, Westminster, Southwark, fo. 3; De Castro, pp. 27, 130, 232; John Sainsbury, *Disaffected Patriots. London Supporters of Revolutionary America 1769–82* (Kingston, Montreal and Gloucester, 1987), pp. 157–8.
23. O'Brien, *Great Melody*, pp. 235–6, 241; Donovan, 'Military origins', p. 87; Watson, *Gordon*, pp. 35–6.
24. Edmund Burke, *The Works of the Rt. Honorable Edmund Burke* (Rivington, London, 1815), vol. VI, pp. 248–9.
25. John A. Woods, *Correspondence of Edmund Burke. IV. 1778–82* (Cambridge, 1963), vol. IV, fn. p. 246.

26. Edmund Burke, 'Speech at Bristol, Previous to the Election, 1780', *Works*, vol. III, p. 409.

27. W.S. Lewis, W.H. Smith and G.L. Lam, *Horace Walpole's Correspondence* (London: Oxford University Press, and Newhaven: Yale, 1965), 6 February 1780, vol. 25, p. 11; Vincent [Holcroft], *Narrative*, p. 11.

28. E. Gibbon to Dorothea Gibbon, 8 June 1780, in J.E. Norton, *The Letters of Edward Gibbon. Vol. 2. 1774–82* (London, 1956), vol. II, p. 245.

29. Cole to Walpole, *Walpole's Correspondence*, vol. ii, p. 226.

30. O'Brien, *Great Melody*, pp. 80–1, 86, 145, 147; Black, *Association*, p. 168.

31. Gibbon to Dorothea, 27 June 1780, *Letters*, vol. ii, p. 245.

32. See Frans De Bruyn, 'Theatre and Countertheater in Burke's *Reflections on the Revolution in France*', in Steven Blakemore (ed.), *Burke and the French Revolution: Bicentennial Essays* (Athens and London: University of Georgia, 1992), p. 23.

33. Burke, 'Speech at Bristol', p. 417. Perhaps it was for this reason, as he said, that 'a very great part of the lower and some of the middling people of this City . . . rather approve than blame the rioters', quoted in Black, *Association*, p. 167.

34. Burke to Loughborough, 15 June 1780, *Correspondence*, vol. IV, pp. 248–50.

35. Mitchell, *Writings and Speeches*, p. 14. Antoine Gorsais also described him as *l'apologiste* de Newgate and de la Bastille'.

36. Quoted in de Castro, *Gordon Riots*, p. 44; see also, Vincent, *Narrative*, p. 28.

37. Walpole to Lady Ossory, 23 June 1780, *Horace Walpole's Correspondence*, vol. 33, p. 201; Vincent, *Narrative*, p. 39.

38. Burke, 'Speech at Bristol', pp. 420–1.

39. Sir William Wraxall, *Historical Memoirs of My Own Time*, 2 vols, (London: Cadell and Davies, 1815), vol. i, p. 348.

40. Charles Coleman Sellers, *Patience Wright: American Artist and Spy in George III's London* (Middletown, Conn: Wesleyan UP, 1976), p. 147; de Castro, *Gordon Riots*, pp. 218–19. These included the auctioneer John Greenwood, Dr Oliver Smith, John Temple, Ben Bowsy and Thomas Lloyd.

41. [Holcroft] Vincent, *Narrative*, p. 44.

42. Wraxall, *Historical Memoirs*, pp. 337–41.

43. Burke, *Letter to a Noble Lord* (1796), in Robert A. Smith (ed.), *Burke on Revolution* (New York and Evanston: Harper, 1968), p. 234.

44. See Israel Solomons, 'Lord George Gordon's Conversion to Judaism', *The Jewish Historical Society of England – Transactions: Sessions 1911–14* (London, 1915), esp. pp. 240–64 for numerous examples of this anti-semitic literature.

45. Iain McCalman, 'New Jerusalems: Prophecy, Dissent and Radical Culture in England, 1786–1830', in K. Haakonssen (ed.), *Enlightenment and Rational Dissent* (CUP, forthcoming).

46. *Memoirs of the Life of Sir Samuel Romilly, Written by Himself with a Selection for His Correspondence Edited by His Son*, 3 vols, (London, 1840), Romilly to Roget, 12 April 1782, vol. i, pp. 217–18. For some of his other anti-ministerial activities in the immediate aftermath of the riots, see British Library Additional MS 5870, Newspaper cuttings, fo. 189; Additional MS 37835, George III's Correspondence with J. Robinson, November 1779–November 1784, fo. 196.

47. See *The Times*, 12 August, 4, 7 November 1786; and the retrospective
     satirical dialogue between Gordon and Nicholson in *Town and Country
     Magazine*, October 1790.
48. PRO PC1/3127, *A Letter to His Grace the Lord Archbishop of Canterbury
     Occasioned by the Excommunication of the Right Hon. Lord George
     Gordon for Nonconformity to the Mandates of the Spiritual Court of
     London* (1787), also Calvinus Minor, *An Appeal to the Scots; in Which the
     Spiritual Court of the Church of England, is Demonstrated to be Opposite
     to the British Constitution and a Part of the Pillar of Popery* (1786);
     Watson, *Gordon*, pp. 67–8; *Gentlemens' Magazine* (1786), p. 993; *The
     Times*, 8 November 1785, 6 July 1786 (a rare, if not unique, defence of
     Gordon by the paper's columnist), 9 March 1787, letter to Gordon on
     behalf of persecuted Dissenters, signed William Roe.
49. *Annual Register* (1787), Appendix to Chronicle, p. 247. See also, *A Letter
     from . . . Lord George Gordon to the Attorney General of England . . .*,
     James Ridgway, London, 1787; PRO TS 11/388/1212, King vs Lord
     George Gordon, Botany Bay –Informations for a libel; *The Prisoners
     Petition to the Right Hon. Lord George Gordon to Preserve Their Lives
     and Liberties and Prevent Their Banishment to Botany Bay* (Wilkins,
     London, 1787); Watson, *Gordon*, pp. 80, 105–6; George, *Catalogue*, vol.
     V, no. 6992, p. 325; no. 7127, p. 387.
50. *The Times*, 4 January 1788. For some early examples of anti-semitic specu-
     lations associated with Gordon, see George, vol. V, no. 8249, from
     Rambler's Magazine, 1 October 1785; *The Times*, 7 September, 11
     November 1785.
51. George, *Catalogue*, vol. V, no. 7628. It is worth noting that many of these
     same themes were also canvassed in the satirical dialogue between the
     bearded Jew Gordon and Margaret Nicholson published in *Town and
     Country Magazine*, October 1790.
52. Watson, *Gordon*, pp. 69, 75.
53. Mary Thale (ed.), *Selections from the Papers of the London Corresponding
     Society, 1792–99*, (Cambridge University Press, Cambridge, 1983), pp.
     xxii, 24, 50–1. See also the two realist-style prints with key engraved by
     the young radical Richard Newton for his employer, William Holland, who
     was in gaol with Gordon. 'Soulagement en prison; or comfort in prison',
     William Holland, 30 August 1793, and 'Promenade in the State Side of
     Newgate', William Holland, 5 October 1793; Watson, *Gordon*,
     pp. 81–2, 87–8, 143; Lord George Gordon, *The Memorial which Lord
     George Gordon Has Written in the Prison of Newgate*, London, 1789, p.
     xiv.
54. *The Times*, 28 January 1790.
55. *The Times*, 11, 14 November 1789. For a satirical pamphlet which simi-
     larly links Gordon, Price, Priestley and the revolutionary sectaries of the
     seventeenth century, see [Thomas Hastings], Rabbi Solomon, *Regal
     Rambler; or, Eccentrical Adventures of the Devil in London* (London,
     1793), pp. 12–29, 96–9.
56. PRO TS 11/46, 'Rex vs P. Stuart – libels against Marie Antoinette, 1784'.
     For earlier pornography against the French Court from exiles in London,
     see Mann to Walpole, 8 July 1780, *Walpole's Correspondence* (London
     and New Haven, 1971), vol. 25, p. 71; Sara Maza, 'The Diamond Necklace
     Affair Revisited (1785–6)', in Lynn Hunt (ed.), *Eroticism and the Body*

Politic (Baltimore, 1991), pp. 65–70; Robert Darnton, *The Literary Underground of the Old Regime* (Cambridge, Mass., 1982), pp. 30–5.

57. *An Address to the Public Explaining the Motives that Have Hitherto Delayed the Publication of the Memoirs of Madame La Motte* (London, 1789), esp. pp. 8–30, 35; *Memoirs of the Countess de Valois de la Motte* (London: James Ridgway, 1789); *Memoirs of Jane St Remy de Valois*, 2 vols (London: John Bew, 1791). For comment on the circulation of the memoirs, see also *The Times*, 3, 10 February, 20 May 1789.

58. On Cagliostro and Gordon in London, see Lucia (pseud.), *Life of Count Cagliostro* (London, 1787), p. vii; Claire Williams (ed.), *Sophie in London, 1786. Being the Diary of Sophie von la Roche* (London, 1933), pp. 139, 148–9; Gordon, *Letter to the Attorney General*, p. 22.

59. *Public Advertiser*, 22 August 1786.

60. Gordon, *Letter to the Attorney General*, p. 16. See also, PRO TS 11/388/1212, 'Informations on Lord George Gordon – Defamatory Libels on Queen Marie Antoinette'; Watson, *Gordon*, pp. 36–7, 81. According to Watson he had been introduced to the Queen in Paris in 1782, but rather than being dazzled by Burke's celestial vision had been disgusted by the court flattery, hypocrisy and luxury at a time of extreme popular misery.

61. Frances Mossiker, *The Queen's Necklace* (New York: Simon and Schuster, 1961), pp. 529–30.

62. Lynn Hunt, 'The Many Bodies of Marie Antoinette: Political Pornography and the Problem of the Feminine in the French Revolution', in Hunt, *Eroticism and the Body Politic*, pp. 108–30.

63. Watson, *Gordon*, p. 91.

64. Quoted in Solomons, 'Gordon's Conversion', p. 259.

65. *The Times*, 9 June, 7 July 1786. Nicolas Ruault produced a lurid pornographic account of this event. Jeanne la Motte also made much of her indignity promising to put an imprint of shame on the brow of the Queen to match the one burned on to her breast. Mossiker, *Queen's Necklace*, pp. 485, 528.

66. Quoted in de Castro, *Gordon Riots*, p. 247. See also, 'The Meretricious Friar', *Town and Country Magazine*, xvii, (1780).

67. Solomons, 'Appendix', 'Gordon's Conversion', p. 271.

CHAPTER SIX

The Example of America a Warning to England? The Transformation of America in British Radicalism and Socialism, 1790–1850[1]

Gregory Claeys

The secession of the American colonies from Great Britain laid the grounds for that form of egalitarian republicanism which eventually became the norm for European politics, as well as being widely if less successfully emulated elsewhere.[2] During the seven year war of independence, French involvement on the American side clearly accelerated that desire for liberty which was to underpin the French Revolution,[3] an even more startling event to contemporaries in so far as it involved not a break from, but eventually the overthrow of an ancient monarchy; and in so far as it took place in circumstances of great social inequality, well-developed commerce and luxury, and a long tradition of monarchical and aristocratic privilege. But French developments did not prevent the 'American model'[4] from remaining profoundly influential to British radical thought during the 1790s and the subsequent century. The young USA's swiftly growing opulence, cheap land, light burden of taxation and social and political freedom for the majority was typically described as:

> this Eden of the new world, where every man possessed in abundance, which was the fruit of moderate labour and industry; where no man was very rich, nor very great . . . Above all, a baneful luxury, which engenders diseases, that not only embitter life, but poison the very source of it, is there unknown. They have no wants but such as nature gives, and which may be easily supplied by a moderate degree of labour. Life is simple, and therefore it is happy.[5]

Such imagery lay at the heart of the appeal of Thomas Paine's immensely popular *Rights of Man* (1791–92), which centrally claimed that cheap republican government encouraged popular opulence, blamed poverty in Britain on the burden of corrupt taxation in support of placemen and senseless wars, and helped to displace earlier political models, like the Anglo-Saxon, Jewish and Spartan constitutions.[6] Crucial to this argument was the notion that while territorial circumstances were clearly different in the USA, this did not account for popular opulence there, which instead was indebted to republican institutions. As the reformer Daniel Stuart put it in 1794:

> I contend that there is a sufficiency of acres in Europe to make every man as comfortable as the American farmer, and that the extent of territory in the New World does not alone prevent indigence among the people. It is the Spirit of their Government, which encourages not only agriculture, but Manufactures and Commerce, and discourages War.[7]

The imagery of the golden land to the west proved a powerful magnet to British emigrants throughout the next century, not least during the 1790s, when perhaps 100 000 mostly liberal artisans left to cross the Atlantic. To many radicals and liberals, America remained a beacon of republican virtue, democratic constitutionalism and private enterprise – secure proof that prosperity and democracy marched hand in hand.

Yet despite the persistent appeal of this vision, the American Utopia became tarnished, at least for some, surprisingly quickly. Paine himself had promised that it might be 'a thousand years' before American social inequality, corruption and poverty matched that of Europe. However, it was evident to some by the early 1820s that the rapid pace of American development was beginning to engender considerable social problems. I want here to trace, very briefly, how increasing American inequality became a crucial bone of contention in radical debate between 1820 and 1850. My central concern is to demonstrate that there emerged in this period a *negative* model of America as a commercial society writ large which radicals initially found implausible and distasteful, but which became central to the socialist case for a collectivist solution to property ownership and management. By the 1840s, this view of America became increasingly persuasive to mainstream radicals as well. Its origins lay both in the conservative critique of democracy, and in the new socialist political economy of the 1820s which purported to offer an economic model to explain the necessary failure of competitive capitalism.

If radicals writing during the great pamphlet debate over reform in the 1790s perceived flaws in the American social and political system, they were naturally reluctant to disclose such fears. But, slavery aside, there were in fact relatively few social problems to point to. A crucial bone of contention was why this was the case. Radicals, of course, thought popular sovereignty and democratic constitutionalism were the cause. Loyalists were keen to argue that this was because circumstances in America were very different from those in Europe, and especially Britain. As one of Paine's critics put it:

> from the peculiar nature of landed property, America is likely to continue in a long progressive state; that even centuries may elapse

before it becomes stationary with regard to accumulating national
wealth; that, during this period, a certain and plentiful subsistence,
and even the means of accumulation will be secured to all who can
labour: They will, therefore, have the means of preserving a certain
degree of equality among their citizens, for a much longer period
than is ever likely to be attainable in Europe.[8]

For loyalist writers like Arthur Young, the fact that America did not yet
possess a class of indigent poor meant that its political institutions were
simply inapplicable to Britain.[9] Radicals broadly shared this confidence
in American prosperity, but maintained to the contrary that republican
institutions might be adopted in Britain. But despite their general enthusiasm, radicals sometimes questioned the reality underlying this powerful
symbol. The London Corresponding Society lecturer John Thelwall, for
example, wrote a letter, introduced at his trial as evidence of his extremism, which was considerably more critical than any of his published
statements on the subject. Here, aligning himself, as 'a Republican and a
true Sans-Culotte', with the 'men of the Mountain' (Jacobins) in France,
Thelwall assailed Americans for having 'too great a veneration for property, too much religion, and too much law'.[10] But such charges, where
acknowledged at all, were usually quickly rebutted. Joel Barlow, for
example, retorted that the view 'that the people of the United States manifest a great attachment to property, considered as *wealth*; and merely for
the purpose of parade; that though their government is American, their
manners are European' was 'true only in a limited sense. The influence of
riches in that country, even on the minds of those who possess them, is by
no means so great as it is in Europe'.[11]

Whether such observations, if true, would remain valid was to become
a point of considerable contention. From the turn of the century four distinctive viewpoints on the American social and political system emerged.
Until well after mid-century, as we will see, most radicals persisted in seeing America as a 'beacon of freedom' from which much could be learned.
Conservative writers, on the other hand, were anxious to advertise the
worst traits of the new democracy, including what was long assumed (on
the model of the French Revolution) to be its tendency to degenerate into
political despotism.[12] Commonly throughout this period, too, aristocratic travel accounts and Tory commentators lamented that the ascendancy of the common people had quickly engendered intellectual
conformity and cultural mediocrity.[13] These themes, albeit treated more
sympathetically, would enter mainstream liberalism through Alexis de
Tocqueville's *Democracy in America* (1836–40) and John Stuart Mill's
On Liberty (1859). Finally, socialist and 'agrarian' writers took up the
increasing evidence that poverty, corruption and social distress were
rapidly developing in the new nation in order to argue that the funda-

mental flaw in modern civilization lay not in the omnipresence of monarchies and aristocracies but in the system of private property and free
competition.

That American social equality was eroding quickly was evident to some
even during the revolutionary period. As early as 1784, the Abbé Mably
had hazarded the view that America was 'inclined towards an aristocracy'.[14] Not all, of course, were unhappy at this prospect, and Federalists
like John Adams lauded the virtues of inequality during the constitutional debates of the late 1780s as loyalists would do in Britain a few
years later.[15] But many Britons who emigrated to the USA in the 1790s,
there 'to a man' becoming Jeffersonian radical democrats (as Richard
Twomey has shown) were critical of the growing inequalities and
'aristocracy' they encountered,[16] and passed this inheritance to the
Jacksonian Democrats of the 1830s. Such perceptions none the less
remained rare in Britain itself at the time; the comment was unusual that
speculators and monopolists had taken over trade in Britain, and 'Even
America seems falling into the same track, she is even now permitting
aristocracy to creep in under the name of trade.'[17]

The first major theoretical statement of this critical trend is to be found
in the physician Charles Hall's *The Effects of Civilization on the People
in European States* (1805).[18] In the tradition of Spartan and Rousseauist
anti-commercial republicanism, Hall dismissed the central Painite
assumption that trade integrated societies by fulfilling common needs,
insisting instead that it exacerbated the conflict of interest between the
rich and poor, who as buyers and sellers of labour had 'in every case, [an]
opposite' interest respecting wages. Offering one of the earliest attempts
to calculate the proportion of the value of their labour the poor received
(one-ninth, after profit, rent and taxes had been subtracted), Hall broke
sharply from the Painite stress on the burden of state taxation as the
cause of poverty, and, by pin-pointing the rapacity of the property-
owning classes in general, clearly pointed the way to the later socialist
analyses of capitalism. In his analysis of 'power', centrally, Hall
described control over the poor's labour as the source of all other power,
effectively reducing the social structure to relations of labour in which
economic power was automatically translated into other types of social
and political control. The wealthy were thus an aristocracy wielding
legislative, judicial, ecclesiastical and other forms of power regardless of
governmental form. To Hall it thus mattered little whether 'modern gov-
ernments' were republics or monarchies. All were 'supported by wealth
in the hands of a few', and were monied aristocracies in all but name.
Against Paine and others, Hall thus dismissed even popular political control as irrelevant, and was probably the first British republican writer to

criticize the '*rising aristocracy of the American States*', where wealth 'universally . . . puts power into the hands of those that have it'.[19]

Hall's analysis commenced a profoundly important critique of the USA as a model for the great inequalities inherent in modern commercial republics generally.[20] In the three decades after 1820, this was principally developed by the followers of the early socialist Robert Owen, most of whom were hostile to competition and private property.[21] I have argued elsewhere that the American model was central to the 'anti-political' stance of many Owenites, of whom it was said that 'Their dogma was social, as opposed to political reform – their argument, that political reform would not effect one important change in the condition of the people – their instance, America.'[22] Yet this proposition, when presented to radicals, could be shockingly novel. The Leeds Chartist and Owenite John Francis Bray, for example, began *Labour's Wrongs and Labour's Remedy* (1839) with the aim of demonstrating complete superiority of the republican system, but then rewrote it completely on realizing that America had beggars as well, and concluded that 'the equality of rights which is thought to be enjoyed by the people of the United States is so enjoyed only in imagination'.[23]

Many Owenites would none the less quarrel with Owen about the immediate virtues of political reform; and this became a highly contentious issue in the late 1830s and 1840s. Many Owenites refused to follow Owen's claim that a radical reform of Parliament was useless, and, abjuring Owen's peculiar brand of perfectionism, accepted the parliamentary struggle and election by ballot of government officials. Most also conceded that the economic analyses of the older radicalism were now outdated, and that the effects of competition and the growth of machinery had invalidated the view that the heavy taxation associated with 'Old Corruption' chiefly caused poverty. From this perspective there emerged a new 'social radicalism' which sought political reform chiefly in order to secure 'social ends' like co-operation, communities and land nationalization. Even those socialists sympathetic to political reform, however, conceded in their many debates with the Chartists between 1835 and 1850 that it was possible to demonstrate 'the startling anomaly of a political constitution in America, framed on the principles of the radical politicians, co-existing with commercial embarrassment – a distressed labouring population and a continual struggle between the wealthy and poorer classes, as to who shall be master, and who the slave'.[24] In other words, American developments had proven that prosperity did not automatically flow from republican government.[25] Indeed, as Charles Bray put it in 1841, the condition of the poor in America was exactly what could be expected from the results of untrammelled freedom of trade;[26] America, as the Owenite William Hawkes Smith wrote in 1838, was simply 'with all its boasted institutions . . . as liable as the old country to ruinous alterations in its commercial undertakings'.[27]

During the 'sectarian' phase of Owenism in the 1840s, when millions of tracts were distributed, the notion that competition created poverty and kept wages down in the USA[28] became the official line for Owen and his immediate circle, who hoped to draw substantial support from Chartism by proving that achieving universal suffrage would not eliminate poverty.[29] The official journal of the Owenite movement, the *New Moral World*, contended frequently that liberty and equality were simply impossible where private property existed.[30] Owenite writers did not assert that social conditions were actually worse in America, only that political power rested with the wealthy *despite* republican institutions, and that the worst state was that 'where popular political economy has been most generally reduced to practice'.[31] The pervasiveness of this analysis clearly undermines the supposition that the Owenites were chiefly 'preoccupied with the concept of America as a pre-industrial, egalitarian working men's utopia, and were reluctant to admit that it was in any way an acquisitive and competitive, rather than a co-operative, society'.[32]

Though it engendered an impressive body of literature, Owenism none the less remained a marginal social movement among the great waves of reformism of the period between 1815 and 1850. While its analysis of America did have a subversive effect upon the economic analysis of the radical parliamentary reformers, this was slow to develop and the radical attitude towards America early in this period was overwhelmingly positive. T.J. Wooler's *Black Dwarf*, for instance, noted in 1818 that while there was some misery in the USA, its workers possessed full rights, and their industry ultimately brought them a comfortable subsistence.[33] Against conservatives, too, there was widespread insistence that prosperity in America was due not to favourable local circumstances, but to its form of government, as Percy Shelley insisted in *A Philosophical View of Reform* (1819).[34]

For the working classes a major source of American life and conditions through the mid-1830s was William Cobbett, who as Peter Porcupine had written against 'the wretched traitor and apostate'[35] Paine (whose bones he would later exhume and return to Britain in 1819), and lambasted the new USA during the French Revolution debates. After his conversion to radicalism in 1804, Cobbett wrote much more positively on America, though he continued to oppose 'unprincipled' American republicanism, and did not begin to praise internal American institutions until about 1812.[36] As early as 1816, Cobbett recognized that 'the writers on the side of corruption' emphasized distress in the USA because this seemed to prove that heavy taxation in Britain was not the cause of distress there.[37] Conservatives, Cobbett stressed, thus saw 'the example of America' as the greatest threat to stability in Britain.[38] Cobbett thus typically contended at this time that American labourers were three times better off than their British counterparts, and that even the lowest of the former enjoyed 'an easy and happy life'.[39] Cobbett was, however, prepared to detail the destructive influence of paper money and the banking system in the United States,[40] and by the 1830s, increasingly acknowledged the 'monstrous mischiefs produced in the USA by the use of paper money', including pauperism, criminality and debt.[41] None the less he also usually insisted that there were great differences between the effects of economic distress in America and in Britain,[42] notably that it caused no real misery in the new world.[43]

Like Cobbett, most radicals believed that America had higher real wages than Britain. The crucial issue, however, was what accounted for this. Some reformers took a more strictly economic viewpoint of this question; the *Reformists' Register* in 1817, for instance, thought this was because 'the quantity of marketable labour is comparatively small'.[44] Most, however, like the *White Hat* in 1819, continued the analysis popularized by Paine in the 1790s, which ascribed prosperity to 'cheap government'.[45] Similarly the *Penny Papers for the People* in 1830 insisted that Americans were happy and prosperous largely because their government was inexpensive. Even where economic distress was acknowledged, moreover, radicals often refused to associate it with the form of government in America. As T.J. Wooler put it in 1820:

> distress has pressed heavily on the Americans. Their trade has experienced a severe revulsion. Their agricultural produce has wanted markets; and all the evils of a paper system have been felt in the United States. No-one thought of blaming the government, because every one knew the government was blameless. It had neither caused the evils by unnecessary and destructive wars, or by enormous taxation, nor had it aggravated them, by a total neglect of economy; or by the insult of those who petitioned it for redress. Take the lesson that America affords, ye would-be despots of Great Britain.[46]

This continued to be the leading trend in radical papers and pamphlets until the early 1830s, with more stress being given to the advantages than the problems of American labour. At the height of the trades' union agitation of the early 1830s, for example, *The Gauntlet* emphasized that labourers could secure a comfortable subsistence with light labour,[47] while the Grand National Consolidated Trades Union paper, the *Pioneer*, claimed that deductions from labourers' wages in America were for their own benefit.[48] Various pro-emigration pamphlets also circu-

lated in these years among radicals who naturally had an interest in tout-
ing the advantages of American life.[49]

From the mid-1830s, none the less, there was a growing radical awareness of inequalities in the USA. President Jackson's efforts to counter the
strength of banks were followed closely,[50] and the view was increasingly
put forward, especially where the influence of Owenite propaganda had
made itself felt, that America proved that 'to the industrious many, one
form of government is about as good as another'.[51]

These divergent trends were exacerbated during the Chartist years by
the growing real distress in America, on the one hand, and the success of
Owenite and other socialist writers in persuading radicals that this
implied a genuine weakness in the radical economic programme. Most
Chartist papers, predictably, were extremely pro-American, and did not
fail to contrast 'the material well-being of Americans with the ragged
poverty of the great body of Englishmen'.[52] The London Working Men's
Association termed America a 'beacon of freedom',[53] while *McDougall's
Chartist Journal* claimed that universal suffrage had been a great success
in America, with 'nothing but prosperity' resulting from it.[54] Emigration
proponents like Edward Gibbon Wakefield who stressed the superior
advantages of American conditions were given much space in Chartist
papers,[55] while more conservative travel accounts were similarly dismissed.[56] Where Chartists did acknowledge American economic distress,
they also insisted that democracy made the solution of such problems
easier. The *Brighton Patriot* in 1839, for example, argued that:

> the Government of America, really emanating from the people, and
> the people themselves, have discovered that their independence is a
> mere phantom, and whatever the public in England may be taught
> by the generality of the newspaper press, they may depend on this,
> that the President, Congress, and people of America are determined
> on having a gold and silver currency, and nothing else, let their con-
> sequences be what it may be to the commercial world.[57]

By the late 1830s, and especially where Owenite influences are
evident, a more critical view of America became more common. This
sometimes caused overt tensions among Chartist audiences. In 1838 the
Northern Star, for instance, reported that the Owenite and moral force
Chartist William Lovett had said in a speech that 'In America, after fifty
years of freedom, the people are still slaving for others – the money-
mongers if you please – and that mostly because of the want of knowledge,' and noted that this was followed by 'hissing'.[58] Yet such charges
were becoming more persuasive and more frequent. By the early 1840s, a
more subtle Chartist reposte to such attacks emerged in the claim that
America had in fact never achieved universal suffrage, since it had 3
million slaves.[59] Even Feargus O'Connor by 1844 said that the USA had

never had a republic because of slavery.[60] This line of criticism, in fact, can be traced from this period until the outbreak of the American Civil War, when former Chartists offered a relatively sophisticated analysis of the failure of a slave-ridden republican system whose origins lay in an aristocratic landholding system unchanged since the seventeenth century.[61]

The increasingly sharp nature of Chartist criticisms of America in the mid-1840s corresponded with the shifting nature of Chartist strategy after 1842, when Feargus O'Connor began to give the Land Plan priority over the immediate achievement of the Charter. As unemployment worsened, too, the linkage of the land question to industrialization became more prominent. Thus by 1844, the editor of the *Northern Star* asserted that the USA had two classes composed of idlers and workers, and that, as in England, capitalists monopolized the benefits of machinery.[62] Soon it would contend, even more pessimistically, that both the American and French Revolutions had failed for the same reason: the working classes had failed to gain land.[63] The development of an agrarian league in America thus met with a warm response from the paper.[64]

After the quiescent years of 1845–47 these major trends re-emerged during the outburst of Chartist enthusiasm which occurred in 1848. Some reformers, like Joseph Barker, remained adamant that American prosperity was due to republican principles, not merely unlimited land.[65] Similarly, a major article in the *Power of the Pence* in 1848 entitled 'America and England Contrasted. Social Influence of Democracy in America' also ascribed American prosperity to democratic institutions.[66] Even critical tracts like R.W. Russell's socialistic *America Compared With England* (1849), which denounced the evils of competition in the United States, linked American prosperity to its form of government.[67] The 'red republicans' of 1848, however, like George Julian Harney, were equally certain that a social revolution of the majority against the minority was necessary in the USA.[68] But even among these, some, like Marx's friend Ernest Jones in 1853, generously asserted that the USA was 'that Republic where, with all its faults, man is still free, whether he chooses to use his liberty or not'.[69] The growing litany of critics in the late 1840s, however, now included new types of radical like the anti-communist republican W.J. Linton, devoted to the Italian patriot Guiseppe Mazzini, who described America as 'the worst monarchy and aristocracy of mere wealth'.[70] Christian communitarians and socialists were similarly critical. Robert Pemberton, author of *The Happy Colony*, (1854), for example, wrote that 'America is a striking and grand example of the false system of making money the sole power and moving agent of our existence – the fundamental good, instead of united labour.'[71]

From 1848, thus, more pronounced criticisms of American developments are clearly evident. After Chartism declined, in fact, most radicals
seem to have become disillusioned with America as well. The influential
radical publisher G.W.M. Reynolds notably contended that if superior
conditions prevailed in America, this resulted solely from 'territorial and
local advantages', and not a better social and political system.[72] This was
a striking inversion of crucial and popular radical assumptions over the
past half century. The most important radical journal of the era,
Reynolds's Newspaper took a sharp line on the USA for the next decade
and beyond, maintaining that while the USA had great advantages, its
Senate, Presidency and tyranny of capital should be abolished, and the
land nationalized. By 1857 the paper even asserted that some workers in
New York might be in 'as pitiable a predicament as the workers of this
country'.[73]

This cursory overview of the emergence of a negative image of America
among early nineteenth-century British radicals and socialists has not
focused on the analytic implications of the debate over American social
and industrial conditions. Yet it was clear, if often more obliquely than
overtly, that the socialist (and Tory) challenge to the radical assumption
that republicanism and prosperity went hand in hand implied the need
for a considerably more perceptive account of political economy, if not
the acceptance of a measure of economic determinism in which forms of
government took a distant second place to the workings of economic
laws. For it was central to both the Tory and socialist critique of the
radical interpretation of America that there was no necessary connection
between governmental forms and economic conditions whatsoever.
Tories like Robert Southey had argued at the end of the eighteenth
century, in the light of the debate over Paine's *Rights of Man*, that 'men
fell into the strange mistake of believing that the facilities of subsistence
in America were owing to its form of government'.[74] Malthus had
insisted in 1798 that the Painite view that taxation was the sole cause of
distress could be disproven by reference to America.[75] This assumption
would be incorporated into most forms of liberal political economy
thereafter.

In this sense, though their reasoning and aims of course differed
sharply, the position adopted by most classical liberal political econo-
mists and most socialists respecting America was identical. But it was
only by the 1840s, as evidence began overwhelmingly to mount about
increasing distress in the new republic, that much of the case for the
analytic separation of democracy from economic liberty was conceded
by leading radical propagandists. Thereafter, from the 1850s onwards,
America became increasingly seen as the prototype of an untrammelled

capitalist economy in socialist thought. This was notably the presumption of Marx, who viewed the availability of much free land and a relatively small population as the chief causes of American exceptionalism in the 1850s and 1860s, and by 1880 saw the closing of frontier and rise of an American proletariat as ending this exceptionalism.[76] By the end of the nineteenth century, the political determinism of the radical republicans, a mainstay of enthusiasm in the French revolutionary era, thus found few proponents. The logic of capitalism had defied republican virtue. Democratic inequality was as destructive as monarchical inequality, and social theory had to be adjusted accordingly.

Notes

1. This article draws on themes explored in my *Citizens and Saints. Politics and Anti-Politics in Early British Socialism* (Cambridge University Press, 1989). I remain grateful for John Harrison's characteristically cogent examination of its arguments when it was presented as a doctoral dissertation in 1982.

2. There is an immense literature on the general impact of the USA on Europe. On the role of America in political thought prior to the period discussed here, see for example, Werner Stark, *America: Ideal and Reality. The United States of 1776 in Contemporary European Philosophy* (Kegan Paul, Trench, Trubner & Co., 1947); Ivan Doig, *Utopia and America. Dreams and Realities* (Hayden Book Co., 1976); Arthur J. Slavin, 'The American Principle from More to Locke', in Fredi Chiappelli (ed.), *First Images of America* (University of California Press, 1976), pp. 139–64. General perceptions of America in nineteenth-century Britain are detailed in Alan Nevins, *America Through British Eyes* (Oxford University Press, 1948); Frank Thistlethwaite, *The Anglo-American Connection in the Early Nineteenth Century* (University of Pennsylvania Press, 1959); W.S. Shepperson, *British Emigration to North America. Projects and Opinions in the Early Victorian Period* (Blackwell, 1957); Max Berger, *The British Traveller in America, 1836–1860* (Peter Smith, 1964), ch. 4; G.D. Lillibridge, *Beacon of Freedom: The Impact of American Democracy upon Great Britain 1830–1870* (University of Pennsylvania Press, 1954); D.P. Crook, *American Democracy in English Politics, 1815–50* (Clarendon Press, 1965); Charlotte Erickson, 'Agrarian Myths of English Immigrants', in O.F. Ander (ed.), *In the Trek of the Immigrants* (Rock Island, 1964), pp. 59–80; and Henry Pelling, *America and the British Left: From Bright to Bevan* (Adam & Charles Black, 1956).

3. See Joyce Appleby, 'America as a Model for the Radical French Reformers of 1789', *William and Mary Quarterly*, 3rd series, vol. 30, (1971), pp. 267–86.

4. I use this abbreviated form to stand for the many American state constitutions as well as the new federal constitution in place after 1787.

5. Joseph Gerrald, *A Convention the Only Means of Saving Us From Ruin* (3rd edn, 1794), reprinted in my *The Political Writings of the 1790s*, 8 vols, (Pickering and Chatto, 1995), vol. 4.

6. See my *Thomas Paine: Social and Political Thought* (Unwin Hyman, 1989), pp. 86–90. Paine's imagery was still the starting point for commentaries on America half a century later, for example, Thomas Brothers, *The United States of North America As They Are; Not as They Are Generally Described: Being A Cure for Radicalism* (1840), pp. 3–11.

7. Daniel Stuart, *Peace and Reform, Against War and Corruption* (2nd edn, 1794), reprinted in my *The Political Writings of the 1790s*, 8 vols, (Pickering and Chatto, 1995), vol. 4.

8. *Considerations on Mr Paine's Pamphlet on the Rights of Man* (1791), p. 16, reprinted in my *The Political Writings of the 1790s*, 8 vols, (Pickering and Chatto, 1995), vol. 5.

9. Arthur Young, *The Example of France a Warning to Britain* (3rd edn., 1794), pp. 61, 88, reprinted in my *The Political Writings of the 1790s*, 8 vols, (Pickering and Chatto, 1995), vol. 7.

10. *State Trials for High Treason. Part Third. Containing the Trial of Mr Thelwall* (1794), p. 21, quoted in my *The Politics of English Jacobinism: Writings of John Thelwall* (Penn State Press, 1995), p. xxiii.

11. Joel Barlow, *Advice to the Privileged Orders*, Part II (1793), reprinted in my *The Political Writings of the 1790s*, 8 vols, (Pickering and Chatto, 1995), vol. 3.

12. See, for example, the *Quarterly Review*'s warning that democracy and equality would produce a 'despotic tyranny' in America ending in a military despotism like France's before the Restoration, 53, (1835), pp. 550–2.

13. Typical was the *Quarterly Review*'s comment that the low level of intellectual attainment in America would remain as long as 'all power shall depend on the fluctuating will, and coarse passions of an illiterate, conceited, encroaching, and sottish population', 41, (1829), p. 439.

14. Abbé de Mably, *Observations on the Government and Laws of the United States of America* (1784), p. 23. On Mably's views, see Werner Stark, *America: Ideal and Reality*, pp. 35–57.

15. See *A Defence of the Constitutions of Government of the United States* (1787).

16. See Richard Twomey, 'Jacobins and Jeffersonians: Anglo-American Radical Ideology, 1790–1810', in Margaret Jacob and James Jacob (eds), *The Origins of Anglo-American Radicalism* (George Allen & Unwin, 1984), pp. 284–99. On the emergence of Jeffersonian democracy see Elisha P. Douglass, *Rebels and Democrats. The Struggle for Equal Political Rights and Majority Rule During the American Revolution* (University of North Carolina Press, 1955), pp. 287–316, and generally Alfred F. Young, *The Democratic Republicans of New York. The Origins 1763–1797* (University of North Carolina Press, 1967). See p. 574 on the antipathy to 'aristocracy' of the radical anti-Federalists, who grew in strength throughout the 1790s.

17. *The Patriot's Pocket Companion or Complete Yearbook for the Year 1797* (1797), p. 7.

18. I draw here on the analysis offered in my 'The Origins of the Rights of Labor: Republicanism and Commerce in Britain, 1796–1805', *Journal of Modern History*, 66, (1994), pp. 249–90. As early as 1899, H.S. Foxwell noted that 'Hall was one of the first writers to see through the imposture of American liberty, about which Godwin and his friends were so warmly

congratulating themselves' (introduction to Anton Menger, *The Right to The Whole Produce of Labour*, Macmillan, 1899).

19. Charles Hall, *The Effects of Civilization on the People in European States* (1805), esp. pp. 248–59.

20. On the image of America in French socialism, see J.F. Normano, 'Saint-Simon and America', *Social Forces*, 11, (1932), pp. 8–14, and A.S. Tillett, 'Some Saint-Simonian Criticism of the United States before 1835', *Romanic Review*, 52, (1961), pp. 3–16.

21. None the less Owen himself was somewhat ambiguous in his comments on America. He found much to praise about its constitution when the New Harmony community was founded in early 1820s (*Selected Works of Robert Owen*, G. Claeys, ed., 4 vols, Pickering and Chatto, 1993, vol. 2, p. 28), and even in 1845 arguing that 'the United States, through its more free institutions, will take the lead in great national and universal improvements, while Europe and other parts of the world will be compelled to follow its example' (*Communitist* (18), 12 February 1845, p. 69; (6), 12 September 1845, p. 21).

22. Quoted in *Citizens and Saints*, p. 152.

23. John Francis Bray, *Labour's Wrongs and Labour's Remedy* (1839), pp. 18–19.

24. Quoted in *Citizens and Saints*, p. 221.

25. There were exceptions to this view. William Thompson, for example, contended in 1824 that labour had been both most secure and most productive in the USA (William Thompson, *Inquiry Concerning the Distribution of Wealth*, 1824, p. 44). But by the time he wrote *Labor Rewarded* (1827), Thompson had become more critical, and he insisted that 'chicane reigns supreme' in the USA (William Thompson, *Labor Rewarded*, 1827, pp. 15, 43).

26. Charles Bray, *The Philosophy of Necessity* (1841), pp. 362–3.

27. William Hawkes Smith, *Letters* (1838), p. 25.

28. Cf. the widely circulated *Social Tracts* (n.p.,?1838), pp. 1–2.

29. For example, *Poor Man's Guardian*, 4, pp. 460–1.

30. *New Moral World*, 2, (1836), pp. 76–7.

31. Quoted in my *Citizens and Saints*, p. 155.

32. See D.P. Crook's otherwise useful *American Democracy in English Politics 1815–50*, p. 153. Henry Pelling had earlier proposed that 'only a tiny minority of Socialistic writers went so far as to suggest that the individual might suffer severely in America from "the errors of society"' (*America and the British Left*, p. 2). Lillibridge, *Beacon of Freedom*, does not deal with the socialists at all, though he touches on some land reformers (pp. 65–72).

33. *Black Dwarf*, 14 January 1818, p. 22. On the general influence of the American model in British radicalism in this period, see Lillibridge, *Beacon of Freedom*.

34. P.B. Shelley, *A Philosophical View of Reform* (1819), cited in R. J. White (ed.), *Political Tracts of Wordsworth, Coleridge and Shelley* (Cambridge, 1953), p. 219.

35. *Cobbett's Weekly Political Register*, 3, (1), 8 January 1803, p. 3. On Cobbett's conversion to radicalism, see David A. Wilson, *Paine and Cobbett. The Transatlantic Connection* (McGill-Queen's University Press, 1988), pp. 148–83. See also M. Clark, *Peter Porcupine in America: The Career of William Cobbett 1762–1835* (Philadelphia, 1935); and P.W.

Gaines, *William Cobbett and the United States, 1792–1835* (Worcester, Mass., 1971).

36. On Cobbett's contrast of Britain and America, see, for example, G.D.H. Cole, *The Life of William Cobbett* (1947), p. 228; William Spater, *William Cobbett: the Poor Man's Friend*, 2 vols, (Cambridge University Press, 1982), vol. 2, p. 321. On the shift in Cobbett's views, which was associated with rising food prices in Britain, see Ian Dyck, *William Cobbett and Rural Popular Culture* (Cambridge University Press, 1992), pp. 29–31.
37. *Cobbett's Weekly Political Register*, **31**, 10 August 1816, p. 118.
38. *Cobbett's Weekly Political Register*, **37**, 29 July 1820, p. 69.
39. *Cobbett's Weekly Political Register*, **25**, January 1817, p. 119.
40. For example, *Cobbett's Weekly Political Register*, **30**, 6 January 1816, pp. 1–7.
41. *Cobbett's Weekly Political Register*, **83**, 8 February 1834, pp. 321–35.
42. *Cobbett's Weekly Political Register*, **31**, 10 August 1816, pp. 118–21.
43. *Cobbett's Weekly Political Register*, **31**, 9 November 1816, p. 481.
44. *Reformists' Register* (20), 7 June 1817, pp. 623–4.
45. *White Hat* (8), 14 December 1819, pp. 126–7.
46. *Wooler's British Gazette*, **2**, (17), 23 April 1820, p. 129.
47. *Gauntlet*, 10 February 1833, p. 2.
48. *Pioneer*, (1833), p. 87.
49. For example, *Rare News for Labourers; or America and England Contrasted* (1829).
50. For example, *Poor Man's Guardian*, **1**, (1832), p. 636–7.
51. Quoted in *Citizens and Saints*, p. 293.
52. Quoted in G. Lillibridge, *Beacon of Freedom*, p. 53.
53. Quoted in G. Lillibridge, *Beacon of Freedom*, p. 5.
54. *McDougall's Chartist Journal*, 10 July 1841, p. 113; 7 August 1841, p. 152.
55. [Edward Gibbon Wakefield], *England and America. A Comparison of the Social and Political State of Both Nations* (1834).
56. See, for example, Thomas Brothers, *The United States of North America As They Are; Not as They Are Generally Described: Being A Cure for Radicalism* (1840), pp. 51–79, 245.
57. *Brighton Patriot*, **122**, 20 June 1839, p. 2.
58. *Northern Star*, 29 December 1838, p. 8.
59. *Northern Star*, 27 March 1841, p. 1. See also *Bury Observer* (2), May 1850, p. 40.
60. *Northern Star*, 4 May 1844, p. 1. In 1849, a group of Nottingham Chartists criticized O'Connor for being too hard on the USA (*Northern Star*, 10 March 1849, p. 1). Harney responded that while the principles of the republic were good, a few of its citizens were wicked (*ibid.*, p. 5).
61. *Jersey Independent*, **12**, (50), 27 February 1862, p. 2. As early as 1850, Harney had written on the USA that 'Just now the Republic in the West is of small account in the affairs of Europe, and this is just on account of slavery' (*Star of Freedom*, **3**, (116), 14 September 1850, p. 8). *Reynolds's Newspaper* commented similarly in the mid-1850s that a civil war would be a blessing in America, because it had been contaminated by the inheritance of slavery from Britain.
62. *Northern Star*, 1 June 1844, p. 7.
63. *Northern Star*, 10 January 1846, p. 4.

64. *Northern Star*, 27 April 1844, p. 4.
65. *The People* (1848), p. 5.
66. *Power of the Pence*, 16 December 1848, pp. 85–7.
67. R. W. Russell, *America Compared with England. The Respective Social Effects and the American and English Systems of Government and Legislation, and the Mission of Democracy* (1849), p. 177. Russell wrote: 'the opinion generally entertained in Europe, that the condition of the people in America is owing to the sparseness of the population, and the abundance of land, is erroneous . . . their prosperity is solely to be attributed to the excellent constitution and laws which emanate from popular representative government'.
68. *Red Republican*, 22 June 1850, pp. 1–2. See also Harney's comments in the *Friend of the People*, 26 July 1851, p. 268.
69. *People's Paper*, 15 January 1853, p. 1.
70. *English Republic*, **4**, (1855), pp. 65–8.
71. Robert Pemberton, *The Happy Colony* (1854), p. 24.
72. *Reynolds's Political Instructor*, 13 April 1850, pp. 182–3.
73. *Reynolds's Newspaper* (381), 29 November 1857, p. 1.
74. Quoted in *Citizens and Saints*, p. 156.
75. T.R. Malthus, *Essay on Population*, 2 vols (Dent, n.d.), vol. 2, pp. 61–7.
76. See esp. Oakley C. Johnson, 'Karl Marx and the United States', *Main - stream*, **16**, (1963), pp. 3–19, and Robert Weiner, 'Karl Marx's Vision of America: A Biographical and Bibliographical Sketch', *Review of Politics*, **42**, (1980), pp. 465–503.

CHAPTER SEVEN

The Town and Country Divide in English History

Ian Dyck

Five years ago, while in Coventry offering a crash course on modern England to visiting Canadian students, I took a day trip to Brighton where I met up with John Harrison for a downland walk. During our many previous treks we had generally chatted about flora and fauna, wine-making, John's book-binding or the relative size of British and Canadian farm machinery. But this time we entertained matters of the shop, principally the long-term effects of the collapse of communism on academic Marxism and English historical writing. Although anticipating that many historians would soon be doing some fast footwork around the subjects of class, class struggle and even Marxist theory generally, we predicted (or rather I predicted, John being wiser and more temperate than his impetuous student) that class would ultimately remain a master category in English history, and that there would be no need to make any concessions to the parlour games of the post-structuralists. The 'linguistic turn' might eventually happen, I suggested, but it would come about much more slowly than the invasion of the 'Althusserian tank' of 15 years ago.[1] In short, it would be business as usual for English historians.

Needless to say these predictions have not come to pass, for within the past few years the post-structural train has clipped along at almost breakaway speed, jostling much of our theoretical fare of the 1980s: first Marxist class divisions, then Gramscian dialectics between the dominant and subordinate, now the distinctions between popular and élite culture. Even many historians who have stood at the back of the platform have felt the breeze of the passing express, perhaps not to the point of converting them outright to post-structuralism but maybe causing them to think twice before imposing a division or a cleavage where a current or continuity could do. Yet there might be something that can be salvaged from my remark to John; if so it might be this: that post-structuralism will doubtless cause more disruption for urban and industrial historians than for rural and agrarian ones.[2]

For reasons that might be traceable to Marx's own despair and gratuitous comments about rural life and culture,[3] theories of class and class struggle have only been soft-pedalled in English rural history, including by such great historians as Rodney Hilton, Christopher Hill, Eric

Hobsbawm and Edward Thompson. In fact it is only recently that a rigorous interpretation of class has been pressed for nineteenth-century rural England, and even this argument has shown few signs of developing into a substantial school of thought.[4] Most self-proclaimed Marxists have long recognized that English peasants, tenant farmers and country labourers have structured their identities in a great variety of ways, and that class is by no means a universal understanding of social order among English country people. Many rural historians will surely wish to quarrel with the conservative ideological underpinnings of the work of Patrick Joyce, James Vernon or of that champion of gradualism J.C.D. Clark, but it is doubtful that even self-described left-wing historians of rural England would vigorously oppose Joyce's or Vernon's argument that class was only one of many contemporary 'visions of the people'.[5] Keith Wrightson, for example, has emphasized the importance of 'community consciousness' in rural England – a sensibility that he defines in much the same way as Edward Thompson defined class consciousness, though on a more vertical axis. Further, Edward's own *Customs in Common*, together with recent work by Jeanette Neeson and by numerous early modern historians (who always seem to be ahead of modernists in terms of theorizing about rural English society), subtly poses the possibility that 'customary consciousness' was at least as important as class consciousness in the culture and experience of English villagers.[6] This is to say, then, that few rural historians are dogmatically locked into positions on class and class consciousness, and that accordingly they might be well placed to explore 'rural populism' or other modes of 'consciousness' as surrogates or as complements to class.[7]

At the moment it is possible to identify three distinct strands in English rural and agrarian history. The oldest – the 'plough and cow' school – has long focused on field systems, soil types, livestock breeds and rent rolls – thereby constituting a very literal 'history on the ground'. Social and cultural questions have sometimes been asked by the 'plough and cow' school but these have generally pertained to the country house rather than the cottage. Second, there is now at work a new generation of rural historians, many of them associated with the new journal *Rural History*, who are posing social and cultural questions, pursuing innovative methodologies and encouraging close contact across the disciplines. A third strand in English rural historiography – taking its cue from Raymond Williams's *The Country and the City*, published in 1973 – has followed the metamorphosis of structuralism from the early 1970s to the 1990s, emphasizing genre, type, symbol and text. A case might be made that the 'country and city' approach is not really rural history at all but rather a series of studies of representations or imaginings of the rural by the urban élite, usually courtiers and town-based aristocrats. Except for the work of such scholars as Alun Howkins and John Barrell, who have studied images and representations of the rural within a social and cultural context,[8] the 'country and city' school has tended to follow Raymond Williams by producing studies that emphasize literary, élitist and urban perceptions of the countryside. Although many recent studies of landscape symbolism and the 'rural idyll' have duly reminded us of the rural nucleus within Englishness,[9] many of these works have tended to perceive the countryside as a spiritual or ideological refuge for townspeople, even to the point where, according to Martin Wiener, the countryside can be accused of sapping the virility and business acumen of English industrial capitalists.[10] This is not to say that we should ignore urban-based thoughts and perceptions about the countryside but that we should search for ways to incorporate the lives and thoughts of the men and women who lived and learned in the English countryside. This study attempts to make a small step in that direction.

Study of urban-rural contrasts has grown enormously in the humanities and social sciences during the past two decades, ranging from the relationship between *rustica* and *urbana* in classical thought to present debates regarding hedgerows, public footpaths, agricultural subsidies and green belts.[11] Town-country anxieties are, in many societies, a permanent fixture of human relations, including in my native western Canada where cultural and economic differences between rural and urban people are as taken for granted, even by political parties, as are class differences in England. Likewise many notable historians of France, such as Robert Muchembled, Roger Chartier and Eugen Weber, have grounded large and important studies of French cultural history on the premise of a town-country divide, which they regard as more important and fundamental than class differences or divisions between popular and élite culture.[12]

In England a town-country contrast is frequently remarked upon but seldom studied in detail. Raphael Samuel, for instance, has recently observed that the town-country division is a central theme in English letters and 'fundamental to ideas of British national character',[13] but beyond this few cultural historians are prepared to go, leaving micro-study of the town-country relationship to demographers, geographers and economic historians, who understandably have focused on population shifts, trading networks and service exchanges rather than the cultural dimensions of the contrast.[14]

An explanation for this gap in cultural history might be that the town-country debate has an uneven history, that it can be vigorous and dominant in one period, mild and inconspicuous the next. Our lines of vision on town and country can also be affected by who we listen to, and here I must confess to having listened closely for the past while to William Cobbett, one of England's most passionate commentators on country life and conversely one of the most formidable critics of the economies and cultures of towns (he put 'Wen' in the language as a pejorative nickname for London). Perhaps the problem is also one of over-recognition – the town-country contrast is everywhere, including in the air that we breathe; or maybe an aura of sanctity (with the country simply being identified with good and the town with bad) has elevated the rural-urban question into a sort of imponderable metaphysic that is as pointless to interrogate as the existence of God. Whatever the explanation, it seems that we are absorbing rather than studying the town-country relationship, observing its presence and then hastily moving on to conflicts and dialectics that seem more intelligible or significant. Even Marx did this, and so too Gramsci – both discerned a division and conflict between country people and townspeople, even recognizing it as an *ideological* division, but neither Marx nor Gramsci seriously explored the origin or meaning of the divide, perhaps feeling that it was ultimately a stalled dialectic that, unlike class conflict and capitalist development, would have no progressive consequences for social relations.[15] The fact that town and country antagonisms might proceed from populist impulses and that they might sometimes cut across class formations is understandably discomforting for ardent Marxist historians because it puts them in the awkward position of having to override contemporary opinion and to declare the sentiment misguided or illusory. Indeed, some 15 years after completing his study of the perceived division between town and country, Raymond Williams pointedly observed that the two entities are 'indissolubly linked', and that any division between them is the artificial creation of modern capitalism.[16] Perhaps so, but we must not trump popular thought and experience with our ideological verdicts.

It is important to remind ourselves from time to time that town and country have not always been at odds either culturally or economically. While the classical period resembles our own in that it witnessed a great deal of high-handed moralizing about urban vices and rustic virtues, especially by Varro, Cicero and Horace,[17] the medieval period manifests surprisingly little town-country tension. One explanation, of course, is that town and country were highly interdependent during the Middle Ages, that many rural residents worked part time in the towns and that many town-dwellers were part-time cultivators. None the less, as Rodney Hilton has shown, there were still opportunities for town-country tensions, especially in those regions and cities where occupational divisions were quite sharply drawn.[18] And a degree of tension there was, expressed most famously perhaps in John Ball's warning to his fellow rebels to beware of 'gyle' in London,[19] but the post-medieval historian must marvel at the extraordinary degree of collaboration between towns-people and country people during the 1381 revolt. As Rosamond Faith has pointed out, urban and rural participants in the revolt did not always have identical interests, but they collaborated to a remarkable extent, including in provincial and chartered towns as well as in London.[20] Indeed, we are told in *Eulogium Historarium* that the citizens of London called for the city gates to be opened to the rebels, whom they addressed as 'neighbours and friends'.[21] Ball's cautionary note, then, might indeed echo an 'ancient mistrust' between country people and Londoners,[22] but this mutual mistrust or suspicion was not sufficient to forestall a search for a common political platform.

Medieval popular culture also saw the construction of heroes – mostly fictional – who were fair-minded champions of all fair-minded people, whether rural or urban. Guy of Warwick, Bevis of Hampton and Robin Hood (perhaps most surprisingly the latter in light of his rural residency and pursuits) show no interest in upholding town-country antagonisms – indeed one even senses that anxieties or disagreements of this sort would be seen as contrary to the spirit of justice and fair play that the legends exemplify. Even the stories associated with the beloved countryman-cum-mayor Dick Whittington, who, though of higher birth than the chapbooks and songs allow, seems wholly uninterested in promoting town-country rivalry – in fact it is a merchant (usually the most despised of city-dwellers from a country point of view) who befriends Dick upon his arrival in the metropolis.[23] Unlike today, when communities jealously guard their icons and mascots, medieval towns and cities bolstered and personified civic identities by making short- and long-term borrowings from the pantheon of English heroes and heroines, perhaps invoking Guy, St George and the Pindar of Wakefield at once. And while almost all of these heroes and heroines were recognized as coming from humble rural stock, country people seemed not to object to the cultural borrow-ings of the towns, doubtless assuming that popular heroes and heroines were at once local, national and always to be shared.

Even that most beloved of medieval characters, Langland's Piers the Ploughman, harbours no special interest in singling out towns and townspeople for special praise or opprobrium. Piers is decidedly of the view that ploughmen are the most valuable of all workers, and that city folk such as merchants, lawyers and courtiers are responsible for a dis-proportionate amount of the world's grief and vice, but Piers, in the end, like John Ball in 1381, sees value and merit in all occupations, and offers everyone a place in Truth's community. There is indeed a social division in *Piers the Ploughman* but it is not between town and country – it falls between the common labourers (scorned by Piers for their sloth and their idle curiosity in the rhymes of Robin Hood) and the hard-working and

earnest ploughman of the story, who is not a propertyless worker but a
landholder who owns his own plough-team and employs waged labour.
But though class and status tensions are readily discernible in *Piers*,
town-country anxieties are decidedly not: 'The king, with his nobles and
counsellors, decided that the common people should provide them with
resources; so the people devised different trades, and engaged ploughmen
to labour and till the soil for the good of the whole community, as honest
ploughmen should.'[24] Langland's social conservatism stands in sharp
contrast to the democratic spirit of John Ball, but what Piers and the
rebels of 1381 have in common is a resolve to communicate their ideological points in a spirit of fairness and egalitarianism to the Christian
community as a whole, without regard for an urban-rural rift.

What has appropriately been called a 'ploughman' tradition in English
literature and social commentary extended from Langland's day to the
early Elizabethan period.[25] The poets and commentators who wrote
within this tradition were not always respectful towards the culture of
ploughmen but as a rule they singled out husbandry as an especially
valuable pursuit. The Kentish squire John Gower, for example, rebuked
the rebels of 1381, lambasted Londoners as avaricious and fraudulent,
chastised peasants as 'sluggish' and 'grasping' and then proceeded to
honour agriculture as a divinely-ordained calling from Adam forward.[26]
In the anonymous poems 'Song of the Husbandman' (*c*.1300), 'The
Plowman's Tale' (1395), 'God Spede the Plough' (*c*.1500) and 'Vox
Populi, Vox Dei' (*c*.1548) husbandmen and ploughmen are said to
'mayntayne this world' but to have poverty as their reward.[27] Judging
from these works, even townspeople looked upon ploughmen as deserv-
ing of special recognition, partly because of Adam's agrarian career and
partly because the case for husbandry was compelling on secular and
economic grounds. A degree of condescension creeps into the ploughman
tradition when it is invoked as a medium for Lollard and later Calvinist
polemics,[28] most notably when the ploughman is trotted out as a 'common sense' commentator who cannot fathom the doctrine of transub-
stantiation (the rustic speaker in Luke Shepherd's *John Bon and Mast
Parson*, for example, informs a priest that the host is 'but a cake')[29] but
even if disposed to ridicule the ploughman the Lollards and Calvinists
had to show restraint, if only because the presentation of a dim-witted
'defender of the faith' would hardly have been a good advertisement for
religious reform. It is likewise with William Tyndale's celebrated quest to
extend knowledge of the Scriptures to 'the boy that driveth the plough'.[30]
The campaign has a prosaic ring to it but Tyndale seems to have suspected that special effort would be required to ensure that the
Reformation reached the countryside. In the end the Reformation would
prove to be more urban than rural, but the countryside still mattered to

religious reformers, if only as a theatre of ungodliness that required correction and nurture.

The hero of the ploughman tradition is sometimes a literal ploughman whose life consists of tilling the soil and who speaks for all English men and women; other times the ploughman or 'good husbandman' is a metaphor for Everyman. Both of these great traditions come together in Robert Crowley, Thomas More and Hugh Latimer, whose writings can be counted among the last great contributions to the ploughman tradition. These men were not probable candidates to agree on much: Crowley and Latimer were Calvinists, More was Catholic. Crowley was thoroughly urban in his sensibilities and idiom, Latimer rural in his, and More a mixture of both. Yet despite the diversity in the culture and theologies of the commonwealthmen they were in thorough agreement that husbandry was the first calling in the Christian nation and that the customary rights of the rural poor should be upheld, even revered. The commonwealthmen did not arrive at their high regard for husbandry by studying the georgic and pastoral modes of the classical world or by contemplating the allegorical meanings of the Scriptures – their assignment of a high moral and economic worth to husbandmen was a literal, common-sense platform based on experience, honesty and good sense.[31]

The commonwealthmen were not interested in dismantling towns or abolishing urban life. Certainly they wished to see Londoners reduce their vices ('repente O London. Repent, repente', pleaded Latimer[32]) but they did not call for major revisions to the social order or for the countryside to be demographically compensated (enclosures were depopulating the countryside in their view) by forced migration from the towns. In More's *Utopia* everyone works at agriculture and has a craft on the side, but there are a total of 54 cities on the island, 'all spacious and magnificent', and each is provided with food and fuel by happy and dutiful farm workers. In short, the commonwealth thinkers wanted a hard-working, plain-speaking, fair-minded England in which town and country cooperated in a spirit of good will. There was to be no community of goods but customary rights were to be upheld and landowners would simply have to learn, in Crowley's words, that they were 'but stuardes'.[33] Indeed, a common platform on customary rights served to bind town and country on account that not just rural but also townspeople, including many Londoners, depended on use-rights and common land for recreation space and fresh food.[34]

Remnants of the ploughman tradition survive into the Elizabethan period, including on the floor of the House of Commons where in 1601 Robert Cecil candidly remarked: 'I do not dwell in the Countrey, I am not acquainted with the Plough: But I think that whosoever doth not maintain the Plough, destroys this Kingdom.'[35] Even an unabashed townsman such as Elizabeth's first minister could value and honour the plough as fulsomely as any countryman. But Cecil was exceptional, for in late Tudor times the ecclesiastical and moral imagery of the ploughman falls away while the task of promoting husbandry is picked up by courtiers and London-based gentleman writers who valued the plough but not necessarily the ploughman.[36] Most of these writers denounce the use-rights and customary consciousness that the commonwealthmen had sought to keep at the forefront of public attention, beginning with that of the monarch. Thomas Tusser, Gervase Markham, Walter Blith – indeed almost all late sixteenth- and seventeenth-century authors of husbandry manuals (as Joan Thirsk remarks this was 'the golden age for English books of husbandry')[37] – do not in so many words disparage the plough but they discharge Crowley's 'stuarde' principle of land ownership by supporting enclosure of the commons, opposing customary rights and encouraging agricultural improvement for the sake of private wealth. This is not to say that the husbandry writers were ignorant and mean-spirited – Thomas Tusser, for instance, was knowledgeable and caring about many aspects of husbandry and rural life – but that they surrendered to some of the cultural trappings of London and the court by reducing the literal and figurative role of the ploughman in English farming. Agriculture was now principally about thrift and about being absolute master of one's own lands. The well-being of the ploughman and the commonwealth mattered less than formerly,[38] and if the harvest fell short, London's interests were seen to first.[39]

The retreat of the worker within the practical, georgic mode of English rural writing removed a potential counterpoint to the pastoral tradition that swept the Elizabethan and Jacobean courts. Whatever its literary merit, early modern pastoral literature denigrated rural England by populating it with an implausible cast of imports from classical Greece and Rome: nymphs, muses and toga-wearing shepherds. Whereas during the Henrician and Edwardian period there was a meaningful and earnest debate about the relative economic merits of arable and pastoral farming, often couched in terms of the sheep versus the plough, the whimsical authors in the new pastoral mode, showing off their courtly metre and diction, avoided talk of ploughs, pasturage and livestock. In Edmund Spenser's *The Shepheardes Calendar* and Philip Sidney's *Arcadia* the rustic language of country people is held up for ridicule, princes come out of nowhere to defeat shepherds at singing contests (even rustic competence in song is not conceded) and there emerges an insidious division between the spirit of Cain – the wicked one who is consigned to the plough – and his brother Abel, who is awarded the good life as keeper of the 'fleecie sheepe'.[40]

As happened in some miracle plays the story of Cain versus Abel could sensibly be invoked as a motto or parable for a discussion of the relative merits of pastoral and arable farming.[41] Even country workers themselves participated in good-natured banter about the experiences and values of ploughmen and shepherds. The anthropologically inclined John Aubrey drew upon cultural contrasts between pastoral and arable regions in Wiltshire which might go some way towards explaining patterns of allegiance in the civil wars: followers of the plough, he believed, were too manually occupied to attend to political and religious disputes, whereas in pastoral areas the herdsmen and stockmen had more time to read and discuss such matters.[42] Milton and Bunyan, of course, would draw upon the images of Christian pastoral, including Cain versus Abel, to personify temporal and spiritual struggles, but their Eden is everywhere and nowhere, and their shepherds are sometimes lazy and dissolute – not the celestial and immutable phantoms of the Elizabethan pastoral writers. Spenser and Sidney were not interested in drawing a representative picture of English rural life. They plundered rural England for landscapes that appeared authentic but sprinkled them with wistful herdsmen and shepherdesses who embrace the aesthetics of the court and pay special attention to the advice of contemporary literary critics, such as George Puttenham and Thomas Wilson, to emulate 'court talke' rather than 'countrey speech'.[43] The result is not a portrait or interpretation of rural life but a satire of it.

Here and there during the seventeenth century there are heroic attempts to reassemble a practical, ploughman-centred husbandry in the spirit of the old commonwealthmen. Some writers, like Abraham Cowley, seemed to sense that the plough had lately been dishonoured and devalued by a mood of contempt for Cain:

> The three first Men in the World, were a Gardner, a Ploughman and A Grazier; and if any man object, That the second of these was a Murtherer, I desire he would consider, that as soon as he was so, he quitted our Profession, and turn'd Builder. It is for this reason, I suppose, that *Ecclesiasticus* forbids us to hate Husbandry; because (sayes he) the most High has created it. We were all Born to this Art.[44]

The ploughman tradition, however, had few supporters within the Elizabethan, Jacobean and Caroline courts, with the result that an increasingly hard line was taken by the Crown against anti-enclosure protesters and other upholders of customary rights.[45] And in Cowley's comments we can discern an ill omen for the future: an unleashing of occupational rivalry between the Ploughman and the Builder.

The political platforms of 'Court' and 'Country', much debated by historians of the English Revolution, do not directly correspond to the urban and rural worlds: London tended to support Parliament but rural England was highly divided in allegiance.[46] But as the wars progress we see emerging a sort of countryman alliance, perhaps most visible in the Clubman movement, that embodies on one hand a certain disinterest in metropolitan affairs and on the other a cultural and economic bonding of countrymen in support of local rights and customs.[47] This rural solidarity is by no means nationwide (the Diggers, for example, do not represent it: their quest was to unite the poor of town and country), but it is visible in many rural songs and tracts in which country people of all classes and stations announce a resolve to coalesce around common local interests. The inspirations behind this countryman bond might simply be disdain for the destruction brought to rural England by Cavalier and Parliamentarian alike, but doubtless it was sustained by the gradual decline in government support for customary rights. The Caroline Book of Orders and Oliver Cromwell's early reservations about enclosure did not stem the opposition; country people now seemed to be edging towards a recognition that court and Parliament alike were losing interest in the traditions and well-being of rural England.[48]

Londoners, for their part, also seem to turn inward. Their ballads and songs focus upon metropolitan achievements during the wars, while political protesters such as the Levellers express little interest in making common cause with country folk. Metropolitan history was also re-evaluated so that the rebels of 1381 – formerly championed for seeking to unite urban and rural workers – were now described and seen as 'rampant' rustics whom the heroic and civic-minded Lord Mayor, William Walworth, proudly dispelled (or indeed murdered in the case of Wat Tyler) in the proud name of London and the King.[49]

The respective cultures of rural and urban were sharply and uncharitably codified during the Restoration period. Caricatures of Hodge as a stupid and plodding boor who is cheated at every turn during visits to London becomes a favourite theme of metropolitan ballads and broadsides. In 'The Downright Countryman' the ploughman of the piece proudly declares '*I am no London cheat*,' while in the rebuttal, entitled 'The Citizen's Vindication Against the Downright Countryman', ploughmen are denounced as 'bumpkins' and 'clowns' who know only how 'to drive the plough, a *Gentile Curr indeed*'.[50] Good-natured teasing between rural and urban people has a long history in England but the Restoration period sees the beginning of gratuitous and mean-spirited stereotypes, especially of rural workers. In his history of 'unfortunate Hodg of the South' Humfery Crouch describes Hodge as a person of 'little wit, crump-shouldered, crook-backed, goggle-eyed, splay-footed, crooked legs, and so deformed, that he was hated by man, woman and child'.[51] Rustic idiots abound in almost every facet of Restoration culture

– the stage, the court and both high and low literature. Even the few defences and vindications of Hodge that can be glimpsed within the onslaught do not address the cultural and intellectual properties of rural workers - in effect they concede the point about Hodge's imbecility and suggest only that he or she is honest and good at heart.[52]

A central premise of Restoration popular literature is that town and country are two solitudes – economically, socially and culturally. An urban identity is negatively distilled from the anti-countryman literature and more positively from close exploration of the distinctiveness of urban, particularly London culture. Many ballads have such perfunctory titles as 'Praise of London'.[53] From this central position of metropolitan solidarity emerges an even larger literature that commemorates individual trades and crafts. Thomas Heywood, Thomas Dekker, John Taylor and many others composed a remarkable number of broadsides, chapbooks and songs that celebrate merchants, tradesmen and apprentices in general; and they wrote even more works which commemorate and recount the glorious histories of individual craftsmen such as shoemakers, weavers, clothiers, carpenters and tailors.[54] Celebrations of the distinctiveness of artisanal culture can be traced back to Chaucer or earlier – such as in the fourteenth-century song about blacksmiths which makes a compelling case for recognition of their skill, strength and indispensability as makers of swords and ploughshares –[55] but the seventeenth-century 'craft-pride' songs were everywhere in popular urban culture. Some provided potted histories of particular crafts while others, such as some of Thomas Deloney's works, went as far as to create a new genre of 'urban pastoral romance' in which the shepherds are cleared out of Arcadia and 'the gentle craftsman' introduced.[56]

For their part rural people proposed a distinctive rural consciousness, exemplified in such texts as 'The Husbandman and Servant-Man' (mentioned in Chapter 15 by Alun Howkins) wherein the husbandman makes a clear and convincing argument that his occupation is more valuable and relevant to the nation than the servant-man's.[57] Older occupational songs, such as 'The Poore Man Payes for All',[58] do not disappear but they do decline in popularity as the seventeenth century wears on, presumably because they are too generalized for the taste of the day, which called for more occupationally-specific texts such as 'The Painful Plough' – an anthem of farm workers from the seventeenth century to the present:

> Behold the wealthy merchant that trades in foreign seas,
> And brings forth gold and treasure for those that live at ease,
> With finest silks and spices, and fruits and dainties too,
> They are brought from the Indies by virtue of the plough.
>
> For they must have bread, biscuit, rice pudding, flour and peas,
> To feed the jolly sailors as they sail o'er the seas,

Yet ev'ry man that brings them here will own to what is true –
He cannot sail the ocean without the painful plough.[59]

Craft-pride songs and writings continue to have a large currency in rural
and urban England today, and the collecting of them continues. During
the 1950s Peter Kennedy gathered a large cache of occupational songs
which celebrate the miller, farmer, blacksmith, ploughman, waggoner,
carter, hedger, ditcher, miner, weaver, sailor, factory worker and even
the poor beggar.[60] Each craft upholds its dignity and importance without
much protest from the others, but almost every craft understands that the
ploughman has the strongest case of all, and that sooner or later they will
have to follow the collier's example and make express reply to 'The
Painful Plough':

In olden times the farmers used themselves to plough and sow:
It was their glory and their pride to hold the painful plough;
While Johnny led the team along, he'd sing with joyful sound,
Not thinking of the sufferings of the lads that are underground.

The plough's not made without the fire, nor fire without the coal.
D'you see what is depending on a collier lad, poor soul?
You may search the wide world over, their equal is not found;
We cannot do without the lads that labour underground.[61]

There is rivalry but also occupational collaboration, such as between
weavers and farm workers who jointly celebrate the loom and the plough
and who make common political cause in such texts as 'Dialogue and
Song, Between Captain Swing and Jone O'Greenfield: Or the Burning of
Both Houses of Parliament'.[62]

Town and country have not proven easy to bring together in nineteenth-
and twentieth-century England but there have been some noble and
heroic attempts. William Cobbett spent much time discussing antagonisms between urban and rural people but he also attempted to unite
urban and rural workers on a common platform during the trial of
Queen Caroline, the trials of the Tolpuddle Martyrs and during his
tenure with John Fielden as Member of Parliament for Oldham.[63] Shared
political platforms of this nature, whether between the countryside and
London or between the countryside and the industrial city, are neither
large nor numerous during the nineteenth and twentieth centuries, but as
Malcolm Chase has pointed out, we should not ignore the fact that many
industrial workers have sought solutions to social and economic problems 'in and on the land', often urging agrarian reform in the process.[64]
Even late nineteenth-century socialists and industrial unionists – many of
whom can justly be scolded for discounting farm workers – sometimes
bring us up short, such as in a May Day garland for 1895, designed by

Walter Crane and published in the *Clarion*, which pictures Britannia with the banners: 'The plough is a better backbone than the factory', 'England should feed her own people' and 'The Land for the People'.[65]

Yet we must also remember that the town worker's vision of the land, and in turn the rural worker's vision of the city, do not necessarily bind the rural and urban worlds. Many of the so-called folk revivalists of the early part of this century claimed to be in search of authentic peasant culture, but in fact they were not: Cecil Sharp, for example, extracted information from many peasants but his real purposes were to collect primordial remnants of a 'national' culture which had supposedly belonged to the élite in the distant past.[66] It is always easy, of course, to uncover impurity of motive, but we must be mindful that some of the greatest rural artists that England has produced, as John Barrell has shown, were utterly disinterested in rural workers and went out of their way to purge them from their canvasses.[67] The same can be said of much poetry, including some much loved works such as Thomas Gray's 'Elegy Written in a Country Church-Yard'. This is surely one of the most beautiful poems in the language, but the hard fact is that the ploughman is ushered from the horizon in the opening stanza, leaving 'the World to Darkness, and to me'.

The town-country divide is still with us, though the twentieth-century record is one of fits and starts. During the world wars a town-country contrast is not very conspicuous, partly because of the extraordinary capacity of the English to overcome social fissures and divides during moments of crisis. Some of the twentieth-century record, perhaps, can be personified by the farmer-writer A.G. Street. On account of being rejected for service during the Great War (he hastened back from a farming sojourn in Canada to enlist) Street had to defer his patriotic exercises until the Second World War, when as a radio broadcaster he complemented the performances of George Orwell and Winston Churchill.[68] On most topics, especially economic exigencies and agricultural technology, Street was unambiguous and incisive, but not so when treating of interwar and post-war relations of town and country. On one hand Street extolled the changes that had come over Hodge – 'He is more alert. He has a broader outlook on life' – but other times he would criticize farm workers for changing too much and for surrendering to the culture of the towns. The motor car, Street mused, had 'improved understanding between the townsman and his country cousin' – but though suggesting that this was a good thing for 'the nation as a whole', it is doubtful that Street actually believed it, for elsewhere he would proudly define himself as a 'rather narrow-minded countryman' and declare that he had considerably more faith in rural England than in its towns. The townsman, Street complained, is simply 'too idyllic in his ideas about the land', and is woefully ignorant of the hardness and exacting nature of agricultural work. In the end, Street called upon townspeople to discover the 'real countryman'.[69]

The rural poet John Clare, even more than A.G. Street, personifies and articulates many of the themes that have been addressed here. First and most importantly Clare repudiated the Hodge stereotype. He wrote of rural labourers whom he personally knew to be gullible and dim-witted; he wrote of many more who understood their craft to the letter, who held a profound knowledge of nature and who could recite and discuss ballads and tales with great thought and emotion.

Clare's poetry and autobiographical writings testify to the depth of his countryman consciousness. Periodically as a youth Clare had dreamt of becoming 'something better than a ploughman', but he always came back to the plough – first after a year as a shoemaker's apprentice and then after a spell as a gardener.[70] It was in the fields where Clare was happiest; and it was the fields that defined his political world. 'I never meddle with politics' he wrote several times, but this is misleading. Like most farm workers his first concern lay with his parish and district – accordingly he praised local radicals, urged a greater voice for the poor but turned to national politics only to consider matters which directly affected his work and experience, such as Cobbett's programme of agricultural reform. Regarding enclosure, Clare was political to the highest degree – he opposed it and versified his opposition. A customary consciousness – manifested in love of common land and of ancient rights and perquisites – are everywhere in Clare's poetry, indeed a customary consciousness is the very mortar of Clare's verse and prose:[71] 'Old customs O I love the sound However simple they may be What ere wi time has sanction found Is welcome and is dear to me.'[72]

At the behest of his publishers Clare scrambled to list his 'literary antecedents', eventually producing a roll-call that included Shakespeare, Milton, Burns and several of the georgic and pastoral writers of the sixteenth and seventeenth centuries.[73] Among the cast is Edmund Spenser, whose 'Shepheard's Calendar' begs to be contrasted with Clare's poem by the same name. The first and most obvious difference is that Spenser's poem is court-centred and Clare's is rural-centred. Further, Clare signifies that the Elizabethan pastoral mode is a false genre, and he goes his own way by replacing wistful and pompous shepherds with working shepherds, and also by bringing ploughmen into the picture – not idle and delicate ploughmen but ones obliged to traverse 'doughy sloughs' and sink 'anckle deep in podgy sloughs and clay'.[74] Clare did not withhold praise of the shepherd's life – indeed he found the shepherd's toil more peaceful than the thresher's, for example – but pastoral farming was still laborious for Clare, who was ever-mindful of the fact that he had inherited the curse of Adam. Whatever genre or mode that Clare was in – whether writing of his sweetheart Mary or expressing his veneration for tree and flower – his landscape was peopled, not with courtiers disguised as shepherds, but with English workers as they are.

Clare wrote of the distinctive talents of all rural workers: ploughmen, shepherds, threshers, hedgers, ditchers, woodsmen, carters, horse-keepers, thatchers – in Eric Robinson's words, 'no play ever had a richer cast'.[75] Clare, though, admits of no significant cultural division within farm work; the only grand division within his writings falls between 'town' (a word that he applied to nucleated settlements of most any size) and his own parish of Helpstone. During his three trips to London, Clare became the 'Hodge' of urban metropolitan literature, even preparing himself for his visits by reading the broadsheet 'Tricks of London laid open'. Like the countryman visitor of the songs and chapbooks, Clare was attracted and repelled by London; he wanted to satisfy his curiosity but felt surrounded and threatened by thieves and tricksters who were always at the ready 'to pounce on a countryman as a raven on carrion'. Everything, Clare remarked from a Fleet Street window, 'is a wonder'.[76]

Clare's consciousness and cultural devotions were attached to his countryside and to his parish. He lived and personified a town-country divide. Yet Clare could and did rise to levels of identification in which he felt associations with the 'lower orders' as a whole – urban as well as rural. Upon being asked by an insolent patron if 'the lower orders made their courtship in barns and pig-styes and asked whether I did', Clare described himself as 'very vext and said it might be the custom of high orders for aught I knew'.[77] Clare did not bind with urban workers in such a way as to warrant the term class association or class consciousness, but he was not afraid to speak up for his mates in the 'lower orders' when their common interests were at issue.

It has recently been remarked that 'there is no *absolute* contrast between the economies, social life and behavioural patterns of town and countryside' in mid-seventeenth-century England, and that town and country have been 'separately compartmentalized by historians who have developed special interests in either one or the other'.[78] The same can doubtless be said of the entire period of English history – we have a tendency to study urban and rural people in separate spheres. And in some ways this is warranted, but there are moments in England's past when contemporaries experience and perceive town-country dichotomies. The ploughman tradition of Piers and the commonwealthmen, the urban-rural union of 1381 and its latter-day interpretations, John Clare's revisions to the pastoral mode, and even the Hodge stereotype of Restoration literature have a place in the history of popular thought and experience. Town against country and country against town might be a more populist than class-oriented sensibility, but it is not worth less of our attention for that.

Notes

1. See Raphael Samuel (ed.), 'Editorial Note', in *People's History and Socialist Theory* (London, 1981), p. 377.

2. For recent assessments of post-structuralism and the 'linguistic turn' see James Epstein, 'The Populist Turn', in *Journal of British Studies*, **32**, (2), (April 1993), pp. 177–89; Patrick Curry, 'Towards a Post-Marxist Social History: Thompson, Clark and Beyond', in Adrian Wilson (ed.), *Rethinking Social History* (Manchester, 1993), pp. 158–200; James Vernon, 'Who's Afraid of the "linguistic turn": The politics of social history and its discontents', *Social History*, **19**, (1), June 1994, pp. 81–97.

3. Karl Marx, 'The Eighteenth Brumaire of Louis Bonaparte' (1850–2), in K. Marx and F. Engels, *Selected Works* (London, 1968), p. 171; D. Mitrany, *Marx Against the Peasant* (Chapel Hill, 1951), esp. pp. 15, 24–5.

4. Roger Wells, 'Social Protest, Class, Conflict and Consciousness in the English Countryside, 1700–1880', in M. Reed and R. Wells (eds), *Class, Conflict and Protest in the English Countryside, 1700–1880* (London, 1990), pp. 121–214.

5. Patrick Joyce, *Visions of the People: Industrial England and the Question of Class 1848–1914* (Cambridge, 1991); Patrick Joyce, *Democratic Subjects: The Self and the Social in Nineteenth-Century England* (Cambridge, 1994); Patrick Joyce (ed.), *Class* (Oxford, 1995), pp. 3–20; James Vernon, *Politics and the People: A Study in English Political Culture, c. 1815–1867* (Cambridge, 1993), pp. 1–14, 331–9; J.C.D. Clark, *English Society, 1688–1832; idem, Ideology, Social Structure and Political Practice During the Ancien Regime* (Cambridge, 1985).

6. Keith Wrightson, *English Society, 1580–1680* (London, 1982), p. 62; Keith Wrightson, 'Aspects of Social Differentiation in Rural England, c.1580–1660', *Journal of Peasant Studies*, V (1977–78), pp. 33–46; Jeanette Neeson, *Commoners: Common Right, Enclosure and Social Change in England, 1700–1820* (Cambridge, 1993), pp. 1–14; E.P. Thompson, *Customs in Common* (London, 1991), pp. 1–15, esp. p. 15.

7. For recent use of the term 'rural populism' see Simon Miller, 'Urban Dreams and Rural Reality: Land and Landscape in English Culture, 1920–1945', in *Rural History*, **6**, (1), April 1995, pp. 89–102.

8. See, for example, Alun Howkins, 'The Discovery of Rural England', in R. Colls and P. Dodd (eds), *Englishness: Politics and Culture 1880–1920* (London, 1986), pp. 62–88; John Barrell, *The Dark Side of the Landscape: The Rural Poor in English Painting, 1730–1840* (Cambridge, 1980); John Barrell, 'Sportive Labour: The Farm Worker in Eighteenth-Century Poetry and Painting', in Brian Short (ed.), *The English Rural Community: Image and Analysis* (Cambridge, 1992), ch. 6.

9. J. Lucas, *England and Englishness: Ideas of Nationhood in English Poetry 1688–1900* (London, 1990); D. Gervais, *Literary Englands: Versions of 'Englishness' in Modern Writing* (Cambridge, 1993); S. Daniels, *Fields of*

Vision: Landscape Imagery and National Identity in England and the United States (Cambridge, 1993); N. Everitt, *The Tory View of Landscape* (London, 1994).

10. Martin Wiener, *English Culture and the Decline of the Industrial Spirit, 1850–1980* (Cambridge, 1981).

11. See, for instance, A.R. Hall and H.K. Kenward (eds), *Urban-Rural Connexions: Perspectives from Environmental Archaeology* (Oxford, 1994); P. Ambrose, 'The Rural/Urban Fringe as Battleground', in Short (ed.), *English Rural Community*, ch. 9.

12. Robert Muchembled, *Popular Culture and Elite Culture in France 1400–1750* (1978), trans. L. Cochrane (London, 1985), p. 154; R. Chartier, *The Cultural Uses of Print in Early Modern France*, trans. L. Cochrane (Princeton, 1987), p. 347; E. Weber, *Peasants into Frenchmen: The Modernization of Rural France, 1879–1914*, pp. x–xiii.

13. Raphael Samuel, 'Grand Narratives', in *History Workshop Journal*, (29), Spring 1990, p. 130.

14. See, for example, E.A. Wrigley, 'City and Country in the Past: A Sharp Divide or a Continuum?', *Historical Research*, LXIV, (154), June 1991, pp. 107–120; Alan Everitt, *Change in the Provinces: The Seventeenth Century* (Leicester, 1969), pp. 36–45.

15. Antonio Gramsci, *Selections from the Prison Notebooks*, Q. Hoare and G. Nowell-Smith (eds), (London, 1971), p. 91; K. Marx, 'The Class Struggles in France 1848–1850' (1850), in K. Marx and F. Engels (eds), *Selected Works* (London, 1968).

16. R. Williams, 'Between Country and City', in S. Pugh (ed.), *Reading Landscape: City-Country-Capital* (Manchester, 1990), p. 7.

17. A. Wallace-Hadrill, 'Introduction' and 'Elites and Trade in the Roman Town', in A. Wallace-Hadrill and J. Rich (eds), *City and Country in the Ancient World* (London, 1991).

18. Rodney Hilton, *The English Peasantry in the Later Middle Ages* (Oxford, 1975), pp. 85–7.

19. Ibid., p. 22.

20. Rosamond Faith, 'The Class Struggle in Fourteenth-Century England', in R. Samuel (ed.), *People's History and Socialist Theory* (London, 1981), pp. 50–80; R.B. Dobson (ed.), *The Peasant's Revolt of 1381* (London, 1970), part III; R.B. Dobson, 'The Risings of York, Beverley and Scarborough,' in R.H. Hilton and T.H. Aston (ed.), *The English Rising of 1381* (Cambridge, 1984), ch. 5; A.F. Butcher, 'English Urban Society and the Revolt of 1381', in ibid., pp. 84–111; R. Hilton, *Bond Men Made Free: Medieval Peasant Movements and the English Rising of 1381* (New York, 1973), ch. 8.

21. F.S. Haydon (ed.), *Eulogium Historarium*, 3 vols (London, 1865), vol. III, p. 352.

22. R. Hilton, *English Peasantry in the Later Middle Ages*, p. 76.

23. 'An Old Ballad of Whittington and his Cat', in *The Roxburgh Ballads*, 9 vols (Hertford, 1873–90), vol. VII, pp. 585–6; 'Sir Richard Whittington's Advancement', in J. Payne Collier (ed.), *Ballads from Early Printed Copies*, 3 vols (London, 1840), vol. II, pp. 5–10; 'The Famous History of Guy Earle of Warwick' (London, 1682) in *The Complete Works of Samuel Rowlands*, 3 vols (New York, 1880; reprint, 1966), vol. I, pp. 1–86; 'The Life and Death of the Famous Champion of England, St. George' (Pepys 'Penny Merriments', vol. II, Pepys Library, Magdalene College, Cambridge); 'The

Gallant History of the Life and Death of that Most Noble Knight, Sir Bevis of Hampton' (Pepys 'Vulgaria', Pepys Library, Magdalene College, Cambridge); E.A. Horsman, *The Pindar of Wakefield* (Liverpool, 1956). See R.B. Dobson and J. Taylor (eds), *Rymes of Robin Hood* (London, 1976) – still the best work on the Robin Hood rhymes and songs.

24. William Langland, *Piers the Ploughman*, trans. J.F. Goodridge (Harmondsworth, 1978), pp. 28, 43, 260. See also Robin Lister, 'The Peasants of *Piers Plowman* and its Audience', in K. Parkinson and M. Priestman (eds), *Peasants and Countrymen in Literature* (London, 1982), pp. 71–90.

25. David Norbrook, *Poetry and Politics in the English Renaissance* (London, 1984), p. 47.

26. John Gower, 'Vox Clamantis', in *The Major Latin Works of John Gower*, ed. and trans. E.W. Stockton (Seattle, 1962), book V, chs 9–14, esp. p. 208.

27. 'Song of the Husbandman', in T. Wright (ed.), *The Political Songs of England* (London, 1839), p. 152; 'The Plowman's Tale', in W.W. Skeat (ed.), *The Works of Geoffrey Chaucer*, 7 vols (Oxford, 1897), vol. 7, pp. 147–90; 'God Spede the Plough', in R.H. Robbins, *Historical Poems of the XIVth and XVth Centuries* (New York, 1959), pp. 97–8; Vox Populi, Vox Dei, in F. J. Furnivall (ed.), *Ballads from Manuscript*, 2 vols (London, 1868–72).

28. See, for example, *Pierce the Ploughman's Crede* (c.1394), W.W. Skeat, (ed.) (London, 1867); 'The Complaint of the Ploughman' (c.1390) in T. Wright (ed.), *Political Poems and Songs*, 2 vols (London, 1859), vol. I, pp. 304–16; *A Proper Dyalogue betwene a Gentillman and a Husbandman* (c.1530), Edward Arber (ed.), (Westminster, 1895), p. 22; 'A Mery Geste how the Plowman Lerned his Pater Noster' (c.1510), in W.C. Hazlitt (ed.), *Remains of the Early Popular Poetry of England*, 4 vols (London, 1866), vol. I, pp. 208–16.

29. Luke Shepherd, 'John Bon and Mast Parson' (1547–8), in Hazlitt (ed.), *Remains of the Early Popular Poetry*, vol. IV, pp. 1–16.

30. *The Acts and Monuments of John Foxe*, 4th edn., 8 vols, The Reverend Josiah Pratt (ed.), (London, n.d.), vol. V, p. 117.

31. See Robert Crowley, 'The Voyce of the Last Trumpet' (1550) in J.W. Cowper (ed.), *The Select Works of Robert Crowley* (London, 1872), pp. 53–104; 'An Informacion and Petition agaynst the oppressours of the pore Commons of this Realme' (c.1550), ibid., pp. 151–76; Hugh Latimer, *Sermon on the Ploughers* (1549), Edward Arber (ed.), (Westminster, 1903); G. Corrie (ed.), *The Works of Hugh Latimer*, 2 vols (Cambridge, 1844–45). See also John King, *English Reformation Literature: The Tudor Origins of the Protestant Tradition* (Princeton, 1982), ch. 7. Rosemary O'Day and the late G.R. Elton have doubts about the degree of radicalism in the proposals of the commonwealth men – see O'Day's 'Hugh Latimer: Prophet of the Kingdom', in *Historical Research*, 65, (158), October 1992, pp. 259–61 and Elton's 'Reform and the "Commonwealth-Men" of Edward VI's Reign', in Peter Clark, Alan Smith and Nicholas Tyacke (eds), *The English Commonwealth* (Leicester, 1979), ch. 1. To my mind, however, Tawney's arguments continue to hold up – see R.H. Tawney, *The Agrarian Problem of the Sixteenth Century* (London, 1912), pp. 134, 307, 366–7.

32. *Sermon on the Ploughers*, Arber (ed.), p. 22.

33. R. Crowley, 'An Informacion . . .', in Cowper (ed.), *Select Works*, p. 157;

Thomas More, *Utopia* (1516), ed. and trans. R. Adams (New York, 1975), pp. 35, 40, 68, 89.

34. Brian Manning, *Village Revolts: Social Protest and Popular Disturbances in England, 1509–1640* (Oxford, 1988), pp. 22–3; R.C. Richardson, 'Town and Countryside in the English Revolution', in R.C. Richardson (ed.), *Town and Countryside in the English Revolution* (Manchester, 1992), ch. 1, esp. pp. 3–4.

35. Sir Simonds D'Ewes, *The Journals of all the Parliaments during the Reign of Queen Elizabeth* (London, 1682), p. 674.

36. David Norbrook remarks that 'the old "ploughman" tradition became overshadowed in the Elizabethan period by more courtly poetic modes, but awareness of the older tradition was preserved, especially in Puritan circles' (*Poetry and Politics*, p. 47). There were some Puritan supporters of customary rights, such as Philip Stubbes, but not many.

37. Joan Thirsk, 'Plough and Pen: Agricultural Writers in the Seventeenth Century', in T.H. Aston, T.R. Cross, Christopher Dyer and Joan Thirsk (eds), *Social Relations and Ideas: Essays in Honour of R.H. Hilton* (Cambridge, 1983), p. 295.

38. Thomas Tusser, *Five Hundred Pointes of Good Husbandrie* (1580), W. Payne and S.J. Herrtage (eds), (London, 1878); Gervase Markham, *The English Husbandman* (1635); Walter Blith, *The English Improver* (1649); Andrew McRae, 'Husbandry Manuals and the Language of Agrarian Improvement' in M. Leslie and T. Raylor (eds), *Culture and Cultivation in Early Modern England: Writing and the Land* (Leicester, 1992), ch. 2; Thompson, *Customs in Common*, pp. 202–2, 269, 299.

39. John Walter and Keith Wrightson, 'Dearth and the Social Order in Early Modern England', in P. Slack (ed.), *Rebellion, Popular Protest and the Social Order in Early Modern England* (Cambridge, 1984), ch. 6, esp. p. 113.

40. See 'The Shepheards Calendar' (1579) and 'Prosopopoia: or Mother Hubberds Tale' (1591), in *The Poetical Works of Edmund Spenser*, 5 vols, J. Payne Collier (ed.), vols I, V; Philip Sidney, *The Countess of Pembroke's Arcadia (The Old Arcadia)*, J. Robinson (ed.) and *The Countess of Pembroke's Arcadia (The New Arcadia)*, V. Stretkowicz (ed.), (Oxford, 1987); Alastair Fowler, 'The Beginnings of English Georgic', in *Renaissance Genres*, B.K. Lewalski (ed.), (Cambridge, Mass., 1986), pp. 105–25; Anthony Low, *The Georgic Revolution* (Princeton, 1985); John Barrell and John Bull (eds), *The Penguin Book of English Pastoral Verse* (London, 1974), 'Introduction'; Louis Adrian Montrose, 'Of Gentlemen and Shepherds: The Politics of English Pastoral Form', in *English Literary History* (1983), vol. 50, esp. pp. 415–25.

41. *The Complete Plays of the Wakefield Master*, ed. J.R. Brown (London, 1983); 'The Second Shepherd's Pageant', in A.C. Crawley (ed.), *Everyman and Medieval Miracle Plays* (London, n.d.), pp. 81–108.

42. John Aubrey, *The Natural History of Wiltshire*, John Britton (ed.), (London, 1847), p. 11; see also David Underdown, *Revel, Riot and Rebellion: Popular Politics and Culture in England 1603–1660* (Oxford, 1987), p. 73.

43. Thomas Wilson, *Arte of Rhetorique* (1553; reprint: New York, 1982), pp. 45–6, 153, 162–4, 329; George Puttenham, *The Arte of English Poesie* (1589; reprint: Menston, 1968), pp. 68–9.

44. Abraham Cowley, 'Of Agriculture' (c. 1640), in *Essays, Plays and Sundry Verses* (Cambridge, 1906), p. 403.

45. Joan Thirsk, 'Enclosing and Engrossing', in *The Agrarian History of England and Wales* (Cambridge, 1967), vol. IV (1500–1640), ch. IV, esp. pp. 206, 213, 237; E.P. Thompson, *Customs in Common*, pp. 194, 201–2, 268–76, 299–301; Underdown, *Revel, Riot and Rebellion*, ch. 5; Paul Slack, 'Books of Orders: The Making of English Social Policy, 1577–1631', *Transactions of the Royal Historical Society* (1980), vol. 30, pp. 1–22.

46. For a discussion of literature on the subject see Kevin Sharpe, *Criticism and Compliment: The Politics of Literature in the England of Charles I* (Cambridge, 1987), pp. 5–15.

47. Underdown, *Revel, Riot and Rebellion*, p. 72, chs 5, 7; John Morrill, *The Revolt in the Provinces: Conservatives and Radicals in the English Civil War, 1630–1650* (London, 1876), pp. 88–110, 196–200.

48. See Hyder E. Rollins (ed.), *Cavalier and Puritan: Ballads and Broadsides Illustrating the Period of Great Rebellion 1640–1660* (New York, 1923); J.O. Halliwell (ed.), *The Loyal Garland: A Collection of Songs of the Seventeenth Century* (London, 1850); Charles MacKay (ed.), *The Cavalier Songs and Ballads of England* (London, 1863); Anon., *Rump: Or an Exact collection of the Choicest Poems and Songs Relating to the Late Times* (London, 1662).

49. For John Lilburne's view of the 1381 rebels see W. Haller and G. Davies (eds), *The Leveller Tracts, 1647–1653* (Gloucester, Mass., 1964), p. 427; John Cleveland, *The Rustick Rampant* (1658); Thomas Deloney, 'How *Wat Tyler* and *Jack Straw* rebelled against King *Richard* the second', in F.O. Mann (ed.), *Deloney's Works* (Oxford, 1912), pp. 413–15; Richard Johnson, 'Sir William Walworth', in *Nine Worthies of London* (1592), in *The Harleian Miscellany* (London, 1811 edn), vol. VIII, pp. 437–61.

50. London: printed for P. Brooksby (c.1672) in *Roxburgh Ballads*, vol. VII, pp. 267–70, 278.

51. Humfery Crouch, 'A Pleasant History of Unfortunate Hodg of the South' (1655), p. 1. In 'Downright Dick of the West; Or, The Plow-Man's Ramble to London' a countryman who is cheated and derided in London calls out: 'Why should these fellows run Husband-men down? You can't live without us in city or town' (*Roxburgh Ballads*, vol. IV, part II, pp. 385–7).

52. See, for example, 'The Ploughman's Praise: In a Dialogue between a Mother and her Daughter; which Daughter Resolves to Forsake a Wealthy Squire, and Marry Roger the Ploughman for his Plain-Dealing' (*Roxburgh Ballads*, vol. VIII, pp. 681–3).

53. 'The Praise of London' (1632) in W.G. Day (ed.), *The Pepys Ballads*, 5 vols. (Cambridge, 1987), vol. II, pp. 219–21.

54. *The Dramatic Works of Thomas Dekker*, 5 vols, F. Bowers (ed.), (Cambridge, 1955); *All the Workes of John Taylor the Water Poet* (London, 1630); Thomas Heywood, 'The Four Prentices of London' (1615) in *The Dramatic Works of Thomas Heywood*, 6 vols, R.H. Shepherd (ed.), (1874; reprint: New York, 1964), vol. II; Louis Wright, *Middle-Class Culture in Elizabethan England* (Ithaca, 1935), ch. 2; Charles Camp, *The Artisan in Elizabethan Literature* (New York, 1924); Charles MacKay (ed.), *A Collection of Songs and Ballads Relative to the Prentices and Trades of London* (London, 1841).

55. Anon., 'The Blacksmith', in Mary Ashraf (ed.), *Political Verse and Song*

from Britain and Ireland (London, 1975), p. 33.

56. On the genre of 'urban pastoral romance' see Laura Caroline Stevenson, Praise and Paradox: Merchants and Craftsmen in Elizabethan Popular Literature (Cambridge, 1984), p. 185. For Deloney see 'The Gentle Craft' (1637) and 'Jack of Newbury' (1597).

57. Madden Collection of Ballads, 5 (II), Cambridge University Library; British Library 1876 d. 41, fo. 45 (London: Catnach). The ballad dates to the mid-seventeenth-century at least, and there were earlier variants such as 'The Ploughman's Glory' (Bodleian Library, Harding Collection of Broadsides).

58. 'The Poore Man Payes for All', (c.1650), (Roxburgh Ballads, vol. II, pp. 334–8).

59. There are many versions of this song. The one cited here is from Roy Palmer (ed.), The Painful Plough (Cambridge, 1974), pp. 54–5.

60. Peter Kennedy (ed.), Folksongs of Britain and Ireland (London, 1975), part XI. The BBC also collected many occupational songs during the 1940s and 1950s.

61. 'The Collier Lads' (c.1820) in Ian Watson, Song and Democratic Culture in Britain (London, 1983), p. 101.

62. Harland Collection, Manchester Central Reference Library. The approximate date of the ballad is the 1830s.

63. Ian Dyck, William Cobbett and Rural Popular Culture (Cambridge, 1992), ch. 8.

64. Malcolm Chase, 'The People's Farm': English Radical Agrarianism 1775–1840 (Oxford, 1988) p. 3; see also p. 15.

65. Jan Marsh, Back to the Land: The Pastoral Impulse in Victorian England from 1880–1914 (London, 1982), p. 24.

66. Cecil Sharp, English Folk Songs: Some Conclusions (London, 1907), 'Introduction'; Cecil Sharp, English Folk Songs (London, 1920), 'Introduction'; Gillian Bennett, 'Folklore Studies and the English Rural Myth', in Rural History, 4, (1), April 1993, pp. 77–91, esp. p. 83; Georgina Boyes, The Imagined Village: Culture, Ideology and the English Folk Revival (Manchester, 1993).

67. John Barrell, The Dark Side of the Landscape; John Barrell, 'Sportive Labour', in The English Rural Community, passim.

68. A.G. Street, Farmer's Glory (1932; Oxford, 1983); Pamela Street, My Father, A.G. Street (London, 1969).

69. 'The Agricultural Labourer' (1933) and 'The Townsman and Countryman' (1933) in A.G. Street, Wheat and Chaff (London, n.d.), chs 7, 26. See also Street's introduction to England Today in Pictures (London, n.d., c. 1947).

70. John Clare, 'The Autobiography 1793–1824', in The Prose of John Clare, J.W. and Anne Tibble (eds), (New York, 1951), pp. 55, 32, 18.

71. Eric Robinson and David Powell, John Clare (Oxford, 1984), p. 448; 'Fragments', in The Prose of John Clare, Tibble and Tibble, (eds), p. 221; 'Apology for the Poor', in Robinson and Powell, Clare, pp. 445–7; 'Sketches in the Life of John Clare Written by Himself and Addressed to His Friend John Taylor Esqr March 1821' in John Clare's Autobiographical Writings, Eric Robinson (ed.), (Oxford, 1986), p. 7. Regarding Clare's view of enclosure see 'The Mores' in ibid., p. 168: enclosure 'trampled on the grave/of labours rights and left the poor a slave'.

72. Clare, The Shepherd's Calendar (1824), E. Robinson and Geoffrey Summerfield (eds), (London, 1964), p. 126.

73. Clare, 'Natural History Letters' in *The Prose of John Clare*, Tibble and Tibble (eds), pp. 174–5; 'Sketches in the Life of John Clare', in *Autobiographical Writings*, E. Robinson (ed.), pp. 1–26.
74. Clare, *The Shepherd's Calendar*, p. 31.
75. Eric Robinson, 'Introduction', in *John Clare's Autobiographical Writings*, E. Robinson (ed.), (Oxford, 1983), p. xi.
76. 'Autobiographical Fragments' in *Autobiographical Writings*, E. Robinson (ed.), (Oxford, 1983), pp. 48, 129–46.
77. Eric Robinson, 'Introduction', in *Autobiographical Writings*, p. xi.
78. R.C. Richardson, 'Town and Countryside in the English Revolution', in R.C. Richardson (ed.), *Town and Countryside in the English Revolution* (Manchester, 1992), pp. 2–3.

CHAPTER EIGHT

Popular Preaching and Millennial Expectations: the Reverend Robert Aitken and the Christian Society, 1836–40

Malcolm R. Thorp

One of the significant historical contributions of John Harrison has been his astute study of the social dimensions of millennial expectations in Britain from 1780 to 1850. Given Harrison's interests in the lives of common people, his explorations naturally concentrated on the popular, largely self-educated adventist millenarians, whose writings were scorned and ridiculed by those of higher social status. Obviously Harrison's study included a number of respectable millenarians, such as the Reverend Edward Irving, whose writings found influence on the popular level. Another such millenarian was the Reverend Robert Aitken, the celebrated revivalist preacher of the 1830s, whose movement, the Christian Society, found considerable support among plebeian elements during the years 1836–40.[1] In many ways, Aitken's millennial writings exemplify various themes developed in the writings of John Harrison.

This essay explores Aitken's career in the decade of the 1830s, when he was recognized as perhaps the greatest popular preacher in Britain. It was during this time that Aitken used adventist rhetoric as an explanation for Britain's social and political ills. This essay seeks to identify the major themes of his millennial teachings, focusing attention mainly on their social implications. Indeed, most of Aitken's writings tend to be derivative rather than original; and in many respects, his sermons explore similar themes found among various writers associated with the Albury group.[2] Still, Aitken was an important popularizer of millennial doctrines and, in some circles, his name was synonymous with the Second Coming.[3]

Robert Aitken (1799–1873) was born into a pious Scottish lowlands family. His father, a schoolmaster of a sternly Calvinist disposition, sent Robert to the University of Edinburgh to follow this profession. However, during his years at the university (1816–19), Aitken fell under the influence of the saintly Bishop Elgin of Moray and was confirmed into the Church of England in 1821.

Two years later, Aitken was ordained a deacon. Shortly after, he was appointed as a curate at Whitburn, near Sunderland. During his residency at Whitburn, Aitken also assisted his brother, who operated a village school. In the following year, 1824, he was ordained a priest at Durham. His sermon delivered on this occasion might be characterized as a pious defence of sacerdotal authority, in which the power of the modern ministry was said to be the same as that exercised in the primitive church, although he acknowledged that gifts of the spirit were lacking in this generation.[4] In the same year, he married Ann Elizabeth Eyres, the daughter of a wealthy Warrington soap manufacturer. Since the marriage apparently improved Aitken's financial situation, money was no longer an obstacle to fulfilling his widening aspirations. But his wife's delicate health necessitated a move from the bitter cold of the north-east to the parish of Braddan, near Douglas, on the Isle of Man. There was no immediate clerical appointment open here for Aitken, excepting the rather lowly position of honorary curate. But, for some reason, which has not been fully explained in various accounts, Aitken engendered the wrath of the local bishop and lost his appointment at St George's chapel in 1833.[5] With no prospects of church preferment, Aitken turned to farming as well as preaching in local Methodist chapels, several of which he helped to endow. He also opened a boarding-school for young boys, which evidently held some promise of success.

However, Aitken's spiritual condition was unsettled. Sometime around 1834 he experienced a religious crisis – a disturbing thought kept recurring: 'You fool! Were you sent into the world with no higher purpose than the draining of a bog.' While he was composing a treatise on the Atonement, in which he pondered Christ's human nature in the great sacrifice, Aitken heard an 'inward voice' tell him, 'You are making a Gospel for god, instead of believing God's gospel.' Startled and perplexed, he fell to his knees and prayed, only to be told by the spirit, 'All thy righteousness is as filthy rags.' Over the next fortnight, Aitken remained in agony. Finally, on the sixteenth day, he prayed mightily: 'Now Lord, let me see thy salvation.' He then fell into a deep and peaceful sleep. He awoke with joy of assurance flooding his soul.[6]

Evidently this experience convinced Aitken to cast his lot with the Methodists and, like Wesley of old, take the message of salvation to the common people. Soon afterwards, Aitken began to preach in Liverpool and in the industrial towns of Lancashire, where he soon acquired a large following. At the same time, he acted as an arbitrator in the dispute among the Manchester Wesleyan Methodist Association. Aitken, however, attempted to impose rather than arbitrate a settlement, and his tactless efforts produced further polarization rather than healing.[7]

In 1835 Aitken apparently attempted to gain entrance into the mainline Wesleyan Methodist church. He wrote to Jabez Bunting, the tsar of Methodism, requesting an hour interview, presumably for the purpose of presenting his case for ministerial acceptance. But the meeting apparently never occurred, and Bunting rejected his application for ministerial status. Moreover, in the 1835 Methodist conference, Bunting expressed his views that, 'Mr Aitken's proceedings would end in division.'[8] It is not difficult to understand Bunting's rationale, for Aitken's preachings created scenes of disorder and 'overwrought enthusiasm', which were popularly associated with Primitive Methodist revivals.[9]

Rebuffed by the Methodists, Aitken united his followers together in a congregation of his own making. Beginning with just nine members in January 1836, the Christian Society (as this new body was called) grew to upwards of 1 500 souls by October of that year.[10] During the next two years the society expanded into a formidable force, with chapels throughout the industrial north and the Staffordshire potteries. In 1837 Aitken also opened two large churches, as well as several smaller chapels in London. Wherever Aitken went his popular style of oratory seared the hearts of his hearers, and the multitudes overflowed the seating capacities of his chapels. His wonderful physique, distinct personal presence and magnificent voice captivated his audiences, which often clamoured for salvation during these revivalistic scenes.

Aitken's success, however, was based largely on personal charisma, and not the uniqueness of his doctrines. Aitken relied heavily on biblical literalism and the heritage of John Wesley, although he asserted that contemporary Wesleyans were 'living beneath their privileges' and had become too worldly. The Christian Society was not unlike other Methodist splinter groups of the time. Emphasis was on the possibility of salvation by grace regardless of the blackness of the sinner's heart. Aitken's success lay in the fervour of this message, which included a sincere concern for the 'damnation of unnumbered millions who have souls as precious and as immortal as my own'.[11]

Although Aitken displayed sympathy for bringing the common people to a knowledge of God's power of redemption, in other respects his Christian Society was decidedly against working-class culture. Indeed, Aitken stated that within the movement preference should be given to members in commerce and 'favoritism towards members in employment'. He likewise decried against participation in popular politics, especially movements critical of the political establishment and those aimed at extending political power to the working classes.[12]

There was also a strong emphasis on teetotalism and abstention from the use of tobacco, as well as not 'singing those songs, or reading those books, which do not tend to the knowledge or love of God'. The wearing of costly apparel was frowned upon. Moreover, Aitken displayed a rigid adherence to strict sabbatarianism.[13] In short, the popularity of the Christian Society, emphasized in its extreme social conservatism, might suggest an undercurrent of disenchantment with the political radicalism normally associated with the working classes of the industrial regions of England. But it is also possible that many working-class Aitkenites (as was common throughout Methodism) simply overlooked the appeals to middle-class deference and took from the society what they wanted, namely manifestations of the spirit and saving grace.

Aitken essentially offered common people a different sense of identity, one based on respectability through moral responsibility and personal worth, as well as on Christian perfectionism and a renunciation of worldly aspirations. Aitken boldly declared: 'The professors of religion of the present day are lovers of the world, conformers to the world, havers of creature-comfort and aspirers after respectability.'[14] To him, life was an ascetic pilgrimage through darkness and sin, the only joy to be found in obedience to eternal decrees, which meant keeping in harmony with every jot and tittle of the word of God.[15] In short, Aitken played the role of an Old Testament prophet by warning of the lures of Babylon and predicting Britain's impending millennial doom, although Aitken's impassioned pleas lacked the poetic grandeur found in the best of his type.

Aitken was both the strength and the weakness of this movement. While there can be no doubt of his personal charisma as a preacher, Aitken was authoritarian in his approach to church organization. Yet curiously enough, he did not systematically pursue rigid supervision and control of the various Christian Society congregations. From the very beginning there were conflicts over Aitken's efforts to circumvent procedural rules that he had established at the outset. For example, his efforts to dismiss John Bowes as minister over the Hope Street congregation in Liverpool ended in an acrimonious conflict in which at least half of the congregation sided with the dispossessed minister.[16]

Shortly after Aitken's death in 1873, the Reverend Frederick Hockin reported that Aitken, during the 'Tracts for the Times' controversy in the 1830s, had fallen under the influence of a nonconformist preacher in London.[17] Unfortunately Hockin did not elaborate on this incident, and the meaning of his statement remains obscure. But, in his autobiography, John Bowes printed a number of letters that he received from Aitken during 1837 and 1838. Thus, on 20 November 1837, Aitken wrote to Bowes concerning the difficulties of arranging for the Reverend Timothy Matthews of Bedford coming into the Aitkenite ministry. Other sources also confirm that Matthews had gone to London to converse with Aitken about joining with him.[18] Indeed, Matthews eventually was able to leave

Bedford, at least temporarily; and he preached at the Aitkenite Hope Street Liverpool chapel at least 85 times in 1839 alone.[19] What is the significance of the liaison between Aitken and Matthews? The difference between these two renegades from Anglicanism must have been enormous. Aitken was a theological Armenian and a Methodist in his own eclectic way; Matthews was more of a biblical primitivist, even fundamentalist, to the point that he began practicing adult baptism at the time of regeneration.[20]

In 1832 Matthews had been deprived of his chaplaincy at the Bedford House of Industry, ostensibly because of his conversion to millenarianism and his belief in spiritual gifts. While this was part of the story, Matthews's dismissal also centred on his acceptance of ordination from G.A. West as a bishop in the Primitive Episcopal Church.[21]

Following his removal, Matthews had quickly organized a primitivist church at Bedford containing about 600 souls. During this time, he became aware of the imminence of the Second Coming. According to Matthews's wife, Ann, a learned Jew had used an old Hebrew Bible to convince Matthews that the world was 5 993 years old, and that only seven years remained before Jesus would come down in glory.[22]

Not long after the arrangement between these two men was formulated, Aitken came to espouse the doctrines of the second advent. Aitken stated in his book, *The Second Coming*, that he had converted to millennialism. He contended that previously he had been one of the most strenuous – even violent – opponents of this doctrine: 'I imagined that it was mere offspring of vain theorising and speculative minds, and that Satan had most successfully made use of it, as a lure to entice enterprising spirits from the more solid, and absolutely essential, concernments of religion.' He claimed that he would have remained a disbeliever had God himself not taught him 'and that too directly, and not through human instrumentality' the doctrine of the millennium.[23]

Regardless of Aitken's explanation, his conversion to millennialism was, presumably at least in part, influenced by the religious environment of the 1830s – a time when various millennial schemes were legion.[24] Furthermore, given the growing liaison between Aitken and Matthews (whatever the exact nature of this arrangement might have been), it is plausible that Matthews was somehow instrumental in Aitken's conversion to the doctrine.[25] Certainly there was a broad pattern of similarity in the adventist teachings of both men. And it might be inferred that Matthews never would have agreed to join the Aitkenites unless he and Aitken had reached some accord on the vital issue of the second coming.

In *The Second Coming* Aitken declared that the doctrines of the Lord's second advent were the key to the prophetical scriptures in both the Old and New Testaments. Although Aitken was obviously influenced by such traditional millennial sources as Daniel, Micah and Revelations, he does not expostulate on any one given text. Instead, he presents a generalized version of the millennium that is marked by a lack of specific biblical references. But Aitken was not interested in prophetic details, and instead used the Second Coming doctrine to launch a savage attack on early Victorian society and the religionists of his day. He also believed that the political establishment was guilty of destroying the Christian underpinnings that had bonded society together for centuries.[26]

Aitken rejected post-millenarianism, based on the notion of a gradual improvement in society. He argued that churchmen and dissenters, as well as Bible societies and missionary societies, all tell the same story of 'increasing piety' and 'extending success' – in other words, that the world is on the mend and such improvements will continue until the world will be filled with the Glory of the Lord. Aitken argued that this idea was an illusion, because the church will coexist with anti-Christianity – the wheat and tares will grow together until the great and dreadful day of the Lord. To him, the churches of the day were entirely corrupt and were doomed for destruction. At the Second Coming the Lord will claim His own from the true believers of all denominations, and the wicked will be rooted out.

As with Matthews, Aitken expressed a great urgency in preaching the millennial message because the last days were upon society and this was a time of prophetic warning: 'I feel as if death or life was in every word; and every time I make the enquiry – Watchman, what of the night – the answer cometh with an increasing thrill to my soul, the morning cometh, and also the night.' Thus the message was one of preparing the way for the great and glorious day: 'Ministers of Christ . . . to your knees for oil – to your bibles for light; away with every trapping of worldly policy; strip your party – coloured robes of Satan's weaving; take to your locusts and wild honey; have done with the poisonous dishes of man's providing.'[27]

Satan, of course, knew about the eminence of the Lord's advent and would do all in his power to thwart professing Christians in their efforts to hasten the day. Therefore, a greater diligence and obedience was needed than in former times. In addition, it was the snare of the devil that promoted speculative minds to ponder the details concerning the manner of the Saviour's reign, such as formulating foolish calculations concerning the precise time of His coming. Aitken was not interested in determining a timetable for events that would lead to the millennial reign. All that was certain was that in due time, the events predicted in the Bible would transpire in their proper order. Simply stated, details were not important to Aitken, whose millennial writings lacked the fervid biblical imagery of many of the popular and revolutionary millenarians.

References in *The Second Coming* also show that Matthews and

Aitken agreed on the lack of spiritual gifts within the churches. No longer were the miraculous powers of healing, prophecy and divine signs manifested within Christianity: 'What has become of the angel messenger, who so frequently appeared to the primitive Christians? Where is the confidence and brotherly love that made all things common; and where is the selling of all that we have, and becoming a disciple of the Lord Jesus?' Christians were now part of the world – not set off from it. The love of ease had replaced trials and tribulations. In short, 'Apostacy – apostacy – apostacy, is engraven on the very front of every church'.[28]

How did society compel a former politically and socially conservative minister to become obsessed by chiliastic doom? Aitken resorted to the metaphor of 'mystical Babylon', which typified society of the day and was doomed to destruction. Like Babylon of old:

> It is Christendom of the present day, and as sure as ancient Babylon is now levelled with the dust, and her sons and daughters numbered with the dead – as sure as her children within her were slain, or led into captivity, so sure, if there be a God in heaven, will the Lord visit our iniquities with his vengeance, and so sure shall those churches, that now extol their heads, and say, 'I sit as a queen, and shall see no sorrow,' so sure shall they endure the vengeance of an angry and an insulted God.[29]

To Aitken this was an age dominated by the sins of sabbath-breaking, whoredoms, prostitution and drunkenness. In short, moral laxity was tolerated. In addition, the enemies of truth (that is, secularists and complacent Christians) were prevailing – those he referred to as the 'Bible-despising, gospel-hardened inhabitants of this land'. Aitken was also appalled by the amount of wealth and affluence spent on luxuries, and he railed against the 'pleasure-loving and world-loving sinners', including the supposed Christian shopkeepers who were obsessed with increasing their treasures. Aitken's nonconformist criticism extended to the affluence within the Church of England: 'Come with me to Lambeth Palace – tell the number of its turrets – count its splendid halls and its painted chambers – give a tongue to these appendages of state, these contributors to luxury, and say – OH! say – What are all these calculated to teach a pleasure-loving and world-loving sinner!' Nor were dissenting ministers spared, for he questioned whether ministers salaried at £500 or even £100 were really worth what they were paid. Such materialism was Satan's way of providing for the damnation of souls. In an adjacent key passage, Aitken attacked the party spirit prevalent at this time, as well as the secularizing policies of the churches. Presumably Aitken refers to the rather weak posture of the Christian denominations who were faced with a government bent on pursuing policies that would lead to further secularization of society.[30]

Aitken carried even further his attack on the liberal political establishment with the publication of his 1839 sermon, 'An Exposition of the 101st Psalm'. 'From the Crown of the head of the nation, to the sole of the foot', the British people 'are covered with wounds, and with bruises, and putrefying sores'. Those serving in the Government, he contended, were guilty of 'immoralities'. But what does all this suggest? Aitken specifically referred to governmental actions that result in the banishing of Christianity from government, as well as attacks on the Church as a divine society. From here Aitken went forth to warn of millennial doom – that the Lord will 'rise up early' and destroy the wicked of the land.[31]

Like other religious conservatives, Aitken was fearful that liberals were encroaching on theism and the underpinnings of a Christian society.[32] It was a common belief in the 1830s that Christianity had been dealt devastating setbacks with the passage of Catholic emancipation and political reform between 1829 and 1832. Parliament was seemingly secular, even non-Christian, in its approach. After 1833, the Whigs gallantly took up the cause of ecclesiastical reform, which appeared to many (such as John Keble and the Tractarians) to be so ominous as to raise the cry that the Church was in danger. Interestingly, Aitken was said to have been strongly influenced by such Tractarian views.[33] Never since the days of Queen Anne had church questions sparked such controversy over a broad spectrum of opinion.

As David Hempton has suggested, government attempts to promote religious peace by legislation produced a variety of responses by several religious groups. One response included a move toward premillennialism as a way of voicing opposition to the politics of this confused age.[34] Robert Aitken's Christian Society surely fits this pattern. The extent to which Aitken was disturbed by the politics of the time can be seen in a comment made just a few years later:

> Do the religionists of our day recognize the doctrine of the divine rights of kings, or the divine appointment of government? Do they account it sinful to evade laws which they do not approve, or to oppose a government which is not of their political creed? Their avowed principles are, the people ought to be consulted; the government is responsible to the people! We have a right to dictate! We have a right to overawe, by making demonstrations of our numerical strength![35]

Sacred principles, such as duties of submission and obedience, were being repudiated in an age of mass demonstrations and extended political power.

While rejecting the measures of political and religious reform undertaken by the state, Aitken believed that the last days would be preceded by the spirit of reform within the hearts of true Christians – the return to the spirit of Elijah, followed by that of John the Baptist. While the nation was doomed to destruction prior to the Second Coming, individuals could be saved through the regeneration of the spirit. Indeed, the key event that was to precede the second advent was the building of a 'Zion society'. This called for a new church order, built on the foundation of Christ, with apostles and prophets as the second row of the foundation:

> Every member of the church must be like Christ; and the life, and purpose, and policy of the church, must be that of the precious foundation ... Such a Zion the Lord will build, such a church the Lord must have; and he will bring his treasures into it; and his gifts as well as his graces shall be there; and he will gloriously manifest his presence and his power there ... By the power of such a church, the Lord will, subjugate the kingdoms of the earth; through such a church the earth will be filled with the glory of God.[36]

In another sermon Aitken contended that:

> God had declared he will never destroy the earth any more by a flood; but this world and these heavens are served to be burned. And I thank God it is so. Men talk about the earth being made the theatre of the glory of God; I thank God this place of sin is to be burned; I have no love for it; it is odious to me, because it is the theatre of sin.[37]

This passage and others suggest that Aitken had a rather morbid preoccupation with destruction. Although it would be easy to resort to psychological explanations for such an obsession, John Harrison reminds us of the danger involved in reducing millenarians to the level of the deranged. Such explanations are usually detrimental to an understanding of the social context of ideas, especially when we consider the widespread acceptance of such beliefs.[33] None the less, it might be suggested that Aitken's renunciation of the world suggests acute anxiety brought about by his failure to cope with a real world composed of wheat and tares. In this sense, Aitken's vision was that of a perfectionist who could not tolerate the growing secular tendencies of an age forced to compromise over religious values.

Apparently it was not until September 1839, at the annual conference of the Christian Society, that Aitken's new views of millennial doom were brought before the Society for official consideration. The conference proceedings mention that Aitken told the group that the Society had previously neglected millennialism. To set matters straight, it was announced that this doctrine would be part of the Society's beliefs. According to Aitken, there was not the slightest possibility that the world would become regenerated prior to the second advent. Instead, the emphasis was on apostasy and destruction – both familiar Aitken themes. However, Aitken did carry the discussion in a new direction by dispelling any figurative notion of Christ's Second Coming and by expostulating on the theme of millennial glory. In addition, we learn of Aitken's commitment to the literal restoration of the Jews and the rebuilding of Jerusalem that figures in events prior to Christ's coming.[39]

The other significant aspect of Aitken's discussion concerns events following the advent. Up to this point, Aitken's sole focus had been on the events that were to precede the glorious day. But here he spelled out the theocracy that was to be established and the pouring out of the spirit on all flesh that lived to see Christ's glory. In this state there shall be 'a free and immediate intercourse with the Redeemer'. And in millennial society 'pure benevolence' will be universal, and all will be restored to primeval purity.[40] As we have observed, Aitken's millenarian perspectives were typical of his time. Certainly the political overtones of his sermons often reflect the concerns of such groups as the Albury circle and individuals like Edward Bickersteth, who shared with Aitken fears for Christianity following Catholic emancipation and parliamentary reform, and many others suspected political intrusions into church affairs by secular-minded politicians. In addition, millennial expectations were spawned by fears of social decay, growing political radicalism and the decline of religious influences in society, a view that Aitken promoted.[41] Aitken likewise saw salvation emanating from a tiny minority who would act as harbingers of the Lord in the last days.

But what is interesting is Aitken's reference to an 'Elijah spirit' which was to be followed by that of John the Baptist, as well as the building of a 'Zion society'. While the language here appears to emanate from radical millenarian sects, such as the Mormons and the Southcottians, Aitken's interpretation lacked the detailed prophetic timetable common to such groups. In the case of the Latter-day Saints and other biblical fundamentalists, Elijah and John the Baptist would actually make physical appearances before the last and dreadful day.[42] From the context of Aitken's brief passages on Elijah, there is no indication that he believed in such a literalism. It is interesting to note that Elizabeth Vaughan, the self-styled Southcottian prophetess, wrote to Aitken to inform him that the spirit of Elijah had already warned the British nation (in 1792), when Joanna Southcott began her public ministry.[43] Regardless of his pronouncements concerning the exact fulfillment of prophecies, Aitken was more interested in general conditions than in predicting future events.[44] Indeed, it was the present, not the future, that most interested Aitken.

In August 1840, Mormon apostles who had recently come to London to preach their version of the millennial gospel attended a sermon by Aitken at Zion's Chapel, Waterloo Road and were favourably impressed. Wilford Woodruff wrote:

> The Rev. R. Aitken ... of London says, As the prophecies concerning the birth, life, & death, of our Lord were litterly [sic] fulfilled at his first Coming, to the division of his garments and to the casting of lots upon his vestures so evry [sic] prophecy & promise respecting his second Coming, throne, kingdom, reign judgment, power, with the Changes predicted in the world, elements, nature, condition of animals and the like, Shall be literally accomplished.[43]

To be sure, one of the Mormon missionaries recorded that Aitken lacked the proper spirit. But they agreed on the power of his message and there was a meeting of the minds concerning the millenarian content of his message.[46]

Although Aitken had been identified in the past as an enemy of the Latter-day Saints, the apostles decided to visit him in hopes of receiving a favourable hearing. On 7 September, the delegation was received courteously by the Reverend Aitken. According to Heber C. Kimball: 'We conversed with him some time upon the principles of our religion, many of which he acknowledged were correct.' Aitken reaffirmed on this occasion that he believed that the Saviour will soon come upon the earth. As the interview proceeded, Aitken became more remorseful. Wringing his hands like a man in agony, Aitken stated: 'I am sorry that I ever left the Church of England. I have preached and published a great many hard things against the Church of England. I ought not to have done it.' This he repeated several times, which prompted one of the apostles to write: 'I never saw a man in such a state [of despondency] before.'[47]

It is apparent that Aitken was undergoing a profound religious crisis. According to Canon Hay Aitken, his son and biographer, Aitken was then influenced by writings on German mysticism as well as the Port Royalists, which brought to his mind the question of schism with the Church. Aitken began to be tormented by the proposition that he himself had erred by working outside of the Church of England. Soon after, on 20 December 1840, at Hope Hall in Liverpool, he preached his farewell sermon to the Christian Society. There he exhorted believers to press forward, but also warned them of the dangers of divisions within the Christian fold. 'The language of sect and party is,' he contended, 'keep together, strengthen one another, and by every possible means increase your number, for number is power ... But this is not the language of God.' He then said that the Society had long abandoned its first principles without stating what those principles were. From a personal perspective, he concluded that 'too much of my cryings to God have been about you, and too little about my own soul'.[48] According to Hay Aitken's account, a delegation of leading members of the Hope Street Church was sent to the Bishop of Chester to solicit Aitken's appointment as an established minister at this church. But the Bishop insisted on

Aitken's outright submission as a requisite for reinstatement, to be fol-
lowed by a three-year silence. After his agreeing to this proposal, the
Bishop then lifted the three-year ban, and Aitken was reinstated into the
Church of England.[49]

Evidently, Aitken's renunciation of leadership over the Christian
Society also marked the end of his partnership with the Reverend
Timothy Matthews. After the collapse of the Christian Society,
Matthews returned to Bedford and re-grouped his scattered flock.
Indeed, Matthews went on to greater heights of success than in previous
years, winning new converts through his street preaching, especially in
nearby Northampton. But, unlike Aitken, Matthews retained his strong
millennialist and primitivist message. According to his biographer,
Thomas Wright, Matthews taught that 'the [Book of] Revelation is the
only book in these days to keep the Children of God alive. Whoever
neglects that, sleeps, and will be asleep when Jesus comes'.[50] Matthews
even had dreams of retiring to the Holy Land, in order to be closer to
events associated with the second advent. There is no evidence that the
lives of the two charismatic ministers ever crossed again.

But what did Aitken's return to the Church of England signify in terms
of his theological and social perspectives? In many respects, Aitken did
not undergo any fundamental theological transformation. His eclectic
blend of Anglican orthodoxy and methodism continued to raise questions in the minds of church authorities. To the chagrin of many, Aitken
brought his conversion methods into the Church of England, and there
continued to be complaints about spiritual excesses. In addition, he
remained highly critical of the political and religious establishments – a
fact that must have caused some embarrassment, and precluded his
serious consideration for ecclesiastical preferment. Indeed, his attacks on
politically controlled church preferments, and his suggestion of the need
for greater lay participation in parish affairs, were bound to offend conservative elements within the Established Church. Nor was his suggestion for a powerful evangelizing ministry to recover the lost cities – a
particularly attractive proposition to many within the Anglican hier-
archy.[51]

In addition, Aitken continued to rail against what he conceived to be
the wickedness of his generation: 'we may not expect great things in these
last days, of a dispensation which has all along been fearfully characterized by unfaithfulness'. Aitken's High Church theological predilections
likewise influenced his outlook on what he conceived to be the 'self-
indulgent softness, the worldly conformity, and the Antinomian spirit of
modern evangelicalism', a corrosive force that permeated both the
Church of England and the ranks of dissent.[52]

On at least one other occasion, Aitken apparently preached directly on the Second Coming. In 1843 extracts of this sermon, largely borrowed from his 1838 writings, were published by Josua V. Himes, the Boston adventist. Here again, Aitken took up the mantle of a modern-day Ezekiel, attacking the existing religions for 'apostasy from primitive purity and primitive simplicity, and their total want of primitive power'. He proclaimed that one more alarm was about to be sounded throughout the realm, and this last trumpet would either result in a hardening or a conversion of sinners. Not placing much hope on this final call to repentance, he announced: 'Godless, Christless world, your destiny is fixed; your destruction is inevitable.'[53] Perhaps the only distinctively new theme following Aitken's return to Anglicanism was his appeal to Christian unity, which he couched in a millenarian perspective. Hence Aitken continued to preach in favour of a selective regeneration of elements in society, including typical premillennial references to 'the Elijah spirit' permeating into the hearts of 'thousands' and 'tens of thousands' of spiritually minded young men. Thus, may ' "the heart of the fathers be turned to the children, and the heart of the children to their fathers", lest the Lord, when He cometh, instead of hailing us with blessings, "should smite us with a curse" '.[54] To be sure, Methodism was no longer the vehicle for the creation of a new Zion spirit, but was part of the problem that could only be solved through millennial regeneration. The High Church element was now seen as the harbinger of reform among the Lord's chosen that would precede the new dawn.[55] But there can be no question that as the excitement of the troubled decade of the 1830s gradually faded, Aitken's interest in millenarian themes likewise receded into the margins of his thought. If millennial expectations were not entirely abandoned, it is safe to say that the sense of eminence was all but lost.

Notes

1. J.F.C. Harrison, *The Second Coming: Popular Millenarianism, 1780–1850* (London, 1979).
2. W.H. Oliver, *Prophets and Millennialists: The Uses of Biblical Prophecy in England from the 1790s to the 1840s* (Oxford, 1978), pp. 124–49.
3. *Times and Seasons*, 12 October 1840.
4. R. Aitken, *Sermon Preached at Whitburn Church* (Bishopwearmouth, 1824), p. 5.
5. E.V. Chapman, *Rev. Robert Aitken*, (n.p., 1982), pp. 1–2, V. Roach, 'The Story of Eyreton Castle', *Isle of Man Examiner*, 2 October 1970.
6. C. Woods, *Memoirs and Letters of Canon Hay Aitken*, (London, 1928), pp. 20–3.
7. R. Aitken, *An Address to the Preachers Office – Bearers and Members of the Wesleyan Methodist Societies* (London and Manchester, 1835); D.A. Gowland, *Methodist Secessions: The Origins of Free Methodism in Three*

Lancashire Towns: Manchester, Rochdale, Liverpool, (Manchester, 1979), pp. 6, 106–7.

8. John Rylands Library, Manchester, PLP 28/2; B. Gregory, *Side Lights on the Conflicts of Methodism . . . 1827–52* (London, 1899), p. 210.

9. D. Thom, 'Liverpool Churches and Chapels', *Historic Society of Lancashire and Cheshire: Proceedings and Papers,* vol. 4 (1851–5), pp. 182–4; *Liverpool Review,* 14 June 1887. For a more sympathetic view of these meetings see T. Stephenson, *Calumny Refuted: or the Rev. Mr Aitken's Sermon Vindicated, from the Aspersions Cast Upon It by Dr Curron* (Douglas, IOM, 1832) pp. 25, 27.

10. *Laws, Regulations and General Policy of the Christian Society, in Connection with the Rev. R. Aitken,* (n.p., 1836) pp. 50–1.

11. *Laws,* pp. 4–5, 8; John Rylands library, PLP 1/28/1.

12. *Laws,* pp. 27, 38, 39; J. Bowes, *The Autobiography or History of the Life of John Bowes* (Glasgow, 1872), p. 185.

13. *Laws,* pp. 27, 38.

14. R. Atkins [sic], *A True Picture: or a Thrilling Description of the State of the Churches Throughout Christendom* (Boston, 1843), p. 7.

15. R. Aitken, 'The Origin, Universality and Consequences of the Apostacy of Man', *The Christian Preacher,* vol. 3 (1839), pp. 11–12.

16. Bowes, *Autobiography,* pp. 197–202.

17. *Church Times,* 3 September 1875.

18. Bowes, *Autobiography,* p. 186; Church of Jesus Christ of Latter-day Saints, Salt Lake City, Utah, Historical Department (hereafter HDC): Joseph Fielding to his sisters, 2 October 1837; M.R. Thorp, 'Early Mormon Confrontations with Sectarianism, 1837–40' in R.L. Jensen and M.R. Thorp (eds), *Mormons in Early Victorian Britain* (Salt Lake City, 1989), p. 65.

19. T. Wright, *The Life of T.R. Matthews* (London, 1934), pp. 44–5.

20. Thorp, 'Early Mormon Confrontations', pp. 51–5; HDC, MS 2779 .

21. J. Varley, 'A Bedfordshire Clergyman of the Reform Era and his Bishop', *Publications of the Bedfordshire Historical Record Society,* (Bedford, 1978) vol. 57, pp. 127, 134–5; Bedfordshire Record Office, MC 136.

22. HDC, Ann Fielding Matthews to Mr and Mrs [Joseph] Fielding, 18 March 1833.

23. R. Aitken, *The Second Coming: A Sermon* (London, 1839), p. 4.

24. Harrison, *The Second Coming* pp. 163–206; Oliver, *Prophets and Millennialists:* G. Underwood, *The Millenarian World of Early Mormonism* (Chicago, 1993), pp. 127–38.

25. G.J. Adams, *A Few Plain Facts, Shewing the Folly, Wickedness and Imposition of the Rev. Timothy R Matthews* (Bedford, 1841), p. 9.

26. Aitken, *The Second Coming,* pp. 5–6.

27. Ibid, p. 22.

28. Ibid, pp. 25–6; Thorp, 'Early Mormon Confrontations', p. 52.

29. R. Aitken, 'God's Vengence upon the Wicked'. Sermon preached 19 May 1839, *The Christian Preacher,* vol. 3 (1839), pp. 4, 6–7.

30. Aitken, *The Second Coming,* p. 16.

31. R. Aitken, 'An Exposition of the 101st Psalm', *The Christian Preacher,* vol. 4 (1839).

32. Oliver, *Prophets and Millennialists,* pp. 140–1.

33. See entry in *Dictionary of National Biography,* vol. 1.

34. D. Hempton, *Methodism and Politics in British Society, 1750–1850* (London, 1987), p. 181.
35. [R. Aitken], *Sermons for the Times. 'The Pollution of the Temple'* (London, 1842), p. 13.
36. *Latter Day Saints' Millennial Star*, 3 February 1843, pp. 172–4. A large section of Aitkens 'Sermon Preached at the Opening of Zion Chapel, Waterloo Road, London on Sunday 2 December 1838' is reprinted in this article. This sermon is listed in G.C. Boase and W.P. Courtney, *Bibliotheca Cornubiensis: A Catalogue of the Writings of Cornishmen* (London, 1874), vol. 1, p. 561, but I have been unable to locate an extant copy.
37. Aitken, *The Second Coming*, p. 21.
38. Harrison, *The Second Coming*, p. 217.
39. *Extracts from the Minutes of the Fourth Annual Convocation of the Christian Society, in Connection with the Rev. Robert Aitken, AM, held at Liverpool, in September 1839* (London, 1839), pp. 6–7.
40. Ibid.
41. Oliver, *Prophets and Millennialists*, pp. 136–41; E. Bickersteth, *Practical Guide to the Prophecies* (6th edn, London, 1839).
42. For a summary of Mormon Millenarianism and a comparison with other popular movements in America and Britain see Underwood, *The Millenarian World; also the Quarterly Journal of Prophecy*, **1**, (1849), p. 332, and 'The Coming of Elias', in **2** (1850) pp. 90–1.
43. E. Vaughan, *A Refutation of the Sermon Preached by Robert Aitken, of Zion Chapel, Waterloo Road, upon the Second Coming of Christ* (London, 1839), p. 3.
44. Aitken's lack of specificity was a factor in turning at least one Aitkenite local preacher, Alfred Cordon, from the Christian Society to the Mormons: see HDC, Journals and Reminiscences of Alfred Cordon, MS 1831, pp. 8–11.
45. S. Kenney (ed.), *Wilford Woodruff's Journal*, vol. 1 (Midvale, Utah, 1983).
46. HDC, 'Journal History', 10 September 1854, p. 8.
47. HDC, Heber C. Kimball to Edward Martin, 11 September 1840.
48. Woods, *Memoirs*, p. 23; R. Aitken, 'Believers Exhorted to Press Forward', *The Pulpit* vol. 38 (1840).
49. Woods, *Memoirs*, pp. 26–8.
50. Brigham Young University, Diary of Joseph Fielding, pp. 94, 96; Wright, *Life of TR Matthews*, p. 83.
51. *Church Times*, 3 September 1875; C. Bodington, *Devotional Life in the Nineteenth Century* (London, 1905), p. 86; R. Aitken, *Hints, Suggestions and Reasons for the Provisional Adjustment in the Church Rate* (London, 1859), pp. 12–20.
52. R. Aitken, *The Teaching of the Types. Tracts for the Clergy and the Earnest-Minded* (Oxford, 1854) p. 124.
53. Atkins [*sic*], pp. 13–15.
54. Aitken, Hints, p. 58.
55. Aitken, *Teaching of the Types*, p. 124.

CHAPTER NINE

Who were 'the People' in 1842?

Dorothy Thompson

In his history of the common people, John Harrison recalls the story of little Joseph Arch, at the age of seven, peeping through the keyhole of the parish church to watch the adults receiving holy communion. The sight of the separation of the congregation by class, with the labourers going humbly to the altar rail after their social betters had received the host gave him a sudden and immediate awareness of the divisions in his society and 'the iron entered into my poor little heart and remained fast embedded there'[1]. By 1842, the year I want to look at in this essay, the teenage Arch was risking his job as well as the charitable gifts of food, blankets and coal on which labouring families relied in times of bad weather or ill-health, to attend the dissenting services held in semi-secrecy in the open air or in the shelter of farm buildings. His quarrel was not with the tenets of Christianity nor, at least initially, with the terms in which it was presented by the Anglican church; it was certainly not with the language of the Bible or the Book of Common Prayer. He was alienated by the context in which these things were offered to the villagers. The language of religion, as in other situations that of politics, has to be seen in precise context if it is to illuminate the actions of the people employing it.

This is not the occasion to enter into an extended argument about any of the questions relating to the 'language' of popular politics which are being debated in some quarters. By looking at a small number of specific expressions I want to raise some of the questions which have to be asked about the use of 'language' as a major historical source. To what extent does the language of politics have a fixed set of meanings irrespective of who is speaking and under what constraints, who is being addressed, who is reporting the speech, and what forms of communication other than verbal are involved such as dress, accent and gender? Put in this simple form the question appears absurd. Every one is aware for example that an order in a public house in a mining district in the nineteenth century for a pint of beer and a whisky chaser would not raise an eyebrow if it was given by a miner, but the same order in the identical words given by an unaccompanied young lady would cause an uproar. An order for tea and scones in a posh London hotel would see the roles reversed, if indeed the unconventional customer in either case could manage to gain admission to the premises; signals given by dress, bearing and gender would have decided the question of their treatment before a word had been spoken. The words alone tell us little about the social issues involved.

Much of the recent discussion about political rhetoric does, at base, lack the essential element of context. The idea of a democratic anti-court rhetoric originating with the 'country party', picked up by Wilkes and Cartwright in the eighteenth century, dominating the political language of post-Napoleonic war political radicalism into Chartism and beyond, carries with it the idea that the programmes of the various political or social movements which employed versions of this rhetoric were basically the same, and that a programme has the same meaning in the mouths of a small aristocratic clique as on the banners of a procession of 10 000 armed coal and iron workers in South Wales. But at any particular moment in history, the meaning given to words and phrases is influenced by precisely the factors which too many of the 'language' school of interpreters set aside, the class, the interest and the power relations of those who employ them.

It is a truism that words, slogans and concepts have very different force at different times in history. As Marc Bloch remarked many years ago: 'To the great despair of historians, men fail to change their vocabulary every time they change their customs.'[2] In the arena of politics, words and concepts are continually being contested. The concept of 'the people' was very widely used by politicians of all shades during the nineteenth century. There may have been moments towards the end of the century when it assumed an over-arching classless national meaning in line perhaps with its use in the USA. In Britain however, in the 1840s it can only be understood in the context of a class-divided society. To read it as a neutral classless term would be to misread the politics, parliamentary and popular, of the period.

In her speech from the throne at the opening of Parliament in February 1842, the Queen spoke of 'the continued Distress in the Manufacturing Districts of the Country' and of 'the Sufferings and Privations which have resulted from it'. She expressed her confidence that the deliberations of Parliament and the measures which they proposed would be 'directed by a comprehensive Regard for the Interests and permanent Welfare of all Classes of my Subjects, and I fervently pray that they may tend in their Results to improve the National Resources and to encourage the Industry and promote the Happiness of My People'[3]. It is hard from this not to conclude that the people in the last phrase are the lower classes of her subjects whose industry needs promoting rather more than that of the higher orders. For virtually all of those who spoke in the parliamentary debates in the course of the year, the expression 'the people' was unequivocally reserved for the lower orders. Thus Peel, Prime Minister in the new Tory administration, praised 'the forebearance of the people' in the distressing times, but deprecated 'motions making the government responsible for providing them with sustenance and employment'.[4] Among the more radical Whigs, Charles Pelham Villiers, anti-Corn-Law enthusiast and younger brother of the Earl of Clarendon, pointed out that 'the people, being neither Whig nor Tory, were disposed to think that the monopolies springing out of what they termed class legislation had so far exhausted their means and restricted their energies as to be answerable for the decline of this great industrial nation'[5]. Charles Brotherton, manufacturer, believed that 'the people were beginning to understand the causes of their distress' which he saw as poverty and lack of sufficient food; he declared that his own principle would always be 'perish party but give the people bread'.[6]

This use of the people to mean the excluded, the unenfranchised was widely used. Ebenezer Elliott's *People's Anthem* embodies it

> When wilt thou save the people?
>   O God of mercy! when?
> Not kings and lords but nations!
>   Not thrones and crowns but men?
> Flowers of thy heart O God are they!
> Let them not pass like weeds away!
> Their heritage a sunless day!
>   God save the people!

In 1861 Lord John Russell defined 'the people' as 'the working classes' when he had been converted to a limited extension of the franchise.[7] If this usage was challenged, it was among old-fashioned extra-parliamentary Tories, not among the political spokesmen of any parliamentary group. James Vernon cites a speaker at a Devonshire Conservative banquet in 1837 as demanding: 'What did the radicals mean by talking about the people? . . . in the list which these liberal philosophers have drawn up, who do they call the people? They exclude the lords, the clergy, the landowners, the merchants and even their old companions the Whigs . . .'[8] In the political debates of 1842 no one challenged the usage which excluded those categories.

The Chartist petition of 1842 consisted of the six points of the People's Charter with around 40 accompanying paragraphs. A petition calling for reforms in line with the six points – for an extension of the suffrage, shorter parliaments and vote by secret ballot had been introduced earlier in the year. It had received little support but little hostility either. The Chartist petition was received very differently by speakers from both major parties. The Chartists were not allowed to speak to their own petition. The proposal that a delegation representing the signatories be received at the Bar of the House was put, debated and thoroughly defeated. The case for hearing the Chartists was put by the small group whom Oastler called the 'philanthropic' radicals, as opposed to the 'philosophic' or free-trade variety[9]. On nearly all the subjects that divided the Chartists from the Leaguers, these three took the Chartist side. Duncombe, radical old Etonian nephew of Lord Feversham, who was said to have spent £40 000 to gain his earlier parliamentary seat, was by 1842 sitting for the radical London borough of Finsbury. Engels described him as 'the representative of the working-men in the House of Commons'[10] and he certainly spoke up consistently on behalf of the Chartists, as well as presenting forcefully the case for the admission of their representatives to speak to their petition. Thomas Wakley, Duncombe's fellow member for Finsbury, had referred to himself, in proposing an amendment in favour of the secret ballot to the Queen's speech in 1837, as 'a representative of labour'.[11] A radical who refused to use any of the normal electoral devices, even including canvassing, Wakley was a surgeon by profession, editor of the campaigning *Lancet*. He spoke with a strong provincial accent – that of his native Dorset, and was not above entertaining the House with anecdotes in the vernacular.[12] John Fielden, whose strong provincial accent was also remarked on – it was held to be so strong as to make his contributions in the House all but incomprehensible to southerners – was the head of the largest cotton manufacture in Europe; he had declared in his initial election address in 1833 that 'nothing but an anxious solicitude to see the people restored to their just rights, and especially the labouring population of society greatly improved could have induced him to enter Parliament'.[13] These three were the main supporters of the petition in the House, and were joined in the division lobby by fewer than 50 assorted radicals and eccentrics.

None of these parliamentary spokesmen could be held to have been using the actual words of the working people who had drawn up and signed the petition. These appeared only in the text, nearly every para-graph of which refers to 'the people'.[14] Addressed in the accepted form to 'the Commons of Great Britain and Ireland in Parliament assembled' the petition announced itself as 'The petition of the undersigned People of the United Kingdom', and proceeded to show 'That Government origi-nated from and was designed to protect the freedom and promote the happiness of and ought to be responsible to the whole people.' In almost every one of the itemized grievances 'the people' are taken to be the unen-franchised, alternating with expressions such as 'working men' or specific groups such as agricultural labourers where particular hardships are being emphasized. Only in the Irish section can the term perhaps be read as having a wider significance: 'That your petitioners complain of the many grievances borne by the people of Ireland; and contend that they are fully entitled to a repeal of the Legislative Union.' Even here, though, it could be argued that it was the unenfranchised Irish, not the property owners there whose interests were being pressed. The term otherwise is used unambiguously:

> That the only authority on which any body of men can make laws and govern society, is delegation from the people . . . That your Honourable House, as at present constituted, has not been elected by and acts irresponsibly of, the people . . . your Honourable House has enacted laws contrary to the expressed wishes of the people; and hitherto has only represented parties and represented the few, regardless of the miseries, grievances and petitions of the many.

Macaulay's contention during the debate on the Chartist petition, that universal suffrage 'would be fatal to all purposes for which government exists and for which aristocracies and all other things exist, and that it is utterly incompatible with the very existence of civilisation'[15] is by now well known. The response of Peel to the 1842 petition was hardly less comprehensive:

> The petition tells me that it is wrong to maintain an Established Church – it says that £9 million of money are annually abstracted from the people for the purpose of maintaining the church. The petition tells me that the people of Ireland are entitled to a repeal of the union. The petition draws a most invidious comparison between the expenses of the Sovereign and those of a labourer. I say the petition is altogether an impeachment of the Constitution of this country and of the whole frame of society.[16]

Lord John Russell, the presenter of the 1832 Reform Act and the proponent of the 'finality' of its provisions, added his voice to the condemnation of the petition:

> I do not think in the present state of popular education – I will not say whether a standard of education sufficiently high can ever be obtained among the labouring classes – but in the present condition of the people at large, I do not think you could be sure that there might not be, in the state of popular ferment on the occasion of some general election, Members returned to this House whose votes would be favourable to the destruction of our institutions, and would shake the security of property.[17]

These responses suggest that it was the context, particularly the extra-parliamentary context of the petition which produced the response, rather than the wording or the specific objects for which it called.

Within Parliament, then, the 'the people' were clearly seen as the lower orders, the labouring population, whose demand for the vote was associated with at best disrespect for authority and at worst with the intention to overthrow the whole edifice of parliamentary government. Outside, too, the authorities in general seem to have used it in the same way. Thus

Lord Chief Justice Denman, addressing 150 Chartists in the dock, in September, complained:

> Unfortunately it was a matter for astonishment and lamentation, that after all that had been done to enlighten and educate the people – and, he would fearlessly add – to improve their condition and improve their comforts – there should be found in this country men, by the hundred and thousand, ready to assemble together for the absurd, the insane, the suicidal purpose of throwing men in their own circumstances out of employment and thus increasing terribly the distress which unhappily existed.[18]

The return of the Tories to power in the autumn of 1841 had released some of the more radical elements among the liberals from their support of the Whig government. The Anti-Corn-Law League and Daniel O'Connell's Loyal National Repeal Association became active in the country and used some of the tactics of the Chartists. The League in particular was not above appealing for support to working men and even contemplating what Villiers referred to as 'the brickbat argument'[19] to drive home their belief in the connection between protection and the depression. Much of their language sounded as subversive as that of the Chartists, while some of their tactics went even further in appearing to defy the legal limits of political activity. But their campaigning in 1842 failed signally either to win over any substantial section of the radical working men or to establish a common 'populist' rhetoric which could have transcended class barriers.

The story of the relations between the League and the Chartists has been told often and well.[20] Historians of different approaches have agreed in seeing the gulf between the two movements and their failure to unite to pressurize the Tory government as being a matter of class relations in the manufacturing districts rather than a clash of ideas. The Chartist petition itself took into account the long-standing radical support for the repeal of taxes on food, but put it into a broader perspective:

> your petitioners deeply deplore the existence of any kind of monopoly in this nation; and whilst they unequivocally condemn the levying of any tax upon the necessaries of life, and upon those articles principally required by the labouring classes, they are also sensible that the abolition of any one monopoly will never unshackle labour from its misery, until the people possess that power under which all monopoly and oppression must cease; and your petitioners respectfully mention the existing monopolies of the suffrage, of paper money, of machinery, of land, of the public press, of religious privileges, of the means of travelling and transit and a host of other evils, too numerous to mention, all arising from class legislation, but which your Honourable House has always consistently endeavoured to increase instead of diminish.[21]

On the side of the League there was little in the way of a shared social identity, although there were a number of attempts to convince the working men of a unity of interest between the classes on the issue of Corn-Law repeal. A letter sent to all Members of Parliament in June began: 'the great bulk of the people, the customers of each other and of all the other classes, are becoming too poor to purchase, and thus they cease to consume'.[22] Here clearly, the people are as usual the lower orders, not the whole of the non-aristocratic population. It is in fact in the material put out by the League that the most consistent rhetoric of class is to be found. There were occasions on which they pleaded a common interest between the middle and working classes and others on which they offered leadership to the lower orders. I can find none in which they elided the two into a single populist category. What is more, although the tactics of the League in the early part of the year were disruptive of parliamentary conventions – as when they set up an alternative gathering as a kind of anti-parliament, or marched 500 strong upon the House of Commons and attempted to invade the lobbies, such behaviour produced nothing of the alarm and heavy condemnation which greeted the Chartist petition. Duncombe complained when the Home Secretary defended the arrest and imprisonment of a group of Midland Chartists:

> If the language used by Mason at that meeting was seditious and was sufficient to justify the constables to interfere and disperse the assembly, why did not the police break up and disperse other bodies of men, at whose meetings language infinitely stronger than any that Mason used was daily heard? Why not break in and disperse the meeting of the delegates of the Anti-Corn-Law League which was held daily within a stone's throw of the House of Commons?[23]

Although the rhetoric of some of its speakers annoyed local magistrates, on the whole they were allowed much greater latitude than were the Chartists, hundreds of whom served prison sentences for speeches made during 1842. Not a single member of the League was charged, although if rhetoric alone is being discussed, it has to be admitted that that employed by the Leaguers often ran the Chartists pretty close. It would indeed be difficult to find Chartists competing with the speech quoted by Kitson Clark given by the Leeds Liberal J.C. Nussey in October 1841, in which 'he begged to remind Queen Victoria that the heads of better sovereigns had rolled in the dust, and declared that, unless the condition of the people were bettered, the flag of revolution would be hoisted and the streets swim in blood'.[24] Young Mr Nussey's speech appears to have been listened to and reported in the local press without any apparent concern on the part of the authorities.

Whigs, Tories and Leaguers responded to the spoken and written word according not only to the content but to the class of the speaker.

They used the concept of class continually. Thirty-year-old John Bright, alarmed by the strikes and demonstrations among the workers in his native Rochdale, wrote an open letter 'To the Working Men of Rochdale'. In it he told them that any attempt to increase wages or to shorten hours was to go against the laws of nature. On the question of the suffrage there was more room to manoeuvre:

> Against the obtaining of the charter the laws of nature offer no impediment, as they do against a forcible advance of wages; but to obtain the charter *now* is just as impossible as to raise wages by force.
>   The aristocracy are powerful and determined; and, unhappily, the middle classes are not yet intelligent enough to see the safety of extending political power to the whole people . . . The aristocracy regard the Anti-Corn-Law League as their greatest enemy. That which is the greatest enemy of the remorseless aristocracy of Britain must almost of necessity be your firmest friend.[25]

Richard Cobden, in some ways more sympathetic in his language at this time to the hardships of the working population hoped that 'the capitalists of Lancashire were sufficiently enlightened as to their own interests to know that the worst thing for them would be to have a badly remunerated working population; for, as Burke said "We are all the pensioners of the working classes" '.[26] When it came to the organized workers, however, Cobden did no better with them than Bright. In a letter to Wilson in late 1841, he spoke of having tried to get some action going in Birmingham, where the Complete Suffrage Union (CSU) was strong and joint action between middle and working classes on the Corn Law questions seemed possible. But he was pessimistic:

> The active workers in their association seem to be *working men*. Hitherto the leading and middle classes seem to have done very little . . . I called along with Jos. Sturge upon Collins and two other leaders of the *new move*, but they are not a whit more reasonable upon our question than the O'Connorites . . . Our only plan is to leave the two Chartist factions to fight with each other & raise up a working class party of repealers independent of both.[27]

By June 1842 Edward Watkin was writing to Cobden reporting the failure of the attempts to foster collaboration between the classes by means of the CSU:

> The radicals who went with us before have now joined the Charter Association . . . and the poor, faithful, but ignorant and bigoted fellows who supported the Corn Law repeal as a better thing than Chartism have been disgusted at what their poor brains consider a piece of cowardly conciliation & now give very lukewarm support.[28]

There are many examples of attempts by the Leaguers in the immedi-

ate aftermath of the Tory victory to establish a joint opposition based on
Corn Law repeal. In all cases the Chartists took the opportunity to get
universal suffrage motions past and the collaboration was stillborn. For
example, a meeting called in Manchester Town Hall by local shopkeepers to consider the bad state of trade in June was attended by so many
people – reported as between 10 000 and 12 000 – that it had to be
adjourned to Stevenson Square. Here the platform was heard only after
the intervention of the Chartist James Leach who called for a hearing of
the shopkeepers' case. Their resolution was put to the meeting asking the
government to 'extend our commerce and repeal those laws that prevent
the importation of food'; James Leach responded with an amendment
proposing the adoption of the Charter. He wanted to know 'if the Corn
Laws were repealed to-morrow, what power would the people have to
protect themselves from class legislation any more than they had now?'
After the Chartist resolution was carried with only a handful of dis-
sentient votes the meeting dispersed. Next day placards appeared in the
city calling another meeting, this time by ticket only, which should
consist of 'shopkeepers, traders, innkeepers, cottage-owners and retail
dealers exclusively' to consider the original resolution.[29] Co-operation
between the two bodies foundered not on rhetoric or incompatibility of
political concepts, but on the fact that in each community the Anti-Corn-
Law case was put by employers, merchants and traders, while that of the
Chartists was put by working people. As Gammage commented many
years later:

> There was, whatever may be thought of the policy – something
> heroic in the attitude assumed by working men on this question. It
> was a battle of the employer and the employed. Masters were aston-
> ished at what they deemed the audacity of their workmen, who
> made no scruple of standing beside them on the platform, and con-
> testing with them face to face their most cherished doctrines.
> Terrible was the persecution they suffered for taking this liberty.
> Loss of employment usually followed, but it was in vain that their
> employers endeavoured to starve them into submission.[30]

It was not only in their confrontation with the League that working
men began to enter public areas which had hitherto been the domain of
the property-owning and educated classes. The early years of the Chartist
movement saw the invasion of parish churches;[31] the later years of the
decade saw some attempts to penetrate the vestries, nominally open to all
parishioners, but in fact usually the preserve of men from the rank of
shopkeeper upwards. The Chartists began to assert a local working-class
presence, particularly on occasions on which the church rate was discussed. Benjamin Wilson made it clear in his reminiscences how uncom-
fortable an individual workman could feel at such meetings.[32] In 1842

the workmen used the power of numbers to boost their confidence, as they did with their taking over of anti-Corn-Law meetings. At Keighley in July the vestry met to lay the parish rate for the coming year:

> At five minutes to eleven Mr Busfield, the parish parson, attended by a group of pot-bellied landlords, two magistrates, two or three brandy-spinners, two auctioneers, a deputy constable, a number of bum bailiffs, lawyers and others to the number of thirty, entered the church. At eleven the vestry door was opened and in rushed the working men to the number of three hundred.

The meeting was adjourned to the churchyard, but was finally abandoned without a rate having been set.[33] Like the overturning of anti-Corn-Law demonstrations, this episode illustrates a victory of numbers over custom and protocol. The working man attempting to enter an area to which he had nominal rights found himself often at the mercy of the symbolic power of language which Pierre Bourdieu has anatomized.[34] The words used in the conduct of the institutions of local authority carry quite different weights according to who is using them. The problems experienced during the gradual entry of working men and then of women into these institutions illustrates the ways in which 'official language' was used as an instrument of class power. As with all the considerations of language the exact context and the status of the speaker or writer is at least as important as the actual words used.

To a large extent, the Chartists used the term 'the people' interchangeably with 'the working classes'. Thus George White, writing to Thomas Cooper in August at the height of the disturbances of that summer described one confrontation:

> My house has been surrounded with police these two nights and a warrant has been issued for my apprehension. I have nevertheless marched with the sovereign people, and addressed them in defiance of their warrant. There was some ugly work last night. My bodyguard chucked a raw lobster [policeman] into the canal and the town has been paraded by soldiers, our lads cheering and marching with them like trumps.[35]

To the Chartists, the Leaguers and to politicians in general, 'the People' in 1842 were the working class. Is it possible however, to see in the Chartist use of 'the people' a less restricted definition than that of those to whom it meant, effectively, working men? Historians in the nineteenth century tended to masculinize expressions like 'crowd' and 'movement' while the earliest labour historians tended to present 'class' as a basically masculine expression. In looking at some of the Chartist attitudes to women it may be possible to suggest that for some at least of the speakers and writers 'the people' included both sexes, and it is certainly clear that the female participation in the Chartist activities was an aspect which

surprised and shocked even some of those among the higher classes who
were sympathetic to the movement.

In his speech in support of the Chartists' right to be heard at the Bar of
the House, Duncombe found the number of women signatories to the
petition something of an embarrassment. He described them as 'the
signatures of a considerable portion of the wives of the industrious
classes'[36] and maintained that they, together with the signatures of young
people below the age of 21, demonstrated the support of the petition by
whole families. But the assumption that all the female signatories were
wives or mothers of male Chartists does not square with the admittedly
few indicators we have of the occupations of Chartist women. They seem
to have included as well as female members of Chartist families (who
were in any case often the instigators of radical ideas and activity) single
women such as servants, textile operatives, shopkeepers and innkeepers
as well as women housekeeping for other family members. Women had
been urged to join the National Charter Association from its foundation,
and their presence at all the major demonstrations at least up until the
mid-1840s is well attested. In 1842 indeed there was probably a greater
number of women actively participating in the strikes and demonstrations than at any other period. For the young John Bright, Quaker textile
manufacturer and Anti-Corn-Law Leaguer, the women's actions were
the first sign of real revolt. He wrote to his brother-in-law: 'About 2,000
women paraded the town this morning singing hymns. The men are gone
to other towns and villages to turn all the hands out. Has the revolution
commenced? It looks very probably. The authorities are powerless.'[37]
When the strikers marched into Rochdale later the same day they were
headed by 'women, eight or ten abreast singing lively songs'. However,
when Bright decided to intervene by writing a letter to the strikers, it was
to the working *men* that he addressed himself.[38] Eye witness accounts of
the summer of 1842 make the participation of women in the demonstrations very clear. In his book on the general strike of that year Mick
Jenkins gives five pages of episodes involving women, mainly from
Lancashire and the potteries.[39] The Chartist crowd, like the workforce in
the manufacturing districts included both sexes.

Benjamin Disraeli made not only the central character in his Chartist
novel a woman, but included women of the factory districts among the
most political and argumentative of the Chartists. In his novel, *Sybil* published in 1844 but based on the events of 1842, two kinds of working-
class women are portrayed: the lively, independent factory girls, ardent
Chartists, if anything more courageous than their male companions,
ready to use any weapons, including their sexual favours, to further the
cause, and the miserable, exploited women of the mining and metal-
working districts, beaten by their menfolk and exploited by grasping

employers and by tommy and badger shops. Her Chartist father speaks regretfully of Sybil's talk of taking the veil, but goes on:

> but, if I lose her, it may be for the best. For the married life of a woman of our class in the present condition of our country is a lease of woe . . . slaves, and the slaves of slaves! Even woman's spirit cannot stand against it; and it can bear up against more than we can master.[40]

Fortunately Sybil turns out to have noble blood and so is able to make a good marriage, but one of the factory girls remains single and becomes a capitalist herself rather than surrender her independence by marrying. Disraeli was an astute observer and saw many things that were missed by less politically-minded novelists who dealt with the Chartists. In spite of the active participation by women, especially in the textile districts, Chartism never had a specifically female agenda, indeed quite contradictory statements can be heard, as they were later in the century within the women's movements.

In May 1842 the publication of *First Report of the Children's Employment Commission* had a great effect on public opinion. The conditions in which women and children worked in many of the manufacturing districts provided ammunition for radical politics and for humanitarian campaigns. Many issues were involved in the attempts to regulate the labour of women and children. Working-class activists in the short time movement made no secret of the fact that they wanted a reduction of working hours for all, but it was easier to win support among middle- and upper-class philanthropists for a campaign to limit the hours of women and children. In many cases arguments for such a programme included not only a protest against the physical exploitation of the weaker members of society but arguments based on the destruction of the working-class family. Richard Oastler was in a debtors' prison in 1842, put there by his former employer largely because of his activities in opposition to the 1834 Poor Law and his campaign against child labour in the factories. He published his journal the *Fleet Papers* from prison and conducted a running argument with the League on economic matters while also carrying on his campaign for factory reform. One of his most frequent accusations was that the factory employers, by always seeking the cheapest labour, fractured traditional family patterns by employing the women and children and leaving the men to care for the house and babies. In April he published extracts from the journal of Mark Crabtree, a West Riding radical, who had just returned from a tour of the factory districts. Crabtree gave accounts of women working to support unemployed husbands or fathers. He also described the women's clubs that were growing up:

> Female clubs are composed of a certain number of females (married
> and single), generally about fifty or sixty in number, who hold their
> meetings weekly at public houses. The ostensible purpose of these
> clubs is to protect each other from want in case of sickness, a provi-
> sion also being made in case of death. These objects are laudable and
> praiseworthy; but on a nearer view of the subject, we find evils
> attached to these clubs, which more than counteract any benefit
> resulting therefrom.
>
> It may easily be imagined what will be the consequence of fifty
> women meeting together in a public house, and enjoying themselves
> in drinking, singing and smoking for two or three hours, and then
> being brought in contact with a number of men assembled in some
> other part of the house, the husbands, waiting for their wives to go
> home, and the young men through curiosity or worse intentions.
> Immediately after the breaking up of the club the women and men
> get intermixed in the tap room and other parts of the house, and then
> commences a series of discourses of the lowest, most brutal and dis-
> gusting language imaginable; and if, as is sometimes the case, the
> husbands should bethink themselves of the family at home, and urge
> the wife to depart, she will generally show signs of vexation and
> insist on having her own way in these matters. He, poor man, *well
> knowing that HIS livelihood depends on HER labour* is obliged to
> submit and quietly wait her pleasure or go to his neglected children
> alone.[41]

It is more than probable that among the women in the clubs of which
Crabtree wrote were many of the 'hen radicals' at whom the respectable
papers jeered. These were the women who were out on the streets in the
factory districts and throwing stones at the soldiers in the Calder
Valley.[42]

There was certainly very much more talk about women's rights and
the possibility of women's suffrage among the Chartists than in any other
political discourse that was around in England in that year. The idea,
moreover, was seen as a challenge to the upper classes. John La Mont
wrote in the *English Chartist Circular* that it was time:

> to suggest . . . such changes as the . . . extension of the suffrage to
> sane-minded males of 18 years of age instead of 21, already provided
> by our Charter; and the enfranchisement of females – notwithstand-
> ing the amount of blackguardism, folly and coercion which will be
> arrayed against this extension by the aristocratic *debauchés*.[43]

But in the same journal Elizabeth Neesom who, with her husband, ran a
Chartist school in London in 1842 was writing regularly against drink
and tobacco. The two voices – that of the independent working woman
and that of the woman defending the working-class family against the
factory system, the Poor Law and the drink trade can both be heard,
though too often filtered through the observations of men or through the
programmes of different reform campaigns. The arguments are not

necessarily mutually exclusive, for the women's manifestos which most clearly claimed political rights for women also complained of the 'soul and body degrading toil' to which women and their children were forced when their husbands' wages were inadequate or work was not available for men.

For many, if not most, of the Chartists 'the People' clearly did include not only men but also women and children. Among the extra-parliamentary radicals it may have had in this respect a different and wider meaning from that used by their opponents and supporters within the political system. Nevertheless the concept had clearly, in 1842, to be taken in nearly every case, to mean the working people or the working class. It was a divisive and never a unifying term.

Notes

1. J.F.C. Harrison, *The Common People* (London: Fontana, 1984) p. 282.
2. Marc Bloch, *The Historian's Craft* (Manchester, 1954) p. 57.
3. *Hansard*, vol. LXI, 3 February 1842. (Oddly, Her Majesty's speech is printed with capital letters for nearly all the nouns – a practice not followed in the reporting of Members' speeches.)
4. 1 July 1842, reported in Joseph Irving, *The Annals of Our Time from June 20, 1837–February 28, 1871*, p. 112.
5. A Member of the Cobden Club, (Ed.), *The Free Trade Speeches of the Rt. Hon. Charles Pelham Villiers M.P.*, (London: Kegan Paul French and Co. 1883) p. 322.
6. *Hansard*, vol. LX, 17 September 1841.
7. *The Times*, 24 July 1861. Cited in Jonathan Parry, *The Rise and Fall of Liberal Government in Victorian Britain* (Yale University Press, 1993) p. 209.
8. Speech at Totnes Conservative Banquet, from *The Western Luminary* 23 January 1837. Cited in James Vernon, *Politics and the People* (Cambridge University Press, 1993) p. 314.
9. *Fleet Papers* 12 March 1842 and *passim*.
10. Frederick Engels, *The Condition of the Working Class in England in 1844* (London: George Allen and Unwin, 1892 edn), p. 17.
11. Charles Brook, *Thomas Wakley*, (London: SMA, n.d.), p. 24.
12. One of No Party, *Random Recollections of the House of Commons* (London: Smith Elder and Co., 1836) pp. 252–4.
13. Joshua Holden, *A Short History of Todmorden* (Manchester University Press, 1912), pp. 163–4.
14. *The National Petition of the Industrious Classes* (Leeds, 1842). The petition is printed in *Hansard*, vol. LXV; there is a copy of the original flysheet at the Working Class Movement Library in Salford. All the quotations below are from the petition and are not separately footnoted.
15. *Hansard*, vol. LXIII, 3 May 1842.
16. Ibid.
17. Ibid.

18. Irving, *Annals of Our Time*, 5 September 1842, p. 119.
19. Lucy Brown, 'The Chartists and the Anti-Corn-Law League' in Asa Briggs (ed.), *Chartist Studies*, p. 364.
20. Norman McCord, *The Anti-Corn-Law League 1838–46* (London, Unwin 1958); Lucy Brown, in Briggs, *Chartist Studies*.
21. *The National Petition of the Industrious Classes* (Leeds, 1842). Printed in *Hansard* vol. LXV.
22. H.J. Leech (ed.), *The Public Letters of the Rt Honourable John Bright, M.P.* (London: Sampson Lowe, Marston and Rivington, 1885) p. 332.
23. *Hansard*, vol. LXV, 4 August 1842.
24. *Leeds Intelligencer*, 2 October 1841. Cited in G. Kitson Clark, 'Hunger and Politics in 1842', *Journal of Modern History*, **25**, 1953, pp. 355–74.
25. H.J. Leech (ed.), *Public Letters*, p. 336.
26. *Hansard*, vol. LXV, 17 September 1842.
27. Cited in Norman McCord, *The Anti-Corn-Law League*, pp. 115–16.
28. Ibid.
29. *Northern Star*, 6 August 1842.
30. R.G. Gammage, *History of the Chartist Movement* (London: Truslove and Hanson, 1894), pp. 216–17.
31. Eileen Yeo, 'Christianity in Chartist Struggle, 1838–42', *Past and Present* (81), May 1981, pp. 109–39.
32. Benjamin Wilson, *The Struggles of an Old Chartist* (Halifax, 1887) p. 7.
33. *The Northern Star*, 30 July 1842.
34. Pierre Bourdieu, *Language and Symbolic Power* (1st English Edition, 1992).
35. George White to Thomas Cooper, 24 August 1842. Cited in Irving, *Annals of Our Time*, p. 117.
36. *Hansard*, vol. LXIII, 3 May 1842.
37. Unpublished Correspondence, John Bright to Duncan McLaren, 12 August 1842 in Rochdale Libraries Local Studies Collection. Cited in John Cole *Conflict and Cooperation*, (Littleborough: George Kelsall, 1994) p. 32.
38. H.J. Leech (ed.), *Public Letters*, pp. 334–40.
39. Mick Jenkins, *The General Strike of 1842*, (London: Lawrence and Wishart, 1980), pp. 213–17.
40. Benjamin Disraeli, *Sybil or the Two Nations* (1844, Penguin edn, Harmondsworth, 1954, pp. 136–7 and *passim*.
41. *Fleet Papers* 9 April 1842.
42. For these events in the Calder valley see D. Thompson, *The Chartists* (London, 1984), pp. 292–5.
43. *English Chartist Circular*, **2**, (88).

CHAPTER TEN

'We Wish only to Work for Ourselves': the Chartist Land Plan

Malcolm Chase

With more than 70 000 weekly subscribers at its peak, the Chartist Land Plan ought to have attracted more attention from historians. Even those largely responsible for what might be termed the rehabilitation of its promoter, Feargus O'Connor, as a serious politician have fought shy of any close engagement with the Land Plan. Epstein's biography significantly stopped short of it, though its section on O'Connor's agrarian ideas is a notable exception in a historiographical pattern that has generally alternated between condescension and hostility. *The Chartist Experience* (1982) virtually ignored the Plan, even though this collection was consciously cast as the successor to the pioneering *Chartist Studies* of 1959. It is still to McAskill's essay in the latter that the reader requiring a broad and dispassionate treatment of the Chartist Land Plan must turn.[1]

The treatment accorded the Land Plan by historians derives directly from its contemporary reception at the hands of critics of O'Connor. R.G. Gammage's verdict that the Plan was the principal 'great folly which was to contribute to the disgrace of the Chartist movement' stuck fast.[2] The historiography of Chartism has been conditioned by a need to frame an explanation for the movement's failure; at the same time generations of historians, habituated to seeing the history of the labour movement almost as an apostolic succession, have been quick to dismiss the Chartist Land Plan as an irrelevance. Hovell's verdict that it was 'not a real Chartist scheme' is the most conspicuous example of this tendency, which has persisted long after the main tenets of his scholarship have been challenged.[3] 'Absurd and doomed to failure from the start', wrote A.L. Morton (from a very different perspective to Hovell's), 'it took up energy that might have been better spent'.[4] There has been a striking degree of unanimity across more recent historical treatments of the Land Plan. It has been dismissed as 'unquestionably reactionary', 'crack-brained', and 'harebrained'[5]; as 'utopian' and 'nostalgic' (as if these terms preclude need for further analysis[6]; and in recent influential textbooks as 'the greatest distraction of all' and 'the most ambitious deviation of all'.[7] Even recent work of substance on Chartism generally can still disappoint by the paucity of attention paid to the scheme,[8] while fuller and more sympathetic accounts have on the whole either been descriptive narratives, or preoccupied with the topography of the Chartist settlements.[9] For a more considered approach we have to look both beyond Britain and to some more neglected reaches of Chartist historiography: the cumulative portrait within Edouard Dolléans' *Le Chartisme* of 1912–13 remains the lengthiest of the Land Plan ever published, while Bachmann's *Die Agrarreform in der Chartistenbewegung* of 1928 is still the only book-length treatment of its subject.[10]

It is helpful to recount this historiography in order to appreciate how understanding the Land Plan has been impeded by a tendency to 'whig interpretation', inclined to dismiss it as a wrong turning and in extreme cases condemn it for impeding the forward march of labour. Even so, how is it that, at the heart of the earliest mass movement of industrial workers, an agrarian analysis of social problems – and an agrarian prescription for them – could exercise so persuasive an appeal?

'We seek not to be rich in this world's goods – we wish only to work for ourselves so that we may enjoy the fruit of our toil, without being subject to a tyrant master.' So wrote William Loveless to his brother George, the Tolpuddle Martyr, in December 1847, concerning his membership of the Chartist Land Plan. We are afforded this glimpse of William, anticipating 'an opportunity for a brief sojourn in this world before passing on to "a better land"', in John Harrison's *The Second Coming*.[11] An agricultural labourer, Loveless had recently joined the branch of the National Land Company (its official title at this time) in the Dorset town of Bridport. 'Mr O'Connor ... anticipates locating 30 thousand in 7 years from the commencement', he wrote to his brother: but in common with some 70 000 other members, William Loveless was not among the 234 that O'Connor had managed to settle before the National Land Company was wound up in 1851. By then the whole enterprise reeked of futility: with more efficient management the Company might have located some 300 further members within its life span, but no more. The actuary to the National Debt calculated that 115 years would have been necessary to settle the full membership. Mortgages had been miscalculated, an almost millennial plenitude of agricultural produce envisaged and thus revenue from rentals had been grossly overestimated.[12]

In its almost limitless vision and heedless enthusiasm, the Chartist Land Plan seems almost at one with the millenarian speculations of William Loveless and his contemporaries. Loveless did not however equate the Land Plan with the millennium, and neither did his contemporaries; but if there is one thing above all that the work of John Harrison teaches us, it is to listen to that which is unfamiliar. 'It is not easy for the historian to hear the voices of the people, for they have left relatively few records, and their views and opinions are drowned or crowded out by the louder and more insistent voices of the educated classes.'[13] In the case of the Land Plan, the drowning and crowding out was done not only by condescending and frequently hostile contemporaries, but also by Feargus O'Connor himself. 'Possessing lungs of brass and a voice like a trumpet', in Ramsden Balmforth's memorable phrase, O'Connor has somehow to be disentangled from those who supported the Plan.[14] The current state of Chartist historiography differs markedly from the situation even 15 years ago, in that O'Connor is now taken seriously and his words heeded instead of being dismissed as demagoguery and bluster. However, the Land Plan presents a particular problem of interpretation: here more than on any other facet of Chartism, O'Connor's personality is stamped comprehensively. It may well be that, had the term Chartism not been coined, historians would have termed the movement O'Connorite radicalism yet it is none the less possible to envisage Chartism without him. Without O'Connor, however, the Land Plan would be inconceivable.

This is not to suggest that there would have been no interest among Chartists in getting 'back to the land' without O'Connor: radical agrarianism had a long pedigree. Furthermore, from the 1820s there was a multitude of land schemes of one kind or another, part of a general proliferation of 'self-made social institutions' among British wage-earners.[15] The Land Plan has to be seen in this social context, as well as within the political context of Chartism, if it is to be properly understood. What marks it out is firstly its size, with a peak of some 70 000 weekly subscribers making payments towards shares which entitled them to a place in the regular ballots for allotments of land. Each cottage smallholding was to be one of hundreds, on estates bought on behalf of the Plan; and each was to pay an economic rent into a fund from which further estates would be purchased. The scheme's huge success, in terms of the support that it attracted, had never been anticipated. 'The number of names overcame us,' said the hapless legal clerk detailed to compile the register of shareholders.[16] The second distinguishing feature of the Land Plan is a function of its size, and of its association with Chartism and the *Northern Star* in particular. There is a wealth of information, still yet to be fully fathomed, particularly in the newspaper's weekly reports from branches, in the shareholders' register with its 20 000-odd entries,[17] and in the evidence of the Parliamentary Select Committee appointed to investigate it. Over them all resound the very substantial echoes of that voice like a trumpet, Feargus O'Connor's weekly letters in the *Northern Star*, his polemics against the Plan's detractors and his only book of substance, *A Practical Work on the Management of Small Farms*.

How far can – or should – we seek to discount the voice of O'Connor in studying the Land Plan? The relationship between the radical platform and its audience was a complex one, and to summarize it as demagoguery

is both lazy and patronizing. As historians become more critically aware
of language and communication (both verbal and non-verbal), there is an
increasing appreciation of the subtleties of platform rhetoric. It was two-
way: it reflected as much as it directed the aspirations of the audience.
The notion of audience is itself problematic: those who attended the mass
rallies and meetings at which O'Connor spoke were participants in a
drama rather than passive recipients of a message. Standing before them
clad in the fustian cloth of the manual worker, O'Connor made heavy
usage of the first person and of rhetorical questions, which are intrusive
on the printed page but which were essential elements in his success as
platform leader. 'I have brought you out of the land of Egypt, and out of
the house of bondage,' he told a meeting in the schoolhouse at
O'Connorville on Mayday 1847:

> And must I not have a cold and flinty heart if I could survey the scene
> before me without emotion? Who can look upon those mothers,
> accustomed to be dragged by the waking light of morn from those
> little babes now nestling to their breasts. (Here the speaker was so
> overcome that he was obliged to sit down, his face covered with
> large tears, and we never beheld such a scene in our life; not an eye in
> the building that did not weep.) After a pause Mr. O'Connor
> resumed: Yes, this is a portion of a great feature of my plan to give
> the fond wife back to her husband, and the innocent babe back to its
> fond mother. (Here the speaker was again compelled to pause, and
> delivered the remainder of his address sitting down.)
>   See what a different race I will make – see what a noble edifice for
> the education of your children. (Cheers.) While a sectarian govern-
> ment is endeavouring to preserve its dominion, and fostering sectar-
> ian strife, I open the sanctuary of free instruction for the unbiased
> training of youth, and woe to the firebrand parson who shall dare to
> frighten the susceptible mind of infancy by the hobgoblin of religious
> preference. (Tremendous cheering and waving of hats.) Let the
> father nourish, and the fond mother nurture, their own offspring
> (cheers) and then we shall have a generation of FREE CHRISTIANS.
> (Loud cheers.)[18]

Modern secularization still does not completely blunt the opening
biblical imagery. Yet this was more than just imagery: it cast the 'you' of
the address in the role of Israel, a chosen people against whom are contrasted, in an inversion of the establishment view of Chartism, the fire-
brand parson and a narrow sectarian government. Robust anticlericalism
of this kind was deep-seated among those who became Chartists. The
focus upon familial, especially maternal, relationships draws on other
deep-seated popular emotions, identifying factories with the reversal of
the natural order of labour and home life. It is the role of fathers to nourish (that is, provide sustaining food for), and of mothers to nurture, their
children. O'Connor made explicit on many other occasions that 'this

system of hiring women, to the rejection of men must naturally debase the character of both, by reversing their natural positions and making the husband a dependant upon the labour of his wife, while his creditable support of her and the family should constitute his greatest pride'.[19]

O'Connor's sentiments on this occasion, as on so many others, show how powerful the idea of independence was among Chartists: independence from the caprice of undemocratic government and a state church, and independence from industrialism's 'house of bondage' (which for males also involved independence in direct economic terms from women). Patrick Joyce has observed how the cluster of ideas around the notion of the cottage economy – 'ideas of independence, of what was "natural", and of what were the proper social relations between master and worker' – served mill hands and domestic workers alike as 'a powerful critique of the factory system'. Joyce rightly sees O'Connor as a particularly powerful advocate of those ideas.[20] The key to O'Connor's popular and emotive leadership of Chartism, especially in the Pennine textile districts, was his capacity to reflect back to his audiences their own perceptions of their position in society and their aspirations to improve upon it. He may have been more articulate, his delivery was certainly highly personal and theatrical (even melodramatic, but therein lies a further clue to his appeal): yet in a real sense his words were their own.[21] In effect O'Connor gave them a new voice, literally so when his weekly letters in the *Northern Star*, themselves largely dictated, were read out aloud in Chartist pubs and halls.

The Land Plan was itself a bold non-verbal statement – the most visible and powerful means of communicating the cottage economy ideal conceivable. The sheer fact of the Land Plan, its estates and O'Connor's energetic promotion of it, were the most powerful embodiment of the independence argument of all. When this was amplified through events such as 'The People's Jubilee' (the significant title of the official opening of the first Chartist estate), and by engravings showing the estates in sylvan settings after the manner of topographical views prepared for aristocratic patrons, the result was a powerful and intoxicating statement about Chartism's potential potency as an agent for change.[22] Aspects of Chartism's history that at first sight appear mildly risible, have to be understood in this context where actions could and often did speak louder than words:

> The first object that met our view, was a huge tri-coloured banner floating, high above an immense chestnut tree, bearing the inscription 'O'Connorville'; and secondly, Rebecca, the Chartist Cow, like the sacred cows of old, clothed in her vesture of tri-colour, rendered holy by the popular voice, which is the voice of God.[23]

The extensive literature generated by the Land Plan allows us to listen further to this popular voice, not necessarily only as O'Connor articulated it, though inevitably he looms large. By introducing the Land Plan into the Chartist movement O'Connor, rather than imposing upon it a maverick of his own devising, was developing aspects of the legacy of ideas which Chartism had naturally inherited from early radical policies. The institutional origins of the Chartist movement in campaigns concerning factory reform, the New Poor Law, and parliamentary reform reinforced an overall tone that was stridently anti-establishment; and that establishment, overwhelmingly, was landed. Furthermore the thrust of Chartism's economic critique was primarily against excessive wealth. This, rather than industrial capitalism *per se*, was the target, and hence the principal source of oppression was perceived as the landed aristocracy, its powers and privileges. Of course Chartism – including the Land Plan – did criticize and interrogate developments in industrial production. But Chartists' perceptions of the process of industrialization were subjective and untutored by hindsight. It was experienced as a threat to workers' independence and status, defined at the workplace by skill (a concept extending well beyond the conventionally-defined skilled trades), and in the domestic sphere by a moderately comfortable subsistence. Participation in the Chartist Land Plan seemed capable both of restoring discretion over the process of work while securing the material basis of domestic comfort through the acquisition of a cottage holding.

Chartism's criticism of excessive wealth was thus more than merely a moral critique of society, but one which embraced the roots of economic and political inequalities as well. Since the movement's inception, land redistribution had been widely seen as among the most immediate and pressing issues a democratic parliament would need to confront.[24] Correspondingly, there was a lively interest in land schemes which might achieve locally what parliamentary legislation would eventually achieve nationally. The decaying textile centre of Cirencester was probably the first Chartist locality to consider the formation of an 'Agrarian Company' in August 1840, following a call by O'Connor to establish 'Chartist Agricultural Associations – Five-Acre Associations – or Landed Labour Associations'.[25] Indeed much of the initial momentum behind the Chartist Land Plan came from key local activists, often steeped in the radical agrarian tradition of the pre-Chartist years: in Manchester James Leach; in London's East End the veteran Spencean and socialist Allen Davenport; in Cheltenham Thomas Sidaway; in Bradford James Arran, and in north Lancashire William Beesley. The advice of two such provincial figures – both of them Owenites – James Hobson of Leeds and Thomas Martin Wheeler of west London, was critical to O'Connor at the formative stage of the Land Plan, and to Wheeler should probably go the credit for the lion's share of the *Practical Work on the Management of Small Farms.*[26]

It was provincial support of this nature that largely secured approval for the Land Plan at the Birmingham Convention of 1843; but we should note too the consistency before then with which both the *Northern Star* and other Chartist newspapers covered 'The People's Question – The Land! The Land!'[27] Indeed, so strong was the interest in agrarianism among Chartists that the Land Plan can be credited with sustaining the movement as a whole during the doldrum years of the mid-1840s. It is not surprising to find O'Connor demanding 'where Chartism would be but for the Land? I may ask you where it was from 1842 to 1845, when the breath of Landism was breathed into its nostrils and gave it fresh vitality'? But the Middleton Chartist who wrote of 'The Resurrection of Chartism' spoke for many communities, as successive local studies have shown.[28] Chartism's success in mobilizing in 1848 owed much to an underlying infrastructure largely derived from the Plan which had taken-off nationally the year before. In ensuring that the 1848 Petition was borne on a wagon constructed from timber felled on the company's estates, O'Connor once again revealed his grasp of non-verbal communication.[29]

The Land Question was central to Chartism, then, politically as the fulcrum for the distribution of wealth and power in society, and organizationally as an issue that gave it renewed momentum after the frustrations of 1842. Yet this only goes part way towards understanding the function of agrarian issues in Chartism. What was the intellectual substance that lay beneath rhetoric such as, 'the accomplishment of the political and social emancipation of the enslaved and degraded working classes being the peculiar object of the Society'? Central to the Plan was a sense of a widening division in society which, with increasing momentum, was propelling it to the verge of disaster. Such a perception was, of course, far from unique to Chartism in the 1830s and 1840s: it was most obvious in Owenism, the influence of which was manifest in the literature of the Land Plan, and in Chartist thinking on land generally: 'We know of nothing but such a system of co-operative unity as is involved in home colonisation, that is capable of preserving the country from inevitable destruction. Let the people be drawn from the manufacturing districts, and located upon the land.'[30] The *Practical Work on the Management of Small Farms* drew conspicuously on contemporary Owenite and phrenological theories of the formation of human character:

> The system which I propose would at once develope [*sic*] all the virtues of our nature, while I defy the devil himself to invent one so calculated to foster and encourage all those vices to which man is

heir, as that which I labour to destroy. Never lose sight of this one
irrefutable fact, that man is born with propensities which may be
nourished into virtues, or thwarted into vices, according to his training. That system which I propose would nourish those propensities
into virtues.[31]

However, even a cursory glance at the contrasting layout of the
Chartist and Owenite communities confirms that their underlying ideologies were sharply divergent. It was the central function of the family as
the socializing force that dictated the topography of Land Plan settlements: two-, three- or four-acre individual holdings, with a cottage at the
centre of each – the diametrical opposite of the Owenite geography of
settlement, the communitarian basis of which reflected Robert Owen's
antipathy to the family, 'the main bastion of private property and the
guardian of all those qualities of individualism and self-interest to which
he was opposed'.[32] Different, too, was the place of women in the two systems: Owenism committed to equality and domestic emancipation, and
the Land Plan emphatic as to the domestic, 'natural' role of the mother.
The design of the Chartist cottages, with the kitchen the largest of the
domestic rooms, is itself eloquent on this issue – expressive of both the
traditional pattern of home life and of woman's place at its centre. For
O'Connor, and for many of his followers, the crisis of the 1840s was as
much a crisis of the family and male authority as anything else, and 'sexual difference was intimately bound up in notions of labour, property
and kin in popular radical thought'. The Land Plan can be seen as a key
part of the rolling-back of that autonomous female participation in
politics which was as notable at the beginning of the Chartist movement
as it was absent at its close.[33]

Idealization of the family and of the domestic sphere was just one
aspect, albeit crucial, of the socio-economic vision of the Chartist Land
Plan. That vision, as has already been suggested, turned on the perception of the 1840s as a period of crisis and deepening division in society.
One of the principal means through which that division was conceptual-
ized was in the dichotomy of the natural versus the artificial. This vocabulary was deeply rooted within radicalism, and agrarian radicalism in
particular.[34] It achieved its widest currency in the Chartist Land Plan, for
example in the words of the Manchester power-loom weaver
Christopher Doyle:

it was the duty of the government of the country to cause the waste
lands to be cultivated so as to give employment and food to those
who were willing to labour, but who were too often, as at the present
time, in consequence of the artificial state of the labour market,
thrown out of employment in large masses, to the great injury of
society at large.[35]

When the first Land Plan members from Preston secured their allot-ments, the local branch celebrated their being 'taken from the miseries naturally attendant upon the present artificial labour market, and placed in a position for a fair development of their capabilities of labour when applied to the cultivation of the natural resources of this country'. 'God gave you the land, and told you to cultivate it,' added O'Connor, 'and to make you labourers he made natural labour, but the devil made you arti-ficial labour. (Cheers.)'[36]

This usage of *natural* and *artificial* links the Land Plan to the long-established radical agrarian strategy of promoting labour's relative scarcity, as O'Connor crisply put it to 'thin the artificial labour market by employing thousands who are now destitute, and constituting an idle reserve to enable the capitalists to live and make fortunes upon the reduc-tion of wages'. Capitalism created an artificial market in which labour was suppressed through its inability to command an adequate, and thus *natural* wage. The connotations of the natural wage, however, extended well beyond mere adequacy. The artificial market depended on the divorce of workers from the land, whereon they would otherwise be able to secure a living through natural labour – that is labour that is indepen-dent, God-given and in community with nature. The age-old concept of the innate dignity of agricultural labour reinforced this analysis of con-temporary market conditions.

> When I see a man with his foot upon a spade, I think I recognise the image of his God, and in him that character which even the Malthusian deigns to assign him – A MAN STANDING ON HIS OWN RESOURCES ... In his own little holding he recognises the miniature of nature.

The artificial market was not simply that of factory labour: it extended to every sector of the economy where an 'idle reserve' needed to be elimi-nated before labour could command its natural wage. The standard for the latter was a decent subsistence, honestly derived from work on the land. A 'natural' wage was not, therefore, incompatible with even factory employment, and all industrial workers stood to gain if an exodus to the land were to drive up wages. This is the key to the exalted predictions made for the Land Plan: 'The capitalists who make fortunes by other men's labour shall henceforth hire that labour in the free labour market, wherein every man will have arrived at a knowledge of its full value.'[37]

Thus, in the words of Thomas Frost of Croydon, 'the Land Question resolves itself into a unity of interests among all men whether they are shareholders or not'.[38] Furthermore it was claimed that workers in the artificial market would purchase the surplus produce of the Chartist allottees, deriving improvements in the quality of provisions along with the elimination of profiteering farmers and middlemen, drawing from O'Connor the gleeful observation, 'I NEVER EXPECTED THE BLOOD-SUCKERS WOULD LIKE THE NATURAL STATE OF MAN'.[39] Yet it was precisely the isolation of the Chartist colonies from market centres, and the inability of the colonists to generate surpluses beyond their subsistence needs, that attracted contemporary ridicule; but we need to understand that the roots of the illusory fecundity of the colonies were sustained by more than simply O'Connor's rhetoric alone. 'The potentiality of material abundance', noted by John Harrison as fundamental to the Owenite case, was also central to radical agrarianism and to the Chartist Land Plan, and for the same reasons.[40] It was seen as a stinging rebuttal of Malthus; it provided grounds for an acceptance of mechanized production; and it constituted a focus for the cross-fertilization of the Land Plan with millennial expectations. Closely related to it was the assertion of the efficacy of spade husbandry, one of the few objects of complete unanimity between the three great radical figures, O'Connor, Owen and Cobbett.

The general advantages that contemporary supporters anticipated from the Plan were, therefore, the gradual demise of the artificial labour market, the restitution of a balance in the relations between the sexes and the restoration of the family as the fulcrum of social life, all these in the context of an improved standard of living. The latter, though, was defined in more than simply material terms, important though the anticipated fertility of land under smallholder cultivation was. The inevitable corollary to a view of deepening crisis in society was a degree of nostalgia: 'What was England then? A great national family, the several branches consisting of agricultural weavers and weaving agriculturalists: of producers and consumers regulating demand and supply, and living united in hand and heart in *small agricultural communities*.'[41] The specific appeal here to the memory of weaver-farmers reflects the base of O'Connor's support in the Pennine textile districts. No less significant, however, are the underlying preoccupations: the scale of society, its setting and the status of those within it. That the setting should be rural is self-evident, but this was more subtle than simple escapism. First the countryside was clearly associated with a natural society. Secondly, the view that independence and self-determination were more readily secured in a pastoral context was a pervasive one, in Britain as well as America (where, of course, it was central to Jeffersonian thinking). Thirdly, 'the grand principle of self-reliance' was a key attraction to the Plan to those whose sense of self-reliance at the workplace was rapidly being eroded not only by factory production but more generally by changes in working practices and in the scope for exercising their independent judgement. O'Connor refined this outlook in a consistent advocacy of what he termed 'the principle of individualism against that of centralisation'. 'I tell you that no other channel to secure individualism is open but the Land.' The ideas at work here need 'unpacking' carefully.[42]

It has already been pointed out that the topography of the Chartist estates diametrically opposed that of Owenite communities: this reflected not only the perceived centrality of the family as a productive and socializing force, but also Chartist suspicions of centralizing tendencies generally. The emphasis on individualism against centralization, paralleling as it did that on the natural against the artificial, can be seen as part of that abiding suspicion of forces controlling economy and society which were centralized and, therefore, unaccountable – the twin evils of state power and monopoly. O'Connor went so far as to claim that 'the present Labour system of England is one huge system of Communism'.[43] The phraseology may be inimitable, but O'Connor was reflecting a widespread perception among Chartists that the contemporary crisis was contingent upon centralizing tendencies in politics and economy. Thus the concept was extendable to urbanization, to the aggregation of labour in ever-larger units of production; to the concentration of land ownership, and to the exclusive appropriation of legislative power by the propertied. The Charter itself, which would have effectively established a system of democracy through mandated delegates (re-elected annually and thereby wholly accountable to their constituencies), embodied this perception politically, just as the Chartist Land Plan – by devolving control of production – was to have done so economically.

The inelegant and protracted demise of the Chartist Land Plan has been well rehearsed in previous studies. It has been linked to the collapse of O'Connor's personal health and finances, to his diminishing political authority after 1848 and by implication to the decline of the Chartist movement as a whole. However, Chartism was in the grip of secular political and economic trends and it is implausible to ascribe its demise directly, or even partially, to the Land Plan. The death of Chartism in 1848 has in any case been greatly exaggerated. Furthermore continued interest in the land question during the 1850s derived in part from the Plan, and from the discussion of reforms to the system of landed property which it had stimulated. Acceptance of land nationalization as a prominent part of the programme adopted by the Chartist Convention of 1851 should be seen in this context; so too should the espousal of agrarian schemes, in opposition to emigration, by Ernest Jones and his supporters at the Labour Parliament of 1853–54. At least 300 land societies, George Harrison of Nottingham claimed there, had emerged since the winding up of the Chartist Land Plan: 'around Nottingham there were half-a-dozen ... that proved that land schemes properly conducted had not

failed. (Hear, Hear)'. 'The wish to improve their condition by the possession of land is taking root in the universal heart of the working classes,'
claimed Thomas Cooper in 1850, a claim which has considerable force if
the take-off around the same time of freehold land and building societies
is borne in mind.[44]

The collapse of the Chartist Land Plan did not, then, mark the collapse
of popular interest in 'back to the land' schemes. What it did constitute,
however, was a watershed in the evolution of working-class associational
forms, the need for sound financial and actuarial management being
among the most obvious of the lessons learnt from it. The conclusion that
the Plan's chances of success were impeded by the attitude of the State
was also widespread, which led to a greater realism in framing mutual
societies either to operate within the parameters of the law or, if not seeking legal registration, to derive relative security through modest scope
and size. From the well-known figure of Thomas Martin Wheeler, once
secretary of the Land Company and subsequently manager of the Friend-
in-Need Life and Sick Assurance Society, to unheeded grass-roots leaders
such as James Maw of Middlesbrough, a founding trustee of the town's
Equitable Permanent Benefit Building Society, the active participation
of former Land Plan supporters in mutual organizations after 1850 is
striking.[45]

Where the Chartist Land Plan did mark a closure was in the demise of
popular belief in the potentiality of material abundance. It can be seen
also as ending literal acceptance of a reclaimable natural state, derived
from the paradigms of Locke and the popular enlightenment. Though the
appeal of 'back to the land' remained powerful, the Chartist Land Plan
marked the effective end of agrarian fundamentalism. On the other hand
it was part of a rapidly evolving popular culture of home-centredness, a
culture which sought in the home a compensatory sphere for diminishing
control and status at the workplace: 'the ideal of domesticity as an idyllic
ending to the melodrama of the working-class struggle', as Anna Clark
characterizes it.[46] It is not too fanciful to see in the growth of home
ownership, and in working-class home-centredness generally, a vestigial
agrarianism, no longer intent on subverting the wider economic and
social system but rather on creating spaces within that system that
would be insulated from its worst effects. For all its intentions to destroy
the artificial economy, therefore, the Chartist Land Plan cannot be
completely disaggregated from the contemporary growth of building
societies. The rhetoric of domesticity was a key element in its promotion.
Although, as we have seen, William Loveless sought 'a brief sojourn in
this world before passing on to "a better land" ', the motives of others for
joining the Land Plan may have been more mundane. On Teesside, for
example, shareholders were both younger and more likely to be sharing

the home of their parents or 'in-laws' than non-shareholders with a record of Chartist activity.[47]

In this we can detect a shift that parallels the outlook of the labour movement as a whole after 1850 as, in Edward Thompson's vivid phrase, 'the workers having failed to overthrow capitalist society proceed to warren it from end to end'. As a historical process it went back much earlier than the final defeat of Chartism, but the later 1840s marked the take-off of a wide range of workers' self-made social institutions, building societies not least among them. Ultimately the Land Plan must be seen in this context: situated on the cusp of the warrening process, melding the ethos and practical procedures of the new mutualism, along with the transcendent ambitions of both the wider Chartist movement and the agrarian tradition of which it was part. Therein lay both its uniqueness and the conditions for its downfall.[48]

Acknowledgements: I have been interested in the Land Plan for a long time, during which I have benefited from many discussions about it; but my thanks are especially due to Shirley Chase, to Jamie Bronstein, and to my special subject students on the Local and Regional History degree programme at the University of Leeds, particularly Margaret Moss and Gillian Oakley.

Notes

1. James Epstein, *The Lion of Freedom: Feargus O'Connor and the Chartist Movement, 1832–1842* (London, 1982), pp. 249–62.
2. R.G. Gammage, *The History of the Chartist Movement* (1854; London, 1969 edn), p. 269.
3. Mark Hovell, *The Chartist Movement* (Manchester, 1918), p. 32.
4. A.L. Morton, *A People's History of England* (London, 1938), p. 425.
5. John Saville, *Ernest Jones, Chartist* (London, 1952), p. 24; Morton, *People's History*, p. 424; R.K. Webb, *Modern England* (London, 1980 edn), p. 262.
6. Norman Gash, *Aristocracy and People* (London, 1979), p. 212; Harold Perkin, *Origins of Modern English Society* (London, 1969), pp. 237, 390; Malcolm Thomis, *The Town Labourer and the Industrial Revolution* (London, 1974), p. 99.
7. Edward Royle, *Chartism* (London, 1980), p. 37; E.H. Hunt, *British Labour History* (London, 1981), p. 226.
8. James Epstein and Dorothy Thompson (eds), *The Chartist Experience: Studies in Working-class Radicalism and Culture, 1830–60* (London, 1982); Dorothy Thompson, *The Chartists* (London, 1984), pp. 299–306.
9. The main estate-centred histories are: W.H.G. Armytage, *Heavens Below* (London, 1961), pp. 224–37; Peter Searby, 'Great Dodsford and the Last Days of the Chartist Land Company', *Agricultural History Review*, **16**,

(1968); A.M. Hadfield, *The Chartist Land Company* (Newton Abbot, 1970); Denis Hardy, *Alternative Communities* (London, 1979), pp. 75–105; Kate Tiller, 'Charterville and Chartist Land Company', *Oxoniensia*, 50, (1985). Important exceptions to this pattern should, however, be noted: D.J.V. Jones, *Chartism and the Chartists* (London, 1975), especially its analysis of Land Plan schareholders, pp. 134–7; John Saville's introduction to the 1969 Cass reprint of Gammage's *History*, pp. 48–62; Eileen Yeo, 'Some Practices and Problems of Chartist Democracy', in Epstein and Thompson (eds), *The Chartist Experience*, pp. 345–80.

10. Edouard Dolléans, *Le Chartisme*, 2 vols (Paris, 1912–13), vol. 2, pp. 278–301, 328–36, 348–54, 367–86; Fritz Bachmann, *Die Agrarreform in der Chartistenbewegung: eine historisch-kritische Studie uber die doktrinen des englischen Sozialismus von 1820–50* (Bern, 1928); see also Heinrich Niehuus, *Geschicte der englischen Bodenreformtheorien* (Leipzig, 1910).

11. J.F.C. Harrison, *The Second Coming: Popular Millenarianism, 1780–1850*, (London, 1979), pp. 224–5; on the Land Plan in Dorset see Roger Wells, 'Southern Chartism', *Rural History*, 2, (1), (1991), pp. 51–5.

12. Select Committee on the National Land Company, *Parliamentary Papers* (Reports from Committees) Session 1847–48 (398), XIX, evidence of Finlaison, q. 4541.

13. Harrison, *The Second Coming*, p. xiii.

14. Ramsden Balmforth, *Some Social and Political Pioneers of the Nineteenth Century* (London, 1900), p. 189; for Balmforth see below, pp. 211, 217.

15. Malcolm Chase, *'The People's Farm': English Radical Agrarianism, 1775–1840* (Oxford, 1988). The useful phrase 'self-made social institutions of British wage-earners' is J.H. Clapham's, *An Economic History of Modern Britain: The Railway Age, 1820–1850* (Cambridge, 1939).

16. S.C. National Land Company, evidence of Chinery, q. 186.

17. Provisional registration documents for the National Land Company, and lists of shareholders, BT/41/474–6, Public Record Office, Kew.

18. *Northern Star*, 8 May 1847.

19. Feargus O'Connor, *A Practical Work on the Management of Small Farms*, (London, 2nd edn, 1845), p. 19.

20. Patrick Joyce, *Visions of the People: Industrial England and the Question of Class, c. 1848–1914* (Cambridge, 1991), pp. 32–4, 97–101, quotation from p. 32.

21. For a suggestive reading of English popular politics in terms of the melodramatic forms of political imagination, see James Vernon, *Politics and the People: A Study in English Political Culture, c. 1815–1867* (Cambridge, 1993).

22. For jubilee see Malcolm Chase, 'The Concept of Jubilee in Late-eighteenth and Nineteenth-century England', *Past and Present*, 129, (1990), pp. 132–47, esp. note 31; O'Connorville: *The First Estate Purchased by the Chartist Co-operative Land Company*, British Library (Bloomsbury), Map Library, MAPS 162.S.1.

23. 'Chartist Jubilee: Grand Demonstration to the People's First Estate, "O'Connorville"', *Northern Star*, 22 August 1846.

24. *Northern Star*, 19 October 1839; *English Charter Circular* 128 (n.d. [1843]); *London Democrat*, 18 May 1839.

25. *Northern Star*, 16 May, 29 August 1840.

26. *Northern Star*, 31 October and 21 November 1840, 29 October and 5 November 1842, 30 September 1843; Allen Davenport, 'The Social Sun', *Reasoner*, **1**, (1846), p. 158; William Stevens, *A Memoir of Thomas Martin Wheeler* (London, 1862), p. 25; Thomas Frost, *Forty Years' Recollections* (London, 1880), p. 96; John Saville, 'Thomas Martin Wheeler', in J. Bellamy and J. Saville (eds), *Dictionary of Labour Biography* (London, 1986), vol. VI, pp. 266–9; Owen R. Ashton, 'Chartism in Gloucestershire: The Contribution of the Chartist Land Plan, 1843–50', *Transactions of the Bristol and Gloucestershire Archaeological Society*, **104**, (1986), p. 205. See also Allen Davenport, *The Life and Literary Pursuits of Allen Davenport: With a Further Selection of the Author's Work* (M. Chase, ed., Aldershot, 1994; first pub. 1845), pp. 45–6, 53–4, 61.

27. The title of an article by 'A Working Agriculturalist of West Suffolk', *English Charter Circular*, **128**, (n.d. [1843]).

28. *Northern Star*, 23 August 1843; G.J. Barnsby, *The Working-class Movement in the Black Country* (Wolverhampton, 1975), pp. 136–41; R.B. Pugh, 'Chartism in Somerset and Wiltshire', in Briggs (ed.), *Chartist Studies*, p. 212; J. Cannon, *Chartists in Bristol* (Bristol, 1964), p. 12; Frost, *Forty Years*, p. 96; A.J. Brown, *The Chartist Movement in Essex and Suffolk* (Colchester, 1979), p. 10–cf. 'Essex and Suffolk Land and Chartist Union', *Northern Star*, 8 April 1848; Geoffrey Crossick, *An Artisan Elite in Victorian Society: Kentish London, 1840–1880* (London, 1978), pp. 201, 203, 208; Keith Wilson, 'Chartism in Sunderland', *North East Labour History*, **16**, (1982); Malcolm Chase, 'Chartism, 1838–1858: Responses in Two Teesside Towns', *Northern History*, **24**, (1988), p. 163.

29. *Northern Star*, 11 March 1848.

30. Editorial (by Hobson?), *Northern Star*, 1 January 1842.

31. O'Connor, *Practical Work*, p. 20.

32. J.F.C. Harrison, *Robert Owen and the Owenites in Britain and America: the Quest for the New Moral World* (London, 1969), pp. 59–60.

33. Sally Alexander, 'Women, Class and Sexual Differences in the 1830s and 1840s: Some Reflections on the Writing of Feminist History', *History Workshop*, **17**, (Spring 1984), p. 136; Dorothy Thompson, 'Women and Nineteenth-century Radical Politics: A Lost Dimension', in Juliet Mitchell and Ann Oakley (eds), *The Rights and Wrongs of Women* (London, 1976), pp. 112–38. See also Anna Clark, 'The Rhetoric of Chartist Domesticity: Gender, Language and Class in the 1830s and 1840s', *Journal of British Studies*, **31**, (January 1992), pp. 62–88.

34. Chase, *People's Farm*, pp. 143–4.

35. *Northern Star*, 1 January 1848.

36. *Preston Chronicle* quoted in *Northern Star*, 18 March 1848.

37. O'Connor, *Practical Work*, pp. 40, 149.

38. *Northern Star*, 24 July 1847.

39. *Northern Star*, 30 January 1847.

40. Harrison, *Robert Owen*, p. 68. The implications of material abundance for radical thought are further explored by Noel W. Thompson, *The People's Science* (Cambridge, 1984), pp. 181 ff., and in Chase, *The People's Farm*, esp. pp. 134–43.

41. Feargus O'Connor, *'The Land', the Only Remedy for National Poverty and Impending National Ruin: How to Get it; and How to Use it* (Leeds, Labourers' Library, nos 2 and 3, 1841), p. 14.

42. 'The Land and the Charter', *The Labourer*, I, (1847), p. 81; *Northern Star*, 9 November 1844, 11 November 1848.
43. *Northern Star*, 18 November 1848.
44. *People's Paper*, 18 March 1854; *Cooper's Journal*, 17 January 1850; Malcolm Chase, 'Out of Radicalism: The Mid-Victorian Freehold Land Movement', *English Historical Review*, 106, April 1991, pp. 319–45.
45. John Saville, 'Thomas Martin Wheeler', in J. Bellamy and J. Saville (eds), *Dictionary of Labour Biography*, vol. 6 (1982), p. 268; Malcolm Chase, 'Chartism and the "Prehistory" of Middlesbrough Politics', *Bulletin of the Cleveland and Teesside Local History Society*, 55, Autumn 1988, pp. 24 and 29.
46. Clark, 'The Rhetoric of Chartist Domesticity', p. 87.
47. Chase, 'Chartism, 1838–1858: Responses in Two Teesside Towns', p. 163.
48. Edward Thompson, 'The Peculiarities of the English', *Socialist Register* (1965), pp. 310–62; revised version in *The Poverty of Theory* (1978); cf. John Saville, *1848: The British State and the Chartist Movement* (Cambridge, 1987), pp. 208–10.

CHAPTER ELEVEN

'Temperance in All Things': Vegetarianism, the Manx Press and the Alternative Agenda of Reform in the 1840s

John Belchem

In *Learning and Living*, John Harrison looked beyond extra-parliamentary agitation and 'pressure from without' to uncover an alternative framework of early-Victorian reform endeavour. Focusing on Leeds, he revealed the 'higher idealism' of the 'Truth-Seekers', middle-class reformers like Dr F.R. Lees, January Searle and James Hole who opened their minds, bodies and journals to a plethora of advanced or 'faddist' causes. These eclectic experimenters in social innovation drew inspiration from communitarianism, co-operation, associationism, transcendentalism, 'physical puritanism' and all manner of progressive creeds of individual and social betterment. However, their commitment to progress, their faith in reform as a law of nature, soon led to a concentration of energies on an essential preliminary, adult education.[1] This study is concerned with a transitional and neglected phase in this development: the attempt to project vegetarianism as the symbolic defining issue of 'compleat' reform in the 1840s and the use of the cheap Manx press to propound its virtues.

Vegetarianism appeared on the agenda of individual reform under the auspices of the temperance movement, the cause which first took advantage of Manx publication. By using Manx taxation and postal privileges, temperance reformers were able to avoid the 'taxes on knowledge', to continue the campaign for a cheap press that mainland publishers, veterans of the 'war of the unstamped', had been forced to abandon in 1836.[2] Free of stamp duty, paper duty and advertisement tax, papers published on the Isle of Man were entitled to free postage throughout mainland Britain, a privilege extended to include re-postage in 1840. Papers could thus be sent post-free to mainland agents for wider distribution through the post at no further cost.

Three broad groups of reformers took advantage of these arrangements, each looking to the medium of the cheap press to redefine the reform agenda of early-Victorian Britain.[3] The first group promoted individual behavioural reform, a project that soon extended from temperance to vegetarianism and beyond into a bewildering array of 'alternative' remedies and regimes, physical and mental. The second group, closely associated with William Shirrefs, the most entrepreneurial of the Douglas-based printers and publishers, sought to encourage the burgeoning 'new model' organizations of early-Victorian Britain. As popular politics and associational culture became more formalized, print took precedence over traditional oral and visual modes of communication.[4] The third group comprised those radicals who wished to expurgate earlier errors and excesses, to replace the transient tumult of the collective mass platform by individual commitment to rational reform. All groups benefited from Manx publication and postal privileges: through distribution of inexpensive propaganda; by the production of cheap 'in-house' journals for members in affiliated friendly societies, amalgamated trade unions and political organizations; and by the packaging of news in cheap and attractive formats to reach the individual family home. At a time of commercialization – the rise of the penny dreadful, the advent of the family magazine, and the dominance of the lurid Sunday press – the Manx press pointed towards the higher ideals of mid-Victorian Britain, providing its readership with the information and instruction to allow their personal and political development within the privacy of the home.[5]

Although the temperance reformers led the way, the first Manx-produced temperance publication, the *British Temperance Advocate and Journal*, lacked the popular touch. However, circulation improved following its re-launch in 1842 as the *National Temperance Advocate* when printing and publishing arrangements were transferred to William Robinson, then the best-equipped printer in Douglas.[6] This was the foundation for the prolific partnership between Robinson and Dr F.R. Lees, the Leeds-based editor of the *National Temperance Advocate*. Together they launched a remarkable range of Manx-produced papers, 'new age' publications specializing in 'alternative' reform. Their joint publications included: the *Teetotal Topic*; the *Long-Pledge Teetotaler*; and the *Truth-Seeker, Temperance Advocate and Mona Journal of the Water-Cure*, subsequently re-titled the *Truth-Seeker: Devoted to Free Discussion on Temperance, Hydriatism, Dietetics, Physiology, Animal and Agricultural Chemistry, Education, National and Social Economy, Mental and Moral Philosophy, Biblical Criticism, and Theology.*[7] Vegetarianism came to the forefront in 1847 when Lees, apparently considering emigration to America, sold his interest in another joint publication, the *Truth-Tester, Temperance Advocate, and Manx Healthian Journal*, to William Horsell, secretary of the newly established Vegetarian Society.[8]

The title of the journal was left unchanged, together with its commitment to 'free discussion on anatomy, physiology, dietetics, temperance, hydropathy, and other questions affecting the social, physical, intellectual and moral health of Man', but Horsell gave immediate priority to vegetarianism. As promoted in the *Truth-Tester* vegetarianism was synonymous with 'temperance in all things', the key principle of individual reform:

> Some months ago our mind was forcibly impressed with the desirableness of possessing a periodical devoted more exclusively than any at present before the public, to the important subject of TEMPERANCE IN ALL THINGS, as contributing to the physical, mental, and moral well-being of man . . . Thinking it would greatly promote our object if we could get it printed and published in the *Isle of Man*, and avail ourselves of the peculiar privilege of Free Postage enjoyed by such Manx papers as have obtained government sanction, communications were opened with Dr F.R. LEES, the late Editor of this periodical, which resulted in arrangements for transferring that paper into our hands . . . We propose to advocate TEMPERANCE in its most enlarged acceptation, including the entire abandonment of Alcoholic Drinks, Animal-Food, Tea and Coffee, Drugs, Tobacco and Snuff, and Condiments . . . While we seek to assist in the confirmation of the thousands of our Teetotalers in truths, the ABC of which they have already learnt, we aspire also to assist in leading them on to the acquisition of the whole Alphabet. Having taken their *ticket* (the pledge), and entered the *carriage* (teetotalism), we offer our service to conduct them to the *terminus* (health, happiness and long life) in safety.[9]

A recent recruit to the cause – and a pioneer jogger – Horsell had enjoyed remarkable health since his conversion to vegetarianism on reading Shelley in 1843:[10]

> since becoming a vegetarian I have never had a day's illness, and have never taken a particle of medicine . . . I am not only able to accomplish more than I ever could, but I do it with a vast increase of enjoyment; for, to me *labor is a real enjoyment*; and sometimes, in the morning, after I have taken my cold bath, I have so much elasticity and vigor, that I hardly know what to do with myself, and I have actually been obliged to run at the rate of six or seven miles an hour in order to expend the physical energy of my system.[11]

With a convert's zeal, Horsell dedicated himself to vegetarian proselytizing, regretting that this crucial issue had been ignored by Chambers and other popular educators. An indefatigable propagandist, he seemed empowered by criticism that he was ahead of his time:

> Their cry is, you go *too fast and too far* – the people are not ready for your extreme views. Perhaps not, and they never will be if left to you and to themselves. We must use all lawful and peaceful means to prepare them, the best of which are agitation and enlightenment.[12]

To spread the message – and to prevent the financial difficulties encountered by earlier vegetarian publications such as the *Healthian* and the *New Age* – Manx postal advantages were exploited to the full. A special commission scheme was introduced, encouraging 'agents' of the *Truth-Tester* to take out bulk subscriptions, 'it being understood that the parties shall receive their order in a parcel, and that we shall not incur the trouble and expense of sending single papers to the address of their subscribers'.[13] Members of the Vegetarian Society were subsequently enjoined to buy as many copies as possible 'for distribution to friends and acquaintances through the post . . . We speak in perfect freedom from all interests save those of the love of Vegetarian truths'.[14] Further to assist the requisite dissemination and instruction, considerable space was devoted to alphabet reform, phonetic shorthand and other 'practical developments of phonological science' for 'the rapid interchange of ideas among all classes'.[15] Here Isaac Pitman lent support. An early member of the Vegetarian Society, Pitman drew attention to 'the intimate connection between the low sensuality of the working-classes, and their ignorance of reading and writing':

> They would always eat flesh, when they could get it, until they were
> instructed as to the deleterious effects of such a course of life; and
> how, he would ask, were they to be instructed, if they could not
> read? . . . The introduction of a simple mode of learning to read, such
> as the Phonetic system presented, which would effect the object in
> from twenty to thirty hours, would put them in a position to under
> stand all that had been written on that important subject; and when
> they understood the matter, those of them who loved truth and
> acknowledged it as the standard of duty, and did not make them
> selves alone a law unto themselves, would become supporters of the
> Vegetarian system.[16]

In October, within a few months of taking over the journal, Horsell published a special supplementary issue to celebrate and report the establishment of the Vegetarian Society, of which he was appointed secretary.[17] Following a preliminary gathering in July at Alcott House, Ham Common (a pioneer vegetarian institution established in 1832), the first Vegetarian Conference and Festival was held on 30 September 1847 at Horsell's residence, Northwood Villa, near Ramsgate. Non-sectarian in membership and agitational in purpose, it marked an important departure in British vegetarianism. Among the most distinguished of the 150 or so founder members was Joseph Brotherton, the veteran Radical MP, whose commitment to the cause dated back to the schism within Swedenborg's Church of New Jerusalem and the formation of the Bible Christian Church with its stress on total abstinence and strict vegetarianism.

Other members of the sect, most notably the Ancoats-based minister and Chartist, the Reverend James Scholefield had sought to broaden the message by publishing cheap recipes, explaining that the Bible Christians' abstention from animal food 'is done not only in obedience to the Divine Command, but because it is an observance which, if more generally adopted, would prevent much cruelty, luxury, and disease, besides many other evils which cause misery in society'.[18] In non-denominational manner, the Vegetarian Society propounded these and other benefits through the standard mechanisms of early-Victorian agitation: lecturers were appointed to tour the country; organization was co-ordinated through a network of local secretaries; and foundation texts, such as Graham's *Science of Human Life* were reprinted in serial form as supplements to Horsell's journal which under its new title, the *Vegetarian Advocate*, provided monthly 'Vegetarian Intelligence', a record of educational, agitational and recreational activities. Aware of the advanced nature of their cause, the Society decided against insistence on a strict 'pledge': prospective members were asked simply to comply with 'a declaration of qualification, attesting abstinence *"for one month, and upwards, from the flesh of animals as food"*, and expressive of the wish (presuming it has been found good so to abstain) to join in disseminating information on its advantages'.[19]

For members of the new society, vegetarianism was much more than a programme of dietetic reform, although much of the early pamphlet propaganda consisted of simple recipes, 'the necessary information to facilitate the progress of those desirous of making an experimental essay of the good of Vegetarianism'.[20] While carrying the mission of reform into the domestic sphere, vegetarians did not question traditional gender roles. One of the most successful vegetarian pamphlets which went through several editions was specifically addressed to the working man's wife:

> The duties which devolve upon the matron of every house, however humble, are such as deeply affect not only the health, disposition, character, domestic happiness and prosperity of the household, but nationally and collectively, may be said to exercise a powerful influence over the social, religious, and even political institutions of the country.[21]

As propounded in the rarefied columns of the *Advocate*, vegetarianism embodied the higher idealism of the 'conscientious principle', the essential philosophy of individual reform:

> By Vegetarianism we do not imply a *mere* system of abstinence from eating the flesh of animals, for such a system has always been the practice of a vast majority of the human race; by Vegetarianism we mean that system which has been adopted by prophets and philosophers at different periods of the world, as calculated to increase

the freedom and consequent power of the intellectual and moral faculties . . . It is a Vegetarianism of the *mind* as well as of the *body* . . .
its tendency is to keep constantly alive the *conscientious principle*. If
a man abstain from a certain kind of food for *conscience sake*, it
reminds him every day of the connexion between his outward conduct and his inward feeling: his sense of justice, of mercy, or of
truth.[22]

In claiming this high ground of principle, vegetarians engaged in competitive bidding, seeking to outdistance other forms of 'expressive' reform.
Thus despite frequent collaboration, members of the Vegetarian Society
criticized the inadequacies of colleagues in the peace movement, not least
Joseph Sturge, acknowledged leader of the 'moral radicals'.[23] In the
words of the Chartist vegetarian Charles Neesom:

They might rest assured that their work would never be complete,
until the carnivorous passions of men were subdued by the mild and
peaceful principles of the Vegetarian system. Joseph Sturge, that
excellent champion of moral reform, had said, he held the life of a
human being so sacred, that he would not preserve his own at the
expense of that of his fellow man. He could not understand, unless
from ignorance of the Vegetarian principle, how a man of such
humane feelings could reconcile the taking life by proxy from any
sentient being, and eating parts of its mangled body, whilst the earth
abounded with a supply of all things needful for human food.[24]

Vegetarianism was the very acme of moral reform, the overarching
issue which, as Alderman Harvey of Salford evinced, embraced all other
concerns of progress and improvement:

Every Vegetarian with whom he was acquainted, was a zealous
advocate of the Peace, Temperance, Education, Sanitary, Financial,
and Parliamentary Reform Movements. The reason was, their system being deeper and wider than those, comprehended them all. He
did not know a Vegetarian who would sanction the grants for keeping up standing armies, and increasing the navy and ordnance.
(Applause.) No! The Vegetarians sought to remove the cause of war,
by taking away a principle (*sic*) incentive to the war spirit. They
sought to remove intemperance, by taking away a great cause of the
thirst for intoxicating liquors. They sought to promote education by
taking away its greatest barrier – sensual indulgence. They promoted
Sanitary Reform, by removing pig-sties, and slaughter-houses, as
well as other nuisances. They promoted Financial Reform, by adopt-
ing a true system of economy, individually and nationally; and they
would secure Parliamentary and all other good reforms, by raising
the moral and social condition of man, by the practice of that truth
which made men free. (Applause).[25]

A test issue for middle-class moral radicals, vegetarianism carried
similar symbolic significance for dissident Chartists, attesting to their
wholehearted commitment to the 'new move'. Having abandoned the

'demagogic' Chartism of the mass platform, the new movers gave priority to regimes of individual reform.[26] The veteran ultra-radical Charles Neesom, previously notorious for his advocacy of physical force, discovered a new lease of life and a new outlook on reform on conversion to vegetarianism:

> taking into consideration the favorable change which has taken place in me, physically and mentally, since my adoption of the vegetarian system, I have to regret, exceedingly, that I did not take it up in my youth rather than in my old age . . . while I go to the utmost extent in aid of every reform, whether religious, civil, political or social; yet at the same time I am well persuaded, that if reform does not commence with the individual, no legislative enactments will ever produce it (applause) . . . we should hear little about the desire to make laws restricting the hours of labor, because, if the working classes will adopt my *bill of fare*, and act upon it as I do, they will find that they would get a greater supply of necessary food in six hours' labor, than they do now in twelve or fourteen. Hence, before we ask for legislative enactments, let individuals, and all of us, use our best endeavours to aid ourselves in social improvement to the best of our abilities.[27]

Vegetarianism, then, aspired to superiority in the alternative agenda of reform. From this vaunted position, its advocates encouraged other progressive causes. Horsell retained his enthusiasm for hydropathy and used the columns of his vegetarian journals to publicize services on offer at Northwood Villa. While his wife continued to run a 'family school' for children's 'moral, intellectual and physical improvement',[28] Horsell converted the rest of the premises to accommodate the Ramsgate Hydropathic Infirmary. The antithesis of aristocratic mineral spas like Bath, hydropathic establishments offered a return to the simple God-given laws of nature, a regime which appealed to the sensibilities and principles of moral radicals or 'anti-everythingarians'. To complement the water cure, hydropathic doctors insisted on total abstinence, simplicity in clothing and avoidance of undue stimulation at balls or the theatre.[29] However, as Horsell discovered, the provision of hydropathic facilities was an expensive business. Northwood Villa seemed an ideal location, convenient for the railway station while enjoying a 'beautiful, retired, airy and healthy situation, with an extensive view of the sea'. Horsell soon spent the £100 allocated to him on pumps, baths and tanks; thereafter, he had to rely on his own resources for the erection of a steam-engine and construction work to deepen and increase the capacity of the well. Regretting their 'inexperience', the Committee of the Ramsgate Hydropathic Infirmary issued an urgent appeal for funds:

> they very much underrated the necessary outlay, which deficiency having been supplied by William Horsell, at the greatest incon-

venience to himself, they feel themselves bound to make an effort to
reimburse him, particularly as the unforeseen and extraordinarily
high price of provisions has necessarily operated most seriously to
his disadvantage.[30]

Unfortunately, these financial difficulties at Northwood Villa coincided
with the first steps to remove Manx postal and publishing privileges.

What prompted the authorities to plug the Manx loophole, however,
was not the vegetarian and temperance press but the radical outpourings
of Shirrefs and Russell, 'a sad jumble of bye-gone chartism, heathenism,
atrocious socialism, and abominable vandalism'.[31] Shirrefs's steam press
was the first to exploit the new market for 'in-house' associational
journals, launching the *Odd-Fellows Chronicle* in October 1844. Encouraged by its success, he began a more ambitious venture, the *People's
Press, and Monthly Historical Newspaper*, a 32-page journal offering
'first class healthy Intellectual Recreation, Amusement and Instruction,
at a price unprecedentedly low, and within the easy reach of the industrious classes'. Readers were informed of the progress of improvement
through 'practical philanthropy', the work of 'Public Health
Associations, Dwellings for the Working Classes, Model Lodging
Houses, Model Villages, Model Farms, Irish Amelioration Societies,
Sewage Companies, Dormitories, Baths and Wash-houses, Literary
Institutes, Ragged Schools, and other Ameliorative, Reforming and
Regenerative Establishments'.[32] At the same time, the paper ventured
beyond the conventional curriculum of popular education and improve-
ment, as Shirrefs, unrestrained by the no-politics rule of the Oddfellows,
displayed his Chartist sympathies.

A stern critic of the futility of mass platform agitation, Shirrefs looked
forward to a new kind of movement, a radical party of principle and
commitment, of self-sacrifice and self-respect: 'Show you are worthy of
political rights, by sacrificing something to obtain them; and fit your-
selves for the day which, be it near or far, will surely come.'[33] He was
joined in this mission by an array of talented contributors, several of
whom – George Jacob Holyoake, Goodwyn Barmby, Dr Bowring and
others – were members of the People's Charter Union, a group of
advanced moral-force reformers first brought together in the People's
International League to propound Mazzini's ideas and principles.[34]

Having attracted a talented team of contributors, Shirrefs then offered
them the use of his Manx facilities for their own publications. Thus, in
August 1848, the first 'communist' journal, the Barmbys' *Apostle and
Chronicle of the Communist Church*, was printed by Shirrefs and Russell
at the Manx Steam Press, Douglas, 'published gratuitously, from the pro-
ceeds of the Propaganda Fund of the Communist Church'. Catherine
Barmby looked to the principles of the Church, 'communism of goods as

a religious duty – common property as a political right', to secure 'Woman's Industrial Independence'.[35] Holyoake and Linton arranged for Shirrefs to print and distribute their *Cause of the People*, a high-minded Mazzinian journal informed by the 'inward conscience of the Universal Duty of the Suffrage'. Amid the excitement of revolution in Europe, they looked to elevate radicalism by removing 'hindrances to the progress of our cause, all these hindrances, which have made Chartism hitherto an AGITATION rather than a MOVEMENT'.[36] Furthermore, Shirrefs undertook a number of external commissions in 1848, including the *Labour League*, the journal by which the National Association of United Trades intended to co-ordinate all trades' endeavour to offer 'a complete and effectual plan of individual, associative and legislative agitation'.[37]

Shirrefs's success was in marked contrast to the sad fate of Bronterre O'Brien, ideologue of the radical unstamped and the 'schoolmaster of Chartism', whose estate in the Isle of Man was wound up in May 1848.[38] A disaffected activist, O'Brien had left London for Douglas in 1844, seeking to use the publishing and postal privileges to challenge the 'demagogue-tyranny' of both Feargus O'Connor and Daniel O'Connell. Committed to 'national reform' through land nationalization, efficient currency, public credit and equitable exchange, O'Brien was a vituperative critic of anything less. This was poor business sense for a radical printer and publisher. By condemning the 'palliatives' pursued by trade unions, benefit societies and other organized forms of working-class collective mutuality, he denied himself the regular business and solid support that Shirrefs was able to attract. Out of step with changes in working-class collective behaviour, O'Brien was finally forced to abandon his *National Reformer and Manx Weekly Review of Home and Foreign Affairs* in May 1847 after 110 weekly issues.[39]

Shirrefs, by contrast, continued to prosper and expand. Profits from his multifarious journals and other commissions were ploughed into an impressive local weekly newspaper, the *Isle of Man Times*. In championing the cause of domestic reform, the paper displayed considerable impatience for mainland 'improvement': 'Here we are in the Isle of Man, within sight of the shores in Britain, governed by institutions dissimilar in every respect, and ages behind those of the countries by which we are surrounded.'[40] To effect the necessary changes, the *Isle of Man Times* advocated a controversial course: 'Union with England, free Municipal Institutions in the Isle of Man, coupled with the continuance of our present Fiscal privileges.'[41] This was not a prescription to please the Manx establishment. Furthermore, there was much spite and envy on the island at the success of the upstart *Isle of Man Times*. Peter Curphey, one of the main Douglas printers, sought to silence Shirrefs by exposing his 'fraudulent' abuse of Manx privileges, accusing him of 'defrauding with *malice prepense* Her Majesty's Exchequer, independent of grossly inter-fering with the honest exertions of our over-taxed British brethren by dint of frontless trick and cheatery'.[42]

Other interests soon became involved in the controversy. The *Athenaeum* complained of the abuse of postal privilege in the Isle of Man and the Channel Islands:

> For instance, a London speculator sets up his printing-presses in one of these Islands; and, by availing himself of the rapid communication now open with the capital, is enabled to flood the country with his second-hand article at a price – seeing that he filches the matter, is called upon for no advertising duty, and has all his carriage done for nothing in the post-office – with which the legitimate journalists can-not compete.[43]

The government soon decided to legislate against such 'literary-smug-gling'. On 4 September 1848 an Act was passed granting the Postmaster-General *discretionary* powers to charge newspapers published in the Channel Islands and the Isle of Man with 'Rates or Duties of Postage, not exceeding the Rates to which such Newspapers would be liable if they were Letters'.[44]

Rather than run the risk of expensive postage, most organizations who used Manx facilities made prompt arrangements for mainland publica-tion.[45] Horsell, however, delayed the transfer, hoping that the govern-ment might first be persuaded to introduce a compromise proposal, a special halfpenny stamp for 'small newspapers':

> No one can now complain of the penny stamp on newspapers which sell at 4d., 5d., or 6d. each; it is but a fair return for the privilege of a free postage: but when a small periodical . . . selling at from 1d. to 2d. each, become liable to the same charge for postage . . . it becomes a heavy tax on private effort, as well as on these valuable means of improving the condition of the people.[46]

Pending the introduction of such a stamp, the *Vegetarian Advocate* con-tinued to be printed and published in Douglas, risking the continuance of discretionary free postage. In April 1849, however, the Post Office sud-denly issued an order for postage at the full 4d letter rate. After lobbying this was reduced to 1d for 'old-established and properly so-called local papers' – papers in the Manx language were still to enjoy free postage[47] – but by this time Horsell had decided to follow the example of the temper-ance press and transfer to mainland printing and publication.[48]

Free postage was forfeited but otherwise the transfer to London from 'a distant Island' allowed an expansion of activities, most notably a new central office and the establishment under Horsell's management of 'a depôt for the sale of Vegetarian Publications' at Aldine Chambers,

Paternoster Row.[49] Andrew Russell, Shirrefs's former business partner, moved across from Douglas to print the *Advocate* until April 1850 when Horsell took personal charge of printing and publishing. However, he no longer had the field to himself. Eschewing any suggestion of competition or rivalry, the *Vegetarian Messenger*, a new journal published by Fred Pitman, defined its purpose as preparatory and complementary:

> As we aim more at completeness in the information we convey, than at variety of articles, we shall sometimes devote a whole number to a single report or essay, so that it will, in fact, frequently constitute a very cheap edition of what would, under other circumstances, be published only in an expensive form; and thus the *Vegetarian Advocate* remains the medium of information, more particularly to Vegetarians, such as condensed accounts of meetings and transactions of the Vegetarian Society, the *Vegetarian Messenger* will be adapted to, and largely distributed among, the members of the various religious and philanthropic societies, and those friends to whom Vegetarians may desire to impart a knowledge of their system.[50]

As it was, however, the *Advocate* seems to have ceased publication at the end of the second volume in August 1850, despite announcing plans for a new fortnightly format.[51] The *Messenger* duly became 'the organ of the society'.[52]

Horsell turned to pamphlet-writing, providing vegetarians with a vade-mecum to answer all possible queries and objections, even from sceptical Malthusians:

> We do not husband our resources. Adopt the Vegetarian System at once, and we shall not only vastly improve in health, strength, sobriety, intellectuality, and morality; but we shall have 'bread enough and to spare', even with ten times the amount of our present population. But this is not all; vegetarianism augments the comforts of its votaries, by increasing their means of subsistence: while it produces thoughtfulness and providence in the management of their own affairs, and a feeling of humanity towards others. There will be less *selfishness*, extravagance and competitiveness, which will prevent reckless marriages, and thus put *natural* checks upon the excessive increase of population.[53]

At the same time he moved premises and broadened his stock from pamphlets, journals and books to cater for the expanding demand for vegetarian products. Members could purchase special cocoa – available in homoeopathic, vegetarian and dietetic forms – and his patent flour and wheat meal from his Homoeopathic Pharmacy and Vegetarian Depot at 492 Oxford Street, where he also operated a 'phrenological museum'.[54]

For vegetarians and other truth-seekers, learning and living took place within a counter-culture of expressive endeavour. In facilitating and servicing the cultural agenda of alternative reform, however, Victorian enterprise was no less important than higher idealism. As the promoter of vegetarianism, Horsell exemplified the requisite resourcefulness through his exploitation of offshore fiscal advantages and his subsequent niche-marketing of alternative or ethical products.

Notes

1. J.F.C. Harrison, *Learning and Living 1790–1960: a study in the history of the adult education movement* (London, 1961), pp. 118–51.
2. On the 'unstamped', see the two splendid studies, P. Hollis, *The Pauper Press. A Study in Working-Class Radicalism of the 1830s* (Oxford, 1970); and Joel Wiener, *The War of the Unstamped. The Movement to Repeal the British Newspaper Tax, 1830–1836* (Ithaca, 1969).
3. John Belchem, 'The Neglected "Unstamped": The Manx Pauper Press of the 1840s', *Albion*, **24**, (1992), pp. 605–16.
4. John Belchem, 'Radical Entrepreneur: William Shirrefs and the Manx free press of the 1840s', *Proceedings of the Isle of Man Natural History and Antiquarian Society*, **x**, (1992), pp. 33–47.
5. Raymond Williams, *The Long Revolution* (London, 1965), pp. 72–4; R.D. Altick, *The English Common Reader. A Social History of the Mass Reading Public 1800–1900* (Chicago, 1957), pp. 332–9; and James Vernon, *Politics and the People* (Cambridge, 1993), ch. 3.
6. Brian Harrison, ' "A world of which we had no conception." Liberalism and the English Temperance Press, 1830–1872', *Victorian Studies*, **13**, (1969), pp. 135–6.
7. Robinson was also associated with James Hole and the Leeds Redemption Society for whom he printed and published the *Herald of Redemption* (1847–48).
8. William Horsell, *The Science of Cooking Vegetarian Food; and also, the Rise and Progress of the Vegetarian Society* (London, 1856), p. 87.
9. 'Future Objects and Designs', *Truth-Tester*, new series, **i**, (1847).
10. William Horsell, *The Science of Cooking Vegetarian Food*, p. 87.
11. 'Report of the First Annual Meeting of the Vegetarian Society', *Vegetarian Advocate*, **i**, (1848–49), p. 14.
12. 'Too Fast and Too Far', *Truth-Tester*, new series, **i**, (1847), p. 113.
13. 'Important', *Truth-Tester*, 15 December 1846.
14. 'Progress of the Movement: General Remarks', *Vegetarian Advocate*, 15 December 1848.
15. See, for example, the report of the South London Phonetic Society, *Truth-Tester*, new series, **i**, (1847), p. 124.
16. 'Second Annual Meeting of the Vegetarian Society', *Vegetarian Messenger*, **i**, (1849–50), p. 11. Pitman was one of the vice-presidents at the Society's banquet at Manchester Town Hall, 12 July 1849.
17. 'Supplement', *Truth-Tester*, 22 October 1847. James Simpson was appointed president and William Oldham treasurer.
18. Reverend J. Scholefield, *The System of Vegetable Cookery, as used by the Society of Bible Christians* (Manchester, 1839), p. xiv.
19. See Horsell's annual reports as secretary of the Vegetarian Society, 1848–50, in *Vegetarian Advocate*, **i**, (1848–49), pp. 5–6, and *Vegetarian*

Messenger, i, (1849–50), pp. 4–15, 135. The first issue of the *Vegetarian Advocate* ('Late Truth-Tester') was published in Douglas on 18 August 1848, 2d. post-free.

20.   A Vegetarian (pseud.), *To the Members of the Vegetarian Society* (Great Malvern, 1847).
21.   *The Penny Vegetarian Cookery: or Vegetarianism Adapted to the Working Classes*, 4th edn, (London, n.d.), p.2.
22.   'Vegetarianism and Education', *Vegetarian Advocate*, 15 February 1849.
23.   For Sturge and the peace movement, see Alex Tyrrell, *Joseph Sturge and the Moral Radical Party in Early Victorian Britain* (London, 1987).
24.   See Neesom's speech, 'Second Annual Meeting of the Vegetarian Society', *Vegetarian Messenger*, i, (1849–50), p. 14.
25.   'Vegetarian Soiree at Worcester', *Vegetarian Messenger*, i, (1849–50, p. 126.
26.   This is to suggest the need to examine aspects of the 'new move' beyond Brian Harrison's study of 'Teetotal Chartism', *History*, lviii, (1973), pp. 193–217.
27.   'Report of the First Annual Meeting of the Vegetarian Society', *Vegetarian Advocate*, i (1848–49), p. 16.
28.   See, for example, the advertisement in *Truth-Tester*, 15 November 1847.
29.   Tyrrell, *Joseph Sturge*, pp. 184–5.
30.   'Report of the Ramsgate Hydropathic Infirmary', *Truth-Tester*, 15 January 1848.
31.   'The Deformed Transformed', *Manx Liberal*, 5 May 1849. For Shirrefs, see Belchem, 'Radical Entrepreneur'.
32.   *People's Press*, (27), December 1848.
33.   'Topics of the Month' and 'The Tenth of April', *People's Press*, (19), June 1848.
34.   The most successful of the moderate Chartist groups of 1848, the People's Charter Union was to transform itself into a pressure group lobbying for the repeal of the newspaper duties, see C.D. Collet, *A History of the Taxes on Knowledge* (London, 1933), ch. 5.
35.   'Woman's Industrial Independence', *Apostle and Chronicle of the Communist Church*, August 1848. For details of the Barmbys and their 'Church', see Barbara Taylor, *Eve and the New Jerusalem: Socialism and Feminism in the Nineteenth Century* (London, 1983), pp. 172–82. Vegetarians, by contrast, did not question traditional gender roles.
36.   *Cause of the People*, 24 June 1848, quoted in F.B. Smith, *Radical Artisan. William James Linton 1812–97* (Manchester, 1973), p. 80.
37.   *Labour League*, 2 December 1848. See also John Belchem, 'Chartism and the Trades, 1848–1850', *English Historical Review*, 93, (1983), pp. 562–9.
38.   A. Plummer, *Bronterre. A Political Biography of Bronterre O'Brien 1804–1864* (London, 1971), pp. 177–9, contains little information about O'Brien in Douglas: it is a topic that deserves extensive treatment.
39.   I have been unable to locate the first series, nos 1–75 (November 1844–April 1846). This is surely one of the most important radical papers to have gone missing.
40.   *Isle of Man Times*, 20 February 1847.
41.   *Isle of Man Times*, 5 June 1847.
42.   *Isle of Man Times*, 29 January 1848. Relations between Shirrefs and Curphey deteriorated rapidly following 'A Row with the Local Press', *Isle of Man Times*, 16 October 1847.

43. 'Our Weekly Gossip', *Athenaeum*, 15 January 1848.
44. *An Act for rendering certain Newspapers published in the Channel Islands and the Isle of Man liable to Postage*, 11 and 12 Vict., Cap. cxvii.
45. See, for example, *Temperance Gazette*, October 1848.
46. See the editorials in *Vegetarian Advocate*, 15 December 1848 and 15 April 1849.
47. *Manx Liberal*, 9 June 1849.
48. See the notices 'To Our Subscribers', *Vegetarian Advocate*, 1 June and 1 July 1849. London publication began on 1 August 1849.
49. 'Introduction', *Vegetarian Advocate*, 1 September 1849.
50. 'Introduction', *Vegetarian Messenger*, i, (1849–50).
51. 'To Our Readers and Subscribers', *Vegetarian Advocate*, 1 August 1850.
52. Horsell, *Science of Cooking Vegetarian Food*, p. 87.
53. William Horsell, *The Vegetarian Armed at All Points: In Which the Theory is Explained; the Chief Arguments Advanced; and the Principal Objections Answered* (London, 1852), pp. 32–3.
54. See the innumerable advertisements for his wares in Horsell, *Science of Cooking Vegetarian Food*.

CHAPTER TWELVE

Will the Real Mary Lovett Please Stand Up?: Chartism, gender and autobiography

Eileen Janes Yeo

In *Learning and Living*, J.F.C. Harrison places William Lovett among the 'famous names of self-educated working-class leaders'.[1] Lovett partly secured his own niche in the radical hall of fame by publishing an auto-biography in 1876 with the splendid title, *The Life and Struggles of William Lovett in His Pursuit of Bread, Knowledge and Freedom*, a source which has shaped the views of generations of historians.[2] For 49 years, William was married to Mary. In his autobiography, he called his wife 'my second self; always my best adviser and truest friend'.[3] The first edition of his *Life*, including appendices, contains 473 pages. Guess how many pages were devoted to Mary? Roughly, six. I am not trying to score cheap points at William Lovett's expense, particularly since he says more about Mary than most radical men say about their wives. Rather I want to probe how and why Chartist sources, even the apparently subjective and intimate autobiographies, systematically conceal women.

To make the probe, I will have to go a circuitous way around and explore the difficult situation both of Chartist men and women in public territory. Few Chartist letters remain, so historians work largely with printed sources which Chartists produced deliberately for public con-sumption and therefore as part of the huge struggle they were waging over public space, public assembly and public speech whether oral or written. Although written later, Chartist autobiographies can usefully be seen as a continuing part of this working-class contestation of the public sphere. But precisely because they were written later, they sit in a com-plex relationship with bourgeois attempts to create a public domain for men in binary opposition to a private sphere which was women's place. A working-class challenge for the bourgeois public realm could go hand in hand with an increasing acceptance of the bourgeois division between separate spheres. This ambiguity started in the Chartist years and contin-ued during the mid-century when the ideology of separate spheres became so dominant that it constituted cross-class common sense and helped to structure working-class autobiography.

Telling a life story is never only a personal affair. Autobiography involves the interplay between personal experience of social processes and the cultural conventions for understanding and communicating it. Far from being individual and idiosyncratic, autobiography usually draws on shared conventions of cultural narrative whether the conventions are already available, actively being created, or being borrowed and adapted by new groups for new purposes.[4] Chartists writing autobiography commandeered genres which were dominated by other classes and tried to put them to new uses. But all cultural narratives involve selection, which means prioritization of some themes and elimination of others, inclusion of some kinds of episodes and exclusion of others. Unfortunately women are the gaping hole, the missing presence in terms of writing autobiographies or appearing in them. Vincent, in his study of working-class autobiography, ascribes their silence to a lack of self-confidence and their increasing exclusion from most forms of working-class organization which would train and stimulate them to self-expression.[5] I would like to take the argument further and explore the cultural politics which impelled robust men and energetic women into public speech and into public silence. Using the Lovetts as an epitome, I will start by exploring the problems of Chartist men with public space and public speech and analyse Lovett's autobiography in this connection. Next I will spotlight the even more acute problems for working-class women in the public arena. Finally I will return to Lovett's autobiography and try to breathe some life into the few remains or mentions of Mary to see what she can reveal about the silent majority of Chartist wives.

Chartist men, and public space: a site of struggle

The Chartists waged a wide-ranging class struggle over public representation in at least two senses. They fought both for political representation in the narrow electoral sense and for self-representation, that is the direct and unmediated articulation of their views and demands. At a time when political rights and powers rested on a property qualification and when the doctrine of virtual representation enabled the enfranchised minority to act for the excluded majority, a situation which lasted largely until 1918, the Chartists claimed direct citizenship on the basis of (male) humanity. As Tom Paine had put it, in words repeated on Chartist banners, 'Every man has a right to one vote in the choice of his representatives, and it belongs to him in the right of his existence, and his person is his title deed.'[6] The Chartists appropriated the dominant Constitutional rhetoric and defined themselves as the People, both 'the source of political authority' and 'the Voice of God'. After the victory of Parliament in the seventeenth-century revolution, the People had become the key political and rhetorical category and the contest shifted away from the Crown versus the People to a conflict over who should be included within the People and who left out. By May 1839, a separation which had begun in 1832 became divorced when Chartists expelled the middle classes from the People and reserved that designation for the 'working', 'industrious', 'productive' or 'useful' classes and their friends.[7] The Chartists redefined their class enemies as 'vulture tribes', 'the factions' and even 'the rebels', devaluing them as parasitic, divisive and destructive.[8]

Chartist activity can usefully be seen as a drama of self-representation. Chartists both acted out their political role as the People and previewed the kind of public sphere they wished to create. The term 'public' has many meanings but for the Chartists two of the most important designated what the People did and the visibility of what they did. The Chartists named their political forms and functions accordingly. They did not hold the mass demonstrations that historians write about but instead called 'public meetings' where true 'public opinion' could be articulated by the People assembled together openly in public.[9] They held county hustings modelled on parliamentary elections where they voted for delegates to the General Convention of the Industrious Classes sometimes called the 'People's Parliament' in contradistinction to the 'Imperial Parliament'. How far the Chartists had moved public politics, both in terms of working-class visibility and their appropriation of the concept of the People, can be seen in two episodes involving the Anglican Church. In the eighteenth century, the discontented poor would have come secretly in the dead of night to nail an anonymous list of grievances to the door of the parish church and in this way recall the wealthy to their duty within a moral economy. By contrast, in August 1839, the Chartists staged highly visible demonstrations by cramming the parish church during Sunday worship, after proclaiming that 'the parish church is our own; and we will for the last time go to hear the parson, before the people take possession of their own public property'.[10] The 'manly' willingness to stand up publicly for what you believed and be prepared to take the consequences formed an important part of Chartist masculinity.

The consequences were often harsh. The ruling classes regarded Chartist claims to be the People as presumptuous and preposterous. A kind of political schizophrenia developed over the right to occupy public space and exercise public speech. In many places, magistrates posted placards denouncing Chartist public meetings as 'illegal meetings': they labelled the Chartist People as the mob and treated Chartist public speech as sedition.[11] The Bull Ring Riots in Birmingham in July 1839 were one of the earliest episodes of confrontation which had national resonance and which involved William Lovett. For safety's sake, the convention had moved to Birmingham. None the less the magistrates, who had defended the right to public assembly in the Bull Ring in 1832 and who had supported Chartism only a few months before, now outlawed Chartist meetings. They imported London police whose brutal behaviour succeeded only in provoking full-blown riots. Lovett, the Secretary of the General Convention, was arrested on a charge of seditious libel for writing protest resolutions, the first of which read:

> A wanton, flagrant, and unjust outrage has been made upon the people of Birmingham by a blood thirsty and unconstitutional force from London, acting under the authority of men who, when out of office, sanctioned and took part in the meetings of the people; and now when they share in public plunder, seek to keep the people in social slavery and political degradation.[12]

After his trial, at which he conducted his own defence by invoking 'the right of public meeting' and denouncing 'the attack upon the people', Lovett went to prison for a year. Again showing the incompatibility of views from above and below, Lovett continually protested that he was a political prisoner but was being treated like a common criminal. Even when first arrested, he petitioned the House of Commons to protest at being subjected to indignities like having 'a common felon' cut his hair.

Lovett fearlessly asserted his identity as one of the People. He never flinched from public assertiveness whatever the price. His autobiography is filled with the 'Public Addresses' he wrote or endorsed while active in a succession of movements and associations. His sense of the public space where he, a London cabinet-maker could legitimately speak, extended worldwide. The London Working Men's Association, which introduced 'the mode of *international addresses* between the *working men* of different countries', to give just two examples, sent one 'Address to the Canadian People' in 1837 starting, 'Friends in the cause of freedom, brothers under oppression, and fellow-citizens living in hope' and another 'Address to the Working Classes of Europe, and especially to the Polish People' (1838) which opened with the salutation, 'Brethren'.[13]

Lovett knew that the ruling classes would not allow this assertion of citizenship into their version of reality or history. He later wrote his autobiography partly to inspire young men to carry on the public political struggle for inclusion, since he regarded the 1867 franchise reform 'as but partial, compared to what it ought to be'.[14] He also wrote his life story in a way which would provide a people's history and safeguard and introduce into the public record the documents often concealed by official eyes:

> Little is found in history, or in our public papers, that presents a fair and accurate account of the public proceedings of the Working Classes: for if the Whig and Tory papers of the day ever condescend

to notice them, it is rather to garble and distort facts, to magnify faults and follies, and to ridicule their objects and intentions ... In consequence of this unjust system the historians and writers of a future day will have only garbled tables to guide them ... and hence a caricature is oftener given of the industrious millions than a truthful portrait.[15]

Yet in telling his own life story, Lovett distorted the 'truthful' picture because of the conventions of political autobiography. His autobiography seems to contain several books. In the first chapter, before he became active in the public political world of radical associations, the book is full of women. Discussion of childhood allows family and women to come into focus even in political autobiography. Indeed Lovett was raised in Cornwall entirely by women. His father drowned before he was born and his mother, Kezia worked hard to support both William and his grandmother. For some time, William went to live with his great-grandmother, aged around 80, who taught him to read. His mother came to visit them once a week. When his energy proved too much for the elderly woman, he went to live with his grandmother's sister. After his mother remarried, to a miner whom neither he nor his grandmother liked, William set up house with his grandmother.

But as soon as William left Cornwall for London and more especially once he became involved with the co-operative movement and the fight against the taxes on knowledge, the book virtually shifts gear. Apart from the few pages about Mary to which I will return, the rest concerns, to borrow the title of Lord Snell's later autobiography, *Men, Movements and Myself*.[16] Lovett told his story within the organizing convention that there was a public sphere of associational life for men and a private world of the family where women and children lived.[17] The private world of the adult did not qualify as the subject of autobiography. The distinction between the public and private spheres was being codified in a particular way in this period by the middle class. Working-class radicals, urgently trying to establish their public place, adopted some of the same conventions.

Working-class women and public space: moving with caution in a dangerous zone

If public space was problematic for working men, it was ten times more treacherous for working-class women. In this period, a 'public woman' meant, simply, a prostitute. At this time, middle-class people, who were defining their class identity in terms of sharply divided roles for men and women, were aggressively trying to impose these models on working-class people as well. The middle class argued that their superiority rested on the sober Christian responsibility of their men who not only pursued an occupation in the public world of business or politics but who protected their weaker dependents including women, children, servants and even employees. The role of middle-class women was to preside in the domestic realm of family and home, the abode of peace and love, while men went into the abrasive public sphere full of competition and conflict.[18]

The evangelical party in the Anglican Church powerfully articulated the view that women and men had different human natures and separate spheres of social life. By 1840 evangelicals had come to dominate the State Church in many urban areas, and evangelical beliefs also pervaded most other bourgeois Protestant groups. How strongly the religious groups pressurized working-class women to adopt bourgeois ideals of femininity was illustrated by the encounter between the Reverend Francis Close and the Chartist women who demonstrated in his church on 12 September 1839. Reverend Close, nicknamed 'the Pope of Cheltenham', had great social power in his town: he stopped the railways from running on Sundays and got the horse races closed down. He also became a notorious class warrior hounding working-class radicals of any stripe: it was he who brought a blasphemy prosecution against socialist missionary George Jacob Holyoake.

Confronted with the women Chartists in his church, Reverend Close preached them a theological riot act. He told them that God had cursed women threefold because Eve had tempted Adam. First women had a body and nerves which felt pain more sharply, second they suffered pain in childbirth and third they had to endure being ruled by their husbands.[19] This situation lasted until God chose Mary to give birth to Jesus which changed everything and enabled women to return to their former paradisical level. If women had been forced to be obedient to their husbands before, they could now cheerfully volunteer to be obedient to their husbands!

> The centre of all your virtues, and the fountain of all your influence in society, is your home – your own fireside – it is amongst your children, it is in the bosom of your family, and in that little circle of friends with whom you are more immediately connected that your legitimate influence must be exercised; there you are born to shine. ... Be the pious mother; be the obedient wife; yield that voluntary and cheerful submission to the wishes of your Husband, which was extorted from you, till Christ removed the curse![20]

Women who strayed beyond the magic domestic circle not only unsexed but dehumanized themselves. They made themselves foreign in the dual sense that they become diabolical as well as unEnglish: Close depicted them as satanic witches and vampires like the 'women of Republican France' who 'became more ferocious fiends than even the men themselves; plunged more deeply into crime, glutted themselves with blood, and danced like maniacs amidst the most fearful scenes of the Reign of Terror!'[21] If the Chartist women had not quite understood his meaning, Reverend Close stressed that it was bad enough for women to support the radical politics of their male kin but

> now, alas! in these evil days – these foreign days on British soil, not content with this, women now become politicians, they leave the distaff and the spindle to listen to the teachers of sedition; they forsake their fire-side and home duties for political meetings, they neglect honest industry to read the factious newspapers! and so destitute are they of all sense of female decorum, of female modesty and diffidence, that they become themselves political agitators – female dictators – female mobs – female Chartists![22]

Not only did this kind of barrage come from above, but some working men did not feel happy about having 'a reading wife'. In places where women had the largest amount of space for public self-expression, like the Woman's Page of *The Pioneer*, even the editor's wife, Frances Morrison, felt reluctant to go into print. She waited some weeks before responding to a London Mechanic's wife with the advice that women had the duty to 'get knowledge' as mothers: 'your children's your own, your country's interest demand it'.[23]

Chartist women did not buckle under hostile pressures. The reportedly 300-strong Cheltenham Female Patriotic Association no doubt knew just what response they would provoke in their Close encounters![24] But they did move through an increasingly complex field of force. On the one hand, Chartist women drew upon and further developed existing traditions of female militancy in which women had featured in their family roles. As family consumers, women had taken a prominent part in eighteenth- century food riots over fair prices and then in boycott strategies right through to the Chartist exclusive dealing policy which urged trading only with shopkeepers sympathetic to the cause. The success of this tactic largely depended upon the female Chartist associations which came into existence in 1839. Chartist women were also mobilizing a tradition of a family and community presence in public demonstrations, marching behind the banners they had so painstakingly made, most recently in two campaigns which highlighted family issues, the movements against the New Poor Law and in favour of a Ten Hours Factory Bill. Women had also formed their own groups in earlier reform movements, trade unions and friendly societies.[25]

However, Chartist women were also moving in territory which bourgeois ideologies were increasingly and vociferously declaring off limits.

And male radicals, intent upon establishing their own public place, not only used every legitimating rhetoric – religion, constitutionality and legality[26] – but sometimes also borrowed bourgeois notions of gendered respectability to reinforce their position on the moral high ground. Some Chartists resisted women's suffrage partly in order to ensure maximum credibility: antagonists often tried to discredit Chartist demands by describing Chartist crowds as being composed largely of women and boys.[27] The permissible extent of women's presence in public politics was scrutinized and contested. At one extreme, delegate William Carpenter proposed that Mary Lovett should take over the secretaryship of the convention when William was arrested:

> such a step would have a great effect upon the minds of the people and especially of the females, in different parts of the country when they saw that a woman like Mrs. Lovett was ready to step into the gap made in the Convention by the arrest of her husband, the women everywhere would be encouraged and excited to do in like manner.[28]

Yet, although elected, she apparently never served. At the other extreme, even the issue of whether women should appear at public festivities became contentious. Radical tailor and Benthamite, Francis Place begged William not to expect Mary to attend the dinner in August 1840 to celebrate his release from gaol: 'she is much too respectable a person to be made a silly show off and I know nothing that so much degrades modest women as these exhibitions of them'. William refused to collude with this extreme gendering of the public sphere and held instead to the usual radical practice of wives being present at public festivities:

> this is a similar affair to that was got up for Hetherington and Cleave at which a great number of respectable women were present and Mrs. Cleave and Mrs. Hetherington among the rest: and if the same order is to be preserved in the forthcoming occasions I cannot see any impropriety in my wife being present with the others. In fact her absence at such a time would seem to imply that I was less indulgent to my wife than other men; either that I was too proud or too unkind to afford her the gratification which my friends' wives and daughters enjoyed.[29]

In characteristic fashion, Mary herself decided the issue, by expressing 'her unwillingness to attend'.

Given the manifold pressures, it is little wonder that Chartist women conducted themselves with circumspection in their public writing. This writing mainly took the form of addresses from women's groups published in the *Northern Star* newspaper. Using the public address form on such a scale was unprecedented for women: the content was carefully framed. Women usually presented themselves as 'glorious auxiliaries' who were entering the public political arena precisely to defend the well-being of their families. The main way of becoming a public woman and a good woman at the same time was to present yourself as a militant family member acting on behalf of adult male kin or children. In a typical example of these eloquent but stylized addresses, the Female Political Union of Newcastle addressed their

> FELLOW COUNTRYWOMEN, – We call upon you to join us and help our fathers, husbands, and brothers, to free themselves and us from political, physical and mental bondage, and urge the following inducement to our friends.
>
> We have been told that the province of woman is her home and that the field of politics should be left to men, this we deny; the nature of things renders it impossible, and the conduct of those who give the advice is at variance with the principles they assert. Is it not true that the interests of our fathers, husbands and brothers, ought to be ours? If they are oppressed and impoverished, do we not share those evils with them? If so, ought we not to resent the infliction of those wrongs upon them? We have read the records of the past, and our hearts have responded to the historian's praise of those women, who struggled against tyranny and urged their countrymen to be free or die.[30]

This address moves in several contradictory directions. On the one hand, the women claim a public role, a nationwide stage and a history of struggle as their own; on the other they are aware of the disapproving eyes which watch them and partly for that reason underline their responsible family concerns. The women are certainly extending their public role but also at the same time restricting it by their family pose which might prove reversible and involve retiring from the public stage once tyranny had been overthrown.

It was unlikely that such women would write autobiographies. Even in the most encouraging of times, women have had enough difficulty conceiving their lives in terms of coherent development which leads in a clear direction, a formula common in male autobiographies even if coherence is achieved through great effort as the outcome of struggle and overcoming obstacles. Julia Swindells points out how several nineteenth-century women writers with literary ambitions drew on literary genres like fiction, romance and melodrama to articulate lives which had 'no simple advance, no simple route or progress, but a continuous, precarious adaptability signified from the brink of despair'. The women tended to represent this muddled passage in terms of melodrama full of intense crises, swooning sickness and total collapses.[31] Labelled as and demoted to amateurs, their writing was judged to be less than literary. Only recently, in the late twentieth century, has a high literary value been placed on women's autobiographies which use a plurality of interpretive devices in order to express multiple selves and fragmented lives.[32]

One hundred years before, the interdiction shadowing women's entry into the public sphere, which included prohibitions around public speaking, compounded the difficulties. These restrictions raised fences round the dominant form of spiritual autobiography, despite growing assumptions of women's exceptional religiosity. Two kinds of problems bedevilled this form, especially for middle-class women, in the nineteenth century. As Linda Peterson shows, spiritual autobiography, as exemplified in John Bunyan's works *Grace Abounding* and *Pilgrim's Progress*, called for a particular hermeneutic skill which 'read' the experiences of an individual's life using biblical texts for interpretation and guidance.[33] The problem for women was not so much that they lacked the capacity to make such interpretations but rather that they were not permitted the public authority to speak the language of biblical types. Peterson gives the illuminating example of Wesley's advice to a woman who felt the call to preach. While approving short exhortations, Wesley cautioned her: 'never take a text, never speak in continued discourse without some break, about four or five minutes'.[34]

The second set of problems had to do with the fact that the very coherence given to a life by the narrative framework of spiritual autobiography could deprive that life of spiritual authority. A means of sharing the good news of salvation, spiritual autobiography generally started with a 'before' phase of sinning, then a conversion experience and an aftermath of joy. But the stage of sinning, particularly if sexual misdemeanour was involved, could undermine the authority of the writer. Even though fictional, Elizabeth Gaskell's novel *Ruth*, about a total innocent seduced by her employer who redeems herself by means of a true Christian life and sacrificial motherhood, was considered so unsuitable a theme for public literature that even the author did not keep a copy in the house in reach of her children.[35] Rather than write public autobiography, committed Christian women, especially evangelicals whose faith demanded constant spiritual self-examination, tended to keep private spiritual diaries. Women also used two further genres for self-expression – family memoirs (a kind of feminization of autobiography by making it familial) and the autobiographical novel, which could, as in the case of Charlotte Bronte's *Jane Eyre*, display considerable hermeneutic skill.[36]

Increasingly from the mid-nineteenth century onwards, women who deliberately made a public career, like Harriet Martineau, or who became active in public campaigns in the women's movement, like Frances Power Cobbe or later Emmeline Pankhurst, began to conceive their lives as appropriate for the conventions of autobiography.[37] Martineau was one of the few Victorian women who defined herself and made her living as a professional writer and was unique in achieving her first real success with that most public of sciences, political economy.

According to Peterson, she was one of the very few women to challenge the formula of spiritual autobiography by substituting a rival interpretative framework in which the positivist stages of history (theological, metaphysical, scientific) repeated in her individual life (ontology recapitulates philogeny!).[38]

None the less it is also important to register that Martineau was very sensitive to public/private divisions and very careful and deliberate in negotiating them. For example, she prohibited the publication of private letters and so could present the production of an autobiography as an 'unquestionable' duty![39] She secularized the idea of a calling (with the People standing in for God) and used the techniques of melodrama to justify and describe her passage into the public sphere. Unconsciously manipulating the double meaning of 'want' both as need and desire, she thought it imperative to bring out her *Illustrations of Political Economy* because 'the work was wanted, – was even craved by the popular mind' ('the people wanted the book') and because she also 'thought of the multitudes who needed it, – and especially of the poor, – to assist them in managing their own welfare'.

But her passage was not smooth. She made her way through the slough of despond of publishers' rejections: 'day after day, I came home weary with disappointment, and with trudging many miles through the clay of the streets, and the fog of the gloomiest December I ever saw'. But she persevered: 'night after night, the Brewery clock struck twelve, while the pen was still pushing on in my trembling hand'. Finally the conditions of publication became so harsh and demanding that she nearly collapsed:

> I now felt almost too ill to walk at all. On the road, not far from Shoreditch, I became too giddy to stand without support; and I leaned over some dirty palings, pretending to look at a cabbage bed, but saying to myself, as I stood with closed eyes, "My book will do yet."[40]

The moment of greatest trial brought the greatest spurt of transforming effort: 'I wrote the Preface to my "Illustrations of Political Economy" that evening; and I hardly think that any one would discover from it that I had that day sunk to the lowest point of discouragement about my scheme.' Instead of suffering a breakdown, she achieved a breakthrough. Finally she triumphed: even Lord Brougham had to admit that the Society for the Diffusion of Useful Knowledge has been 'driven out of the field by a little deaf woman at Norwich'.[41] Deafness enabled her to stand apart from mainstream bourgeois femininity as did her unmarried state. She declared herself 'probably the happiest single woman in England',[42] attended by her little family entourage of mother and aunt and, as money accumulated, a servant.

Working-class women had much more complicated tasks to juggle.

When working-class women finally started to write their life stories after activity as late nineteenth- and early twentieth-century socialists and suffrage campaigners, they revealed the complex constraints of their family duties as well as the problems of public territory. Hannah Mitchell, in *The Hard Way Up*, not only told how her husband and his friends would stand as bodyguards to protect her while she held outdoor suffragette meetings and transgressed the prohibitions about women speaking in public, she also delivered the famous verdict that 'no cause can be won between dinner and tea, and most of us who were married had to work with one hand tied behind us'.[43] Her autobiography focused not only on the politics of housework but the housework of politics. She told how she organized the household and family work, with the help of the customary women's mutual help networks made up of neighbours and relatives, so as to free time to carry on a public political work.[44] All political activists, men as well as women, have this problem even though it goes unacknowledged because both men and women collude in assigning the family and domestic work to women alone. Yet this solution has always created further problems for women, by making yet more difficult their public activism and their public utterance.

Will the real Mary Lovett now please stand up?

Mary Lovett did not play a public role in the Chartist movement except for the one day when she seems to have held the office of Secretary to the Convention. This pattern repeated in other families and much about Mary Lovett seems typical including the fact that she rarely stepped into the public eye. William's few pages of description can be read carefully to suggest a number of things about Mary. She came from the world of respectable artisan families (her father had worked as a carpenter) and she reproduced this in turn. Before she married William, she first kept house for her single brother and when he married, she became a ladies maid, the position of highest status for a young woman in service. She married William when he was working as a cabinet-maker; their daughter Mary eventually married the son of a carpenter. Their son-in-law, a compositor by trade, ruined his eyesight while setting small music type and turned to keeping a tobacco shop while their daughter then tried to make her way on the stage.[45]

Mary had definite opinions and showed considerable initiative. She wrote in a clear legible script, and in a fluent easy style, denoting a modicum of education and a feeling of reasonable comfort with words. Jutta Schwarzkopf has given an account of the Lovett marriage in which she portrays William as 'extremely paternalist' and Mary as showing 'a

pliability and devotion to her husband that bordered on self-abnega-
tion'.[46] I am not convinced by this portrait of Mary and feel that
Schwarzkopf may be extrapolating more from Lovett's ideology about
woman's role than reading between the lines for the dynamics of his marriage. Mary was no cipher, and at strategic moments in their life together
she either called the shots or was consulted about decisions in a strikingly
respectful way. Mary first met William in the church where she was wor-
shipping and he just visiting to see a celebrated preacher and thereafter to
see her. Upon discovering the real difference in their religious views,
Mary 'candidly declared that she could not conscientiously unite her des-
tinies with any man whose opinions so widely differed from her own' and
promptly broke off their engagement. Poor William was desolate: 'I tried
to summon some little philosophy to my aid, but philosophy I believe has
little control over this strong and powerful passion; and months elapsed
before I recovered sufficiently from the shock to resume quietly my usual
avocations.' In a typical William-like way, he tried to forget by throwing
himself into public activity: he joined 'several associations literary, scientific and political' and recommended this medicine 'to all those who may
experience a similar heart-rending disappointment; for such pursuits
serve to excite and strengthen one set of faculties to enable them to overcome the force of another'. A year later, just when William was managing to gain back some control over himself, Mary took the initiative
again and sent him a Christmas card which expressed the hope that he
had changed his views. This communication reopened their relationship
with a 'controversial correspondence ... the result of which was that our
religious opinions became perfectly satisfactory to one another'. It is
unclear just what they did agree – possibly to differ and respect each
other's conscientiously held views.[47]

Certainly from then on, William took great pains to familiarize Mary
with everything he learned, thought and did. He presented this in a kind
of condescending way, talking of 'enlightening and instructing her', as
though she were a pupil and he a teacher. But we already know the penalties for William of not being candid and clear, frank and fair with Mary.
A very different tone appeared in his prison letters where he gave advice
as a suggestion rather than as an instruction, usually asking her to think
over what he had said and tell him her views or take the decision herself.
Thus when he was very anxious about his daughter's health, suggesting
she be sent down to his mother-in-law's, he added 'consult, however
your own feelings on the subject' or, when he told her that his poor
health and his radical politics would make it difficult to resume cabinet-
making and that he had 'a plan to open a shop of some description, such
as the book line', he ended by asking her to 'turn the subject over in your
mind and give me the benefit of your opinions respecting it'.[48]

Once married, Mary became the exemplary artisan's wife, although she quickly lost her health through childbearing. First, she looked after the family and domestic duties which included tragic moments, for example, when their youngest child Kezia died and when their eldest, Mary, became so weak that she went to the country for two years to stay with her grandfather. Like the wives of other respectable artisans, Mary also brought income into the household. She took the initiative immediately after marriage and tried to run a series of little businesses to augment the family income, especially to provide for sickness and old age. First she started a bakery shop which failed; then she took over William's job as storekeeper for the first London co-operative store – at half his pay. In the meanwhile William was unemployed and seemingly did little in the way of childcare because Kezia's death resulted from a fall from a nurse's lap during this time. When William came out of prison, too weak to take up cabinet-making again, he opened a bookseller's shop which Mary managed so as to free him for political activity.[49]

As the wife of a Chartist, Mary had yet another layer of responsibility laid upon her already doubly demanding life. A radical's wife carried a triple burden. Besides doing the domestic and family work and bringing extra income into the household she also had to be prepared to make sacrifices for the cause and endure the hardship which came from being victimized for political activity. Early in their marriage, as a punishment for protesting against the militia laws, all their household goods were seized. William's later year in prison brought great material and emotional suffering to the family. Mary received support from a public subscription but had to manage cleverly to make ends meet. She assiduously sent William all the literature he wanted but went to some lengths to get it cheaply: trying to procure Dr Southwood Smith's *Philosophy of Health*, she wrote to Place 'if you can put me in the way of getting a copy without buying it I will thank you, If not Mr. Watson will get it for me at trade price'.[50]

Mary indefatigably looked after William's interests: every time she received his letter from gaol, she immediately forwarded it to Francis Place with a cover note and also scurried around London on Williams' behalf seeing to petitions to get his condition improved, organizing for a doctor to examine him in gaol, shuttling back and forth to Warwick Gaol from London in any season.[51] Only her daughter's recurrent illness which affected little Mary's eyes, or the expectation that William might imminently return could keep her at home: although William wished her to visit Place, 'I am afraid to leave home lest he should come in my absence – don't laugh at me.'[52] The stress wore her down in the end. Both Mary and William continually expressed their anxiety when letters were delayed. Their hopes of an early release were dashed when the Home

Secretary attached unacceptable conditions requiring the prisoners to be bound over 'to be good boys' for a year. Finally just before his prison term had come to an end, Mary cracked. She thought he was dying. In a hasty note, with smudged handwriting and broken sentences, she scribbled: 'I fear William is too ill ... I am sure I shall never see him any more. Can nobody do anything for him – but I fear it is too late.'[53] Luckily, he was alive if not well and came home shortly afterwards.

Upon his return, Mary once more disappeared behind the veil of William's words: he wrote to Place briefly that they were all well and then, at much greater length, gave accounts of the depressed state of the trades of Cornwall, where the Lovetts had travelled to visit relatives and to recuperate. Mary seemed to prefer this public anonymity. She did not serve in the convention, nor did she attend William's welcome-home dinner. It is not even clear whether she was present some years later when she received public recognition as the model Chartist wife. On 23 February 1848, when the London radicals gave William a tricolour purse containing 140 gold sovereigns, they also paid tribute to the unswerving support of 'Mrs. William Lovett' with a silver tea service:

> We give it to her, because we know that never, even when the whole of their little property was sacrificed, did she breathe a single murmur or complaint (*loud cheers*). And in the hour of severer trial ... when prison walls divided her from his love and attention – an hour of trial peculiarly severe to a woman deeply attached to the man with whom she was united, feeling that her domestic happiness might be blighted and destroyed by her husband's bold assertion of political principle, and the inevitable consequence of severe punishment, yet, even then, she shrank not, but patiently rejoiced, far happier in being the partner of the courageous William Lovett, than if surrounded by luxury, and united to a man who had swerved from his duty (cheers). Therefore it is to her we present this portion of the testimonial. We present it to Mrs Lovett as an offering of respectful affection and regard.[54]

To great applause and 'waving of handkerchiefs by the ladies', William then collected and acknowledged the gifts on behalf of them both.

Who was the real Mary Lovett? Of course, we shall never know. Every generation of historians will reinterpret her significance, if they want to know about her at all, and find her elusively disappearing behind the hardening divide between public and private spheres. None the less we catch glimpses of an affectionate, intelligent and energetic woman probably stronger than even her husband's account suggests. Despite poor health, she carried out a complex round of duties and proved full of courage in times of misfortune. She may not have been the most publicly active Chartist wife. Nevertheless Mary's support was the indispensable springboard which freed William to act and to endure the penalties for his actions. From gaol he gave some idea of her importance to him telling her that 'while all goes well with you and Mary I shall not repine' and insisting that 'my books, my wife and my little one will constitute my only fortune when I get out'.[55] Helpmates and comforters, symbolic of what made life worth living and what made Chartism worth fighting for, however much 'hidden from history', the Mary Lovetts of their time provided a vital force which held together and energized the Chartist movement.

Notes

1. J.F.C. Harrison, *Learning and Living* (London, 1961), p. 44.
2. J. Wiener, *William Lovett* (Manchester, 1989), pp. 1–3, details some of the good press Lovett has received from historians like Hovell, Beer and Tawney, while arguing the need for a more complex assessment.
3. W. Lovett, *Life and Struggles of William Lovett in His Pursuit of Bread, Knowledge, and Freedom*, intro. R.H. Tawney, (London, 1920), vol. II, p. 450. All references to this text will be to the 1920 edition.
4. Autobiography has become a subject for cultural and critical theory. Some of the most trenchant works include P. Dodd, *Modern Selves. Essays on Modern British and American Autobiography* (London, 1985), especially his ch. 'Criticism and the Autobiographical Tradition'; L. Stanley, *The Auto/biographical I. The Theory and Practice of Feminist Auto/biography* (Manchester, 1992). Some of the most helpful work on cultural narrative has been written by scholars addressing issues in oral history, e.g. L. Passerini, *Fascism in Popular Memory. The Cultural Experience of the Turin Working Class*, trans. R. Lumley and J. Bloomfield, (Cambridge, 1987), pt. 1; R. Samuel and P. Thompson (eds), *The Myths We Live By* (Routledge, 1990), p. 78 for Al Thompson's exposition of the Popular Memory Group's concept of composure. See also note 32 below.
5. D. Vincent, *Bread, Knowledge and Freedom. A Study of Nineteenth-Century Working Class Autobiography* (London, 1981), p. 8.
6. *Northern Star* (hereafter cited as *NS*), 29 September, 27 October 1838.
7. E.g. *NS*, 24 July 1841 for the Sunderland toast: 'every human being was one of the people, or, if there was to be any exception, it must be made in favour of those justly called the working classes'.
8. An editorial referred to 'the whole complex of the vulture tribes whether denominated "upper", "middle", or "trading", classes who feed upon the vitals of the people', *NS*, 31 August 1839. A Blackburn banner read: 'A Faction may be rebels, the people never', ibid., 13 July 1839; the Female Political Union of Newcastle complained that 'the working men who form the millions, the strength and wealth of the country, are left without the pale of the Constitution, their wishes never consulted and their interests sacrificed by the ruling factions, ibid., 2 February 1839.
9. *NS*, 6 July 1839 for Feargus O'Connor on public opinion; Lovett based his trial defence around the 'right of public meeting' and 'public opinion', *The Charter*, 11 August 1839. For the earlier history of public meetings as a vehicle for expressing public opinion, see H. Jephson, *The Platform. Its Rise and Progress*, (London, 1892), vol. 1, pt. 1.

10. *NS*, 27 July 1939, 'Great Moral Demonstration' (Stockport); for the eighteenth century, see E.P. Thompson, 'The Crime of Anonymity', in D. Hay, P. Linebaugh, J. Rule, E.P. Thompson and C.Winslow, *Albion's Fatal Tree: Crime and Society in Eighteenth Century England*, (London, 1975), pp. 278–9, 301–2.
11. E.g., *Bradford Observer*, 15 August 1839. I discuss this ongoing encounter more fully in E. Yeo, 'Christianity in Chartist Struggle, 1838–1842, *Past and Present* (91), (1981), pp. 110 ff. and in E. Yeo, 'Culture and Constraint in Working-Class Movements, 1830–1855', E. and S. Yeo (eds), *Popular Culture and Class Conflict* (Brighton: Harvester, 1981), pp. 156 ff.
12. Lovett, *Life*, vol. 1, p. 223; for haircut, ibid., p. 226. His opening remarks in his defence were peppered with the word 'public': If there is any principle of justice left, which was wont to distinguish our forefathers, it was the loud and general expression of public opinion against public outrage and public wrong. It had never been the boast ... of English Freedom, that all must submit to the wholesome chastisement of public opinion whether the offender be prince or peasant, whether he be armed with wealth or invested with power. Public opinion is the great tribunal of justice ...': *The Trial of W. Lovett, Journeyman Cabinet-Maker ... 6 August [1839]* (London, 1839), pp. 8–9.
13. Lovett, *Life*, vol. 1, pp. 100, 109, 154; also p. 132 to the 'Citizens of the American Republic', addressing them 'in that spirit of fraternity which becomes working men in all the countries of the world' and assuring them that '*the mutual instruction and united exertions* of our class in all countries rapidly advance the world's emancipation'. For replies to Addresses issued in the 1840s, see letter from the Polish Commune of London to the ... Meeting of the People of England ... 6 June 1844 and the Reply of the Precursor Society on Behalf of the People of Ireland, MS. 753, Lovett Coll., Birmingham Central Library Archives.
14. Lovett, *Life*, vol. II, p. 414.
15. Ibid., vol. 1, p. xxxi.
16. H. Snell, *Men, Movements and Myself* (London, 1936), tells the story of his development from an agricultural labourer to a Labour MP and then peer.
17. Catherine Hall delineates a public sphere of associational life including voluntary as well as statutory organizations, 'Gender Divisions and Class Formation in the Birmingham Middle Class, 1780–1850', in C. Hall, *White and Middle-Class. Explorations in Feminism and History* (Cambridge, 1992), pp. 101–3.
18. L. Davidoff and C. Hall, *Family Fortunes. Men and Women of the English Middle Class, 1780–1850*, (London, 1987), explores the importance of gender division in bourgeois class formation.
19. Reverend F. Close, *A Sermon. Addressed to the Female Chartists of Cheltenham, Sunday 25 August 1839, on the Occasion of their Attending the Parish Church in a Body* (London, 1839), pp. 3–4.
20. Ibid., pp. 14–15.
21. Ibid., p. 14.
22. Ibid., p. 17.
23. *The Pioneer*, 8 February 1834, p. 191. My thanks to Helen Rogers for drawing this to my attention.
24. *Western Vindicator*, 29 June 1839.

25.   For earlier traditions, see D. Thompson, 'Women and Nineteenth Century
       Radical Politics: a lost Dimension', in J. Mitchell and A. Oakley, *The Rights
       and Wrongs of Women*, (Harmondsworth, 1976), pp. 116 ff.; also M.
       Thomis and J. Grimmett, *Women in Protest, 1800–1850*, (London, 1984).
       C. Hall, 'The Tale of Samuel and Jemima: Gender and Working-Class
       Culture in Early Nineteenth-Century England', in White, for the gendered
       experience of Peterloo.

26.   For the Chartist desire to remain legal see my, 'Some Practices and Prob-
       lems of Chartist Democracy' in J. Epstein and D. Thompson, *The Chartist
       Experience. Studies in Working-Class Radicalism and Culture, 1830–
       1860*, (London, 1982), pp. 360 ff.; for religious and constitutional legiti-
       mation, see my 'Christianity'.

27.   For other male Chartist views on female suffrage, see D. Jones, 'Women
       and Chartism', *History*, (1983), vol. 68, pp. 8–9; D. Thompson, *The
       Chartists. Popular Politics in the Industrial Revolution* (Aldershot, 1984),
       pp. 124 ff.; J. Schwarzkopf, *Women in the Chartist Movement*, (London,
       1991), pp. 60–2.

28.   *The Charter*, 14 July 1839. Subsequent Convention sessions show a num-
       ber of men serving in the post.

29.   F. Place to W. Lovett, letter dated 16 July 1840, p. 678; Lovett to Place
       reply, letter dated 20 July 1840, p. 684, Francis Place Collection, Pt. II, Set
       55, Working Men. Reform. Case of Lovett and Collins, 1839–41, British
       Library, Dept of Printed Books; Harvester Microfilm, 'Radical Politics and
       the Working Man in England', reel 19. Ladies tickets for the meeting and
       ball cost 2s. 6d., men's 3s.

30.   'Address of the Female Political Union of Newcastle', *NS*, 9 February 1839,
       closely echoed by the Birmingham Female Political Union, *The Charter*, 10
       November 1839. Schwarzkopf (1991), pp. 199–200 gives a selected list of
       such addresses in her footnotes. The fullest analysis of such texts is M. de
       Larrabeiti, 'Conspicuous Before the World. Radical and Political Discourse
       in the Women's Addresses to the *Northern Star*', a chapter in a forthcoming
       book I am editing on 'Radical Femininity. Women's Self-Representation in
       Social Movements in the 19th and 20th centuries'.

31.   J. Swindells, *Victorian Writing and Working Women. The Other Side of
       Silence*, (Minneapolis, 1985), pp. 149, 152.

32.   To give just two of many examples, C. Wolf, *A Model Childhood* (London,
       1983), features herself in the present and interrogates the process of mem-
       ory as well as trying to recall her repressed Nazi childhood. C. Steedman,
       Landscape for a Good Woman. A Story of Two Lives (London, 1986),
       reviews the interpretative devices for talking about working-class lives
       while recounting the life stories of herself and her mother. Stanley (1992),
       pp. 13–14 discusses these issues as does Dodd (London, 1986), pp. 2 ff. on
       the dangers of moving to the centre of the literary canon and pp. 9–10 with
       reference to R. Fraser's autobiography *In Search of a Past. The Manor
       House, Amnersfield, 1933–1945* (London, 1984), which 'interrogates not
       only the past but also two of the major discourses (oral history and psycho-
       analysis) which offer to articulate the past'.

33.   L. Peterson, *Victorian Autobiography. The Tradition of Self-Interpretation*
       (New Haven, 1986), pp. 6 ff. for useful exposition of the hermeneutic
       method, pp. 126 ff. and especially 130 ff. for women's difficulties with
       hermeneutic tradition.

34. John Wesley quoted in ibid., p. 130. D. Valenze, *Prophetic Sons and Daughters: Female Preaching and Popular Religion in Industrial England* (Princeton, 1985), pp. 11, 277, shows female preaching lasted longer in non-Wesleyan groups but declined rapidly after 1850 as cottage religion was replaced by chapel.
35. E. Gaskell to Anne Robson, letter (n.d.) in J.A.V. Chapple and A. Pollard (eds), *The Letters of Mrs Gaskell*, (Manchester, 1966), no. 148, p. 221.
36. Peterson (1986), p. 124 on available genres, pp. 133–5 on *Jane Eyre*.
37. F.B. Cobbe, *The Life of Frances Power Cobbe, by herself*, 2 vols, (Boston, 1894), E. Pankhurst, *My Own Story* (London, 1914).
38. Peterson (1896), p. 137.
39. H. Martineau, *Autobiography*, 3 vols (London, 1877), vol. 1, pp. 1–4 for her distinction between public and private writing.
40. Ibid., pp. 171, 160, 161.
41. Ibid., pp. 176, 171.
42. Ibid., p. 133.
43. H. Mitchell, *The Hard Way Up*, (London, 1977), pp. 128, 130.
44. Ibid., pp. 125–6 for the description of how she organized the day of work as a Poor Law Guardian with the help of her neighbour Mary Hartley, her niece and her son.
45. Lovett, *Life*, vol. 1, pp. 37–9, vol. II, p. 451. Her handwriting can be found in the letters to Francis Place cited below.
46. Schwarzkopf, *Women*, pp. 171, 173; A. Clark, 'The Rhetoric of Chartist Domesticity', *Journal of British Studies*, vol. 31 (1992), p. 71.
47. Lovett, *Life*, vol. 1, pp. 38–9.
48. W. to M. Lovett, letter dated 24 June 1840, p. 609; 17 October 1839, p. 92. All the letters involving Mary and William cited here and below are in the Place Coll., full reference in note 29 above.
49. Lovett, *Life*, vol. 1, pp. 41, 43, vol. II, pp. 250, 451.
50. Ibid., vol. I, p. 67 for distraint of goods; M. Lovett to F. Place, letter dated 11 October 1839, p. 82; one subscription was raised to support Mary and her daughter, another was reserved for William when he left prison: any surplus would go to pay off a debt owing on a coffee shop venture, F. Place to Mrs M. Gaskell, dated 27 January 1840, p. 156; also *The Charter*, 25 August 1839 for the public meeting setting up the subscriptions.
51. M. Lovett to F. Place, letter dated 30 January 1840, p. 158 for a visit to Warwick gaol; *Memorials of Correspondence Relating to Lovett and Collins*, contain five of Mary's communications, on 19, 30 October, 16 November, 5, 7 December 1839; for her efforts to get William's physician to Warwick Gaol to examine him, J. Watson to F. Place, letter dated 11 December 1839, p. 230.
52. M. Lovett to F. Place, letter dated 24 April 1840, p. 504; also 5 October 1839, p. 75.
53. M. Lovett to F. Place, letter n.d., p. 610. Place wrote 'your wife is ill adapted for being the wife of a politician who runs risks as you have. She is sadly afflicted', letter to W. Lovett, dated 27 June 1840, p. 614.
54. *Speeches delivered at the Soirée etc ...*, in Proceedings of the Working Man's Association, pt IV, p. 241, Lovett Coll., Birmingham Public Library.
55. W. to M. Lovett, letter dated 29 November 1839, pp. 192, 193.

CHAPTER THIRTEEN

The Mysteries of G.W.M. Reynolds: radicalism and melodrama in Victorian Britain

Rohan McWilliam

G.W.M. Reynolds (1814–79) was a man of mystery.[1] Chartist, novelist, journalist, pornographer, he pursued many careers and lived an immensely public life. Yet we know remarkably little about this man who was one of the leading Chartists during its dying fall, who founded *Reynolds's Newspaper*, the most successful and enduring working-class newspaper of its day and who, as author of *The Mysteries of London*, was arguably the most popular novelist of the nineteenth century. Reynolds spoke in many voices. He came close to urging revolution through physical force but also devoted much of his life to producing domestic romances for a largely female audience. Reynolds was that rarity among radicals, a leader at ease with the multitudinous forms of popular culture in Victorian Britain.

Moreover, this peddler of cheap fantasies provides the key to a pressing historical question: what happened to Radicalism between the end of Chartism and the coming of Socialism? Historians have tended to assume that 1848 was a major watershed, the end of a radical tradition going back to Paine and the beginning of a period dominated by consensus and class collaboration; but it is becoming increasingly clear that the older tradition with its emphasis on democracy and constitutionalism survived into the mid-Victorian period and beyond. Radicalism after 1848 was characterized as much by continuity as by discontinuity. It was absorbed into radical liberalism and became a source for the early Labour party. This is borne out if we look at the leading communicator of radical arguments in the mid-Victorian period. Reynolds's significance is that he kept the old radicalism alive in what was admittedly an unpropitious time for oppositional politics. Issue after issue of his publications attacked the undemocratic nature of the Victorian state and blamed social evils on the aristocracy. Reynolds has often been patronized or dismissed but the increasing amount of research on him suggests that historians are coming to terms with his importance in Victorian popular politics.[2]

Yet while Reynolds kept radicalism alive, he was also different from other Radicals. Such figures as George Howell and the Trade Union

Junta represented the values of respectability. Some of Reynolds's writings, composed for the self-improving labour aristocracy, were in this vein. *Reynolds's Miscellany*, commenced in 1846, was aimed at readers 'imbued with a profound spirit of inquiry in respect to Science, Art, Manufacture, and the various matters of social or national importance ... '.[3] But *Reynolds's Miscellany* does not fit neatly into the canon of Victorian improving literature because it combined educational articles with stories that verged on pornography. *Wagner the Wehr-Wolf* contained illustrated scenes where half-naked women beat themselves in the depths of a convent. Part Respectable Radical, he was also one of what Steven Marcus calls 'the other Victorians'.[4] How can we reconcile this contradiction in his output?

A study of Reynolds suggests that respectability in Victorian Britain was skin deep. As Peter Bailey has shown, it was a form of self-presentation dependent on context and role-playing.[5] Thus Reynolds helped construct an audience that had 'high' cultural aspirations but 'low' desires at the same time. In common with the music hall and the pub, he exploited an area of popular culture that combined respect for domesticity with sexual titillation. Yet Reynolds was also a throwback to an earlier age, representing a continuity of the unrespectable tradition of radicalism that flourished in London journalism during the early nineteenth century, combining politics with pornography.[6] Although his writing was tamer than his predecessors', his use of sex made him relatively unique among contemporary writers. Reynolds's fiction presumably sold because of its titillating appeal, but the use of sexuality also had a political context. Reynolds used sexual crime to reveal the evils of the aristocracy, to demonstrate that it was the upper class that was not respectable. Never an original thinker, Reynolds employed a technique in his fiction that earlier radicals had used. He became a literary blackmailer exposing the private vices of the aristocracy to public view. In this sense, Reynolds's politics can be reconciled with his use of sexual adventure. His publications addressed the labour aristocracy and persuaded it that, for all its susceptibility to titillation, it was the only truly respectable class in society, a device used by the popular press down to the present day.

Reynolds wrote within the 'mysteries' tradition of fiction that became popular throughout Europe and the United States in the 1840s. The 'mysteries' novel dramatized the fear of the 'dangerous classes' in the city, mixing Gothic romanticism with social realism.[7] The genre was initiated by the French novelist, Eugene Sue, who lived a parallel life to Reynolds. His serial, *Les Mystères de Paris* (1842), dealt with the sufferings of the poor in the modern city. Researching the novel, Sue visited poverty-stricken areas and was converted to socialism by what he found. In 1850, he became a socialist deputy for a working-class district in

Paris.[8] Reynolds followed a similar trajectory. His *Mysteries of London* (1844–48), an imitation of Sue, enjoyed remarkable popularity. Reynolds's advocacy of the rights of the poor in his fiction propelled him, like Sue, into radical politics. But Reynolds also resembled Sue in that his language and politics were refracted through the lens of melodrama. There is little distinction to be made between the language of Reynolds's fiction and the editorials in his newspapers. What Reynolds demonstrates is that the boundaries between fiction, politics and reportage were permeable in the nineteenth century.[9]

Recent work on Reynolds tends to discuss specific aspects of his life in isolation from the rest. Here, I intend to examine his whole career and political ideology, drawing on his speeches, journalism and fiction. To solve the mysteries that Reynolds presents, I will examine his life and then consider the extent to which it is possible to identify a coherent ideology informing his multiple pursuits. Reynolds was like a sponge, absorbing the radical and romantic elements of his culture. Space does not allow for any discussion of the reception of Reynolds's work but his continued success suggests an audience that appreciated the intersection between radicalism and melodrama that he represented. One of the first great figures produced by the shift to mass market publishing, this industrious scribbler managed to embody the kaleidoscope of the popular mind.

George William MacArthur Reynolds was born in 1814 at Sandwich in Kent, the son of a post-captain in the Royal Navy and a descendent of Admiral John Reynolds, the governor of Georgia in 1754–57.[10] On the death of his father in 1822, he was looked after by a guardian and sent to Sandhurst with the intention that he should pursue a military career. Acquiring £7000 on his mother's death in 1830, he opted to embrace a Bohemian life as a writer in Paris. There are allegations that before leaving for France, the 16-year-old Reynolds committed fraud. He borrowed jewels from a shop in London, claiming he had a customer for them but actually used them to pay off his hotel bill. On reaching Paris, Reynolds was apparently punished for gambling with loaded dice. Then, in Calais, he and his brother Edward, pretending to be master and servant, ran up another huge hotel bill and promptly decamped.[11]

Whatever the truth of these claims, Reynolds's French experience proved decisive. He entered Parisian literary circles, became an enthusiast for the ideas of the French Revolution and temporarily adopted French citizenship. He also married the writer, Susanna Frances Pearson. Evidence of early radical inclinations is provided by his first publication, a defence of deism inspired by Paine's *Age of Reason* and published in London by the freethinker Richard Carlile.[12] Using his inheritance, he established the Librarie des Etrangers, helped edit several newspapers and wrote his first novel, *The Youthful Imposter* (1835). However, all these endeavours came to nothing and he returned to London bankrupt in 1836.

What rescued Reynolds financially was the success of his *Pickwick Abroad* the following year, which became the best loved of the contemporary Dickens imitations. It was serialized in the *Monthly Magazine* which Reynolds briefly edited in 1837–38. He was launched upon a literary career that involved the production of several novels a year. Reynolds's French enthusiasms intruded into much of his fiction. *Robert Macaire in England* (1840) featured the adventures of a French bandit while *Alfred* (1839) not only had a French setting but also was supportive of Louis Philippe, a view Reynolds would later retract. Most important of all, he published *The Modern Literature of France* (1839) in which he defended the work of writers such as Sue, Victor Hugo and Georges Sand against charges of immorality. He translated several French works, including *Sister Anne* (1840) by Paul de Kock, an author whose 'racy' novels were often characterized as pornographic. Reynolds's 'high' literary ambitions at this time can be seen in *A Sequel to Don Juan* (1843) which continued Byron's poem and was written in the latter's style.

His political activity in the early 1840s was restricted to a brief involvement with temperance. Reynolds apparently took the pledge after debating with the temperance lecturer J.H. Donaldson in May 1840. He went on to edit *The Teetotaller*, write a temperance novel, *The Drunkard's Progress* (1840) and was a leader of the London United Temperance Association. However, by September 1841, he had become Director-General of the United Kingdom Anti-Teetotal Society and editor of the *Anti-Teetotaller* although this connection proved equally short lived.[13]

Reynolds finally became a household name with the serialization of *The Mysteries of London* (1844–48) for the publisher George Vickers, a specialist in smutty publications, based in Holywell Street, the centre of London's pornographic book trade.[14] This may account for the reputation of Reynolds as a pornographer. He wrote the first two series and then left after a dispute in 1848. Two other writers, Thomas Miller and E.C. Blanchard, were brought in to continue the series (1848–50) though without the same impact. Reynolds meanwhile, in effect, continued his original novel under the title, *The Mysteries of the Court of London*. The serial lasted from September 1848 through to December 1855. The 'Mysteries' cycle therefore ran for over ten years and enjoyed huge popularity. It was read particularly by costermongers and young working-class men and women.[15] Abel Heywood, the Manchester bookseller, noted that 'A great many females read the "Court of London" and young men; a sort of spreeing young men; young men who go to taverns, and put cigars in their mouths in a flourishing way.' Such was their success that there were several dramatizations – at the Marylebone Theatre (1846) and at the Pavilion and Victoria theatres (1847). It is also possible that some of the story-songs in the novel were performed in London's theatres.[16]

The two serials comprise a series of tales that demonstrate the problems of retaining virtue within the labyrinth of the modern city. They derived their tone from Sue's *Mystères de Paris* and Pierce Egan's *Life in London* (1822). Framed by the conventions of Victorian melodrama, Reynolds used the stories as an indictment of modern society with its twin evils of wealth and poverty. The author frequently halted the exciting narrative so that he could rant about the condition of the poor and the contrasts of the city. Reynolds was unusual among contemporary popular novelists in foregrounding his social conscience. He later claimed that the novels were pervaded by 'the most uncompromising republicanism'.[17] The whole of the mysteries cycle is structured by binary oppositions: rich/poor, virtue/degeneracy, urban/rural. Yet the purpose of the stories is to reveal that all classes are united through crime. Thus in the *Mysteries of the Court of London*, the confrères of the Prince Regent recruit thugs on the street to perform their master's evil wishes. It is the centrality of crime that is the key to one of the mysteries of the city. All society is corrupt. Reynolds eschewed representing the poor as virtuous and instead revealed the way in which morality was destroyed by urban squalor. The stories functioned as guides to the habits of the dangerous classes, even including glossaries of thieves' slang.[18]

Reynolds's imagery stressed pollution. Dirt was symbolically central in the novel, possessing shock value and alerting the reader to the need for social reform. The following description of Smithfield is but one of many grotesque scenes that demonstrates Reynolds's agitprop approach to the story:

> In that densely populated neighbourhood . . . hundreds of families each live and sleep in one room. When a member of one of these families happens to die, the corpse is kept in the close room where the rest still continue to live and sleep. Poverty frequently compels the unhappy relatives to keep the body for days – aye, and weeks. Rapid decomposition takes place; – animal life generates quickly; and in four-and-twenty hours myriads of loathsome animaculae are seen crawling about. The very undertakers' men fall sick at these disgusting – these revolting spectacles.
>
> The wealthy classes of society are far too ready to reproach the miserable poor for things which are really misfortunes and not faults. The habit of whole families sleeping together in one room

destroys all sense of shame in the daughters; and what guardian then remains for their virtue? But, alas! a horrible – an odious crime often results from that poverty which thus huddles brothers and sisters, aunts and nephews, all together in one room – the crime of incest . . . These are the fearful mysteries of that hideous district which exists in the very heart of this great metropolis.[19]

Thus, for Reynolds, to understand the mysteries of London, it is important to comprehend that the city is built on incest. Reynolds's concerns with pollution and dirt echo Mayhew's and predate Mearns's *Bitter Cry of Outcast London* (1883). The melodramatic frame of Reynolds's writings also led to perpetual scenes featuring assaults on female virtue, the central theme of Victorian melodrama. In this sense, he prefigured W.T. Stead's construction of London as a labyrinth of sexual danger.[20] Heywood noted that many considered *The Mysteries of the Court of London* to be an 'indecent publication' because 'it draws upon scenes of profligacy as strongly as it is possible for any writer to do, and the feelings are excited to a very high pitch by it'. But he decided the book was not pornographic because 'I do not believe that any words appear that are vulgar.' *The Bookseller* was later not so convinced arguing that Reynolds's fiction was mischievous, making 'the life of a courtesan, or an actress, a life of ease, pleasure and gay delight'. It urged the production of wholesome literature to counter him.[21] The Dublin *Nation* also attacked him as a pornographer in an article titled 'Mr. G.W.M. Reynolds's Dunghill' and denounced him as 'the scavenger of an infamous literature'.[22] Reynolds's fiction was pornographic in so far as it dealt freely with matters of seduction and included scenes of sexuality that were unusual in mainstream fiction. The novels would occasionally include pictures of his heroines in a state of undress. Several even depicted the torture of women. Reynolds admitted that he was an admirer of De Sade but this ceased to be a significant feature of his output after the early 1850s.[23]

The Mysteries cycle was the most politicized of Reynolds's works. His other fiction during the 1840s and 1850s was mainly composed of blood and thunder novels such as *Wagner the Wehr-Wolf* (1846–47) and *The Necromancer* (1852). Many had a historical setting and betrayed the influence of Walter Scott: for example, *Kenneth* (1851) and *The Massacre of Glencoe* (1852–53). However, certain novels featured political themes. *The Soldier's Wife* (1853) was an attack on flogging in the army (which led the military to ban sales of *Reynolds's Newspaper* to soldiers), while *The Seamstress* (1850) was derived from Thomas Hood's 'The Song of the Shirt' and Mayhew's descriptions of the plight of needlewomen. Moreover, Reynolds as a writer always had his eye on the main chance. During the Crimean War, he produced romantic novels with a

Turkish setting: *Omar* and *The Loves of the Harem* (both 1855). Some of these novels were serialized first in the *London Journal* which he edited between 1845 and 1846 and then in *Reynolds's Miscellany* which was modelled on the *London Journal* and eventually sold 200 000 copies a week.[24]

Reynolds's identity as a socially committed journalist and author explains how, in 1848, he found himself catapulted into the leadership of the Chartist movement. Along with 10 000 to 15 000 others, he attended the 6 March meeting in Trafalgar Square that Charles Cochrane called to protest against the income tax. When the meeting was declared illegal, Cochrane failed to turn up. Reynolds was then called to the chair where he drew on his fame as a novelist by saying 'in all the novels and romances he had written, he had never failed to push forward the great rights of the people'.[25] The theme of his address was the current French Revolution which was to become his great political passion. His speech supporting Louis Blanc was cheered by the crowd who then followed him all the way back to his home in Wellington Street from where he addressed it once more. It was the accompanying violence and window-breaking at this meeting that was to lead to the intense policing of the Chartist demonstration on 10 April. The 6 March meeting transformed Reynolds into a major figure on the Radical platform. He was invited to a demonstration the following week on Kennington Common where he maintained his internationalist theme by attacking Louis Philippe. At the same time, the Irish Democratic Federation of Finsbury passed a resolution praising him both as a Chartist and as the author of the radical *Mysteries of London*.[26] On 4 April, he was elected to the Chartist convention at the John Street Institution as representative for Derby, moving an amendment that in the event of the rejection of the petition, the convention should declare its sittings permanent and the Charter the law of the land. The motion failed but Reynolds went on to become one of the leading speakers at the 10 April demonstration. Indeed, Gammage speculated that had an English revolution happened, Reynolds might have been able to take it over. He was certainly notorious during these months. *Punch* attacked him as a pornographer from Holywell Street while W.J. Linton later called him 'the tin-kettle at the mad mob's tail . . .'.[27]

Reynolds was a significant figure during the later years of Chartism, hoping to engineer its revival. However, his reputation as a Chartist remains controversial. W.E. Adams's words are often quoted:

> I do not think . . . that any large number of the Chartists accepted him seriously. O'Connor and O'Brien, Jones and Harney, all had their followers; but Reynolds had no such distinction. Indeed it was rather as a charlatan and a trader than as a genuine politician that G.W.M. was regarded by the rank and file.[28]

While it is true that Reynolds did not generate the personality cult of other Chartist leaders, he clearly remained a major figure in Chartist politics, topping the list in the election for the Chartist executive in 1851. He was proposed as a Chartist parliamentary candidate in 1850 for Finsbury, for Bradford in 1851 and Lambeth in 1852. Ill health apparently forced him to withdraw his candidature in Bradford and to resign from the Chartist executive. This may account for his failure to take a personal role in politics thereafter. His reasons for withdrawal from active political participation may also have been financial. He was constantly bankrupt through the 1840s and even as he was making his mark on the Chartist platform, he was forced to appear in the bankruptcy courts.[29] Reynolds's relationship with the publisher John Dicks during the 1850s apparently put his affairs on a solid financial footing, but his intense literary and journalistic productivity during the decade (he wrote at least 24 novels and edited three periodicals) may not have left much time for politics.

The quality of Reynolds's relationship with other Chartist leaders varied. He supported Bronterre O'Brien and George Julian Harney in opposing an alliance with the middle class. In September 1849, he assisted O'Brien in the creation of the National Reform League for the Peaceful Regeneration of Society, acting as a link to the National Charter Association. On the other hand, Reynolds entered into serious disputes with Thomas Clark and with Ernest Jones who was successfully to sue him for libel in 1859 after allegations by Reynolds of financial impropriety.[30]

Reynolds made two important contributions to late Chartism. First, he was a strong internationalist and enthusiast for liberation struggles in France, Hungary and Italy. But Reynolds's most important bequest was his journalism. In November 1849, he published *Reynolds's Political Instructor*, a weekly paper devoted to political commentary, taking over the radical elements of *Reynolds's Miscellany* (which thereafter became rather apolitical). Reynolds was assisted on the *Instructor* by Bronterre O'Brien and devoted the paper to support for Chartism and internationalism. It was chiefly important as a dry run for *Reynolds's Weekly Newspaper* (later *Reynolds's Newspaper*), a fully fledged popular Sunday newspaper, originally priced 4d., that commenced on 5 May 1850 (taking over from the *Instructor* which ceased publication). The paper was to be the greatest success of Reynolds's career, lasting right up to 1967. It demonstrated his superb understanding of his audience, balancing radical commentaries written by himself and by his brother Edward (who wrote under the name 'Gracchus') with sensationalist stories of horrible murders and train crashes. Reynolds pulled together the diverse strands of popular culture and helped create the basic formu-

lae of mass journalism. By early 1855, the paper was selling 49 000–
50 000 copies per week, but the abolition of the stamp duty that year and
a consequent reduction of the price took sales to 100 000. After the
abolition of the paper duty in 1861, the price was lowered to 1d. and
sales reached 300 000. It was popular in northern industrial areas that
had supported Chartism and, as Virginia Berridge has shown, was
notable for penetrating the unskilled working class.[31]

Reynolds's involvement with the paper after the later 1850s is unclear.
However, it continued to advocate the kind of radical causes of which
Reynolds approved and to employ his melodramatic language. In this
sense, Reynolds can be seen as a major radical figure well into the 1870s.
As late as 1873, he was asked to stand as a Radical candidate in Stoke
and subsequently, Edward Kenealy, the leader of the cause of the
Tichborne Claimant, hoped Reynolds would join him in Parliament as a
Tichborne MP.[32] Despite W.E. Adams's harsh words, it is clear that
Reynolds had some standing as a Radical icon.

Reynolds's wife died in 1858 and his literary output began to decline
thereafter. By this time his publications seem to have obtained for him
the financial security that had earlier eluded him. He brought *Reynolds's
Miscellany* to an end in 1869, despite the fact that it was still in profit,
because he wanted to concentrate on his weekly newspaper.[33] At the time
of his death in 1879, G.W.M. Reynolds, whose early politics were anti-
clerical, was churchwarden of St Andrew's, Wells Street.[34]

Surveying Reynolds's many careers in pursuit of his ideology is problematic. Journalists are not always renowned for consistency and there is no
question that Reynolds was in many ways an opportunist. *A Sequel to
Don Juan* (1843) attacked Chartism as 'humbug' but Reynolds went on
to become a leading Chartist.[35] His volte-face on temperance within less
than a year makes one realize why he was considered untrustworthy.
Even Reynolds's radicalism can be put down to his undoubted flair for
latching on to anything that would sell. On the other hand, looking at his
career from the late 1840s onwards, it is possible to discern certain ideological commitments that were long-lasting and probably genuine.
Reynolds may have been a maverick but his persistence in arguing radical
causes during the mid-Victorian years suggests that he was more princi-
pled than his detractors admit. No cynical opportunist names his sons
Kossuth Mazzini and Ledru Rollin.

In this section, I will examine the components of Reynolds's radicalism, especially his hostility to the aristocracy and to the mid-Victorian
state, as well as his internationalism. These concerns place Reynolds
securely in the radical tradition. The following survey draws on some
unsigned material in Reynolds's newspapers that may not have been

written by him. This is defensible as they conform to his overall line. Furthermore, we know that his papers were a family industry. Not only did Reynolds's brother Edward contribute but he became editor of *Reynolds's Newspaper* on his brother's death (having been *de facto* editor for some years). Reynolds also took care to assemble a staff that was sympathetic to his political opinions.[36]

Reynolds was committed to the six points of the People's Charter which he vainly tried to revive in the 1850s through his journalism. Moreover, he joined Bronterre O'Brien in demanding 'The Charter and Something More'. *Reynolds's Political Instructor* actually proposed adding two new points to the People's Charter: 'the recognition of the rights of labour' and 'the abolition of the law of primogeniture'. The paper explained these points. By the rights of labour it understood 'the axiom that "there should be a fair day's wage for a fair day's work"; and that every man able and willing to work should have work found for him'. The abolition of primogeniture, mortmain and entail was necessary as they 'obstruct the coming together of land and useful labour – and by thus hindering the production of food from advancing at the same rate as the production of people, spread pauperism and misery over the face of the country'.[37]

In keeping with his Chartist principles, Reynolds maintained that the state was unfair and needed to be transformed through the injection of democracy. He welcomed the 1867 Reform Act and supported independent working-class representation. His publications constantly urged that the People's Charter become law. For example, *Reynolds's Newspaper* hailed the abolition of the property qualification for MPs in 1858. The paper was later to claim partial responsibility for bringing several points of the Charter into being.[38] Despite his link with O'Brien, his attitude to socialism was ambivalent. He was an enthusiast for Louis Blanc's *démoc-soc* ideals and sympathized with the co-operative movement. On the other hand, he denied that he was the 'enemy of capital'.[39] Reynolds essentially continued the marriage between eighteenth-century commonwealthman ideas and artisan radicalism. This strain of thought remained an element of Chartist ideology and Reynolds persisted with it. Hence, his main venom was reserved for the aristocracy as the source of social evil. His fiction and his journalism never ignored an opportunity to attack the landowning classes. A Brighton bookseller told William Thackeray that Reynolds was popular because 'he lashes the aristocracy'.[40]

He employed the traditional radical argument that the aristocracy was a parasite on the labour of others. In later life, he claimed that he was driven to write his *Mysteries* cycle in outrage against a system where 'the workers and toilers should have to support the idlers'.[41] He also berated the élite for its heartlessness and hypocrisy. Yet, as was not uncommon in melodrama, some of the heroes and heroines in his fiction were aristocrats themselves. Reynolds did maintain a role for a paternalist aristocracy. The eponymous heroine of *Mary Price, or The Memoirs of a Servant Maid* finishes by marrying Lord Wilberton who comes to spend his time 'personally visiting every house and cottage upon his immense estate, and studying his best to ameliorate the condition of all who lived upon the domain'.[42]

Reynolds's writings demonstrate the continuity of the Norman Yoke form of radical argument. The significance of Reynolds is therefore not just that he was a force for continuity but that he indicates how influential this discourse was right up to the 1880s. Reynolds echoed Paine's personal denunciations of William the Conqueror:

> William of Normandy [was] the son of Carlotta, a tanner's daughter of Falaize, a notorious prostitute – the English world 'harlot' being derived, it is said, from her name . . . Property in the case of the Norman aristocracy was acquired by rapine, murder and violation of all laws, both human and divine; that property has descended by title of heirship down to the holders of the present day; these holders are the descendants of robbers and wholesale plunderers; and the origin of property, therefore, held by many aristocratic houses boasting of their lineage is *robbery!*[43]

Until recently, historians often wrote off this kind of pronouncement as false consciousness or, at best, a form of romantic nostalgia because it did not take seriously the role of the bourgeoisie. However, given the current emphasis on the continuing importance of the aristocracy throughout the nineteenth century, Reynolds should perhaps be reclaimed as someone who was trying to define the real nature of the Victorian state.[44] It is true that Reynolds did not devote much space to the middle classes. However, he was prepared to denounce the cotton lords ('of all despots the most potent and overwhelming') and city financiers cropped up as villains in his fiction. The *Political Instructor* argued 'it is indeed a painful fact that the middle classes have too often proved themselves as hostile and as oppressive as the aristocracy towards the industrious millions'.[45] The fact that Reynolds as a Chartist opposed an alliance with middle-class reformers suggests some grasp of the class system as it had evolved by the mid-Victorian period.

Alongside the denunciation of the aristocracy, Reynolds's politics were essentially republican. Even in his fiction, Reynolds dwelt on the appalling atrocities committed by the royal family. *The Mysteries of the Court of London* was an extended attack on George IV. In itself, this was significant as the Queen Caroline case of 1820–21 was the highpoint of obscene populism in the early nineteenth century. Reynolds's polemical style is comparable to Renton Nicholson's *The Town* (1837–42) and to the early nineteenth-century *chroniques scandaleuses* (confessions of courtesans) which acquired a radical dimension through the Mary Anne Clarke and Harriette Wilson affairs.[46] *The Mysteries of London* also attacked George III, using the legend of Hannah Lightfoot, a quaker woman who was alleged to have entered into a secret marriage with the king and then mysteriously disappeared. This was a traditional item in the radical repertoire and was used constantly to attack the royal family along with the aristocracy.[47] Even at the time of his death, *Reynolds's Newspaper* was running a series of features on 'The British Aristocracy: its origin, progress and crimes' which used the Hannah Lightfoot legend to attack the royal family.[48]

Reynolds's pronouncements on politics were complex. *Reynolds's Miscellany* after 1849 became rather unpolitical and indeed would often feature positive articles about politicians Reynolds was attacking in his other publications. However, if there was a core theme in his work it was the attack on 'flunkeyism' which cropped up constantly and indicates his impatience with the spirit of deference evident in the working class. For example, the Queen's visit to Edinburgh in 1872 was dismissed as 'Great British Flunkeyism'.[49] Reynolds was horrified by what he perceived to be working-class conservatism, such as the support of workers for Lord Palmerston.[50] He was a believer in independent-minded citizens in battle with despotic élites.

Elsewhere, Reynolds's chief political commitment was international-ism, a long-standing radical concern that continued into the mid-Victorian period. *Reynolds's Newspaper* emphasized the importance of French radicalism and Mazzinian nationalism. Reynolds was an endur-ing critic of Napoleon III, the 'Despot-Ape of France'.[51] He opposed the British Empire as it stood because it was organized simply for the benefit of the aristocracy but Reynolds was not necessarily an anti-imperialist. He proposed a benevolent empire that would allow colonial people to develop their own land and so come to appreciate the virtues of citizen-ship. He supported the sepoys during the Indian mutiny and considered their suppression to be an imposition on the artisan pocket. Similarly, he took the radical anti-Russian line during the Crimean war which he con-sidered an avoidable conflict from which England gained nothing. Reynolds declared himself to be in favour of Irish nationalism although he added that 'as an Englishman [he] would be sorry to see Ireland separated from this country'.[52]

Reynolds's greatest passion in terms of internationalism was the United States of America which he saw as a place where the People's Charter really had been put into effect. America was glorified in his news-papers:

> The introduction of the American systems of conveyancing, and the
> abolition of the laws of entail, would, if the Aristocracy were
> deprived of the government patronage now enjoyed by them, cause
> all the great landed estates in the kingdom to be broken up into
> parcels, and sold out to form little farms, the cultivators of which
> would be the owners.[53]

Reynolds praised the fact that the people's representatives in the USA
were seldom wealthy. Although opposed to slavery, Reynolds (like some
abolitionists) actually supported the South at the commencement of the
Civil War on the grounds that it was a conflict about state rights and that
the South was in battle with northern capitalists. However, the paper
changed its allegiance to a cautious support for the North after the
Emancipation Proclamation of 1863. It also denounced English critics of
the Republic during the crisis that followed Lincoln's assassination:

> as for the sneers and sinister predictions of the flunkeys of aristoc-
> racy . . . at the elevation of Andrew Johnson to the presidency – we
> beg leave to remind them that it is not for the nation which has been
> ruled over by a series of German swine – being redolent and reeking
> with every known abomination – drunkards, profligates, and
> scoundrels of the blackest dye – to exult over the supposed humilia-
> tion of the republic . . .[54]

In common with some Chartists, by the 1860s Reynolds's politics had
become broadly radical liberal although he never liked the Liberal Party.
He had great regard for Gladstone because of his Free Trade budgets and
policy of retrenchment. But Reynolds's politics remained fundamentally
more libertarian than liberal. His papers were hostile to all intrusions on
individual freedom (opposing, for example, the Contagious Diseases
Acts) and therefore represent a continuation of the Freeborn Englishman
tradition. Government was regarded as at best a necessary evil. His
approach to religion was anti-clerical, attacking the Church for lecturing
the poor on morality and ignoring the question of wages. However, there
was a broadly Christian theme that ran through much of his fiction.
Unlike many radicals, Reynolds was pro-semitic and devoted several
articles to this theme.[55] *The Jewish Chronicle* was actually moved to
reprint a passage praising Jews from *The Mysteries of London*.[56]

Reynolds's most enduring theme (after the crimes of the aristocracy)
was his opposition to the law and to lawyers who he regarded with
venom. He saw the law in a similar way to Dickens in *Bleak House*, as a
fog that simply mystified the poor individuals who had to make use of it.
Reynolds attacked the élitist nature of the law; this is particularly evident
in the editorials on *causes-célèbres* which distilled from them their political content and revealed the problems of the poor in getting justice in a
court of law. For example, *Reynolds's* commented on the case of Priscilla
Bigadyke, executed for the murder of her husband in 1869 despite the

circumstantial nature of the evidence:

> The woman was poor, ignorant, perhaps immoral and had no
> friends to plead in her behalf. It is not such as she to whom Home
> Secretaries extend mercy. Had she been the wife of a gentleman, a
> member of a family of the ruling class, then scientific evidence would
> have been forthcoming as to her insanity, founded upon her condi-
> tion at the time of the deed . . . Poverty makes all the difference.
> There is only one law; There are two modes of administering it – one
> for the rich and one for the poor.[57]

The Mysteries of London also contained an attack on class law in Britain.
Reynolds complained that 'the wealthy may commit all social offences
with impunity; while the poor are cast into dungeons and coerced with
chains, for only following at a humble distance in the pathway of their
lordly precedents'.[58] It was in this spirit that Reynolds supported the
Tichborne Claimant, a poor man forced to confront an aristocratic state
and an unfair legal system. *Reynolds's Newspaper*'s emphasis on *causes-
célèbres* demonstrates the essence of Reynolds's style. He employed the
sensationalist elements of popular culture to give these apparently unpolitical cases a radical gloss.

After Reynolds's death in 1879, a memorial meeting was held by a
variety of London's radical clubs. Frank Kitz of the Social Club, Soho
moved a resolution praising him for his efforts in the cause of 'right and
justice'. He was seconded by William Morgan of the Manhood Suffrage
League and by Charles Murray who paid tribute to Reynolds's part in
1848 and his subsequent career as a radical journalist.[59] These were the
people who kept Socialism alive during the mid-Victorian years and
formed a connecting thread between Chartism and the late-Victorian
labour movement.[60] This kind of endorsement suggests that Reynolds,
though not a socialist, should be reclaimed as a major figure in the continuity of British radicalism. It is therefore appropriate that the author of
the entry on Reynolds in the *Dictionary of National Biography* was
Ramsay MacDonald.

But Reynolds also represents an opportunity lost for the left. Unlike
many radicals and socialists who came after him, Reynolds was not
hostile to the vulgarity and escapism of popular culture.[61] Indeed, he
embraced mass culture and appropriated its forms for radicalism.
Reynolds was essentially the product of the libertarianism of popular culture and politics. This could take respectable or unrespectable forms but
he straddled both worlds. Reynolds's achievement was to keep radical
ideas alive and to embody the politics of fairness and virtue against an
unjust state. His speeches, novels and journalism represented the values
of radical melodrama.

Notes

1. I would like to thank Dr Kelly Boyd for her comments on this article.
2. The most substantial biographical treatment is Louis James and John Saville, 'G.W.M. Reynolds' in Joyce Bellamy and John Saville (eds), *Dictionary of Labour Biography* (London: Macmillan, 1976), vol. 3, pp. 146–51. Otherwise, the most important work is by Anne Humphreys: 'G.W.M. Reynolds: Popular literature and popular politics' *Victorian Periodicals Review* (1983), vol. XVI, pp. 79–89. See also her 'The Geometry of the Modern City: G.W.M. Reynolds and *The Mysteries of London*' *Browning Institute Studies*, 11, (1983), pp. 69–81; 'Popular Narrative and Political Discourse in *Reynolds's Weekly Newspaper*' in Laurel Brake, Aled Jones and Lionel Madden (eds), *Investigating Victorian Journalism* (London: Macmillan, 1990), pp. 33–47; 'Generic Strands and Urban Twists: The Victorian Mysteries Novel' *Victorian Studies*, 34, (4), Summer 1991, pp. 455–72. On Reynolds's journalism, see Virginia Berridge, 'Popular Journalism and Working-Class Attitudes 1854–1886: A Study of *Reynolds's Newspaper, Lloyd's Weekly Newspaper* and *The Weekly Times*' (University of London D.Phil thesis, 1976). E.F. Bleiler's introduction and bibliography in the reprint of Reynolds's *Wagner the Wehr-wolf* (New York: Dover, 1975) are indispensable as is Donald Kausch, 'George W.M. Reynolds: A bibliography' *The Library*, 5th series, 28, (3), December 1973, pp. 319–26. Other studies include Daniel S. Burt, 'A Victorian Gothic: G.W.M. Reynolds's *Mysteries of London*' in Daniel Gerould (ed.), *Melodrama* (New York: New York Library Forum, 1980) pp. 141–58; Margaret Dalziel, *Popular Fiction 100 Years Ago: An Unexplored Tract of Literary History* (London: Cohen and West, 1957) ch. 4; Gertrude Himmelfarb, *The Idea of Poverty: England in the Early Industrial Age* (London: Faber and Faber, 1984) ch. 18; Richard C. Maxwell Jnr, *The Mysteries of Paris and London* (Charlottesville, Va.: University Press of Virginia, 1992); Cyril Pearl, *Victorian Patchwork* (London: Heinemann, 1972) ch. 4. Other scholars who discuss Reynolds include Eugenio Biagini, *Liberty, Retrenchment and Reform: Popular Liberalism in the Age of Gladstone* (Cambridge: Cambridge University Press, 1992) and Margot C. Finn, *After Chartism: Class and Nation in English Radical Politics, 1848–1874* (Cambridge: Cambridge University Press, 1993).
3. *Reynolds's Miscellany*, 7 November 1846, p. 16: hereafter *Miscellany*.
4. *Miscellany*, 26 December 1846, pp. 113–15; Steven Marcus, *The Other Victorians: A Study of Sexuality and Pornography in Mid-Nineteenth-Century England* (London: Weidenfeld and Nicholson, 1964).
5. Peter Bailey, ' "Will the Real Bill Banks Please Stand Up?": Towards a Role Analysis of Mid-Victorian Working-Class Respectability', *Journal of Social History*, vol. XII (3), Spring 1979, pp. 336–53.
6. Iain McCalman makes this connection in *Radical Underworld: Prophets, Revolutionaries and Pornographers in London, 1795–1840* (Cambridge: Cambridge University Press, 1988), pp. 236–7. See also McCalman, 'Unrespectable Radicalism: Infidels and Pornography in Early Nineteenth-Century London', *Past and Present* (104), (1984), pp. 74–110.
7. Michael Denning, *Mechanic Accents: Dime Novels and Working-class culture in America* (London: Verso, 1987), ch. 6 is an important treatment of the Mysteries tradition.

8. Jean-Luis Bory, *Eugene Sue* (Paris: Hachette, 1962).
9. Anne Humphreys, 'Popular Narrative and Political Discourse in *Reynolds's Weekly Newspaper*'.
10. *Miscellany*, 10 December 1859, p. 369.
11. Captain Vincent to Sir George Grey 9 April 1848: HO 45/2410 A f. 337 (Public Record Office).
12. G.W.M. Reynolds, *The Errors of the Christian Religion Exposed, by a Comparison of the Gospels of Matthew and Luke* (London: Richard Carlile, 1832).
13. G.W.M. Reynolds, *Wagner the Wehr-wolf*, E.F. Bleiler (ed.) (New York: Dover 1975), pp. vii–viii; P.T. Winskill, *The Comprehensive History of the Rise and Progress of the Temperance Reformation* (privately printed, 1881); *Temperance Lancet and Journal of Useful Intelligence*, 2 October 1841, p. 21.
14. McCalman, *Radical Underworld*, p. 220.
15. Henry Mayhew, *London Labour and the London Poor* (London: Griffin, Bohn and Co., 1861–62), vol. 1, p. 25.
16. Select Committee on Newspaper Stamps: Parliamentary Papers 1851, vol. XVII, p. 379; *Miscellany*, 20 February 1847, p. 256; Reynolds to W. Gurnsey, 28 May 1846: British Library Additional MSS 43,382 fo. 43.
17. Louis James, *Fiction For The Working Man, 1830–1850: A Study of the Literature Produced for the Working Classes in Early Victorian Urban England* (London: Oxford University Press, 1963), p. 166; *Reynolds's Newspaper*, 11 July 1875, p. 1: hereafter *Reynolds's*.
18. Reynolds, *The Mysteries of London* (London: George Vickers, 1846–50) vol. 1, p. 35.
19. Reynolds, *Mysteries of London*, vol. 1, p. 43.
20. Judith R. Walkowitz, *City of Dreadful Delight: Narratives of Sexual Danger in Late Victorian London* (London: Virago, 1992).
21. Select Committee on Newspaper Stamps: Parliamentary Papers (1851), vol. XVI, p. 374; *The Bookseller*, 1 July 1868, pp. 447–8.
22. *The Nation*, 6 April 1850, pp. 504–5.
23. Reynolds, *Mysteries of London*, vol. 1, p. 169; Reynolds, *The Modern Literature of France*, 2nd edition (London: G. Henderson, 1841) vol. 1, p. 83.
24. Alice Clowes, *Charles Knight: A Sketch* (London: Richard Bentley, 1892), p. 226.
25. *Northern Star*, 11 March 1848, p. 1.
26. *The Times*, 14 March 1848, p. 8; R.G. Gammage, *History of the Chartist Movement* (Newcastle-upon-Tyne: Browne and Browne, 1894), p. 296; *Miscellany*, 8 April 1848, p. 352.
27. Gammage, *History of the Chartist Movement*, p. 294; *Punch*, (1848) vol. XIV, p. 112; W.J. Linton, *James Watson* (Manchester: Abel Heywood, 1879), p. 65.
28. W.E. Adams, *Memoirs of a Social Atom* (London: Hutchinson, 1903), vol. 1, p. 235.
29. Gammage, *History of the Chartist Movement*, p. 377; *The Times*, 27 May 1848, p. 7, 7 September 1848, p. 7.
30. Thomas Clark, *A Letter Addressed to G.W.M. Reynolds* (London: T. Clark, 1850); John Saville, *Ernest Jones: Chartist* (London: Lawrence and Wishart, 1952), pp. 72–3.

31. Virginia Berridge, 'Popular Journalism and Working-Class Attitudes' pp. 39, 62–6.
32. *Potteries Examiner*, 29 March 1873, p. 6; *Reynolds's*, 29 June 1879, p. 1.
33. *Miscellany*, 19 June 1869, p. 432.
34. Clement Scott and Cecil Howard, *The Life and Reminiscences of E.L. Blanchard* (London: Hutchinson, 1891), vol. I, p. 55.
35. Reynolds, *A Sequel to Don Juan* (London: Paget, 1843), p. 35.
36. *Reynolds's*, 11 July 1875, p. 1.
37. *Reynolds's Political Instructor*, 10 November 1849, p. 2: hereafter *Instructor*.
38. *Reynolds's*, 5 January 1868, p. 3; 11 July 1858, p. 7; 11 July 1875, p. 1.
39. *Instructor*, 15 December 1849, p. 43.
40. W.M. Thackeray, 'Charity and Humour' in *The Oxford Illustrated Thackeray* (London: Oxford University Press, n.d.), vol. 10, pp. 623–4.
41. *Reynolds's* 11 July 1875 p. 1.
42. Reynolds, *Mary Price; Or, The Memoirs of a Servant Maid* (London: John Dicks, 1852), vol. 2, p. 410.
43. *Instructor*, 10 November 1849, p. 5; see Christopher Hill, 'The Norman Yoke' in John Saville (ed.), *Democracy and the Labour Movement* (London: Lawrence and Wishart, 1954), pp. 11–66.
44. David Cannadine, *The Decline and Fall of the British Aristocracy* (New Haven, Conn.: Yale University Press, 1990); Andrew Adonis, *Making Aristocracy Work: The Peerage and the Political System in Britain, 1884–1914* (Oxford: Clarendon Press, 1993).
45. *Instructor*, 10 November 1849, pp. 5, 1.
46. McCalman, *Radical Underworld*, pp. 221–31.
47. Reynolds, *Mysteries of London*, vol. 1, p. 187; John Lindsey, *The Lovely Quaker* (London: Rich and Cowen, 1939).
48. *Reynolds's*, 22 June 1879, p. 2.
49. *Reynolds's*, 18 August 1872, p. 3; see also 8 September 1872, p. 3; 29 September 1872, p. 1.
50. *Reynolds's*, 5 April 1863, p. 1; 14 August 1864, p. 4.
51. *Instructor*, 6 April 1850, p. 170. See also *Reynolds's*, 7 June 1863, p. 1.
52. *Northern Star*, 15 April 1854, p. 6.
53. *Instructor*, 10 November 1849, p. 3.
54. *Reynolds's*, 30 April 1865, p. 1.
55. *Miscellany*, 21 August 1847, pp. 226–27; *Reynolds's*, 11 July 1858, p. 7.
56. *Jewish Chronicle*, 19 March 1847, pp. 101–2.
57. *Reynolds's*, 3 January 1869, p. 4.
58. Reynolds, *Mysteries of London*, vol. 1, p. 2.
59. *Reynolds's*, 29 June 1879, p. 1.
60. Stan Shipley, *Club Life and Socialism in Mid-Victorian London* (London: Journeyman Press, 1983).
61. Chris Waters, *British Socialists and the Politics of Popular Culture, 1884–1914* (Manchester: Manchester University Press, 1990).

CHAPTER FOURTEEN

Owenism and the Secularist Tradition: the Huddersfield Secular Society and Sunday School

Edward Royle

The science of society

Between 1837 and 1845 'a great and spreading sect'[1] was making an impact on industrial towns and villages throughout the Midlands and North of England. These were the followers of Robert Owen, officially known as Socialists. Pursuing the science of society, they believe Robert Owen had revealed the reasons why poverty was increasing amidst the plenty generated by industrialization, and they accepted his view that irrationality and ignorance were responsible for the blight which struck so many in what he called 'the old immoral world'. They looked forward with him to the creation of 'the new moral world'.

The history and significance of this popular form of Owenism as 'a visible social movement with its distinctive institutions, known leaders and widespread institutions'[2] was rescued from the myths of traditional labour history by John Harrison in the 1960s. He not only saw the significance of the movement as a coherent part of Owenism but also interpreted the movement within the religious sectarian framework of early nineteenth-century society.

The social doctrines of Robert Owen contained two principal elements: that the character of man was formed for and not by him; and that the new moral world was to be created through life in 'communities of united interest'. The first element was one of the great truths which the ignorant and irrational were unable to appreciate. Instead, orthodox Christian doctrine taught the sinfulness of mankind and the need for redemption from sin through the blood of Jesus Christ. Sectarian religion blinded people to the real truth which Owen was revealing to them, that mankind was innately good and had the resources in a rationally organized society to commence immediately the new moral world on earth.

Much followed from the doctrine of circumstances. One irrational feature of modern society, preventing the rational distribution of resources for the common good, was individual competition. Individualism, ultimately, was rooted in the nuclear family, the basis of which was the institution of religious marriage. The latter was frequently perpetuated not by love but by legal chains which held particularly women in a form of legalized prostitution long after experience of changed circumstances had banished the vestiges of love and the basis of happiness. Thus Owen arrived at his list of 'Satanic institutions ... the priesthood, the lawyers and magistrates, the military, the unnatural and artificial union of the sexes, individual and national competition and contests and the consequent single family or universally disuniting arrangements of society, and the metal circulating medium of wealth'.[3]

This diagnosis had wide appeal, but many who accepted Owen's ends were dubious about his means and saw less relevance in his vision of a communitarian millennium than in immediate improvements to their lot at home. Co-operative trading ventures were both more immediate and appealed also to workmen and their wives for whom the consolations of Christianity appeared to underpin rather than challenge their efforts to create a better society. Sympathetic political radicals maintained that the reform of society was dependent upon the seizure of political power through manhood suffrage. As one leading West Riding Chartist argued in 1839:

> He advocated Chartism that he might ultimately obtain the innu-
> merable and solid advantages of Socialism with perfect security; and
> it was upon this point only that he and other Chartists differed from
> Mr. Owen, who thought that the advantages of Socialism could be
> obtained and secured sooner than the political objects sought by the
> Chartists could be obtained.[4]

In fact, neither was successful. Owen's attempt to create a model community at Queenwood Farm in Hampshire was to fail amid acrimony and bankruptcy in 1845. The Chartists were to petition for manhood suffrage three times, in 1839, 1842 and 1848, and were to be ignored by the House of Commons on each occasion. Chartists and Socialists alike were compelled to settle for a more gradual reform of both the political and social system.

Rational religion

The form which Owen gave to Socialism in the later 1830s was religious. As he explained to The Friends of Truth in Paisley in 1836: 'This system is derived *solely* from God, or that *Power* which *compels* us to have our *thoughts* and our *feelings*; it is in accordance with all nature ...'.[5] And as the Creed of the New Social System put it in 1838, 'The religion of the New Moral World consist in the unceasing practice of promoting the happiness of every man, woman, and child, to the greatest extent in our power, without regard to their class, sect, or party, country or colour.'[6]

The vehicle for this new religion was the Association of All Classes of All Nations (AACAN), founded on 1 May 1835 as a propagandist organization to prepare the public mind for the new moral world. The next stage came in 1837 with the formation of the National Community Friendly Society (NCFS), at which time the AACAN was given a popular democratic structure based on a network of local branches and classes. Thus Owenism developed at the local level into what might be called an extreme anti-sect which, rejecting religious orthodoxy, espoused an alternative rational and secular theology which had many of the trappings of a religion – with Halls of Science instead of chapels, social missionaries and stationed lecturers instead of ministers and local preachers, ceremonies for the naming of children instead of the rite of baptism, and hymns from the 'social hymn book'. Meetings resembled services, with hymns, readings and sermons. Owen was prophet and Social Father.

This religious form was partly a matter of idiom – it spoke the current language of popular organization, mission and revival as understood by communities experienced in Methodism and chapel life; and partly a matter of antithesis – the religion of the new moral world which would replace that of the old. Religion also provided the means by which those small numbers to whom the true revelation had been granted could protect themselves, psychologically and physically, against their enemies until their moment of victory should come. The sect was an excellent vehicle for survival as well as for mission in the old immoral world.

The years 1837–39 were ones of heady revival and by May 1839 there were over 50 branches situated in the most populous and industrial towns in England and central Scotland. Then, Owen announced that the first stage in the campaign was over. He amalgamated the AACAN and the NCFS to form the Universal Community Society of Rational Religionists. The public mind had now been alerted and the time had come to demonstrate the truth of his message with the acquisition of Queenwood Farm.

Unfortunately for Owen, local men and women who had committed themselves to life in their local Social Institutions and were enjoying considerable success attacking Christianity by playing to the anti-clerical gallery, were not disposed now to sacrifice everything for what seemed the remoter prospect of transforming the world in Hampshire. Energies were divided. When the community failed in 1845, fragments of the local sectarian organization were all that remained of what was now termed the Rational Society. The doctrine of circumstances, shorn of its communitarian values, gave rise to a new individualized ethical system emphasizing the improvability of man through education and a better environment, rejecting alternative theological accounts. It was this aspect of Owenism which, under the leadership of one of the Owenite lecturers, George Jacob Holyoake, became known in 1851 as Secularism.[7] Though most Rational Society branches collapsed with the failure of Owen's practical experiment and the general malaise which afflicted both Owenism and Chartism alike in the mid-1840s, memories, loyalties and some organizations survived to be rallied in the 1850s by Holyoake and other former Owenite lecturers.

The legacy of Owenism

The purpose of this essay is to trace the legacy of Owenite experience in a local context.[8] The possibilities of such an approach were pointed out in 1969 with regard to the society at Failsworth, near Manchester, which survived until 1958.[9] More recently, the Leicester Society, which still exists with a rich collection of minute books, has attracted scholarly attention.[10] But few sources survive for the many other local societies which disappeared, often without trace, towards the end of the nineteenth century. Their history can be pieced together only from odd references in the periodical and newspaper literature of the day.[11] One of the more celebrated and successful of these Victorian societies was to be found in the medium-sized Yorkshire manufacturing town of Huddersfield. Its history can suggest some of the possibilities for understanding radical continuities in the mid-Victorian years.

Both Chartism and Owenism had been strong in the textile districts of the North, and so it is not surprising to find the largest grouping of Secular societies in these same areas.[12] Here, in the Pennine uplands, communities had not been transformed overnight by the onset of industrialization, but had grown slowly – from hamlets into villages, and villages into small towns. A sense of community was still strong in the mid-century years, centred on chapel, public house and co-operative society. The radicals did not recruit from a rootless proletariat, but from among workers with shared experiences of work and culture. In such a community the Secularist could not expect to be a popular figure – the chapel and public house would be unlikely to draw his custom, though he might well be a pillar of the local co-operative society. He would, however, be respected as a man of stiff principles, a natural leader when some burning national or local issue called for radical agitation and organization – one of that type referred to by contemporaries as a 'politician'.[13] In the larger centres there might be a couple of dozen such people; a club would then be formed where discussions could be held. Occasionally, when a national figure came down from London to lecture, a large hall would have to be hired, and the handful of activists would then find that their surrounding communities could produce a thousand people eager to hear G.J. Holyoake, Charles Bradlaugh, Mrs Harriet Law or Mrs Annie Besant.

Huddersfield from Owenism to Secularism

Huddersfield was a centre for Owenism. It had the first AACAN branch in Yorkshire – and the sixth in the whole country.[14] The branch was founded in the spring of 1837 when Lawrence Pitkethly junior, son of the Huddersfield draper who was a leading campaigner against the new Poor Law and for the Ten Hours movement, discretely asked for socialist tracts to circulate among the 24 local readers of the official journal, the *New Moral World*.[15] Between 1837 and 1845 the Huddersfield members paid more in penny membership subscriptions to the Rational Society than any other branch relative to the size of town. At first they met at what they called their Social Institution – actually a room belonging to the landlord of the George and Dragon in Manchester Street – but it soon proved too small for their meetings and their landlord was threatened with the loss of his licence, so a prospectus was issued to raise the funds to build a large hall of their own.[16] The land was secured with some difficulty, since almost all the land in the town centre of Huddersfield belonged to the Ramsden family who were staunch supporters of the Established Church. Nevertheless, a purpose-built Hall of Science was opened in November 1839.[17]

The cost of the Hall and the need to finance the Queenwood Community meant that the local Owenites had a hard time maintaining their cause during a period of severe economic depression. Membership fees peaked in 1840, declined for the next three years, and then showed some recovery in 1844.[18] Support for the community was less enthusiastic, peaking in 1840 but not reviving in 1844 despite the fact that in November of that year one of their members, John Gray, an agriculturalist, secured a place there. Local costs were cut in 1844 when the Hall of Science was let to the Chartists on alternate Sundays, but interest seems to have drifted in that direction the following year as the Chartist Co-operative Land Society captured the imagination.[19] Undaunted by the failure of their community, though, the Socialists celebrated the sixth anniversary of the Hall of Science in November 1845.[20]

During the whole of this time, Huddersfield had not had their own stationed lecturer, but their opportunity came in 1846 when redundant Owenite lecturers were seeking any post they could find. One of the Huddersfield members, Read Holliday, was a manufacturing chemist and he was able to bring to the town the former lecturer from Edinburgh,

Robert Cooper, whom he employed as a clerk. Cooper was not impressed with Huddersfield – it was certainly not like Edinburgh, or even his native Manchester. He described it as 'a mental wilderness' and wanted to move on to London as quickly as possible.[21] He also described Holliday's business ungratefully as 'wanting in respectability'. This was unfair, for it was the presence of upwardly mobile local businessmen like Holliday which gave Owenism and, subsequently, Secularism, their strength and ability to survive.[22]

Cooper's departure came with the sale of the Hall of Science to the Unitarians in 1847. Though temporarily scattered as a branch, the hard core of members remained and were soon again in evidence to continue their advocacy of truth and exposure of error. When G.J. Holyoake came to the town in July 1848, he drew a mixed audience of Chartists and Socialists to the Christian Brethren's meeting room in Albion Street. The Brethren were the followers of Joseph Barker, one time Methodist New Connexion minister and vigorous opponent of Owenism, but now a Unitarian Chartist and on his way to outright – though temporary – unbelief.[23]

When Holyoake revived the remnants of the old Rational Society under the name of Secularism and called a conference in Manchester in 1852, Huddersfield was not one of the 20 societies represented there and it was not until the following year that he was invited to return to the town to lecture. The initiative came from William Harral Johnson, a young ex-Methodist recently arrived from Leeds, who had commenced an agitation in association with Joseph Bowker, an old Chartist and a canvasser of radical books in the area, and William Rowland Croft, a local grocer. He looked for a meeting place for lectures and sought assistance from George Brook, now a prospering dyer, who had been dismissed by his evangelical employers in 1839 for the part he had played in the erection of the Hall of Science.[24] A society, grandly called The Athenaeum Literary and Secular Society, was formed, holding lectures at the Christian Brethren's room, but this seems not to have outlasted Johnson's removal to Blackburn in 1855. Bowker was a proscribed man because of his views, and left the town for Glasgow where he died in 1856.[25]

The Albion Street room was not available on Sundays,[26] which limited the regular activities of those who wished to revive the spirit of the old Rational Society in the town to informal discussions at the Temperance Hotel opened by Joseph Thornton, a former cropper, in the town centre in 1851. Thornton's (which thrived until its proprietor's death in 1887) was described by the local newspaper in 1875 as a place where employers and employees could meet on equal terms, and where all shades of religious and political opinions were welcomed: it was naturally a centre of radicalism and heterodoxy.[27] When Holyoake stayed at Thornton's in 1860, while lecturing at the Philosophical Hall, he commented how 'Huddersfield has taken more care for the reputation of Freethought than I was aware of.'[28]

He also noticed that 'in Huddersfield, chapels are multiplying faster than mills'. This was part of the great religious revival which swept the country in 1860 from Northern Ireland. Secularism, which had been expanding generally in the north of England since 1853, was caught up in the fervour as two great Camp Meetings, attended by several thousand sympathizers from both sides of the Pennines, were held on Castle Hill just outside the town in 1860 and 1861.[29] As a result of the second of these, a meeting was called in the Assembly Room of the Philosophical Hall at which the Huddersfield Secular Society was formed.[30]

Revival on both sides led Christians and Secularists into a new wave of mutual antagonism such as had not been experienced since the early 1840s when Owenites and Christians had clashed. Restrictions were again placed on Secularist meeting places. On 12 January 1862 Mrs Harriet Law, a popular and outspoken lecturer from London, was due to lecture at the Philosophical Hall but the owner objected to the contract and had the doors barred against her. The Secularists forced an entry, whereupon the owner turned off the gas, necessitating a temporary evacuation of the premises. Mrs Law finally managed to give her lectures, on 'The spread of Christianity no proof of its divine origin' in the afternoon, and 'The oppressed and degraded condition of women' in the evening. At tea-time 300 people sat down to tea in a side room to celebrate the opening of the society's Sunday school.[31]

The Huddersfield Secular Society and Sunday school

For the next quarter of a century the freethinkers developed their own style of anti-Christian chapel and chapel culture. Within a year the society had 80 members with a further 100 children in the school; they had a mutual improvement class of 16, a library with over 200 volumes and they could attract an audience of over a thousand to lectures delivered by the young rising star of national Secularism, Charles Bradlaugh.[32] The strength of the society lay in its roots. As W.H. Johnson later recalled:

> Large numbers of Freethinkers were present from all the districts round about Huddersfield. They had travelled from Holmfirth and Honley. Men who had carried in triumph the huge black flag of Paddock which had flaunted in many a struggle when Richard Oastler was Steward of Fixby Hall and the chosen leader of the Ten-

hours' agitation. There were men present who had borne the brunt
of every fight at the old Hall of Science; and who, like George Brook,
had been dismissed from Starkie's [sic] factories a generation before
or who, like Joseph Thornton, had trained up a squadron of
Reformers, or who, like W. Rowland Croft, had kept alive the flick-
ering flame of Secularism . . .[33]

Their aim, announced at a half-yearly meeting in June 1863, was to fulfil
the promise of Owenism which had failed 20 years before. Their president at this time was George Brook, and the leader of the school was
another veteran of Owenism, David France.[34]

   After four years of success and growth, the society acquired the use of
new premises, Senior's Schoolroom in East Parade, which had just been
vacated by the Primitive Methodists.[35] By now they were making an
impact on the town and began to face considerable local opposition.
When the former Philosophical Hall – now the Theatre Royal – was hired
for a lecture from Bradlaugh, the agreement was broken on the grounds
that such contracts with unbelievers were invalid in law. A course of anti-
Secularist lectures was then delivered by the Reverend James McCann,
evangelical curate of St Paul's Church, which in turn led to a six-nights'
debate the following spring between McCann and Bradlaugh.[36] The
publicity this debate occasioned was of great benefit to the society.
Bradlaugh had just reorganized Secularism and asserted his own control
of the movement by establishing the National Secular Society. During the
later 1870s and 1880s this was to be one of the leading radical organizations in the country, though the men of Huddersfield had little directly to
do with it – for reasons which will emerge later in this chapter.

   Despite complaints in 1868 that the society was drifting and attracting
few new members, the Sunday school was thriving and audiences of
1 500 or more could be attracted to lectures if the theatre or some other
large building could be hired for the occasion.[37] By the 1870s, Secularism
in Huddersfield was well established around a nucleus of dedicated freethinkers, some of them veterans of the Owenite movement, running a
successful local society which was something of a mixture of a club and a
chapel, to which was attached a thriving Sunday school. Though membership was tiny when compared with one of the many Christian congregations which met in the town, a wider group of sympathizers could
always be found in Thornton's Temperance Hotel. When a national
lecturer came to town they could fill the largest public hall available, or,
as happened in 1874, draw thousands to an open-air meeting on Castle
Hill – 'this of course including some hundreds attracted by curiosity'.[38]

   By 1874, the Secularists were feeling the need to secure larger premises
to accommodate their lecture audiences and Sunday school anniversary
meetings. At the annual Christmas tea and entertainment in 1875, 140

people sat down to tea in the East Parade schoolroom and afterwards discussed the need to build larger premises. But Huddersfield was owned by
Sir John Ramsden, and Sir John did not like Secularism. Thwarted, they
managed to renegotiate their lease to take their existing premises on a
full-time annual basis, and spent money improving them. But at the
fifteenth anniversary celebrations in 1877, the room was 'crowded to
excess'. In the school there were about 80 boys and girls, with 28
teachers, of whom nearly half were former scholars.[39]

The school continued in this fashion until December 1883, when the
premises proved inadequate for the activities of both a branch of the
National Secular Society and the Sunday school. The latter was squeezed
out and restarted in new rooms some distance away in Brook Street.[40] By
1885, the school was in yet different premises again, in Ramsden Street,
while the Secular Institute in East Parade continued to be used for ordinary meetings. A new approach was made to the Ramsden estate for the
lease on a site for a new hall. Ramsden at first agreed to let a site on East
Parade and the Secularists launched a building fund, but in 1886 he
changed his mind.[41] 'Freethought is thus boycotted in Huddersfield by
one man, who holds the mental life of the town in the hollow of his
hand,' commented G.W. Foote, editor of the national *Freethinker*; but he
went on perceptively to add: 'and there is too much reason to fear that he
is tacitly supported in this instance by the general sentiment of the
Christian population, who always fail to recognise persecution unless it
is directed against themselves'.[42]

The tide was turning nationally against Secularism in the later 1880s
and the weakened Huddersfield society was in no position to counter the
trend. A final meeting was held at East Parade on 22 August 1886, and a
small room was taken not far away in Upperhead Row. After the prize-
giving on 24 October, the Sunday school was 'dissolved until further
notice'. Occasional lectures were given in the new Friendly and Trades
Societies Club in Northumberland Street, although their lecturers had to
enter by the back door on Sundays. The members were disheartened.[43] In
1890 even Bradlaugh could get only a 'fair' audience for a morning lecture on the Eight Hours' Question, and 'slightly less' for his afternoon
lecture on theology.[44] There was a short revival in the early 1890s with
increased lecturing activity, and a successful sick club was started, but
reports of activity thereafter are less frequent than the obituary notices of
deceased members sent in by the secretary who was also treasurer to the
local Oddfellows. In this fashion the society continued a tenuous
existence until at least 1910 when the Secularist, Harry Snell, stood as
Labour candidate in the December general election.[45]

The sociology of Secularism

The life of the Secular Society and its school at their height gives in micro-
cosm not only a view of Secularism at large, but also of other popular
radical and religious institutions. It is therefore worth looking more
closely at the life of this one society both to exemplify the macrocosm
and to test some of the generalizations which sociologists have made
about religion and freethought.

One sociological model, based on Weber, suggests that in all religious
organizations there is a tendency towards routinization, from beginnings
as a sect or missionary endeavour with informal organization, spon-
taneity, and charismatic leadership, to maturity as a church or denomination with an inward-looking, respectable, self-perpetuating
membership. So far as Secularism is concerned, the first type is anxious to
eliminate religion, while the second seeks a substitute religion.[46] This is a
sociological model, not an historical description, but it does have some
validity in historical analysis.

These two opposing types or models – the militant, missionary sect
and the organized, respectable chapel – do not appear in any chronologi-
cal order but rather exist as tendencies within any society or indeed any
Secularist. The Huddersfield society had its militant moments, but in its
heyday those members who emphasized this aspect were in a minority.
When the National Secular Society split in 1877 over Bradlaugh's decision to republish the controversial birth-control work, *The Fruits of
Philosophy*, most of the Huddersfield members came out against him and
worked outside the NSS structure for at least five years. They were the
epitome of moderation and respectability. Only with decline in the 1890s
did they see the need for renewed mission and revival.[47]

Why should moderation have been the dominant characteristic of the
Huddersfield society? Sociologists drawing on American evidence have
tried to link the degree of militancy with the size of community – groups
in small towns having to reach a *modus vivendi* with their neighbours;
those in large towns needing to be militant to be noticed at all. There
seems little British evidence to support this.[48] Probably the four most
respectable and non-militant societies were those in Glasgow, Leicester,
Huddersfield and Failsworth. While concentrating on Huddersfield,
something can be learned from what these four had in common.

First, all four were successful, the three others more so than
Huddersfield. The Leicester society still exists, and the Failsworth
Sunday school closed its doors only in 1958. Success could breed com-
placency and moderation. Secondly, as G.W. Foote noted when he was
president of the National Secular Society after Bradlaugh's death, moder-
ates tended to be dominant where the Owenite legacy was strong,[49] and

this was certainly true of these four societies – especially Failsworth and Huddersfield where the members were also active in those other legacies of Owenism, popular education and the co-operative movement.

Secularism and 'chapel' culture

Huddersfield provides a very good case study of a freethought 'chapel', where the society served its members as a functional equivalent to that chapel life which flourished in the town.[50] Not to be deprived of the consolations of orthodoxy, the Secularists existed on the religious spectrum a little to the left of the Unitarians. In a town where practically every child passed through a Sunday school, the children of Secularists too enjoyed their outings, their treats and their anniversaries with hymns, recitations and prize-givings. There was a small library, an elocution class and a discussion group for mutual improvement. The ladies held their bazaars for 'chapel' funds, and ran their sewing class like any group of chapel ladies. Christian festivals were celebrated with tea-parties and dances, marking the yearly rituals of Christmas, New Year, Shrovetide, Easter and Whitsun.[51]

But more so than many chapels, the Secular society was also a working-men's club and a political organization. In 1873, at the height of the popular republican movement, the society gave birth to a Republican Club. Its secretary, Owen Balmforth, was the son of an old Chartist-Owenite. Three years later, Balmforth made his debut as a lecturer with 'Home Rule for Ireland; what does it mean and should it be granted?' The meeting decided in favour of Home Rule some eight years in advance of general Liberal opinion.[52] The Sunday school also was more than a place for moral education. In an age when elementary education was still not easily obtained, Sunday schools offered classes on week-nights and taught adults as well as children. The Secular Sunday school was no different. One of the best-known accounts of the school at its height comes in the autobiography of Ben Turner, the future textile workers' leader:

> They had two sessions each Sunday, at which we were taught reading, writing, arithmetic, geography, history, elocution, singing, etc. Sometimes there was no school in the afternoons, and noted Secular lecturers came and gave afternoon and evening addresses. It was there I heard Annie Besant, George Jacob Holyoake, Harriet Law, Charles Watts, Dr. Aveling, and many others whose names slip from my memory. I heard Bradlaugh several times; he was a big draw, and they used to engage a big hall for his visit and folks would walk miles to hear him. These Secularists didn't always lecture on Secularism. Many of their addresses were on social subjects like the land question, perpetual pensions, republicanism, home rule, etc., and I learnt

a bit about many subjects, but more still, I learnt how to learn about these things. Anti-religion didn't enter much into it, but we were not orthodox religionists, and our workmates, etc., were always running us down as young infidels. It was at this school, through its elocution and singing classes, that I got my further stimulus to reading. I learnt scores of recitations, took part in many little plays, and we held our own debates, when we thrashed things out rudely and crudely, but, by jove! it was rich life for young fellows like me, from fifteen to nineteen years of age.[53]

Turner was a serious-minded, self-improving working youth, and his type gives a further clue to the sober and moderate air which character-ized the Huddersfield society. It is a common observation that people can express their inward aspirations and outward achievements in their reli-gious behaviour – Methodists making good and turning Anglican, for instance. Among the Secularists this sort of movement could take a mem-ber to the Unitarian chapel, but in other cases the rising status of the members simply changed the character of the society and made it more like a Unitarian chapel. One such respectable convert was the solicitor and local historian, D.F.E. Sykes, who obviously had himself in mind when he described the ministry of the Reverend John Thomas of the Fitzwilliam Street Unitarian chapel between 1862 and 1884:

> His philosophical discourses were much appreciated by the most thoughtful and cultured minds of the town and neighbourhood, and it is a significant fact that the less aggressive section of those who had been wont at Senior's School Room to sit at the feet of George Jacob Holyoake, Charles Bradlaugh, George W. Foote, Dr. Aveling, and other lecturers of very liberal views, were more and more attracted to the church in Fitzwilliam Street.[54]

Enough respectable people remained behind, however, to maintain the Secular society in friendly rivalry. Mr Thomas was the chief preacher at the Sunday school anniversary services in 1878.[55]

One indication of the social status of some of the society's members is that the Secularists never seemed short of money. When Ramsden refused the lease for a new site in 1886, donations of £350 and a loan of £500 had already been promised towards the £1 300 expected building costs. Recalling the 1850s, W.H. Johnson wrote that they were always able to pay their lecturers their fees, thanks to half a dozen middle-class people.[56] Such patronage was essential to any working-class venture which did not have a mass membership, but not many local Secularist societies were fortunate enough to enjoy it.

Obituary notices from the freethought press can bring the historian a little closer to who these members were. The source no doubt gives a sample biased towards the elderly and the important, but they nevertheless provide a guide to those people who determined the complexion of the society and ensured its success. In all, there are 37 obituaries, including those of five women. Of the 32 men, reasonably full details are given for half, of whom nine ran their own businesses (mainly shopkeepers). The overall picture is of an elderly, respectable and successful group of gentlemen who, from often humble origins, had risen to positions of commercial and even civic importance in the town.[57]

In her study, *Varieties of Unbelief*, Susan Budd makes a number of suggestions about the national complexion of Secularist membership, using mainly obituary notices and autobiographies.[58] My impression from the same evidence is that her conclusions are a little extreme,[59] and certainly Huddersfield does not conform to her national picture. First, the rank-and-file membership may well have been of the working class, but the local activists seem to have been *petit bourgeois* to a greater extent than she allows. Secondly, whereas she finds an overwhelmingly male movement (only 6 per cent female), in Huddersfield 15 per cent of obituaries were those of women; moreover, in the membership lists given in the *National Reformer* in 1879 and 1880, 11 out of 43 (26 per cent) and nine out of 38 (24 per cent) respectively were women. Dr Budd argues for a low level of family participation and little continuity between generations; again, Huddersfield is different. Perhaps because of the Sunday school, there is evidence both of family participation and of a second generation growing up in 'the faith'. Both of Watts Balmforth's sons were active members. Owen continued so, and remained a Radical Liberal;[60] the other son, Ramsden, like his father joined the ILP and later became a Unitarian minister.[61]

A number of the features of the Huddersfield society were mutually reinforcing. Militant freethinkers were often of the first generation, reacting against former strongly held religious principles and beliefs; those brought up in the Secular Sunday school without such beliefs were likely to be of a more moderate outlook. A respectable society was as likely to attract respectable support as respectable support was likely to turn the society respectable. Even so, to remain with the Secular Society was ultimately an act of defiance and a statement of independence from accepted values and patterns of behaviour.

Conclusion

Huddersfield may not have been typical, but there is equally no reason to see it as wholly untypical. Our image of freethought is often shaped by the contemporary Christian propaganda which projected the 'infidel' as a creature who was immoral in life and bereft in death. It may therefore come as a surprise to see these Huddersfield 'infidels' as a group of respectable tradesmen, with their wives and daughters, running a successful chapel and Sunday school comparable with any Christian denomination in everything except their lack of belief in supernatural religion. To study them is worth while, if only for this.

But the group at Senior's Schoolroom was also the embodiment of a living political tradition, a little to the Radical left of the Gladstonian Liberal Party, but always proudly independent of it, cherishing the ideals of Owenism and Chartism and handing them on to the next generation. The energies once devoted to Secularism were after 1886 absorbed into the wider religious and political life of the town, in the Unitarian chapel, the Friendly and Trades Club, the Co-operative Society, the School Board, the Town Council and both Liberal-Radical and Labour politics.

The existence of this tradition of Secularist Radicalism in Huddersfield throughout the Victorian period, suggests that those historians who have searched to explain discontinuities in working-class history after the defeats of Chartism and Owenism in the 1840s might after all have been asking the wrong questions about the local experience of political and social activism in the Victorian era.[62]

Appendix

Some members of the Huddersfield Secular Society, *c.* 1860–1900:

Armitage, William: d. 8 May 1876, aged 68; seed merchant; supporter of Oastler and Chartism – known locally as 'young Feargus O'Connor'; later a staunch Liberal; sometime president of the Secular Society.

Balmforth, Watts: b. 1826; d. 29 January 1904, aged 78; handloom weaver, retired on savings; old Owenite and Chartist; founder of Secular Society and Sunday school; a staunch Liberal and a member of the Rashcliffe Liberal Club; represented Huddersfield at founding meeting of ILP in Bradford, 1893 for which he suffered reprisals from some Liberals; joined Lockwood Labour Club; continued a supporter of Labour until his death; father of Owen and Ramsden Balmforth.

Berresford, J.H.: buried 9 October, 1912; an atheist and a socialist.

Brook, George: d. December 1880, aged 77; Owenite; president; foreman in dyeing department at Starkey's, but dismissed after 17 years service in 1839 for Owenism; set up in own business and was able to retire when 53; promoter of the Hall of Science; Improvement Commissioner.

Brook, Rebecca: d. 17 June 1865, aged 27; parents Owenites, children educated in the local branch school; continued in Secularism.

Brown, James: d. 2 October 1885, aged 82; musical instrument maker; Owenite.

Chorlton, John: d. 25 November 1876; handloom weaver from Scammonden; Owenite and Co-operator; freethinker for 60 years.

Croft, William Rowland: grocer from Rashcliffe; later Inspector of Nuisances; historian of the Factory Movement.

Denton, Ernest: grocer from Moldgreen; secretary, and later Sunday school treasurer.

Eastwood, Jonas: d. 1874, aged 76; a joiner from Netherthong.

Entwistle, William: d. 15 March 1904, aged 79; 'retired from business for some years'.

Fielding, Henry: letter-press printer (later moved to Oldham); sometime secretary.

France, Mrs David: d. 9 September 1882; wife of David France [an old Owenite; vice-president and Sunday school superintendent; address in 1883 was Freehold Street].

Green, George: d. 31 March 1876, aged 57; from Honley; 'He was one of the old Socialists; and by trade he was a weaver, but owing to his energetic character, he has very successfully carried on business as a stationer and general dealer for a number of years'; a covert supporter, who sent money.

Hirst, Henry: d. 1 March 1880, aged 76; kept Shakespeare Hotel; admirer of Charles Southwell and Ernest Jones (and Shakespeare).

Hirst, Joseph: d. 4 April 1867, aged 27 (of bronchitis); from Lockwood; parents were Owenites; sometime secretary.

Hopkinson, Mrs: d. 25 November 1877, aged 60; from Rashcliffe; wife of Joash Hopkinson; one of her sons was treasurer and her two daughters taught in Sunday school.

Netherwood, Hannah: d. January 1915, aged 87; founder of Secular Society; wife of John, below.

Netherwood, John: d. 11 February 1899, aged 75; committee member and taught in Sunday school.

North, Abraham: d. 29 November 1878, aged 69; active in Ten-Hours movement; anti-Corn Law Agitation; Chartism (O'Connorite; nominated to NCA General Council, 1842); later worked for the Conservatives in elections; committee member.

Ollernshaw, Tom: d. 22 August 1910; had emigrated to Australia, but returned.

Pogson, Joseph: d. 1 February 1884, aged 67; shoemaker from Slaithwaite; freethinker and republican for 50 years.

Priestley, William: d. 1915, aged 75; draper and general dealer; became a socialist in old age.

Redfern, Joseph: d. 14 October 1872; worked for Marsden Gas Co.

Spivey, William Henry: d. 1915, aged 64; painter, paperhanger, gilder, grainer, sign-writer etc.; secretary for 30 years; Oddfellows treasurer.

Studdard, Uriah: d. 1906, aged 84; 'a very old tradesman of this borough' until retirement; committee member.

Thornton, Joseph: d. 11 January 1884, aged 86; cropper and Temperance Hotel keeper; Owenite and Chartist.

Woofenden, David: d. 5 October 1892, aged 79; bookseller, newsagent and bill-poster.

Notes

1. *Quarterly Review*, lxv, December 1839, p. 305, quoted in H. Silver, *The Concept of Popular Education* (London, 1965), p. 229.
2. J.F.C. Harrison, *Robert Owen and the Owenites in Britain and America. The Quest for the New Moral World* (London, 1969), p. 197.
3. Robert Owen's lecture at the Charlotte Street Institution, *New Moral World* [*NMW*], 29 November 1834.
4. *NMW*, 21 December 1839.
5. *NMW*, 17 December 1836.
6. *NMW*, 4 February 1838.
7. G.J. Holyoake, *Rationalism. A Treatise for the Times* (London: Watson, 1845); and *Secularism, the Practical Philosophy of the People* (London, 1854).
8. The legacy is traced generally in Harrison, *Robert Owen and the Owenites*, pp. 235–54 and by E. Royle, 'The Owenite Legacy to Social Reform', *Studies in History and Politics*, 1, (1980), pp. 56–75.
9. F.H. Amphlett Micklewright, 'The Local History of Victorian Secularism', *Local Historian* (1969), pp. 221–7.
10. D. Nash, *Secularism, Art and Freedom* (Leicester, 1992).
11. For an earlier attempt to piece together fragments of the local and regional history of these Owenite remnants, see my *Victorian Infidels. The Origins of the British Secularist Movement, 1791–1866* (Manchester, 1974), pp. 179–95, and *Radicals, Secularists and Republicans. Popular Freethought in Britain, 1866–1915* (Manchester, 1980), pp. 45–71.
12. For locations, see E. Royle, *Victorian Infidels*, pp. 295–7 and *Radicals, Secularists and Republicans*, pp. 337–42.
13. See, for example, the obituary of John Snowden of Halifax, *National Reformer* [*NR*], 7 September 1884, reprinted in E. Royle, *Chartism* (Harlow, 1980).
14. For the history of early co-operation in Huddersfield see R.G. Thornes, 'The Early Development of the Co-operative Movement in West Yorkshire, 1827–1863' (D.Phil. thesis, Sussex, 1984) and 'The Origins of the Co-operative Movement in Huddersfield' in E.A.H. Haigh (ed.), *Huddersfield – a Most Handsome Town* (Huddersfield, 1992), pp. 171–88. For Owenism, see A. Brooke, *The Hall of Science. Co-operation and Socialism in Huddersfield, c. 1830–1848* (Honley, 1993).
15. *NMW*, 25 February, 11 March 1837.
16. *NMW*, 9 December 1837, 17 November 1838.

17. *NMW*, 9 March, 9 November 1839, 28 May 1845; *Northern Star* [*NS*], 6
     April 1839. For further on the Hall of Science, see *Huddersfield Examiner*
     [*HEx*], 4 November 1939, 20, 21 March 1946, and Brooke, *Hall of
     Science*, pp. 28–35.
18. *NMW*, 28 May 1845. Subscriptions were one penny per week per member.
     On this basis the membership of the Huddersfield branch was 5 (1837); 88
     (1838); 80 (1839); 153 (1840); 91 (1841); 57 (1842); 33 (1843); 93 (1844).
19. *NS*, 3 February 1844, 19 July 1845.
20. *Herald of Progress*, 25 October 1845.
21. *Reasoner* [*R*], 10 June, 30 September 1846; R. Cooper to R. Owen, 10 July
     1847, Owen Correspondence no. 1480, Co-operative Union, Manchester.
22. Holliday's business became British Dyes in 1915 and subsequently the
     dyestuffs division of ICI.
23. *R*, 12 July 1848. For Barker, see J. Baylen and N.J. Gossman (eds),
     Dictionary of Modern British Radicals, vol. 2 (Brighton, 1984).
24. *R*, 19 October, 14 December 1853, 10 September 1854, 14 January 1855.
     Johnson's recollections are in *Agnostic Journal*, 7 January 1893; see also
     Yorkshire Tribune [1856], pp. 116–17.
25. *R*, 6 July 1856.
26.   *R*, 1 January 1855; *London Investigator*, March 1855.
27. *HEx*, 29 December 1875.
28. *R*, 12 August 1860.
29. *HEx*, 4 August 1860; *National Reformer* [*NR*], 3 August 1861. For the
     general growth of Secularism in the North, see Royle, *Victorian Infidels*,
     pp. 185–90.
30. *NR*, 30 November 1861.
31. *HEx*, 18 January 1862.
32. *NR*, 30 August 1862.
33. C.R. Mackay, *Life of Charles Bradlaugh, M.P.* (London, 1888), pp. 164–5.
     This libellous biography of Bradlaugh was ghosted by Johnson.
34. *NR*, 20 June, 21 November 1863.
35. The Huddersfield Circuit Primitive Methodist Account Book shows a small
     membership at Senior's Schoolroom from December 1862 to March 1865
     – Kirklees Archives, C311/36. The Secularists moved in on 2 April – *NR*,
     19 March, 9 April 1865.
36. *HEx*, 25 November 1866, 30 March, 6, 13 April 1867; *NR*, 9 December
     1866, 24, 31 March, 7, 14 April 1867. See also H.B. Bonner and J.M.
     Robertson, *Charles Bradlaugh. A Record of His Life and Work*, 2 vols
     (London, 1898), pp. 240–5.
37. *NR*, 12 January, 22 March 1868.
38. *NR*, 12 July 1874.
39. *Secular Chronicle*, 22 November 1874; *NR*, 14 November 1875; *HEx*, 29
     December 1875; *NR*, 30 January 1876; *Secular Review* [*SR*], 3 November
     1877.
40. *NR*, 22 October 1882; *SR*, 15, 22 December 1883, 19 January 1884;
     Freethinker [*F*], 16 December 1883.
41. *SR*, 17 January 1885; *NR*, 18 January 1885, 28 March, 1 August 1886;
     HEx, 15 August 1886.
42. *F*, 15 August 1886.
43. *NR*, 29 August, 12 September, 3, 31 October 1886, 10 April 1887; *F*, 1
     December 1889.

44. *NR*, 28 September 1890.
45. *F*, 3 May 1891, 1 December 1889, 20 March, 11 December 1910. *Reformer*, 15 June 1898.
46. See, C.B. Campbell, 'Analysing the Rejection of Religion', *Social Compass*, **24**, (1977), pp. 339–46.
47. See Sam Standring's report in *NR*, 12 October 1890.
48. N.J. Demerath III and V. Theissen, 'On Spitting Against the Wind. Organisational Precariousness and American Irreligion', *American Journal of Sociology*, **71**, (1966), pp. 674–87.
49. *F*, 7 February 1909.
50. See E. Royle, 'Religion in Huddersfield Since the Mid-Eighteenth Century' in E.A.H. Haigh (ed.), *Huddersfield*, pp. 100–44.
51. E.g., *NR*, 5 May, 23 June, 7, 28 July, 24 November 1867, 14 January 1877, 1 December 1878, 14 January 1883; *SR*, 3 November 1877, 16 March, 9 November 1878. Compare these activities with those of Owenism, described by E. Yeo, 'Robert Owen and Radical Culture' in S. Pollard and J. Salt (eds), *Robert Owen. Prophet of the Poor* (London, 1971), pp. 84–114.
52. *NR*, 4 May 1873; *Secular Chronicle*, 19 March 1876.
53. Ben Turner, *About Myself, 1863–1930* (London, 1930), pp. 47–8.
54. D.F.E. Sykes, *The History of Huddersfield and the Valleys of the Colne, the Holme and the Dearne* (Huddersfield, n.d.), p. 245. The Unitarians had moved from the old Hall of Science to their Fitzwilliam Street chapel in 1854. The old Hall had then passed to the Baptists until 1878 when it was acquired by Conacher's, a firm of organ builders. In 1910 it was a railway mission and has been a warehouse since 1919 – Owen Balmforth, *Huddersfield Industrial Society Limited* (Huddersfield, 1910), p. 27; Brooke, *Hall of Science*, p. 1.
55. *NR*, 29 September 1878.
56. *NR*, 28 March 1886; *Agnostic Journal*, 15 October 1892.
57. See the Appendix for names and brief details of important members.
58. S. Budd, *Varieties of Unbelief. Atheists and Agnostics in English Society, 1850–1960* (London, 1977), pp. 94–6.
59. See E. Royle, *Radicals, Secularists and Republicans*, pp. 127–9.
60. Owen Balmforth (1855–1922): began work as an errand boy, aged 10; educated at the Mechanics' Institute and Secular Sunday School; editor of its magazine from 1875 to 1877; secretary of Huddersfield Republican Club, 1873. After the closure of the Sunday school in 1886 he transferred his energies to the local Unitarians, becoming a teacher with them (1888–98), a member of the Church Committee (1889–1922), and Sunday school superintendent (1898–1907); in 1892 he was elected on to the executive of the Yorkshire Unitarian Sunday School Union; vice-president in 1894. He was a founder of the Friendly and Trades Club in 1886 and secretary from 1888. In 1874 he joined the Huddersfield Industrial Society, where he was employed as a book-keeper. In 1893 he was a founder of the Education Committee, which opened a reading room in Albion Street not far from the old Secularist meeting place, and was chairman until 1902. His politics were Liberal-Radical. He was a founder of the reformed Liberal Association in 1880, an executive member from 1881, and an area vice-president from 1892. He was elected on to the School Board as a Liberal and Secularist in 1883, became chairman of the school attendance commit-

tee in 1893 and vice-chairman of the new local authority Education
Committee in 1903 having been elected a councillor in 1897. He became an
alderman in 1904 and mayor and a JP in 1906. In 1909 he was appointed
salaried Secretary for Education (that is, the local education officer), a post
he held until his death – *HEx*, 4 February, 22 May 1922, 6 October 1967.

61. Ramsden Balmforth (named after his paternal grandmother, not the
     Huddersfield Lord of the Manor) trod a similar path to Unitarianism as his
     brother Owen, but like his father he moved from Liberalism to Labour and
     became an advocate of ethical Socialism. He was elected to the School
     Board as a Labour representative in 1892 and, after a period of study in
     Oxford, became minister at the Fitzwilliam Street Unitarian Chapel in
     1894. In 1897 he emigrated to South Africa – see Robert Perks, 'The New
     Liberalism and the Challenge of Labour in the West Riding of Yorkshire,
     1885–1914', (PhD thesis, Huddersfield Polytechnic, 1985), pp. 58, 86,
     161, 244.

62. For example, see G. Stedman Jones's critical discussion of J. Foster, *Class
     Struggle and the Industrial Revolution* (London, 1974) in *Languages of
     Class. Studies in English Working Class History* (Cambridge, 1983), pp.
     25–75 where he assumes that the problem is to explain the roots of
     reformism, not to question its extent. Since then, some non-Marxist histori-
     ans have begun to write about the more subtle nature of radicalism after
     1850 – see E.F. Biagini and A. Reid (eds), *Currents of Radicalism*
     (Cambridge, 1991) and M.C. Finn, *After Chartism. Class and Nation in
     English Radical Politics, 1848–1874* (Cambridge, 1993).

CHAPTER FIFTEEN

From Hodge to Lob: reconstructing the English farm labourer, 1870–1914

Alun Howkins

The earliest written use of the name Hodge is in Chaucer. There it is used simply descriptively or as the diminutive of Roger [Roger, like Colin, was a common 'name' for a countryman]. Not until the mid-eighteenth century does a note of contempt creep into the usage,[1] and not really before the 1820s does the name Hodge become totally synonymous with backwardness and lack of sophistication. By 1827, though, a correspondent to Hone's *Everyday Book* (1827), when asked about the customs of Purton Old Fair in Wiltshire, replies, with some indignation and not a little hurt pride, 'You seem to think that with the name I still retain all the characteristics and predilections of a *hodge*.[2] In 1837 when 'Hodge' occurs in Thomas Hood's poem 'Agricultural Distress: A Pastoral Report' (whose title consciously mocks the Parliamentary Commissions) as one of the 'bumpkins' taking part in a dialogue after church, he and his friends Dickon, Giles and Colin have become the stock yokels of later urban humour. They don't quite understand what agricultural distress is and thus, take things literally. Agricultural distress is an accident with a cart to one of them, and to another a pig knocking the farmer into a trough. All their 'tales' are couched in what actors call 'Mummerzet', a kind of universal 'oo, arr, ee' accent via which we indicate rural stupidity. So despite a 'progressive' ending the poem comes over as simply mocking.[3]

So, between the late eighteenth century and the 1830s we see an important change in language use. Terms like Hodge become universally terms of contempt expressing a belief that the countryman is stupid. This is not to say that before that date country people were seen as superior but that there was at least a contrast – urban and rural. In a ballad like the 'Husbandman and Servingman', which was in print from at least the seventeenth century, urban and rural are contrasted over some 500 lines ending with the rural as a superior and more important way of life. The Servingman concedes:

> Kind sir! I must confess,
> And grant you your request
> And give you the uppermost hand;

Although it is so painful,
Your calling is most gainful-
I wish I was a husbandman.[4]

In similar vein are songs like 'The Painful Plough' which stresses the primacy of agricultural production, or the folk rhyme, 'The Five Alls':

The King he rules all,
The parson he prays for all,
The lawyer he pleads for all
The soldier he fights for all
The farmer he feeds all, and pays for all.[5]

The consistent use of words like 'Hodge' or 'clodhopper' (another word of a purely descriptive kind until the mid-eighteenth century) as insults semantically marks the real change and deterioration in status and position of the farm labourer between the 1780s and 1830s. As William Cobbett wrote, in calling the labourers 'poor' or worse 'peasants', the élite made them 'a *distinct and degraded class of persons*, who have no pretensions whatever to look upon themselves, in any sense, as belonging to the same *society* or *community* as the *Gentry*' [italics as original].[6] It also marked the triumph of the urban over the rural. When the labourer left the land he got back his status and his pride. The urban worker had power and this was recognized by his enemies. To them, 'the qualities of the swine are cast off with the smock frock'.[7]

By the 1840s this 'very unjust and unfavourable opinion of the character, habits, and practices of the Agricultural Poor' as George Crewe put it, was widely accepted.[8] The famous *Morning Chronicle* reports, especially those from East Anglia in 1849–50 speak of the degraded and backward state of the rural population. Sullen and unable to communicate at all, the labourer was 'a physical scandal, a moral enigma, an intellectual cataleptic'.[9] This view was constantly reinforced by the parliamentary investigations from the mid-1820s onwards. Indeed the 'problem' of the poor is overwhelmingly seen as one of the rural areas. Increasingly the picture presented of the rural poor in these is one of voluntary idleness supported by the Old Poor Law. Sub-Malthusian ideas about the relationship between poor-relief and marriage rates were widespread which added the notion of slyness and deceit to those of immorality. Finally the riots of 1828 in parts of the south and the more general Swing Rising of 1830–31 added the notion of a barbaric and dangerous sub-class.

The mid-century novelists presented the same picture. In Kingsley's novels the rural poor are degraded and defeated. The London radical Alton Locke's description of the Fenland poor would not have been out of place in the writing of a Malthusian reformer:

As we pushed through the crowd, I was struck with the wan, haggard look of all faces; their lacklustre eyes and drooping lips, stoop-
ing shoulders, heavy dragging steps, gave them a crushed dogged air,
which was infinitely painful, and bespoke a grade of misery more
habitual and degrading than that of the excitable and passionate
artisan.[10]

The poor in *Yeast* are if anything worse since they accept their miserable
lot.[11] It is clearest of all, and indeed provides the whole structuring
principle in Mrs Gaskell's *North and South*. Here what is almost a proto-
typical description of the farm labourer is given by the book's
heroine Margaret Hale to a Northern worker with ideas of going 'back to
the land':

You would not bear the dulness of the life; you don't know what it
is; it would eat you away like rust. Those that have lived there all
their lives, are used to soak in the stagnant waters. They labour on,
from day to day . . . The hard spadework robs their brain of life; the
sameness of their toil deadens their imagination; they don't care to
meet to talk over thoughts and speculations . . . they go home
brutishly tired poor creatures! caring for nothing but food and
rest.[12]

We have here the mid-nineteenth century progressive élite characterization of Hodge. His work, far from being ennobling reduces him to animal
status wanting 'nothing but food and rest'. Unlike the quick brained
mechanic, or Kingsley's, 'excitable and passionate artisan', whose techni-
cal or scientific work means he is constantly challenging and changing,
the very timelessness and repetitiveness of agricultural work renders
those who do it stupid. Such a characterization at one stroke devalues
both the man and his work. Later in the same book Margaret Hale
returns to the South, which she has held throughout as being superior, to
confront not only the toil, poverty and stupidity of the inhabitants but
the 'savage country superstition' which demands a cat be roasted alive.
She tries to persuade the woman involved of the illogicality of it but fails.
'Margaret gave up in despair, and walked away, sick at heart.'[13] So the
'north' abandons the 'south' as unsaveable.

Nor was it only that these were middle-class writers. Alexander
Somerville's 'mission' as outlined in *The Whistler at the Plough* in 1852
was to convince the backward labourers and farmers of the south not
only of the virtues of the Anti-Corn Law League but also the superiority
of modern northern and Scottish farming.[14] The urban working classes
looked upon the countryman in the same way. In a remarkably ill-timed
article in January 1872 Lloyd Jones, editor of *The Beehive*, a London
radical paper, looked at the farm labourer:

It would be a waste of time to touch the controversy as to the social condition of the worker in our fields. In intellect he is a child, in position a helot, in condition a squalid outcast, he knows nothing of his past; his knowledge of the present is limited to the fields he works in and the half understood utterances of the rural curate give him the only gleam that comes to him of his future . . . Church and State, so full of contradictory and contrary ideas to others have no meaning whatever for him. These terms in the larger and fuller sense cannot penetrate the solid darkness by which his dull intellect is surrounded.[15]

Even the new more 'balanced' social investigations of the second half of the century did little to alter these views. The series of government reports on the employment of women and children in agriculture in 1843 and then in the late 1860s and early 1870s simply reiterated the conclusions of the 1820s and 1830s. Time and again, at least in the southern and eastern counties, the picture presented was of village after village populated with immoral and degenerate almost sub-human creatures. The Reverend M.S. Jackson, former Curate of Castleacre in Norfolk told the Children's Employment Commission in 1867: 'I have been to Sierra Leone, but I have seen shameless wickedness in Castleacre such as I never witnessed in Africa.'[16] The Beehive thought much the same: 'He has not the active intelligence of the Chinaman, the pastoral independence of the Thibetian [sic], the dignity of the Zulu, the ease and abundance of the South Sea savage, or the unconstrained liberty of the Red Indian.'[17] But by the time The Beehive had published its article things were beginning to change. Literally within a month of publication Joseph Arch had called the first meeting of what was to become the National Agricultural Labourers' Union. The 'helots' revolt, the 'revolt of the field', had begun.

Although historians have now found predecessors in local unions and campaigns, the shock caused by the 'revolt of the field' cannot be doubted. One of the union's own songs put it succinctly when it said:

> The farmer, parson, Lord and Squire.
> Looked on with evil eyes,
> Some looked with scorn and some with ire,
> And some in dumb surprise.[18]

Arch's own autobiography says, with his characteristic drama: 'The whole county was roused and ringing with the news. All the leading papers took notice of this strange thing; they could no longer ignore the fact that a great moral and intellectual awakening was in progress among the down .odden peasantry of England.'[19] 'Moral and intellectual awakening' it certainly was. Arch, and many hundreds like him, saw the question of the labourer in terms of the Hodge stereotype, in the way in fact the urban, artisan radicals of The Beehive saw it. Throughout much of Arch's writings, and indeed through those of many other labourers' union leaders, there is the unmistakable tone of the labour aristocrat lecturing those 'beneath him', those who have not yet, owing often to some moral failing, seen the light. 'Unite for mutual intercourse, instruction and information', said George Rix a local union leader in Norfolk, 'Knowledge is power. Leave off smoking and tippling, and get to reading, thinking, and acting and there is for the working-class of old England a brighter and better day.'[20] Like the preacher he was, Rix also warned against the snares of the world. The farmers are described as Delilahs' who 'have been of late dandling you on their knees'. In the same 'letter' the enemies of the Union are 'Philistines' who will 'Most certainly put out your eyes', eyes one assumes newly opened by the Union.[21]

When the Union finally collapsed in the mid-1890s the explanation adopted by many leaders, including Arch, was again one of almost moral failing on the part of the labour. Arch said in an interview in 1912, 'the Union was *wrecked!*. They broke up their Union and left me without a penny'.[22] Even George Edwards who remained a labourers leader after the collapse of the 1890s bitterly blamed 'Hodge' for the Union's demise: 'In taking my final farewell of you, let it never be said that George Edwards has left you. It is you that have left him . . . I have lost all faith that you will ever manifest an independence long enough to claim your rights.'[23] Yet the labourer had changed. First, the leadership of men like Edwards and Arch did give a section of rural poor a sense of their own worth. Secondly, the assertion of power that the Union represented convinced sections of the élite that the labourer had changed. Finally, the agricultural depression of the late 1870s and 1880s strengthened some aspects of the labourer's position.

The first point first. It is absolutely certain that the Union improved the 'moral and intellectual' position of the labourer. Real gains in wages, hours or conditions may have been limited but the change in what we might call consciousness was more striking. At the most basic level it was expressed in the refusal to accept that the labourer's interest was automatically subsumed in that of the 'agricultural interest'. As Arch said forcibly to the 1881 Royal Commission on Agriculture: 'Do not talk about the good feeling [between master and man]; it is a mockery to the agricultural labourer to talk about it so much; because the farmer had got all he could out of the labourer . . . '.[24] The strikes and less organized forms of conflict, the fights for the votes and the constant local battles over charities, schooling, the game laws and local government which occurred through rural Southern and Eastern England in the years 1872–78 show the extent to which Hodge was beginning to change.

Perhaps more importantly the majority of farmers, in the South and East at least, were convinced that the labourers had 'changed' in a number of ways. They were more difficult to handle, worked less long hours, were unwilling to do overtime or piece work and generally 'uppity'. Henry Overman who farmed 1 300 acres in West Norfolk told the Royal Commission in 1881: 'men do not care to take piece work, or even work longer hours . . . even my good men do not work with the zest they used to work with . . . '.[25] Robert Hartley Lipscomb, who managed an estate of 45 000 acres in Devon said: 'all the farmers agree that they do not get so much work or such good work as they did, and there is a great absence of pride on the part of the labourer in his work'.[26] George Gayford who farmed 1 000 acres on the Norfolk/Suffolk border was even more convinced:

> There is not the willingness to work; I do not know how it is. I worked with my father's people, and if there was a lot of hay in good order in showery weather like this, they were all as anxious as my father to get it in; they would say 'Oh, we will have this hay in to night; never mind if we work an hour or two later; we have short hours in the winter.'[27]

The Reverend Augustus Jessopp, Rector of Scarning in Norfolk, and an often sympathetic observer of the labourer, claimed to see similar changes in the 1870s:

> It is when we come to compare the agricultural labourer of today with him I remember so well, that I notice the most curious and marked changes . . . The truth is the peasantry have begun to have tastes as well as other people . . . All this is so much gain: but there is something on the other side. I do not know that the agricultural labourer is much more of a grumbler than he was, but he is certainly more defiant in his tone and bolder in his self assertion.[28]

Many witnesses before the Royal Commission of 1881 made a direct connection between the unions of the 1870s and this increasing unwillingness of the labourers to behave in the way they 'used to'. In some cases these beliefs reach almost the level of paranoia. Mr Overman told the Commission in answer to the question 'Then who has corrupted the younger men?'

> The agitators in the villages, and the men appointed to look and see that there is not too much work done. I believe on every farm there is a man appointed to put the stopper on. Whenever I find that man he always goes; I never tell him what for, but he always goes.[29]

George Gayford agreed with his questioner that the 'independence and almost insolence' of labourers in the 1870s 'was very marked' and added: 'You were obliged to be very careful what you said to them.'[30] In Devon, according to Mr T.S. Carter a small hill-farmer, things were no better:

> Are the labourers, generally speaking, in that part of the world contented? – No they are not. What are they discontented about? – I do

not think they know. They get the low prints and read about these
nasty agitations in the papers, and so on, and it has a bad effect upon
them. I think that has a great deal to do with it.[31]

At one level this kind of evidence has to be treated with care. It is
clearly idyllicist in the sense that it treats of 'the day before yesterday' and
finds the old ways superior. Yet such evidence is consistent throughout
the Richmond Commission of 1881 and the later Commission of the
1890s. It is also contrary to statements, for example, on the supposed
improvements in manner and deference following 1834, as reported in
similar government papers; in that sense it is not simply a matter of recurring complaint. There is also a sense in which the literal truth of such evidence is anyway irrelevant to this argument. The important thing is that
it clearly had some basis, and that the rural élite began to act on the belief
that the labourer was no longer simply quiescent in his bondage.

This brings up the effects of the agricultural depression on the
labourer. First, wages did not drop as fast as farm prices, which left the
labourer temporarily 'better off'. At this point some of Arch's prophecies
began to come true. Thrift seems to have increased, certainly friendly
society membership was very widespread even in the villages. Also, as
Jessopp notes, that little extra enabled people to indulge in a taste for, as
he puts it, 'leisure . . . I have found them reading novels; they like to see
things looking pretty, they put up neat papers on their walls . . . they buy
pictures such as they are'.[32]

Secondly, and more importantly, the depression brought to the fore
the continuing rural depopulation which had been made worse by the
encouragement of emigration by the labourers' unions. As Mr F.W.
Knight MP, the owner of Exmoor wrote:

> The North Devon labourer . . . is intelligent, thrifty and hard work-
> ing. He is very respectful in his demeanour to his superiors, but per-
> fectly independent. He well knows that the great Welsh coal field lies
> only a few hours sail away from any of the little harbours that dot
> the coast . . . and that among the teeming gangs that work among its
> mines, docks and railroads, he can, at a days notice, get work at
> higher wages than at home . . . Many too have emigrated to America
> and no parish is without its representative in Canada and the United
> States.[33]

Knight's picture of the labourer may be too rosy, but its stress upon independence, skill and freedom of movement is very different from most
accounts written in the 1840s or 1850s, and certainly any written prior
to that.

To some extent then the labourer himself began to reconstruct his own
image and self-respect, often via quasi-proletarian forms of dissent, and
with some help from the economic circumstances of the 1880s. However,

much more important were the changes in attitude among an essentially southern, artistic/intellectual, and urban élite. Their concern with the labourer began in the 1870s when reforming journalists like Richard Heath and Archibald Forbes (who covered the formation of Arch's Union for the Liberal *Morning Chronicle*) picked up first on the appalling conditions in the countryside, then on the 'Revolt of the Field'. In articles like Richard Heath's 'The English Via Dolorosa; or Glimpses of the History of the Agricultural Labourer' (1884) urban intellectuals were presented with both a history of degradation and the first signs of awakening:

> The light has fairly broken, and although the clouds keep gathering, they cannot hide the rising sun. Already the pedestrian wandering in various parts of rural England, fails to see many of the signs of the long night through which the labourers have toiled and suffered. The cottages are rapidly improving, and the labourer begins to look strong and hopeful.[34]

The writings of Heath and others brought the 'problem of the rural areas', to use a favourite phrase of the time, to the attention of the urban élites at precisely the point when the urban areas themselves were perceived as entering a crisis. Briefly, from the publication of Andrew Mearns's *The Bitter Cry of Outcast London* in 1884, the city was seen increasingly as degenerate, producing an inferior breed of humanity which gave a rotten heart to the empire. A mixture of primitive sociology, eugenics and Gibbon's account of the decline of ancient Rome produced an explanation of decay which centred, at least in part, on the superiority of rural life.[35] As Henry Rider Haggard wrote in 1898:

> Heretofore John Bull has been depicted as a countryman and nothing else, a comparison with meaning. If henceforth he is to forsake the soil that bred him, how will he be pictured by our children, drawing from a changed and shrunken model? . . . the practice of Agriculture . . . means more than the growing of grass and grain. It means, among other things, the engendering and achievement of patient, even minds in sound enduring bodies, gifts of which, after the first generation, the great towns rob those who dwell and labour in them. And when those gifts are gone, or greatly lessened, what does history teach us of the fate of the peoples who have lost them?[36]

Gradually, John Bull was elided with the countryman. Historical accounts like those of Heath or Hasbach or Green stressed an almost Cobbett-like history of rural England. In this the 'real' countrymen were the descendents of those dispossessed by first the Tudor enclosures and then the agricultural revolution – the landless labourers. Occasionally old 'yeomen' farmers got a look in but all knew, from Heath and later the Hammonds, that those who farmed rural England were *arrivistes* there only for profit and conspicuous consumption. Therefore, it followed that the real 'heart of England' was the rural labourer.

The construction of the labourer as 'Lob', the ideal and 'real' Englishman, took three basic routes. First, his timelessness and permanence had to be stressed as in Hardy's 'At the Time of the Breaking of Nations': 'Only a man harrowing clods/In a slow silent walk . . . / Yet this will go onwards the same/ Though Dynasties pass.' Secondly, the nature of agricultural work had to be revalidated as against industrial work and, thirdly, the labourer was made the bearer of Englishness.

The idea that the countryman, and the labourer in particular, was in some sense the continuity of all history was of course not new, indeed, that notion is very much there in *North and South*. The difference is that this timelessness is elevated to a virtue. George Sturt in his introduction to *The Bettesworth Book* (1901) writes of Bettesworth the farm labourer as the archetype of the English worker whose descendants 'are carrying on the work begun by the ancestors of a thousand years ago, making England's fields productive and her towns habitable'.[37] Racial origin and type were always a major part of such accounts. The countrymen preserved the true racial type, an absolutely vital concern if the 'urban' stock was to be saved. In Hudson's *Nature in Downland* (a collection 'put together' in 1923 but written earlier) he talks of the meeting of two different 'racial types' in a Sussex pub. The 'Sussex men', the real countrymen were superior:

> they were distant children of those who came with Ella to these purple shores, abandoned by Rome; . . . they had not so greatly degenerated in fourteen centuries as not to be able to drink any dark-eyed and pale-faced young man into the deepest intoxication, or the grave, without themselves experiencing a qualm, physical or mental.[38]

Later in the book a Sussex labouring girl is made the direct descendant of the Romans, 'although her parents and grandparents, and their families as far back as she knew, were all of the working class and their home was the Sussex Downs'.[39] F.E. Green's labourers preserved something more direct, 'I remember once hearing an author', he wrote in 1911, 'distinguished for his knowledge of rural England, telling a company of friends . . . that the descendents of the old English aristocracy were in the main living in labourers' cottages'.[40] Nor were these ideas mere literary conceits. In 1892 the Anthropological Institute, the Society of Antiquaries and the Folk-Lore Society met in London to 'discuss the possibility of making an ethnographic survey of the British Isles'. By the next year the committee issued its first lists of places to study, and produced guides for the largely amateur local societies who would carry out the investigations. However, changes in the nature of anthropology and divisions within the committee meant that the survey was effectively abandoned in 1897. Nevertheless, the notions of original 'races' remained a powerful one.[41]

George Sturt though made the most of this continuity in what he called, in *Change in the Village* (1912), 'the peasant system'. This Sturt argued was a way of doing things handed down through generations which assured the essential continuity at the heart of the village community. It was 'nothing less than a form of civilisation – the home made civilisation of the rural English'.[42] This theme was echoed in that spate of publications on open-field agriculture around this time, many of which stressed values of endurance, co-operation, tradition, local office-holding and continuity of community. Sturt argued that this system had all but vanished but its echoes remained, and should be encouraged. 'Best of all, those customs provided a rough guidance as to conduct – an unwritten code to which, though we forget it, England owes much.'[43] Sturt believed that although the system was vanishing it could serve as the basis for the 'new' order:

> For 'England' is – what shall I say? the stream, the tradition the living continuity, of public opinion, public conduct, public intercourse and behaviour of the English people towards one another and towards the hills and valleys, and waving trees and fair sunshine of this island. It subsists in their Conduct of Life, from minute to minute and century to century.[44]

It was of course this insistence on continuity and 'organic' society which Sturt made much of in his later work and which was picked up by his admirers, especially F.R. Leavis. It was also the theme of countless rural-located regional novels, the numbers of which grew rapidly from the late 1880s.

It would be possible to multiply the examples of those who argued for continuity further. Christopher Holdenby's slightly odd, but in the end true account *Folk of the Furrow* published in 1913[45] begins with both an account of 'continuity' and a fine attack on the idea of the slow and stupid countryman. The more consciously literary productions like John Masefield's book-length poem 'The Everlasting Mercy' which was the poetic sensation of the winter of 1911 stretched the point to near breaking. In this the timeless ploughman is not only some representation of the continuities of history but is also linked to the Christ figure:

> Near Bullen Bank on Gloucester Road,
> Thy ever lasting mercy showed
> The ploughman patient on the hill
> Forever there, forever still,
> Ploughing the hill with steady yoke
> Of pine-trees lightning-struck and broke

And in men's hearts in many lands
A spiritual ploughman stands
Forever waiting, waiting now,
The heart's 'Put in, man, zook the plough.'[46]

At least as important as establishing the timelessness of agricultural work was validating it. To the mid-century writer agricultural work was mindless toil, totally lacking in skill, and indeed that notion remains very late in the day among some writers. In addition repetition, the very basis of traditional practice, led to boorishness and stiffled improvement. The Smilesian account of change was entirely industrial. From the 1870s these views were challenged. First the skill involved in agricultural work was stressed and secondly the argument about repetition was literally turned on its head. Custom was suddenly desirable.

The notion that agricultural work was (and indeed is) highly skilled re-emerges first in the government reports on the Employment of Women and Children in Agriculture of the late 1860s and early 1870s; it is firmly present in the Royal Commission on Agriculture of 1881 and dominates discussion of labour in the reports of the 1890s. This contrast is marked with the censorious and even contemptuous tone of the 1832–34 Poor Law Commission, and the Ricardian economism of other such reports before the 1850s. In all the later reports skill is something 'gone' either because the best men are leaving the land or because the young no longer care to learn. Little's report to the 1881 Commission makes this point in relation to Devon and Cornwall:

> Most old farm labourers can turn their hand to anything, and they can do one or two things well and thoroughly. Unfortunately, nowadays, the young workmen (except the few who take an interest in machinery), do not care to learn their work, nor do they take pride in doing it well.[47]

This valuation though remained 'within' the industry until the 1890s when continued rural migration, and a number of highly influential books on the 'rural problem' took these arguments out of the pages of the 'blue books' and put them in the area of public debate.

Gradually at first, but gaining momentum after 1900 it became a 'new' axiom that, far from being mindless toil, agricultural work was highly skilled. As Christopher Holdenby wrote, 'Good agricultural labour needs as much intelligence as any other Industry if not more . . . "Can't anyone dig?" asked an intellectual friend, when I told him I had "joined the gang". As a matter of fact, good digging, is a very difficult operation . . . '.[48] F.E. Green, one of the best friends the labourer ever had, raised his status even higher:

> Professor Thorold Rogers, one of our greatest authorities on indus-

trial workers, stated in 1878 that the agricultural labourer possessed five or six more qualifications to the title of skilled worker than did the artisan. Professor Rogers might have added even more qualifications than five or six to the title of skilled worker.[49]

If agricultural work was skilled and timeless it was a short step to making custom not a drag on society, something to be rejected and fought against, but rather the very definition of worth. Custom in Sturt's work is the ordering principle, the organic basis of continuity in all human society but in English rural society in particular. Ways of doing things create the social order and are the foundation of tradition:

> Tradition is a form of group life. It tends to composure and conversation in individuals. No industry can long go on without it, peasant industries are stiff with it. Hence it prevails in the country more than London, where individuality most flourishes. But to name the many ancient English industries is to recite the group efforts of the English from time immemorial.[50]

Tradition and custom were preserved, sometimes unknowingly, in the individual. Bettesworth, the Surrey labourer, was such a man to Sturt. Bettesworth knew the history of the area, the old common rights, the traditions of wood gathering and seasonal labour, 'in gossiping about his own life Bettesworth is unawares telling the similar lives, as lived for ages, of a type of Englishman . . . '.[51]

To others the labourer carried more. To Cecil Sharp, the folk song collector or Vaughan Williams, the composer, the English rural poor held the only source of real English music which was still living. In 1912 Vaughan Williams told an audience, 'I am like a psychical researcher who has actually seen a ghost, for I have been among the more primitive people of England and noted down their songs . . . '.[52] Among the rural poor, the 'peasantry' as they were inevitably called, some almost mystic truth was to be found. As Sharp wrote in 1907, 'the music of the common people must always, therefore, be genuine and true; for instinct is their only guide and the desire of self-expression their only motive'.[53]

In a similar, if more complex vein Kipling in *Puck of Pooks Hill* and *Rewards and Fairies* posited an alternative 'moral' history of England which stresses the rural against the urban, continuity against change and the essential and 'unchanging' virtues of certain ways of life and attitudes, characteristically those of the rural against the urban and commercial/industrial. Kipling's rewriting places the real power and continuities of England in the hands of the poor, or at most middling sort, largely of the rural areas: 'Take of English earth as much/As either hand may rightly clutch./In the taking of it breathe/Prayer for all who lie beneath – /Not the great nor well-bespoke, /But the mere uncounted folk . . . '[54] It is the 'uncounted folk' who really make history and who are the bearers of

continuities through time, even if they themselves are only dimly aware
of their role. 'Old Hobby' some time labourer, some time casual worker,
occasionally small Wealden Farmer, knows about Magna Carta: it guarantees the rights of the 'freeborn Englishman'. But Puck, through his
stories explains to the children how it comes about: ' "Well", said Puck
calmly, "what did you think of it?" Weland gave the Sword! The Sword
gave the Treasure, and the Treasure gave the Law. It's as natural as an
oak growing'.[55] At each stage of the process the stories show how it was
the 'mere uncounted folk', acting not through selfish interest but either
through some dimly perceived sense of destiny or more usually through
honesty or loyalty, who shaped England's destiny. This gives a 'natural-
ness' to the whole account very similar, for instance, to Sharp's account
of the origin of 'folk song' or Sturt's of the basis of custom.

Kipling's history is rural and it is southern, as indeed is the project of
many if not most of those who sought to change Hodge. All 'real' events
either happen in the South or are transmitted through it. Crucially in
Kipling the South, therefore in some sense England itself, becomes
Sussex. Again there are similarities. Surrey and Sussex, along with East
Anglia were the bywords for rural degradation and hence for rural recovery. It is very significant that neither Hodge nor his reconstructed self
(nor for that matter Kipling's 'history') found many echoes in the North.

The choice of Sussex is deliberate. That county becomes the cradle of
history because there the real virtues of Englishness are preserved in
people like Hobden and of course the very spirit of England – Puck.
These virtues of Englishness produce in turn the virtues of an organic
society based on a human nexus of friendship and loyalty rather than
class. This is in turn represented through customary behaviour and 'old'
agricultural practices which, like those who perpetuate them, link the
modern world and even the future (Puck speaks to the children as a kind
of mentor) to the better past which is the precise opposite of the contemporary urban/industrial world. As the 'handful' of English earth 'heals'
the individual's sickness in 'A Charm' at the beginning of *Rewards and
Fairies*, so will the history heal society, 'cleanse and purify' it by revealing
among familiar English things the real greatness of the English – 'Every
man a King indeed'.[56]

However, it was not only in literature that the labourer was valorized.
In the visual arts the French 'Salon realism' of the 1880s became the
English 'new naturalism' of the 1890s and 1900s. This, according to
Kenneth McConkey, 'embodied moral and political imperatives, it was
"democratic" and universally legible . . . '.[57] For our purposes two expo-
nents of this 'style' stand out, the painter George Clausen and the
photographer P.H. Emerson. Clausen began in the 1880s painting what
he called 'people doing simple things' and consciously working in the

manner of the 'salon realists' especially Bastien-Lepage. In the area around his home at St Albans, Clausen found 'his equivalent of Millet's Barbizon or Bastien Lapage's Daumvilliers'. The beginnings of Clausen's approach can be seen in his essay on Bastien-Lepage where he writes, 'one reads in his work the life history of the workaday human beings he painted'.[58] The rural poor 'doing simple things' come to stand for the very basis of rural life. Even in his early paintings under the influence of Lepage, and in the phase of 'rustic realism' his labourers are types if not yet symbols. Through his paintings of the 1880s and 1890s we are offered a series of modern rural characters, like those of Lepage or even Millet, who are valorized by being presented in a open and 'realistic' way. Although these pictures occasionally have a moral tone in a conventional way, in 'Allotment Gardens' for instance, with its obvious references to Millet's 'The Angelus', we are asked to take them as 'very true type(s) of English rustic character' or as breathing 'the very life of the fields', to quote two contemporary opinions,[59] rather than as bearers of an obvious exterior meaning. As in Hudson's descriptions of 'peasant types' we are shown a gallery of contemporary rural England which is harsh, perhaps, but ultimately strong. His woman stone picker has none of the horror of Wallace's Stone Breaker of 30 years before with its dead figure at the roadside; his shepherds in 'A Sheepfold in the Evening' are not the rustic swains of pastoral, but nor are they demoralized or sub-human figures. They are 'very true types' of a newly-invented rural Englishness.

In the late 1890s and early 1900s his style changed and the labourer moves from 'type to symbol'. To quote McConkey again, 'His . . . labourers were men whose countenance reflected nature's flux'. In his painting, especially his Edwardian painting 'The Boy and the Man', the worker 'grew up, like the corn itself, and stood against the sky'.[60] In Clausen's writing in this period, especially his lectures published in 1904, we come straight up against a familiar comparison:

> Comparing the 'City man who goes to his office in the mornings by the "tube" with the "average ploughmen"' Clausen felt, the mind naturally refers to the beauty of the great elementary things – the sky, the sunshine, and the hills, rivers field and trees: and in people to those things which suggest beauty, activity and health. We all have a longing for the perfect things.[61]

In the 'Boy and the Man' we see these 'perfect things' in the form of the monumentalized rural worker. Standing against the sky the figures dominate what was Clausen's largest rustic painting to date. Although contemporaries found little 'spiritual' significance in it, surely the meaning is clear in its very scale. There followed in the next few years a series of paintings of rural life and labour, most successfully 'In the Fields in June'

(1914) on the same scale as 'The Boy and the Man' again with two figures, this time haymakers, dominating a flat landscape.

Clausen's paintings found a close parallel in the photographs of East
Anglian life taken by P.H. Emerson. Emerson began taking photographs
in the early 1880s but it was a series of books beginning with *Life and
Landscape on the Norfolk Broads* in 1887 which made his name. He
admired Clausen and Bastien-Leparge, and certainly some of his photographs are in conscious imitation of either or both painters. In his
photographs of East Anglian, and especially Norfolk life, Emerson celebrated the rural poor not as they were but, as Aaron Scharf puts it, as:

> hard working men and women of field and fen, poor but good,
> honest folk content with their lot – a confirmation of Victorian val-
> ues. Indeed the figures in the silvery, dreamlike landscapes are so
> much at one with nature that they appear physically to grow out of
> the earth itself. For the most part they present a benign image – no
> more frightening than nature itself. 'Picturesque labour' is the term
> Emerson used to describe the weary work of the Norfolk reed
> cutter.[62]

Yet there is more than that. In the 'texts' which went with the photographs, and in some of the photographs themselves like 'The Poacher',
as well as his prose writings Emerson took his public into an 'older'
world. Here through pseudo-folk tale and story a world of 'rural characters' is created in which men link backwards, unknowingly through the
generations, to some lost world. Here was the labourer and the marsh-
man truly vindicated. As Ian Jeffrey's description of part of *Marsh
Leaves* (1895) shows:

> Old Wrote, his greatest invention, is more hero than wizard. A pig
> herd and a drinker of pails of beer, old Wrote appears in *Marsh
> Leaves* as a legend in process of formation. Aged and deaf, he
> mutters about a magnificent past when men were giants, Emerson
> sets down the story of a Thor or Odin.[63]

And so finally to Lob. Lob is both a poem by Edward Thomas and one
of the names of Puck. As Puck in Kipling represents something quintes-
sentially English so does the 'character' Lob in Thomas's great poem.[64]
The 'plot' is simple. Thomas goes to look, in Wiltshire, for an old man
whom he had met years before and who had showed him a right of way.
After searching and getting different answers he meets a 'young squire'
who explains that Lob has no existence:

> He is English as this gate, these flowers, this mire.
> And when at eight years old Lob-lie-by-the fire
> Came in my books, this was the man I saw.
> He has been in England as long as dove and daw,
> Calling the wild cherry tree the merry tree . . .

Like the labourer, Lob's ways were silent but ultimately his skills and knowledge great:

> But little he says compared with what he does.
> If ever sage troubles him he will buzz
> Like a beehive to conclude the tedious fray . . .
> Yet Lob has thirteen hundred names for a fool
> And though he could never spare time for school
> To unteach what the fox so well expressed,
> On biting the cock's head off – Quietness is best –
> He can talk quite as well as anyone
> After his thinking is forgot and done.

Crucially he has been and always will be, 'Although he was seen dying at Waterloo/Hastings, Agincourt and Sedgmoor too/Lives yet. He never will admit he is dead/Till millers cease to grind men's bones for bread.'

Lob is not immortal like Kipling's Puck. He is somehow an essence which passes from generation to generation because of their relationship to the land. Lob is not only the labourer, the poem makes him a farmer or even a 'squire'. Yet in the end his essence is that of the labourer, the labourer transformed and ennobled like Clausen's monumental figures in his later paintings. He is not 'unrealistic' though: his back is still bent and he is still poor, but he was in the past both Jack Cade and Robin Hood; knew Shakespeare and Herne the Hunter. He still knows all the footpaths and English names for flowers, can outwit the wisest and the greatest by his own skill and cunning. Lob is a long way from Hodge. The unions made him in part, in part he made himself. Crucially, like Hodge, he is the product of an urban or urbanized rural world and that world's dream of a 'real' and still obtainable past.

Notes

1. *Oxford English Dictionary.*
2. William Hone, *The Every-day Book; or, Everlasting Calendar of Popular Amusements*, 2 vols (London, 1927), vol. II, p. 1210.
3. Thomas Hood, 'Agricultural Distress. A Pastoral Report', in John Barrell and John Bull (eds), *The Penguin Book of English Pastoral Verse* (Harmondsworth, 1982), pp. 498–501.
4. Broadside by Catnach, Madden Collection 5(II), University of Cambridge.
5. From Lillian Howkins, née Lowe, b. Osney Town, Oxford 1913.
6. William Cobbett, *Political Register*, LXXVIII, p. 710. On this period see Keith Snell, *Annals of the Labouring Poor* (Cambridge, 1985), pp. 8–14.
7. Cobbett, *Political Register*, 21 December 1816, pp. 771–2.
8. Sir George Crewe, *A Word for the Poor, and against the Present Poor Law* (Derby, 1843), p. 6.
9. *Morning Chronicle*, 18 January 1850.

10. Charles Kingsley, *Alton Locke, Tailor and Poet* (London: Everyman, 1910), p. 251.
11. Charles Kingsley, *Yeast. A Problem* (London: Eversley, 1890), for example ch. VIII.
12. Elizabeth Gaskell, *North and South*, (Harmondsworth: Penguin, 1970), p. 382.
13. Ibid., p. 478.
14. Alexander Somerville, *The Whistler at the Plough and Free Trade* (Manchester, 1852), see for example vol. I, p. 154.
15. *The Beehive. The People's Paper*, 13 January 1872, p. 1.
16. *PP 1867, XVII*, 'Royal Commission on the Employment of Children in Trades and Manufactures not Regulated by Law (1862), Sixth Report, Evidence on Agricultural Gangs, collected by Mr J.W. White, p. 181.
17. *The Beehive*, 13 January 1872, p. 1.
18. Josiah Sage, *The Memoirs of Josiah Sage* (London, 1951), p. 18.
19. Joseph Arch, *From Ploughtail to Parliament* (new edn, London, 1986), p. 79.
20. *Eastern Weekly Press*, 15 May 1880, p. 8.
21. *Eastern Weekly Press*, 22 March 1879, p. 1.
22. *Labour Leader*, 15 August 1912, p. 523.
23. *Eastern Weekly Leader*, 8 February 1896, p. 2.
24. *PP 1882 XIV*, 'Royal Commission on Depressed State of the Agricultural Interest. Minutes of Evidence', p. 92.
25. *PP 1881 XVII* 'Royal Commission on Depressed State of the Agricultural Interest. Minutes of Evidence', p. 736.
26. Ibid., p. 728.
27. Ibid., p. 676.
28. Augustus Jessopp, *Arcardy For Better For Worse* (London, 1887?), pp. 17–18.
29. *PP 1881 XVII* p. 742.
30. Ibid., p. 676.
31. Ibid., p. 734.
32. Jessopp, *Arcardy*, pp. 18–19.
33. *PP 1882 XVI*, 'Royal Commission on the Depressed State of the Agricultural Interest . . . Devon' p. 23.
34. In Richard Heath, *The English Peasant. Studies: Historical, Local and Biographic*, (new edn, Wakefield, 1978), pp. 55–6.
35. See Alun Howkins, 'The Discovery of Rural England', in Robert Colls and Philip Dodd, *Englishness: Politics and Culture 1880–1920* (London, 1986).
36. Henry Rider Haggard, *A Farmer's Year* (1899), p. ix.
37. George Sturt, *The Bettesworth Book*, (new edn, Firle, 1978), p. 8.
38. W.H. Hudson, *Nature in Downland*, (13th edn, London, 1981), p. 86.
39. Ibid., p. 95.
40. F.E. Green, *The Awakening of England* (London, 1911), p. 306.
41. See James Urry, 'Englishmen, Celts, and Iberians. The Ethnographic Survey of the United Kingdom 1892–99' in G.W. Stocking Jr (ed.), *Functionalism Historicized. Essays in British Anthropology. History of Anthropology (Vol. 2)* (Wisconsin, 1982).
42. George Bourne (Sturt), *Change in the Village*, (Harmondsworth, 1984), p. 69.

43. Ibid., p. 70.
44. George Sturt, *The Journals of George Sturt, 1890–1927*, 2 vols (Cambridge, 1967), vol. II, p. 767.
45. Christopher Holdenby, *Folk of the Furrow* (London, 1913) pp. 17 ff.
46. John Masefield, *The Everlasting Mercy* (London, 1912) pp. 86–7.
47. *PP 1882 XVI*, p. 23.
48. Holdenby, *Folk*, p. 98.
49. F.E. Green, *A History of the English Farm Labourer 1870–1920* (London, 1920), p. 2.
50. Sturt, *Journals*, p. 839.
51. Sturt, *Bettesworth*, pp. 11–12.
52. Quoted in Ursula Vaughan Williams, *RVW: A Biography of Ralph Vaughan Williams* (Oxford, 1964), p. 402.
53. Cecil J. Sharp, *English Folk Song. Some Conclusions* (new edn, 1965), p. 44.
54. Rudyard Kipling, 'A Charm', *Rewards and Fairies*, (London, 1910), p. ix.
55. Rudyard Kipling, *Puck of Pook's Hill*, (pocket edn, London, 1951), p. 303.
56. Kipling, *Rewards*, p. x.
57. Kenneth McConkey, 'Dr Emerson and the Sentiment of Nature', in Neil McWilliam and Veronica Sekules (eds), *Life and Landscape: P.H. Emerson, Art and Photography in East Anglia 1885–1900*, (Norwich, 1986), p. 48.
58. Ibid.
59. See Kenneth McConkey, *Sir George Clausen, R.A. 1852–1944*, (Bradford, 1980), *passim,* for the critical response to Clausen.
60. Ibid., p. 12.
61. Ibid., the quotation is from Clausen's *Six Lectures on Painting* (London, 1904).
62. Aaron Scharf, 'P.H. Emerson. Naturalist and Iconoclast' in McWilliam and Sekules (eds), *Life and Landscape*, p. 28.
63. Ian Jeffrey, 'Fabulous Domains: Emerson as a Writer' in ibid., p. 42.
64. R. George Thomas (ed.), *The Collected Poems of Edward Thomas* (Oxford, 1978).

CHAPTER SIXTEEN

Deciding to Teach: the making of elementary school teachers in the early twentieth century

Phil Gardner

In the closing decades of the nineteenth century and the opening decades of the twentieth, the structures, if not yet the practices of public education in Britain were being transformed. The foundations of a recognizably modern national system of education were rising.[1] Compulsion – a dangerous innovation in the 1880s – was questioned no longer. Fee-paying – a nineteenth century convention which had applied to all forms of schooling – was disappearing from the public elementary sector and would be applied only partially in the new municipal grammar schools which appeared after the 1902 Education Act. Leaving ages were beginning to rise, with a widely mooted universal minimum leaving age of 14 enacted in 1918. Regularity of school attendance was reaching a level that would not be bettered at any later point in the twentieth century.[2] The old, rigid segmentation at the heart of national education in the previous century, though fundamentally preserved, was being modified at its margins as a trickle of working-class pupils toiled up the new, narrow scholarship ladder thrown between the elementary and secondary sectors.[3] For many on the left, the principle of widening opportunity in public education began to raise a prospect of social transformation with a force that would hold until the last quarter of the twentieth century.[4]

These changes have commonly been charted as the effects of progressive legislative and administrative reform, prompted by a combination of liberal benefaction, national expediency and the pressure of organized labour. Each of these was of course important in establishing the formal parameters for change.[5] But the transformation also had an immense and largely undocumented popular dimension which is much harder to investigate and to assess. It is clear however, that from the closing years of the nineteenth century, 'going to school' was taking on a new and defining importance at the centre of the everyday experience of the nation's children – regular, unavoidable, expected and accepted as a fact of national daily life.[6] At the same time, for many working-class parents, the prospect of their children doing well – 'getting on' – at school began to assume a similarly heightened significance. Though learning and scholarship had long been highly valued elements in working-class life, they had traditionally been developed episodically and unsystematically – 'under difficulties' – in a wide range of contexts and through many disparate agencies.[7] What was new in the closing years of the nineteenth century was the movement towards a more general acknowledgement that the formalization and standardization of structures of learning were important and legitimate functions of public policy. Understood in this way, 'school' was finding a new, more intimate place in the commonality of national life.[8] However imperfectly parents perceived the business of the publicly provided schools that their children attended, and however distanced they were from the teachers who staffed those schools, the form of educational success that they defined was coming to be seen as a badge of social pride as well as a potential ticket to a better kind of life.[9] As a consequence, the question of public education found itself higher on the list of popular concerns than ever before.

The character of this change was always complex, frequently uneven and often contradictory; but its magnitude for the lives, prospects and expectations of the British people was profound. Some sense of this is still there for us to see in the architectural record of the period. Survivors of the great redbrick board schools of the late nineteenth century are everywhere in our older towns and cities. We know a great deal about how and why these new buildings came to be built – about the formulation, implementation and administration of national education policy. We also know about the personalities who proposed, designed and engineered this work – the Forsters, the Morants, the Sadlers and the rest.[10] But when we leave the well-illuminated world of policy and political personalities, our knowledge falls away. We know little of how the changing educational landscape was perceived and accommodated by those who were to be most affected by it – by children, by parents and, in particular, by teachers. At the time, the ways in which teachers went about their daily business in the classrooms of the nation's newly built schools were hidden from passers-by by iron railings and lofty windows which denied the casual gaze.[11] A century later, their work remains similarly hidden from the scholarly gaze of the historian. The barriers now however are no longer made from bricks and mortar but constructed from the paucity of historical evidence that we have to work with.

Who were the elementary school teachers? How did they practise their profession? What did their work mean to them? And – the question which we will particularly consider here – how did they come to teaching in the first place? We are by no means devoid of histories of the teaching profession in this period. But they do not address questions of this kind. Their focus is on issues of institutional and organizational formation, for which there is a substantial documentary record.[12] Such work can tell us much. It can, for example, show that with the unprecedented educational expansion after 1870, the numbers of certificated teachers in public elementary schools trebled inside a decade.[13] It can elucidate the chronic professional insecurity and status ambivalence which affected the profession as the newly formed National Union of Elementary Teachers sought to counter and re-fashion traditional perceptions of teaching as the refuge of failures, incompetents and charlatans.[14] It can help us to trace the striking feminization of the profession, dating particularly from the inception of the controversial Revised Code of 1862.[15] It can chart the growing official concern over the social background and educational qualifications of recruits entering elementary teaching which was signalled in the minority report of the Cross Commission and the subsequent departmental enquiry into the pupil-teacher system.[16] All of these are important elements for any understanding of the teaching profession at the turn of the century. But what they have to tell us is essentially about structure and not about agency. They give us this or that piece of the background scenery setting the stage on which the teachers enacted their daily performances. Of the individual actors themselves, they can tell us little. In so far as teachers make any significant appearance in work of this genre, it is in terms either of typification or stereotype, in which attitude and behaviour can be read off from structural imperatives or can be deducted from generalized characteristics of personality.[17]

For a more intimate approach to the classroom life of elementary school teachers at the turn of the century, sources are scarce. Few lifelong elementary teachers sought to commit their professional memories to print.[18] In consequence, we are restricted to a small number of well-known autobiographical fragments written mostly by ex-teachers who subsequently made their way into more elevated political, inspectorial or trade union careers.[19] While these are very valuable, their usefulness is restricted both by the smallness of their number and by the unrepresentative character of the careers of their authors. Yet there is another route by which we might hope to come closer to the working world of the elementary teacher at the turn of the century – and that is the route carved out by the oral historian.[20] Though the teachers of whom we need to learn more have themselves all now slipped beyond the reach of such historians, survivors from the ranks of their former pupils have not. These constitute a group who, more than any other, were in extensive daily contact with the teachers of the early twentieth century. What can we learn from their recollections?

The most important work of oral history in this area is Steve Humphries's path-breaking *Hooligans or Rebels?*.[21] In this work, Humphries evokes the elementary classroom of the early years of the twentieth century through the recollections of former pupils. Their memories are searing. Despite the occasional sympathetic or inspirational individual, teachers collectively emerge as at best culturally and temperamentally unsympathetic to their pupils and at worst as petty, authoritarian and vicious.[22] The recollections of Humphries's respondents portray a picture of fundamental and endemic classroom conflict between teachers and pupils as the former struggled to enforce unchallenged obedience and the latter strove to resist or to subvert it: 'I tried to grab the cane. If you could grab the cane, you could snap 'im across your knees, but you would suffer afterwards 'cos they'd get another teacher in to come an' hold yer hand – one teacher to hold yer, while the other hit 'im proper...'.[23]

The strengths of such recollections are their originality, immediacy and frankness. They take us to the heart of individual experience and classroom interaction in a way that is very rare in histories of education and which is seldom possible through the use of more conventional sources.[24] But there are difficulties too. If we are to use such sources to help us understand life in the past, that is to say, as material to write history as well as to approach individual memory, then they must be employed with the same critical care as any other historical source.[25] When reading oral recollection in this way,[26] we may wish, in particular, to consider both the validity of the data that oral recollection produces, and the degree to which it may legitimately be used to support generalized argument.[27] These difficulties can appear almost as a function of the data themselves. The material can be so rich, so novel, so striking, precisely because it involves the personal recollection of unique moments from an individual life. How to justify this process as generating something other than historically unverifiable anecdote, and how to incorporate individual testimony into historical arguments with generalizing force are problems which have often been raised against oral recollection as a method of historical analysis.[28] One way of responding to these difficulties is through the conventional process of cross-referencing findings against appropriate sources of comparative documentary information. In the case of the study of formal schooling, the extensive official documentary record fortunately allows such systematic comparative analysis to a degree that is not possible for those areas of oral recollection which do not relate to activities so explicitly sanctioned and regulated by the State. Comparison with printed and manuscript sources of this kind is the approach which Humphries principally uses, where it is appropriate, both to support the authenticity of the testimony of his respondents and to assess its representativeness of the school experience for working-class youth as a whole.

There is however a second approach, not available to Humphries, by which we might seek to test the strength of the evidence he cites. Such a method operates not by referring principally to comparative sources of non-oral data, but by invoking other, parallel but quite distinctive sources of oral testimony. In the case of *Hooligans or Rebels?* this would most profitably have taken the form of complementary interview series with the teachers who appear in such unfavourable terms in the recollections of their pupils. We can only imagine how our perceptions of the memories of the latter might be affected if we could read them alongside the memories of the former. The teachers, after all, were the only other witnesses to the kind of events so graphically described by former pupils. But if the teachers of those pupils who figure in the pages of *Hooligans or Rebels?* are now beyond the extent of our reach into the past, an important part of their professional legacy is not – and that is the new, growing generation of elementary school teachers who were still pupils in school at the same time as Humphries's respondents.

In every elementary classroom in the country, alongside those pupils who sought to subvert the school syllabus or to challenge classroom coercion, there was also that small minority who were themselves to become elementary teachers in a few years' time. These were young people who were already starting to form the idea that they might emulate the careers of those figures who stood before them every day. What did pupils such as these think of their teachers? How different, how similar were their perceptions to those of their overtly rebellious classmates? And how might their recollections lead us to revise our historical understanding of the development of the teaching profession in the early twentieth century?

The remainder of this essay seeks to answer these questions. Its findings are drawn from a sample of data produced in a study of the recollections of 44 former pupils, born between the years 1888 and 1917, each of whom went on to become teachers themselves.[29] Each of these individuals spent at least half their school years as pupils in elementary schools; some of them – those who came to teaching by the old pupil-teacher route – attended no other type of school.

We might expect to find that the classroom memories of these teachers in the making would be very different to those in Humphries's sample. After all, given the nature of their recollected experiences, it is hard to conceive that the respondents from the pages of *Hooligans or Rebels?* could have nurtured any wish to model themselves on those who were characteristically their tormentors. One such respondent, for example, was Bob Adams:

> Well, we 'ad one [teacher] an' he was a big pig, a sadistic pig. He delighted in rapping kids' knuckles if you weren't paying attention, daydreaming instead of writing. [Respondent bangs on the table.] 'Wake up boy! Wake up boy!' Anyway, one of my pals there, name

was Been, he 'ad a younger brother, Arnold, in a lower class. And a kid rushed into our class an' said, 'Eh, Tommy Burrows i'n't 'alf 'itting your Arnold, Wilf.' So Wilf Been and Wilf Williams and me got out of our seats an' rushed into Tommy Burrows's class, and he was doing little Arnold. And we jumped on him and we had 'n down an' we was going, 'We'll have you! Leave our Arnold alone . . .'[30]

Is it possible that those pupils who went on themselves to teach also shared experiences such as these? Or, to put the question another way, how typical of their profession at the turn of the century were teachers like Tommy Burrows? The answer which emerges is striking. The image of the brutal teacher is a part of the memories of the future teachers just as it is in the recollections of rebels like Bob Adams. Here is Marion Mortimer, recalling her schooling in Derby, just before the outbreak of the First World War:

> I remember two teachers. One was a Miss Timmons . . . and she was a dragon. She'd never got the cane out of her hand . . . And the head-mistress, Miss Bennett, oh she was awful . . . I can remember one day, I can remember this day so very well. She saw a girl, and her name was Eileen Moorcroft, she saw her not singing so she fetched her out, and as she . . . she used to get into terrible tempers Miss Bennett did. She got . . . her neck reddened and the more . . . the more angry she got, the redder it got. And she was in such a temper with this girl and she caned her terrible . . . And I was so terrified and so upset that I played truant. And I was away from school nearly a fort-night, just going out in the morning, coming back for lunch, going out again in the afternoon, just wandering about.[31]

At about the same time, as an infant in a small school in an Essex village, Grace Bartholomew was being inducted into a similarly cruel regime. Like Marion Mortimer, she was shocked and frightened by the physical power of the teachers.

> Strict disciplinarians I must admit . . . Well, you'd got to behave yourself or you got the cane and that sort of thing which was of course horrifying to youngsters who saw it happen to big boys in the school. Yes, to see big boys having to hold out their hands. We used to sit there and shriek.[32]

A few years older, Miriam Harford remembers her teacher in Standard 7 at a Birmingham elementary school without affection: 'All I remember of him is, if anybody spoke . . . he'd suddenly lose his temper and go down a row, slap!, slap!, slap!, slap!, slap!, slap!, slap!, all the way down. And sometimes you got what you didn't deserve.'[33]

Treatment of this kind was regularly recalled by many respondents either as routine or unexceptional. In this, their testimony strongly confirms Humphries's finding that the extensive application of physical punishment was a ubiquitous and unremarkable characteristic of elementary teachers in the early years of the century.[34] Moreover, many of the future teachers were themselves beaten – sometimes frequently – and some suffered in ways that they felt were particularly cruel or unjust:

> I can remember once when I'd done something – I can't remember what it was – and that was during the War period, so I must have been, say 8 or 9 then and I was made to stand inside the fireguard ... I can remember it was late afternoon and the fire was dying down and I was made to stand inside the fireguard. I never dared to go home and tell my parents because I knew they would have come up to school and created a fuss which no children like ... I knew they would create about the type of punishment that I'd had. I can always remember that.[35]

The mark of Nora Crawford's distress over this incident remains as strong now, nearly 80 years later, as it did at the time. The same is true of Ellen Barton who, as a ten-year-old in 1908, was at school in Tonypandy.

> I can remember one incident whilst reading. The master put another teacher in the classroom – I don't know whether the regular teacher was absent and this one was supplementing. I can always remember him saying, 'Now, if there is anybody who hasn't got their place in the book, you send them in to me.' Now, it was reading round the class – stand up and read a paragraph. Well, I got rather interested in the story, so I turned the pages over and I read it. 'Oh!', I thought, 'Gosh, I don't know where they are' – you had to follow on after the one next to you read, or whoever she pointed to – and she said, 'You haven't got the place have you? Go into Mr Shaw and take the cane with you.' ... So I had to go to Mr Shaw with the cane, and the tears were streaming down my face. I can see it myself now – how I walked out there I don't know ... I've always remembered it.[36]

Even for those who escaped direct punishment, the fear of the teachers was powerful and ever-present. Mary Boston, for example, who was born in the Rhondda Valley in the last year of the nineteenth century, 'Can't remember having the cane, but I dreaded it you know. We were very much afraid of having it. The teachers were strict, very strict'.[37] Such pervasive dread could sometimes develop into a lasting hatred of the elementary school and its teachers. In the case of Marion Mortimer, who had truanted as a result of her revulsion at the uninhibited use of the cane, such feeling was particularly intense. 'Oh I hated it. I hated school all my life. I was never really happy at school at all ... Shall we pass on to the grammar school now?' This last remark is significant. From the turn of the century, the site for the preliminary preparation of teachers was shifting from the elementary to the secondary school. Increasingly, and especially after a new Board of Education regulations in 1907, places at local grammar schools were made available to those pledging themselves to train as teachers.[38] For those who followed this route, the transition from their familiar elementary teachers to those who staffed the grammar schools could be a revelation. The escape from the rigid regime of her elementary school to the more liberal atmosphere of the local grammar school came as the greatest relief to Marion Mortimer. 'Oh, very different. There was no physical punishment I think – I never heard of it.' The characteristically more informal and open relationship between grammar school staff and their pupils doubtless influenced the developing perceptions that the young teachers-to-be had of the role of the teacher. It could not, however, inform the initial decision to teach. For the great majority, this had to be taken at a point when the only professional models that pupils had any knowledge of were their elementary teachers.

How then was it, that having witnessed or endured experiences which could drive their peers to resistance or open rebellion, these pupils were able not only to negotiate the ordeal but were able to cultivate an ambition to become teachers in elementary schools themselves? The answers are complex, but the memories of the future teachers do begin to reveal some important patterns.

The first is that, though these recollections point to the same species of authoritarian classroom regime recreated in *Hooligans or Rebels?*, they are almost entirely devoid of any similar evidence of pupil resistance, either on the part of respondents themselves or their recollected peers. For them, although school might be saturated with feelings of fear and sometimes of resentment, these were seldom focused or catalysed into open acts of rebellion. In their schools, no individual or collective pupil action served to penetrate the traditional bases of classroom power or to shake the grip of the teachers. Cruel regimes did not always lead to resistance; preconditions for rebellion were not always capitalized. In many schools the structure of discipline was, to a greater or lesser degree, successful in its own terms, with children remaining cowed, subservient and deferential. In consequence, those who were to go on to become teachers themselves did so from a background in which their own teachers were seldom challenged, their authority never threatened. Teachers might be secretly disliked and covertly whispered about, but the impact of their magical power to subdue a class was not diminished or exposed; the emperor retained his clothes.

A second feature is that the exercise of unequivocal teacher power could, for some pupils, evoke a kind of admiration alongside a more general revulsion. This was particularly so for clever children from poor or modest family backgrounds where intellectual resources were always likely to be limited. For such individuals, who characteristically found that they enjoyed learning in school and that learning resulted in academic success and teacher approbation, a degree of admiration for teachers was quite common. These, after all, were often the only practical models of labour based on intellectual rather than manual capacity which were available to children seeking to make sense of and to direct their own, often profound, scholastic talent. As such children sat at their desks, studying their teachers as well as learning from them, feelings of fear, revulsion and escape could co-exist and compete with fascination, admiration and engagement. Often the latter overwhelmed the former. The result was that though the flawed examples of particular teachers might be rejected, a higher, often romanticized ideal of teaching itself could be quietly and deeply nurtured.

The most striking expression of such an ideal was a conscious determination to avoid those aspects of observed pedagogical practice which were perceived to be cruel or humiliating. This was, in other words, a projection of an appropriate role for the teacher as seen through the eyes of the clever pupil who enjoyed academic study and intuitively understood how teachers might potentially make it yet more pleasurable. Many of the future teachers pledged themselves that, while they would emulate the academic proficiency of their own teachers, they would do so with a new dignity and sympathy which would respect the sensibilities of children. Such a critique meant that an ambition to teach did not imply a simple desertion to the ranks of the enemy. By promising themselves that they would somehow humanize teaching when their turn came at the front of the class, pupils could continue to share in the general disaffection of their peers for the profession as it was actually practised in their classrooms. At the same time, they could keep open a channel through which to direct their personal ambition in the only available career that could both repay their intellectual interest and offer the chance to extend it further. This was the strategy adopted by Dorothy Tanner, when she was wrongly accused by her teacher of lying. The pain of this experience helped her to think about the transformation of the business of teaching, rather than its rejection. It was 1906; Dorothy was nine years old:

> She said, 'Put your hand up if you've ever been anywhere else but in Yorkshire.' So I put my hand up and she said, 'But you're telling lies. You've never moved from Northallerton.' ... You know that stuck in my mind often when I was teaching ... It made me very careful ... It affected me to some extent, my attitude to children when I taught. Yes, I often thought about it then.[39]

In the same year, though at an even younger age, Miriam Harford learned a similarly hard but equally instructive lesson:

> I decided to become a teacher at the age of 5. I strongly objected to

the way I was treated by one Miss Appleby, my very first teacher. I remember that on my first day in the infants' school I was put into a desk with another girl. Miss A put a cardboard letter 'f' between us and hissed, 'f'. As soon as she'd left us, my companion turned it upside down and said, 'j'. I was the one who was slapped. Outraged and being outspoken, I announced, 'I don't like you.' I liked her still less after retribution had fallen upon my head. I went home and told my mother I had no intention of returning to school. My mother had other ideas. For 2 weeks, I was dragged howling to school. At the end of that time my mother had had enough. I was soundly slapped and told she was having no more nonsense. Thus deprived of any hope of help, I thought things out. I made a solemn vow that I would become a teacher and I would treat my pupils as they should be treated. Having made this decision I never wavered. I owe much to Miss Appleby.

What such testimony reveals is that in classrooms where overt pupil resistance was low, where models of teaching were not catastrophically challenged or exposed by the collective action of the peer group, then it was possible for a pupil such as Miriam Harford to mount her own private mental critique of pedagogical style and practice – to project herself as a teacher in her own mind's eye. As a result, it was possible for new recruits for the profession to emerge even from the most authoritarian and forbidding of classroom settings. And these, moreover, were recruits with real performing potential because they sought explicitly to reject and not emulate fundamental aspects of the teaching that they had been subjected to.

Nevertheless, pupils who found their way into teaching sustained only by this kind of personal critique had to be unusually determined and resilient. For most, some further impetus was needed to accelerate and consolidate the process. Almost always, this came from some intimate and positive contact with the practice of teaching which nuanced or even challenged prevailing pedagogical norms – practice which, in other words, came closer to the pupil's perception of good teaching. Such a contact could be established in two ways. Either, almost at a stroke, a pupil's intellectual energy and personal ambition might be captured by a single exceptional individual whose influence was lifelong and indelible; or, more rarely, a pupil was inducted informally into successful practical teaching in a supernumerary capacity. The first of these could happen at any point in the elementary schooling process; the second, characteristically towards its end.

For pupils who were spiritually captured by the example of a single teacher, there were two moments of particular susceptibility. One came in the earliest days at infant school; the other at the critical moment when the handful – if there were any at all – of scholarship examination entries were being considered. Mary Donaldson is a good example of the first case. For her, the encounter came on her very first day in school in rural Worcestershire, in 1909:

> On Monday morning I went to school. I had to walk up two fields to get to the road and then a mile from the top gate, as we called it, to school, under a lovely avenue of trees of all kinds. And I went into the infants' school. I can still see that room. I learnt my right hand was where the window was and my left hand was where the door was. And the teacher, Miss Lymm, was a wonderful person – so kind, so thoughtful ... That's what made me want to be a teacher because she was so good and I thought, 'Oh, I would like to be like that!'[40]

The early, instantaneous recognition of an ideal model came in a similar way to Gladys Shillingford: 'My father had a cousin and she became a teacher and she came to teach at our school – and teach me. And she had the same surname as I had, you know, and I thought, "I wish I could be like her".'[41]

When, five or six years later in the career of a pupil, it came to the time for entries for examinations for grammar school scholarships, many older elementary teachers, particularly headteachers, simply ignored the issue altogether. Though there was certainly considerable prestige to be accrued in winning places, this had to be balanced against the extra work that entries entailed and the inflation of local expectation that would inevitably result. For such teachers, the old assumptions underlying traditional systemic segregation offered a measure of institutional security, an escape from the demands of educational modernization and an opportunity to cling to unreformed teaching methods based on undifferentiated whole-class teaching rather than on the identification and development of individual ability. For younger, more idealistic teachers fresh from the more optimistic culture of the training colleges, the enhanced scholarship opportunities which resulted from the Act of 1902 and from the subsequent reform of teacher training regulations, presented a welcome challenge. Many future teachers were to be set on their professional path by such individuals. One such was Isabella Potter who remembers,

> Miss Bunting ... the teacher in Standard 4. In those days she was active with the Labour Party and she was keen of course for children to get on. It wasn't the head who bothered, it was Miss Bunting. She chose 4 of us to sit (the scholarship) and she gave us a little bit of extra tuition.[42]

Another was John Evenden:

> The teacher that put me through the (scholarship) exam in Standard 4 was an uncertificated teacher by the name of Ernie Phillips. One of

the finest teachers I've ever come across in my life. To this day I
remember him. He was a great hero of mine. He was a *marvellous*
teacher – there was no other word for it.[43]

As individual teachers and scholarship hopefuls met and worked in
extra sessions after school hours, the bond between mentor and protégé
grew stronger. For teachers, there was the satisfaction of tangible public
success and professional fulfilment in a job where such rewards were
often hard to achieve in any other way. At a deeper level, this was work
which preserved the principle of missionary duty which had been built
into the elementary teaching profession from its earliest days, but which
could reformulate the principle away from a traditional emphasis on
moral or religious regulation towards an expression of the burgeoning
new concern for meritocratic opportunity. For pupils, there was an
escape from normal routines of classroom drudgery and the unexpected
delight both of stimulating academic work under individual tuition, and
the longer term promise of a career devoted to the emulation of the
teacher who was doing so much for them.

Not infrequently, the closer relationship between teachers and pupils
such as these, along with their shared enthusiasm for teaching, led to a
pupil taking his or her first – and unofficial – pedagogical steps under the
teacher's tutelage. Though the old pupil-teacher system was now all but
dead other than in remote rural areas, this kind of informal arrangement
was a clear professional echo of the transmission of grounded pedagogical knowledge which had been at its heart. Norman Wilson's experience
offers a good example of this:

> I was there, 11, with big lads who were 14. I was the little boy, the
> clever little boy in the class ... I had some very good teachers,
> especially I can remember Mr Gellian, and he had me going round
> helping these big lads in my class – helping them, going round teach-
> ing them, showing them how to do different things. I can remember
> doing that.[44]

Another example comes from Edith Thanet, who, at the age of ten, on
those occasions when the infant teacher was absent from her Tredegar
school, was deputed to teach them. Her experience was a particularly
happy one, in a school favoured by a succession of sympathetic and
supportive teachers who collectively made a great impression on Edith:

> Yes, I would have to take the class. I remember one day, the atten-
> dance officer came in and he was also a lay preacher. He had seen
> through the glass partition my performance and on the Sunday when
> he was due at our place to preach, he said to my father, 'You know,
> Edith ought to be allowed to become a teacher – she puts on a good
> show.' Well, I was only ten, and, Oh, I worshipped the teachers ... I
> loved being at school. I really loved learning.[45]

What, in summary, do these memories of pupils who became teachers have to tell us? They certainly confirm that the elementary teaching profession at the turn of the century was still substantially controlled by the principles and practices of a narrow and fundamentally authoritarian pedagogy. But they also show that this pedagogy was neither universal nor static. Many severe and uncompromising teachers were neither cruel nor unjust, and many pupils did not perceive their teachers in a negative light.[46] Moreover, teaching itself was beginning to change.[47] There were a number of policy reasons for this, the more important involving changes in patterns of training and recruitment.[48] But equally significant, though seldom recognized, was the contribution of those individual teachers who strove to liberalize and humanize the practical conventions of their profession. In their time, such teachers may have been few in number, but their historical significance was proportionately very much greater. This is because, by their own examples, they acted both as beacons attracting able pupils into teaching, and also as models of good professional practice. In the midst of a picture of classroom life that was commonly overshadowed by the dullness as well as the brutality of the past, there were enough such individuals to awaken or to enthuse the latent talent of a new generation of teachers – and sometimes to fire their commitment in the long, difficult and continuing struggle for a system of education and a culture of teaching that would promise the best to all the nation's children.

But the impetus for classroom change did not spring only from an enlightened minority of teachers. Pupils themselves played a critically important part. Alongside those who explosively resisted authoritarian teaching, there were, in every classroom, a few who reflected at length on their experience as the recipients of such teaching, and who promised themselves that one day, they would do better. In the long run, it may well have been that these few did as much as any to change the face of classroom life for the school generations that were to follow.

Notes

1. E.J.R. Eaglesham, *The Foundations of Twentieth Century Education in England* (London, 1967); G. Sherington, *English Education, Social Change and War, 1911–20* (Manchester, 1981); D. Muller, F. Ringer and B. Simon (eds), *The Rise of the Modern Education System* (Cambridge, 1987).
2. D. Rubinstein, *School Attendance in London 1870–1904*, (Hull, 1969); J.S. Hurt, *Elementary Schooling and the Working Classes 1860–1918* (London, 1979), pp. 52–74; D. Wardle, *The Rise of the Schooled Society: The History of Formal Schooling in England* (London, 1974), pp. 17–21; J. Harris, *Private Lives, Public Spirit: Britain 1870–1914* (London, 1993), pp. 88–9.

3. M. Sanderson, *Educational Opportunity and Social Change in England* (London, 1987), pp. 18–33; D.E. Reeder, 'The Reconstruction of Secondary Education in England, 1869–1920' in Muller, Ringer and Simon (eds), pp. 135–50; P. Gordon, *Selection for Secondary Education* (Woburn, 1980), pp. 167–78.

4. R. Barker, *Education and Politics 1900–1951: A Study of the Labour Party* (Oxford, 1972); B. Simon, *Education and the Labour Movement 1870–1920* (London, 1965); C. Griggs, *The Trades Union Congress and the Struggle for Education 1868–1925* (Lewes, 1983); J.R. Brooks, 'Labour and Educational Reconstruction, 1916–26: A Case Study in the Evolution of Policy', *History of Education*, **20**, (3), (1991), pp. 245–59.

5. A. Green, *Education and State Transformation* (London, 1990), pp. 300–7.

6. R. Roberts, *The Classic Slum: Salford Life in the First Quarter of the Century* (London, 1971), pp. 129–45; T. Gautrey, *Lux Mihi Laus: School Board Memories* (London, 1937), p. 36; C. Parsons, *Schools in an Urban Community: A Study of Carbrook 1870–1965* (London, 1978), pp. 49–81.

7. D. Vincent, *Bread, Knowledge and Freedom: A Study of Nineteenth-Century Working Class Autobiography* (London, 1981), pt 3; J.F.C. Harrison, *The Common People: A History from the Norman Conquest to the Present* (London, 1984), pp. 287–95; D. Vincent, *Literacy and Popular Culture in England, 1750–1914* (Cambridge, 1989).

8. P. Gardner, 'Schooling, Markets and Public Agency, 1833–1944', in D. Bridges and T. McLaughlin, *Education and the Market Place* (Lewes, 1994), pp. 9–18.

9. P. Gardner, ' "Our Schools"; "Their Schools": The Case of Eliza Duckworth and John Stevenson', *History of Education*, **20**, (3), (1991), pp. 163–86.

10. J. Leese, *Personalities and Power in English Education*, (Leeds, 1950).

11. M. Seaborne and R. Lowe, *The English School: Its Architecture and Organization vol. 2: 1870–1970* (London, 1977), pp. 3–39.

12. A. Tropp, *The School Teachers: The Growth of the Teaching Profession in England and Wales from 1800 to the Present Day* (London, 1957); P.H.J.H. Gosden, *The Evolution of a Profession* (Basil Blackwell, 1972); M. Lawn, *Servants of the State: The Contested Control of Teaching 1900–1930* (London, 1987); H. Kean, *Challenging the State? The Socialist and Feminist Educational Experience 1900–1930* (London, 1990).

13. P. Gordon, R. Aldrich and D. Dean, *Education and Policy in England in the Twentieth Century* (London, 1991), p. 24.

14. B. Bergen, 'Only a Schoolmaster: Gender, Class and the Effort to Professionalize Elementary Teaching in England 1870–1910' in J. Ozga (ed.), *Schoolwork: Approaches to the Labour Process of Teaching* (Milton Keynes, 1988), pp. 39–60: G. Grace, *Teachers, Ideology and Control* (London, 1978), pp. 13–15.

15. F. Widdowson, *Going Up into the Next Class: Women and Elementary Teacher Training* (London, 1980).

16. Parliamentary Papers, *1888 XXXVI* 'Royal Commission on the Elementary Education Acts. Final Report; *PP 1898 XXVI* 'Departmental Committee on the Pupil-Teacher System'; also L. Jones, *The Training of Teachers in England and Wales: A Critical Survey* (Oxford, 1924), pp. 23–4.

17. Comparison with recent advances in contemporary studies of teachers'
     lives is striking. See particularly J. Nias *Primary Teachers Talking: A Study
     of Teaching as Work* (London, 1989); P. Sikes, L. Measor and P. Woods,
     Teacher Careers: Crisis and Continuities (Lewes, 1985); I. Goodson,
     Studying Teachers' Lives (London, 1992).
18. A number of important works have emerged from the community publish-
     ing movement. A good example is N. Bridge, *My Liverpool Schools*,
     (Liverpool, 1992).
19. For example, B. Christian, *English Education from Within* (London,
     1922); P. Ballard, *Things I Cannot Forget* (London, 1937); F. Spencer, *An
     Inspector's Testament* (London, 1938); A. Jones, *From an Inspector's Bag*
     (Cardiff, 1940).
20. Popular Memory Group, 'Popular Memory: Theory, Politics, Method', in
     R. Johnson, G. McLennan, B. Schwartz and D. Sutton, *Making Histories:
     Studies in History, Writing and Politics* (London, 1982), pp. 205–52; L.
     Passerini, 'Women's Personal Narratives: Myths, Experiences and
     Emotions', in Personal Narratives Group (eds), *Interpreting Women's
     Lives* (Bloomington, Indiana, 1989); R. Samuel and P. Thompson, *The
     Myths We Live By* (London, 1990); K. Weiler, 'Remembering and Repre-
     senting Life Choices: A Critical Perspective on Teachers' Oral History
     Narratives', *Qualitative Studies in Education*, 5, (1), (1992); K. Casey, *I
     Answer With My Life* (London, 1993), ch. 1; P. Thompson, *The Voice of
     the Past: Oral History* (2nd edn, Oxford, 1988), pp. 22–71.
21. S. Humphries, *Hooligans or Rebels? An Oral History of Working-Class
     Childhood and Youth 1889–1939* (London, 1981).
22. Ibid., pp. 18, 22, 43–48, 70.
23. Ibid., p. 75.
24. H. Silver, 'Knowing and not Knowing in the History of Education' in
     History of Education, 21, (1), (1992), p. 105.
25. P. Hutton, *History as an Art of Memory* (Hanover, Vermont, 1993).
26. Popular Memory Group in *Making Histories*, pp. 227–9.
27. K. Plummer, *Documents of Life: An Introduction to the Problems and
     Literature of a Humanistic Method* (London, 1983); J. Rose, 'Willingly to
     School: The Working-Class Response to Elementary Education in Britain,
     1875–1918', *Journal of British Studies*, 32, (1993), pp. 114–38.
28. Thompson, *The Voice of the Past*, 101–49.
29. The research was funded by a grant from the Nuffield Foundation, to
     whom I am most grateful.
30. Humphries, *Hooligans or Rebels?*, p. 86.
31. Marion Mortimer, born 1905, Derby; father – master plumber; mother –
     dressmaker.
32. Grace Bartholomew, born 1906, Essex; father – postman; mother – at
     home.
33. Miriam Harford, born 1901, Birmingham; father – toolmaker; mother – at
     home.
34. Also see M. Highfield and A. Pinsent, *Survey of Rewards and Punishments
     in Schools* (London, 1952), p. 56.
35. Nora Crawford, born 1908, Nottinghamshire; father – farmer; mother –
     cheese maker.
36. Ellen Barton, born 1898, Glamorgan; father – colliery electrician; mother –
     milliner.

37. Mary Boston, born 1899, Glamorgan; father – colliery engine driver; mother – at home.

38. Board of Education, *Report of the Board of Education for the Year 1909* (London, 1910), pp. 46–58; also Board of Education, Circular 573, *Memorandum on the History and Prospects of the Pupil Teaching System* (London, 1907); Board of Education, *Report of the Departmental Committee on the Training of Teachers for Public Elementary Schools* (London, 1925), pp. 10–23.

39. Dorothy Tanner, born 1897, Stockport; father – block cutter; mother – dressmaker.

40. Mary Donaldson, born 1904, Glos.; father – butcher; mother – at home. Also see F. Widdowson ' " Educating Teacher": Women and Elementary Teaching in London 1900–1914' in L. Davidoff and B. Westover (eds), *Our Work, Our Lives, Our Words* (New Jersey, 1986), p. 106.

41. Gladys Shillingford, born 1892, Bradford; father – carter; mother – at home.

42. Isabella Potter, born 1906, Cheshire; father – casual labourer; mother – shop assistant.

43. John Evenden, born 1906, Cardiff; father – railway supervisor; mother – at home.

44. Norman Wilson, born 1908, Liverpool; father – shipping clerk; mother – at home.

45. Edith Thanet, born 1911, Tredegar; father – colliery overman; mother – at home.

46. Rose, 'Willingly to School', p. 130.

47. G.A.N. Lowndes, *The Silent Social Revolution* (London, 1937), pp. 155–66.

48. H.C. Dent, *The Training of Teachers in England and Wales* (London, 1975).

John Harrison: a bibliography

Books

A History of the Working Men's College, 1854–1954 (London: Routledge & Kegan Paul, 1954).

Social Reform in Victorian Leeds: The Work of James Hole, 1820–1895 (Leeds: The Thoresby Society, 1954).

Learning and Living, 1790–1960: A Study in the History of the English Adult Education Movement (London: Routledge & Kegan Paul; Toronto: University of Toronto Press, 1961; reprinted London: Gregg, 1994).

(Editor), *Society and Politics in England, 1780–1960* (New York: Harper & Row, 1965).

(Editor), *Utopianism and Education: Robert Owen and the Owenites* (Classics in Education Series, New York: Columbia University Press, 1968).

Robert Owen and the Owenites in Britain and America: The Quest for the New Moral World (London: Routledge & Kegan Paul, 1969). [American edition] *The Quest for the New Moral World: Robert Owen and the Owenites in Britain and America* (New York: Scribners Sons, 1969; reprinted London: Gregg, 1994).

The Early Victorians, 1832–1851 (London: Weidenfeld and Nicholson; New York: Praeger, 1971; reprinted London: Panther, 1971; reprinted as *Early Victorian Britain, 1832–1851*, London: Fontana, 1979).

The Birth and Growth of Industrial England, 1714–1867, Harbrace History of England, Part III (New York: Harcourt Brace Jovanovich, 1973).

(Editor), *Eminently Victorian*, 'People and Opinions' (London: BBC, 1974).

(With Dorothy Thompson), *Bibliography of the Chartist Movement, 1837–1976* (Brighton: Harvester Press, 1978).

The Second Coming: Popular Millenarianism, 1780–1850 (London: Routledge & Kegan Paul; New Jersey: Rutgers University Press, 1979).

The Common People: A History from the Norman Conquest to the Present (London: Croom Helm and Fontana, 1984).

Late Victorian Britain, 1875–1901 (London: Fontana, 1990).
Scholarship Boy: A Personal History of the Mid-Twentieth Century (London: Rivers Oram Press, 1995).

Parts of books

'The WEA in the Welfare State', in S.G. Raybould (ed.), *Trends in English Adult Education* (London: Heinemann, 1959).

'Chartism in Leeds', and 'Chartism in Leicester', in Asa Briggs (ed.), *Chartist Studies* (London: Macmillan, 1959).

'A New View of Mr Owen' in S. Pollard and J. Salt (eds), *Robert Owen: Prophet of the Poor* (London: Macmillan, 1971).

'Robert Owen's Quest for the New Moral World in America', in Donald E. Pitzer (ed.), *Robert Owen's American Legacy* (Indianapolis: Indiana Historical Society, 1972).

'James Hole', and 'Abram Combe', in J. Bellamy and J. Saville (eds), *Dictionary of Labour Biography*, vol. 2 (London: Macmillan, 1974).

'The Iron Machine' in Theo Barker (ed.), *The Long March of Everyman* (London: BBC, 1974).

'Victorian Social Themes' [discussion with Asa Briggs on Chartism and the 1870 Education Act], in *Nineteenth Century Britain* (London: Sussex Books, 1976).

'Robert Owen', in J. Bellamy and J. Saville (eds), *Dictionary of Labour Biography*, vol. 6 (London: Macmillan, 1983).

'Millennium and Utopia', in Peter Alexander and Roger Gill (eds), *Utopias*, (London: Duckworth, 1984).

'Early Victorian Radicals and the Medical Fringe', in W.F. Bynum and Roy Porter (eds), *Medical Fringe and Medical Orthodoxy* (London: Croom Helm, 1987).

'Thomas Paine and Millenarian Radicalism', in I. Dyck (ed.), *Citizen of the World: Essays on Thomas Paine* (London: Christopher Helm, 1987).

'The Popular History of Early Victorian Britain: A Mormon contribution', in Richard L. Jensen and Malcolm R. Thorp (eds), *Mormons in Early Victorian Britain* (Salt Lake City: University of Utah Press, 1989).

'Radical and Social Reform in England, 1830–50', in Wang Juefei (ed.), *Political, Economic and Social Modernisation of Britain* (Nanjing, China: Nanjing University Press, 1989) [in Chinese].

'In Search of Robert Owen', in Chushichi Tsuzuki (ed.), *Robert Owen and the World of Co-operation* (Tokyo: University of Tokyo Press, 1992).

Pamphlets

Worker's Education in Leeds: A History of the Leeds Branch of the Worker's Educational Association, 1907–1957 (Leeds: WEA, 1957).
Underground Education in the Nineteenth Century (Albert Mansbridge Memorial Lecture, University of Leeds, 1971).

Articles

'Remota Justitia', *Tutors' Bulletin*, Autumn 1949.
(with Richard Hoggart and Roy Shaw), 'What Are We Doing?', *Tutors' Bulletin*, Autumn 1948.
(with Richard Hoggart, Roy Shaw and Catherine Reynolds), 'To What Good End?', *The Highway*, **40**, (November 1948 and April 1949).
'Adult Education and Self-Help', *British Journal of Educational Studies*, **6**, (1), November 1957.
'The Victorian Gospel of Success', *Victorian Studies*, **1**, (2), December 1957.
'For the Good of the Association: American Trade Unionism at the Grass Roots', *Bulletin of the British Association for American Studies*, **9**, November 1959.
'Recent Writing on the History of Victorian England', *Victorian Studies*, **8**, (3), March 1965.
'The Steam Engine of the New Moral World: Owenism and Education, 1817–29', *Journal of British Studies*, **6**, (2), May 1967.
'The Owenite Socialist Movement in Britain and the United States: A Comparative Study', *Labor History*, **9**, (3), Fall, 1968.
'Education in Victorian England', *History of Education Quarterly*, **10**, (4), Winter 1970.
'Robert Owen and the Communities', *Robert Owen Bicentenary Association Bulletin* (1971).
'Robert Owen: The Quest for the New Moral World' *The Montgomeryshire Collections*, **62**, pt 1 (1971) [Robert Owen Bicentenary Lecture, Newtown, Montgomeryshire, 1971].
'A Knife and Fork Question? Some Recent Writing on the History of Social Movements', *Victorian Studies*, **18**, (2), December 1974.
'The Portrait', *History Workshop*, **10**, Autumn 1980.
'Owenite Communitarianism in Britain and America', *Communal Societies*, **4**, Fall 1984.

Shorter articles and reviews have appeared in *Adult Education, American Historical Review, Columbia Teachers' College Record,*

The Guardian, Harvard Review of Business History, The Highway, Journal of Interdisciplinary History, Journal of Modern History, Journal of Social History, Labor History, Labour History Review, New Statesman, Political Science Quarterly, Times Literary Supplement, Victorian Studies, Virginia Quarterly.

Index